Hoover's FBI and the Fourth Estate

ʊ

Hoover's FBI and the Fourth Estate

The Campaign to Control the Press and the Bureau's Image

Matthew Cecil

University Press of Kansas

© 2014 by the University Press of Kansas

Published by the University Press of Kansas (Lawrence, Kansas 66045), which
was organized by the Kansas Board of Regents and is operated and funded by
Emporia State University, Fort Hays State University, Kansas State University,
Pittsburg State University, the University of Kansas, and Wichita State University

Library of Congress Cataloging-in-Publication Data

Cecil, Matthew.
Hoover's FBI and the fourth estate : the campaign to control the press and the bureau's
image / Matthew Cecil.
pages cm
Includes bibliographical references and index.
ISBN 978-0-7006-1946-7 (alk. paper)
1. Hoover, J. Edgar (John Edgar), 1895–1972. 2. United States. Federal Bureau of Investigation—History. 3. Journalism—Objectivity—United States—History. 4. Journalism—Political aspects. 5. Government and the press—United States—History. 6. Public
relations—United States—History. I. Title.
HV8144.F43C426 2014
363.25092—dc23
                            2013035680

British Library Cataloguing-in-Publication Data is available.

Printed in the United States of America

10 9 8 7 6 5 4 3 2 1

The paper used in this publication is recycled and contains 30 percent
postconsumer waste. It is acid free and meets the minimum requirements of the
American National Standard for Permanence of Paper for Printed Library
Materials Z39.48-1992.

CONTENTS

ILLUSTRATIONS

PREFACE

My interest in history began as an exercise in imagination. As a high school student, I worked at a restaurant in Brookings, South Dakota, that occupied a former bank building on Main Avenue. One evening during a lull in my work, I noticed two yellowed newspaper pages framed and hanging in a dark corner of the restaurant. Those pages described a daring daylight robbery of the bank by a young couple, Bennie and Stella Mae Dickson. Just a few feet from where I stood, the Dicksons had entered the bank building with their weapons drawn and then escaped with more than $17,000 worth of cash and securities. From that point on, I was hooked on the idea of imagining how that robbery had played out. When I looked across Fourth Street at a small bar called Ray's Corner, I would imagine Bennie Dickson drinking a soda there while he waited for the bank president to arrive early that morning in 1938. When I entered the building to go to work, I was passing through the doorway where Dickson had put his gun in the bank president's back and forced his way in. The front of the restaurant was the lobby where Bennie and Stella Mae had waited, guns drawn, for the vault's time lock to open. An old boardinghouse located a few blocks away on the corner of Third Street and Sixth Avenue still stood, marking the spot where the Dicksons had released their hostage, the bank president. And the intersection of Sixth Street and Medary Avenue, a few blocks farther from the bank, was where Stella Mae had scattered a bag of nails on the road to discourage anyone inclined to follow them.

As a college student at South Dakota State University in Brookings, I discovered more newspaper accounts of the robbery and the subsequent pursuit while doing research for a term paper. Years later, a graduate school assignment led me to request the Dicksons' FBI file using the Freedom of Information Act. Their much-expanded story, including details of Bennie Dickson's 1939 shooting by FBI agents in St. Louis, became my master's thesis. The larger story of FBI public relations, with Bennie and Stella Mae serving as examples of how certain people and cases were used as props in

Bureau public relations campaigns, became the subject of my doctoral dissertation and a series of academic publications. I moved from faculty positions at Purdue University to the University of Oklahoma and then back home to South Dakota State before taking an administrative position at Wichita State University, always carrying an ever-larger collection of FBI files with me.

Along the way, dozens of people helped me hone my interests and maintain my focus, resulting in this exploration of FBI public relations and the journalists and publications the Bureau has identified as its friends and enemies. First of all, thanks must go to the FBI's Freedom of Information/Privacy Act Section. As time has passed, the FOIPA staff have become more responsive and helpful. This sort of historical work, based on many thousands of documents, would not have been conceivable without their help. They do a remarkable job, given the difficulty of the task, the volume of requests, and the legal constraints that guide their work.

I am grateful to my mentors John Miller and Jerry Sweeney of South Dakota State University, Dan Berkowitz of the University of Iowa, Jeff Smith of the University of Wisconsin–Milwaukee, Fred Blevens of Florida International University, and Charles Self of the University of Oklahoma. The administration and my former colleagues at South Dakota State provided tremendous support. Grants that supported this project came from Purdue University, the Gaylord College of Journalism and Mass Communication at the University of Oklahoma, and the Graduate School at South Dakota State University.

Thanks to Michael Briggs, editor in chief, and the rest of the talented staff at the University Press of Kansas. I am grateful to reviewers Betty Houchin Winfield of the University of Missouri and Douglas Charles of Pennsylvania State University's Allegheny Campus for the constructive and thoughtful critiques that greatly improved this manuscript.

I am a historian because my father, Charles Cecil, instilled in me an appreciation of the importance of the past. My mother, Mary, has always provided support and love through thick and thin. My older brother Dan has always rooted for me and believed in me. My sister Amy Cecil Holm patiently and carefully line-edited this manuscript and, to her great credit, even claimed to enjoy it, despite my inability to correctly employ a comma. Finally, my wife Jennifer Tiernan and our son Owen Cecil are sources of unending love and inspiration.

Hoover's FBI and the Fourth Estate

Introduction

Before the Freedom of Information Act opened up J. Edgar Hoover's massive archive of meticulously indexed files to researchers in the 1970s, the FBI enjoyed a unique and lofty position in American society. Hoover and his agents were heroes to many Americans. Tales of the FBI's infallible laboratory and army of honest and professional agents became part of popular culture. Thanks to movies, television programs, books, magazines, and countless news reports, the FBI was widely considered to be an indispensable government agency. It was not always that way.

Created in the early 1900s despite a storm of controversy and fear of federal law enforcement, the early FBI, originally known as the Bureau of Investigation, quickly established itself as precisely the corrupt, out-of-control agency critics feared it would be. It was not until the 1930s that the FBI and Hoover, who was named director in 1924, began a three-decade period of cultural and jurisdictional growth. The arc of FBI power mirrored the arc of Hoover's own life. Scandal and corruption (some of it enabled by Hoover) had nearly sunk the agency by the time he took over as director in 1924. By the late 1930s, Hoover had calmed many critics' fears by removing political cronies, professionalizing the agency, and modernizing its law enforcement techniques. During the 1940s and 1950s, Hoover became a ferocious anticommunist, utilizing the awesome power of the FBI to enforce a specific vision of what it meant to be an American. In the 1960s and early 1970s, Hoover's vitality waned and critics became increasingly willing to attack the Bureau's activities.

Hoover and the FBI first emerged as cultural icons in the mid-1930s when the public became aware of the Bureau through its high-profile battles with enigmatic outlaws such as John Dillinger. Hoover personified the legendary G-man, and he and the Bureau became media darlings. Dramatic FBI cases became the fodder for newspaper and magazine stories, radio programs, and books. The 1940s and 1950s saw Hoover and the Bureau at their most powerful as they rooted out subversion (through both legal and illegal means) and maintained the loyal and outspoken support of a majority of Americans. As Hoover aged, though, his agency failed to shift with the times; the nation had moved beyond the director's Victorian-era worldview, leaving him and the FBI out of step with society. The Bureau's demonization of Hoover's enemies on the Left became increasingly strident and anachronistic as leftists and their antiwar or pro–civil rights messages moved closer to the mainstream. In the years prior to Hoover's death, public criticism of the FBI, once a dangerous and lonely undertaking, had become increasingly common. Hoover's passing in 1972, after forty-eight years leading the FBI, eliminated the primary locus of the Bureau's iconic power and control.

When historians and authors gained access to the FBI's remarkable trove of information, the Hoover legend immediately began unraveling. A culture of secrecy that had shielded the Bureau from scrutiny for decades was removed, replaced with relative openness and limited public access to the information in the FBI files. Initial forays into the files allowed pioneering FBI scholars to sketch out the framework of what lay behind the Bureau's public facade and create a timeline of Hoover's many shameless illegalities and seemingly constant lesser offenses against civil liberties. That reality—of a lawless and uncontrolled Bureau that expended enormous amounts of time and resources policing political thought rather than investigating violations of federal law—confirmed more than six decades of critics' complaints. Americans came to understand that Hoover, hired to clean up the Bureau, had ultimately transformed the FBI into an American secret police force, even as he convinced the public and many in the news media that he was a trustworthy defender of civil liberties.

It is interesting to consider how, in a nation so proud of its watchdog press, a high-profile federal agency managed to hide the reality of its activities for so long. The answer is as complex as the FBI's decades-long deception, but it surely includes failings entrenched in the ideology of journalism and in readers' and viewers' often uncritical acceptance of news as truth.

For the news-consuming public, particularly during times of national crisis, Hoover's stellar reputation likely fulfilled some inner need to believe that good people were working hard on their behalf and that better times lay ahead. For ordinary Americans, the question of how government news emerges from the messy process of journalism and public relations was not, and is not, a common topic of concern. Most of the time, news is a commodity consumed without great thought about how it has been produced. An examination of the requirements of news work and of the relationship between public relations messages and news content demonstrates that the production of news, because it involves human beings, is far from the objective ideal that has come to characterize journalists' defense of their work. Instead, it is a human process that involves myriad choices of what to include, what to leave out, and how to express what is left as a simplified narrative that somehow reflects reality.

What about the journalistic canon of objectivity? As David T. Z. Mindich noted in his study of the development of objective journalism, it is surprising that "years after consciousness was complicated by Freud, observation was problematized by Einstein, perspective was challenged by Picasso, writing was deconstructed by Derrida, and 'objectivity' was abandoned by practically everyone outside newsrooms, 'objectivity' is still the style of journalism that our newspaper articles and broadcast reports are written in, or against."[1]

In fact, modern assertions of objective journalism are a twentieth-century phenomenon. Journalism in the early to middle 1800s was an openly and explicitly partisan or "biased" activity, as newspapers associated with particular individuals or political factions presented their own editorial worldviews. With the advent of the Penny Press in the 1830s, which relied on advertising rather than subscription revenues, newspapers filled their columns less with editorial matter, with its presumed potential to alienate advertisers, and more with relatively unbiased "news." The arrival of the Associated Press in 1848 has sometimes been credited with signaling the rise of "objective" journalism. As journalism historian Michael Schudson suggested, however, the defensive journalistic objectivity that exists today did not begin to take shape until after World War I.[2] In spite of minor challenges to the ideology of objectivity, it remains the core of the news paradigm today.

During most of the twentieth and twenty-first centuries, the objective news paradigm has not been defined by a clear set of guidelines or ethical standards. Objective news is an ideal in which "bias" or a lack of objectivity is minimized. Yet even that watered-down definition, a far cry from the blank-slate arguments of an "objective" scientist, is problematic, according to scholar Robert A. Hackett: "The ideal of objectivity suggests that facts can be separated from opinion or value judgments, and that journalists can stand apart from the real-world events whose truth or meaning they transfer to the news audience by means of neutral language and competent reporting techniques."[3] In journalistic practice, objectivity has become a "strategic ritual," a set of established routines that, if applied properly, allows journalists to protect themselves against charges of bias.[4] In practice, a journalist's concern about how to maintain objectivity has become less a philosophical question than a logistical one. The objectivity journalists speak of and the objectivity they practice may be very different. Though they often speak of "truth" and "reality," in practice, journalists learn to gather and juxtapose competing truth claims and proclaim the result to be an "objective" representation.[5]

Thus, the process of reporting the news is a product of journalists and sources understanding those established routines, as noted by Richard V. Ericson, Patricia M. Baranek, and Janet B. L. Chan in their study of crime news. "Staged performances in both the courtroom and newsroom are packaged as if they are based on more 'natural' events and therefore represent unmediated reality," they wrote. "The realism helps them to constitute the truths of their discourses . . . as if theirs is not one way of seeing but *the way* of seeing."[6] The authors concluded that government news coverage, rather than providing a reflection of reality, often becomes "primarily a public conversation among journalists and government officials with others left to make only occasional utterances and to eavesdrop."[7] In his study of the media's role in the emergence and disappearance of the New Left movement in the 1960s, Todd Gitlin asserted that when considered in the context of law enforcement, that closed conversation ostensibly based on interdependence actually overwhelmingly empowers the police: "When the power to define news is, in effect, turned over to the police, the media are serving to confirm the existing control mechanisms in society."[8] It is the conventions of journalism that create a power imbalance between media and government, Gitlin said. By adhering to those conventions and routines, journalists "systematically frame the news to be compatible with the main institutional arrangements of the society. Journalists thus sustain the dominant frames through the banal, everyday momentum of their routines."[9]

Those understandings of the nature of journalism correspond to contemporary accounts during Hoover's early tenure as director of the FBI. In his 1937 book *The Washington Correspondents*, Leo Rosten observed reporters in order to describe how they produced and reproduced government officials' "way of seeing" through their work routines. According to Rosten, the work of reporters covering government was a vocation of "professional reflexes and individual temperament" rather than any application of objectivity:[10]

It is impossible to generalize about the extent to which news-coloring and news-suppression, based on personal obligations . . . thrive in the capital. It is no secret that some newspapermen are charged by the rest of the press corps as being sycophants to ambitious politicians on or off Capitol Hill; that others are won by the flattery of Representatives, Senators, or administrative officials who call them by their first names, slap them on the back, open the sacred portals of Washington Society to their wives, or ask them for advice on political matters.[11]

Rosten described a Washington culture in which the power in the relationship between reporter and source nearly always tipped in the source's favor, with the scale of the power imbalance corresponding to the source's perceived power and authority. "The Washington correspondent must . . . be careful to remain persona grata with his news sources. In the words of the trade, 'he must keep his sources open,'" Rosten wrote. "He may do this by repaying his informants in the currency of journalism: he may play up a story which casts glory on a good news-source and play down a story which is embarrassing."[12]

According to Rosten, the glorification of informative sources sometimes resulted in a reality so skewed that not even the reporter could parse the truth from the myth. "Reporters often come to believe in the fictional qualities which they assign public figures during that professional delirium which characterizes the daily meeting of deadlines," he wrote.[13]

In that daily delirium, authoritative sources in government wield tremendous and even coercive power in the reporter-source relationship. In his 1973 observational study of news workers at the *New York Times* and *Washington Post*, Leon Sigal noted that authoritative sources utilized public relations strategies to maintain their dominance in the reporter-source relationship. Those strategies included going over reporters' heads directly to editors and publishers, deriding coverage that dared stray from a predefined story line, and laboring to feed reporters a steady stream of information, thus assuring little time for careful analysis of any given story.[14]

The most powerful influence in the public relations practitioner's toolbox, however, is the most obvious one: government sources can grant and withhold access to information as they please, and they often do so based on whether reporters remain compliant amplifiers of the agency's message.[15] According to Bernard Roshco in his 1975 book *Newsmaking*, "These potential news sources largely determine for themselves the degree to which they will be publicly visible. They are usually free to release or withhold newsworthy information as they see fit, unless events draw them into public arenas where an 'audience' of reporters is stationed."[16]

The potency of that weapon is obvious when one considers the nature of journalists' ambitions and notions of professionalism. According to sociologist Warren Breed, who observed reporters and editors as a subculture, journalists learn newsroom policy and standards of professionalism "by osmosis."[17] Through interaction with other journalists, a reporter "learns to anticipate what is expected of him so as to win rewards and avoid punishments."[18] Journalists quickly understand that gaining and maintaining access to authoritative sources equates to successful practice because it demonstrates an understanding of the necessities of journalism.[19] "Knowing sources brings professional status," according to sociologist Gaye Tuchman, based on her own newsroom observations. "The higher the status of sources and the greater the scope of their positions, the higher the status of reporters."[20] Journalists are hired to produce news stories. Authoritative sources provide information that is defined by journalists as newsworthy. Thus, maintaining access to those sources clearly demonstrates mastery of the craft to other journalists. With that mastery, however, comes the risk that access to information may suddenly be cut off, which leads to tremendous uncertainty and may potentially lead to ethical compromises. As Sigal noted, "The very routines and conventions that newsmen use to cope with uncertainty, though, are exploited by their sources either to insert information into the news or to propagandize."[21]

The structure of news "beats" likewise feeds the power imbalance. Reporters are essentially asked to embed themselves in an organization, becoming entirely reliant on that organization for access to information. Yet at the same time, reporters are somehow expected to remain connected to their news organization and abide by its policies and ethical principles. The difficulty of negotiating these two disparate positions makes it likely, according to Sigal, that a reporter may "absorb the perspectives of the senior officials he is covering" and become a press agent for the organization.[22] Based on his observations, Sigal concluded that "the line between role-taking and absorption is a thin one indeed."[23]

According to Sigal, Hoover's FBI relied on the absorption of friendly reporters into the Bureau's culture and worldview. "Political support for the FBI and its autonomy within the Justice Department are due in no small measure to the favorable press it has won itself over the years."[24] In his 1966

This photo of reporters interviewing "Hoover" was provided to SAC Edward P. Guinane of Minneapolis. Guinane's note accompanying the picture read: "Jack Conners, reporter for the St. Paul Daily News gave me this picture and said that it represented the results of the determination of the reporters and photographers in the Ross [kidnapping] case. He said that they were all determined to get a picture of Mr. Hoover and turned this into the city desk as the best they could possibly do." (National Archives at College Park, Record Group 65, Series H, Box 4, Folder 208, #1)

study *The Press in Washington,* Ray Eldon Hiebert likewise highlighted FBI public relations and its assimilation of compliant reporters as a key to the Bureau's lofty status in American society:

> The FBI runs its own public relations office quite independently from the Department of Justice and sets many of its own policies. It has a fine public relations operation; the reputation of the FBI and its director is the best evidence of that. The FBI will answer questions from most newsmen. And, upon occasion, it will leak to those newsmen whom it regards as its friends. Its leaks often produce some of the hottest news stories in Washington, but you can bet your last dollar that such stories

appear where and when they do for certain specific reasons best known to the FBI.[25]

While skillful public relations can tip the balance of power in the reporter-source relationship in the direction of the source, the FBI held even greater powers of persuasion based on its role as a federal investigative and law enforcement agency. During the early days of U.S. involvement in World War II, for example, President Roosevelt placed Hoover and the FBI in charge of federal censorship. Starting with that temporary authority, Hoover used the exigencies of war to expand his efforts to monitor and even investigate journalists, according to historian Betty Houchin Winfield. When columnists Drew Pearson and Robert S. Allen published information in their "Washington Merry-Go-Round" column that disclosed details of U.S. losses at Pearl Harbor, Hoover confronted Allen and urged White House officials to threaten the reporters. "In an unprecedented action, [White House official] Steve Early threatened to stop their column and bar their governmental access," Winfield wrote.[26] For most organizations, the success of their public relations efforts hinges on the authority of the source and the salience of the information, but the FBI's public relations efforts were enhanced by Hoover's iconic authority and backed by the power and capabilities of a federal law enforcement and investigative agency.

Beginning in the mid-1970s, many studies of the FBI have explored what lay behind the Bureau's public image. Broad FBI histories have exposed the Bureau's activities over Hoover's forty-eight-year tenure and created a clear timeline of events and of the director's role in twentieth-century American history. Their judgments have been harsh. Historians Athan Theoharis and John Stuart Cox labeled Hoover's tenure "the great American Inquisition" and concluded that "Hoover had more to do with undermining American constitutional guarantees than any political leader before or since."[27] Historian Richard Gid Powers chronicled Hoover's life and noted that the opening of FBI files to scholars has resulted in a case study of "excessive power run amuck." According to Powers, Hoover's tenure is now remembered for its illegal surveillance, secretive nature, and attacks on political opponents. "The rubble of his reputation buried the man himself even deeper, along with the forces that had produced him."[28]

Following these broad studies, scholars began to look more closely at specific aspects of the Bureau's work, focusing on narrow time periods such as the outlaw era of the 1930s or the FBI's work on specific topics such as obscenity and freedom of expression. One very important activity that helped the FBI maintain its public image—public relations—has been mentioned in passing or alluded to generally in studies of Hoover's Bureau. Scholars have identified something they refer to as "public relations" as an important weapon in Hoover's arsenal, but the topic has not been studied in any great depth or with any thoughtful understanding of the nature or history of the practice of public relations. One aspect of public relations—media relations—was a day-to-day focus of the FBI. Although individual reporters' interactions with the FBI have been studied as part of the larger story of the Bureau, there have been no broad studies of FBI public relations and, in particular, the Bureau's relationships with prominent reporters, editors, publishers, broadcasters, and publications.

This book seeks to add detail and perspective to earlier studies by examining the FBI's public relations tactics and its relationships with selected journalists and news publications. It is important, however, to understand the limitations of this study. Given both the volume of source material in the files and the fact that many files were destroyed by Bureau officials after Hoover's death or as part of the agency's ongoing document destruction program, no history of FBI public relations and journalism can ever be considered comprehensive. This caveat only underlines the importance of public relations to Hoover's FBI. For this book, I reviewed more than 400 files of reporters, editors, publications, and others obtained using the Freedom of Information Act. The source materials for this study totaled approximately 200,000 pages detailing those relationships.

I made a conscious decision not to focus on journalists whose relationships with Hoover have already been explored as part of biographies or other studies. Thus, Walter Winchell and Drew Pearson are not covered extensively in this book. The chapters that follow focus instead on some lesser-known journalists whose work for or against the FBI has not been carefully considered elsewhere. Some of the journalists and publications covered here were chosen because of the remarkable length or depth of their relationships with the FBI. Others were selected because their work, while outside the mainstream, was considered significant enough to merit extensive monitoring or even active investigation by the FBI. The subjects were likewise chosen strategically to exemplify different portions of a period beginning with the creation of the FBI's public relations division in the mid-1930s through Hoover's death in 1972 and the cancellation of the Bureau's most famous public relations showcase, its prime-time television program, in 1975. The book's chapters highlight relationships and controversies that typify the approximately forty-year period of the study. Finally, because of the study's scope and its focus on the news media, I chose not to consider FBI educational campaigns, another key element of Bureau public relations under Hoover.

Chapter 1 explores the crisis of legitimacy created by public concerns about potential corruption and abuse of power in a federal police force. From its creation as the Bureau of Investigation in 1908, the FBI faced questions about its responsibility and utility. Critics' concerns about corruption were proved correct by the outrageous overreach of the Palmer Raids, which rounded up thousands of alleged radicals and communists in 1919 and 1920. It was later discovered that those raids were based on faulty evidence, and nearly all those arrested were released. A young J. Edgar Hoover, assistant director in charge of the Bureau's Radical Division, led the prosecution of the Palmer Raids. Yet for some reason, he was chosen to clean up the organization in 1924. From his perch at the center of the storm surrounding the Palmer Raids, Hoover well understood the importance of maintaining the Bureau's legitimacy.

Chapter 2 reviews the history of public relations and the development of a public relations capability, including the creation of a replicable message template and the establishment of a publicity staff, in the Bureau. After a few tentative steps into the realm of publicity during the late 1920s, the Bureau became a key element of FDR's New Deal war on crime in the mid-1930s. Two journalists, independent author Courtney Ryley Cooper and *Washington Star* editorial page editor Neil "Rex" Collier, collaborated with Hoover and his top lieutenants in creating a template for FBI news stories emphasizing responsibility and science and featuring Hoover as America's careful and reliable top law enforcement officer. With the creation of the public relations–oriented Crime Records Section in 1935 and the establishment of clear lines of public communication authority, Hoover had both a public relations message and a management team to amplify and enforce it.

The remaining chapters explore the relationships between Hoover and several key enemies and friends in the news media over time. Iconoclastic liberal journalists George Seldes, I. F. Stone, Fred J. Cook, and James A. Wechsler figure prominently herein because they represent the Bureau's preoccupation with its enemies in the media. Despite their relatively small circulations, liberal publications such as the *PM* newspaper, *The Nation*, and *The New Republic* were the focus of intensive FBI interest because of their agenda-setting roles. Conservative stalwarts such as columnist George Sokolsky, broadcaster Fulton Lewis Jr., and *Chicago Tribune* Washington correspondent Walter Trohan represent prominent journalists with huge followings who became friends and defenders of the FBI. Other key FBI supporters, including *Reader's Digest* editor Fulton Oursler and *Memphis Commercial Appeal* editor Jack Carley, represent a different kind of Bureau "friend." They were willing to work both as "objective" journalists supporting the FBI and Hoover and as adjunct agents and confidential informants discreetly gathering information for the Bureau. Yet another group of journalists and authors, exemplified by two-time Pulitzer Prize–winning Associated Press newsman Don Whitehead, uncritically helped the Bureau amplify its public relations message through FBI-authorized books. Finally, the Bureau's foray into entertainment television in the 1960s and 1970s represents the ultimate expression of its public relations template, while journalists' critical reactions demonstrate how American culture had shifted while Hoover and the FBI remained frozen in the G-man mold of the 1930s and 1940s.

FBI public relations activities, particularly its work with journalists, are significant because Hoover used public relations to create and maintain an iconic public facade that for decades hid the true nature of the Bureau's work from the public. As the chapters that follow demonstrate, the FBI used public relations techniques and tactics to court and handle its friends in the news media. At the same time, the Bureau monitored and investigated its enemies and (with the help of friendly journalists) actively undermined those who were critical of the FBI. Over the course of several decades, and despite the efforts of critics and many leftist journalists and publications, public relations specialists inside the Bureau and friendly journalists outside managed to construct and maintain the facade of a legitimized FBI that most Americans believed was a protector of civil liberties.

Chapter 1

The FBI's Ongoing Crisis of Legitimacy

On March 6, 1959, FBI director J. Edgar Hoover ordered his staff to investigate whether "subversive factors" in the personal lives of prominent news reporters, editors, and publishers might be at fault for news content that was "discrediting our American way of life."[1] Hoover's request for a background review of key journalists came in the wake of a series of news stories attacking the FBI. Most notable was an in-depth critique of Bureau history by *New York World Telegram and Sun* rewrite man Fred J. Cook that filled the entire October 18, 1958, issue of the iconic liberal journal *The Nation*. Cook suggested that the history most Americans knew from news and entertainment media was suspect: "Is the FBI the perfect organization beyond reproach? Or is it a mixture, part heroic fact, part heroic myth which Americans should try to understand before they worship?"[2]

These kinds of questions had loomed over the FBI from the beginning. But with the emergence of the iconic, all-powerful FBI atop a mountain of publicity in the 1930s, such questions became even more of a threat to the Bureau. Cook's fifty-eight-page article deconstructed the mythical FBI of comic books, detective magazines, radio dramas, newspaper and magazine reports, and motion pictures—an image that Hoover's public relations team had systematically built and maintained for two decades. According to the FBI's carefully crafted public relations narrative, the Bureau was unquestionably a fair, restrained, scientific law enforcement agency and Hoover was an all-American figure above reproach. The FBI seldom made errors, according to Bureau-authored dogma; in fact, it was a vigilant and reliable protector of Americans' civil liberties. Anyone who said otherwise, according to Bureau lore, was likely one of the "10,000 Public Enemies" operating from cells infesting every neighborhood. In the 1930s, those public enemies were the ruthless outlaws who roamed the American Midwest. Later in that decade and for the next thirty-plus years of Hoover's tenure, the Bureau's attention turned to leftist politics, branding critics as communists or at least fellow travelers who were party to an enormous conspiracy to overthrow the U.S. government, starting with Hoover and the FBI.

Bureau critics created an ongoing crisis of legitimacy for the FBI as their attacks occasionally penetrated the army of Hoover defenders in the news media and reached the public. These criticisms focused on FBI crime-control tactics, Hoover's god-like media persona, and the Bureau's harassment of the political Left. It was hardly a fairly waged battle of ideas. Hoover controlled most of the public sphere through effective, ongoing public relations campaigns that seduced reporters, editors, political leaders, and, through popular entertainment, Middle America. Critics found themselves relegated to dissident publications, swimming against a tide of pro-Hoover, pro-FBI publicity that never seemed to ebb. Beginning with the war on crime in the early 1930s, FBI publicity constructed a public image of Hoover and his Bureau as icons of American innovation, good, and power. At a time when Americans were desperate for government to do something right, the FBI's pursuit and elimination of John Dillinger and the other "Robin Hood" outlaws of the Midwest provided a compelling hook on which to hang the Bureau's reputation. Hoover built on that narrative, erecting an FBI built not only on real law enforcement innovation but also on a manufactured public relations foundation that hid mistakes and excesses from public view for nearly forty years.

Cook's criticism hit close to home. He was, by 1958, already well known to the FBI, and his lengthy critique—despite appearing in a small-circulation, niche publication—posed a direct challenge to the legitimacy of the federal law enforcement agency and even identified public relations as a factor in legitimizing Hoover's Bureau:

> Is there a danger in a highly concentrated national police power? Is there danger to civil liberties? To freedom of speech? To the administration of justice itself? These questions have been raised again and again; and always until now, they have been answered in the popular mind in favor of the FBI. J. Edgar Hoover and the agency with which his name is inseparably linked—because in effect he is the agency—have been placed by public sentiment upon a pedestal and made the center of a cult of hero worship.[3]

Cook's critique was specifically aimed at rebutting the 1956 authorized history of the Bureau, *The FBI Story: A Report to the People,* a best seller authored by two-time Pulitzer Prize–winning journalist Don Whitehead. Reviews of the book had helpfully reinforced the notion that Whitehead's work represented the famous journalist's earnest effort, as he said in his preface, to "learn the facts so I could report the inside story of the FBI."[4] In *Commentary* magazine, book reviewer and former Socialist Party leader Norman Thomas supported the objective reporting theme. "It comes close to being a eulogy of the man and the institution," Thomas wrote. "It would, however, be very unfair to dismiss the book with this statement. Unquestionably it is an honest piece of work."[5]

In reality, Whitehead worked out of an office at the FBI's Justice Department headquarters, and all the information he used to write the book was supplied by the FBI's public relations division. He did not interview critics or cite any of the unflattering news reports or books that had appeared during Hoover's tenure. Agents in the FBI's Crime Records Division were allowed to read and edit the manuscript before publication. The result, unsurprisingly, was a reinforcement of the Bureau's preferred themes of science, restraint, and the steady Hoover at the helm, told through a revisionist recap of familiar FBI success stories.

Whitehead's "objective" book rewrote portions of FBI history, erasing, for example, Chicago Special Agent in Charge Melvin Purvis (who fell out of favor with Hoover) from the shooting of Dillinger—the Bureau's defining early moment. The Bureau's side project of routinely tapping telephones and planting bugs as part of its investigations into the loyalty of American citizens was explained as simply common sense, analogous to a businessman checking "every possible source for information as to the honesty and reliability of a prospective employee."[6] *The FBI Story* sold well because of its alleged objectivity—after all, it was written by an award-winning war correspondent—and because twenty years of unwaveringly positive publicity for Hoover and the FBI had made them icons of American culture. Whitehead's best seller simply reinforced the publicly accepted, Bureau-authored canon.

Whitehead sold out his own journalistic credibility to the heroic history of the FBI. Hoover counted on the public's logical conclusion that a famed, objective journalist had reviewed the evidence and verified the Bureau's history as it had always been told. Whitehead's book flew off the shelves, and in 1959 it became the basis for a popular motion picture, also titled *The FBI Story*, starring Jimmy Stewart. And when Hoover moved the FBI story into television in 1965, carefully selected scriptwriters were provided copies of Whitehead's book, the popularly accepted, journalist-vetted story of the genesis of the FBI.

Cook's 1958 reporting in *The Nation* systematically dismantled White-head's *FBI Story*, exposing the Bureau's flaws and errors along with its secret: a twenty-year history of surveilling law-abiding American citizens who happened not to share Hoover's ideology and worldview. Cook raised questions about such revered Bureau myths as the origin of the "G-man" moniker and the shooting of Dillinger. Cook even offered evidence that the efficiency and effectiveness of the FBI laboratory and fingerprint identification sections, though laudable, had been overstated. In countering Whitehead's version of FBI history, Cook undermined the carefully crafted signifiers of the Bureau's preferred self-image and painted a picture of the out-of-control secret police force feared by so many Americans.

For Hoover, who had carefully tended the Bureau's image for decades, such direct challenges could not go unanswered, particularly when they were part of a flurry of criticism. Cook's was just the first of several reports in 1958 and 1959 that found a foothold among Bureau critics. Appearing on television on May 4, 1958, industrialist Cyrus Eaton declared that the FBI's growth in power and authority represented an alarming threat to civil liberties. Of the FBI, Eaton told Mike Wallace: "I think it's had a tremendous buildup. It has enjoyed wonderful propaganda and sold itself in a marvelous way. But I always worry when I see a nation feel that it is coming to greatness through the activities of its policemen. And the FBI is just one of scores of agencies in the United States engaged in investigating, in snooping, in informing, in creeping up on people."[7]

Editor James A. Wechsler of the *New York Post* followed Eaton's broadside with a critical series on Hoover and the FBI that appeared in late 1958. FBI officials dismissed Wechsler and his staff as "iconoclastic liberals" who "deliberately seek to break or destroy the highly favorable images which people have of men and women. In short, they would destroy idols of the people."[8] These attacks, along with Cook's article in *The Nation*, convinced the FBI that a coordinated campaign was under way to undermine the agency's legitimacy. Two months after Cook's article was published, assistant director William Sullivan, in a stunningly paranoid memorandum to another top FBI official, declared that the criticisms constitute, "in reality, a concerted attack on the internal security of the United States."[9] Sullivan's determination, not coincidentally, fit with Hoover's overarching thesis that any criticism of the FBI was a threat to the U.S. government. Like most Bureau officials of the Hoover era, Sullivan had internalized the director's narrow conceptualization of acceptable political thought and speech.

Questions about the FBI's legitimate role in society predated Hoover's tenure and can be traced to the organization's founding as the Bureau of Investigation. The questions that shaped Hoover's administration of the FBI are, in fact, as old as the United States itself and relate to a fundamental dispute over limits on federal power and authority. America is the product of a war for independence that was sold to citizens as a necessary response to tyranny. Fearing the arbitrary nature of centralized authority after gaining independence, the founding fathers created a system of government that placed most powers in the hands of the states and severely limited the power of the national government. Under the Articles of Confederation, the single house of Congress required unanimity to pass laws. No single currency was recognized. There was no authority to create armed forces or to levy federal taxes.

This decentralized government was the natural result of a war against perceived tyranny. It was also a dismal failure. The anemic Articles of Confederation led the founding fathers to author a new constitution, the ratification of which led to a battle over the extent of federal powers. Amendments protecting individual liberties were packaged as the Bill of Rights. Thomas Jefferson's anti-Federalists, fearing the corrupting potential of centralized government power, prevailed, and the Bill of Rights was added to the Constitution. From the Bank of the United States crisis in the 1820s to the Civil War to the health care debate of the early twenty-first century, disputes over the bounds of federal power and the rights of individuals have continued to be a staple of American public discourse. Americans have always had a tendency to fear concentrated federal authority. Thus, many Americans in the early twentieth century questioned the legitimacy and trustworthiness of a federal police force.

According to mass communication scholars, organizations whose output is compatible with society's value patterns—specifically, organizations that demonstrate responsibility and utility—are generally considered legitimate by the public.[10] Over time, such organizations may lessen the likelihood of criticism based on perceptions of power imbalance between the institution and individuals in society.[11] Legitimation strategies often employ public relations messages to reduce concerns about the irresponsible exercise of arbitrary power.[12]

The Justice Department's investigative bureau faced questions about its legitimacy from its inception in the first decade of the twentieth century. The creation of the Bureau of Investigation in 1908 came about only after a

Appointed in 1919 by President Woodrow Wilson, A. Mitchell Palmer was the nation's fiftieth attorney general. Palmer, who served until 1921, is perhaps best known for the controversial raids in which approximately 10,000 alleged radicals were rounded up but few were actually convicted. The 1919 and 1920 Palmer Raids were coordinated by the man Palmer had hired to organize and run the General Intelligence Unit: J. Edgar Hoover. (National Archives at College Park, Record Group 65, Series HN, Box 2, Folder 29, #3255d-A)

public controversy over the abuse of power that could result from centralized police authority. Concerns about President Theodore Roosevelt's accrual of executive power—in particular, a controversy surrounding the assignment of Secret Service agents to what opponents viewed as politically inspired investigations—led to a congressional battle over the Justice Department's need for its own investigative force. The issue became a political circus as the players in the drama sought to publicly adjudicate the dispute. Ultimately, it became clear that the attorney general had the power to order the creation of an investigative bureau, and on March 16, 1909, with the stroke of a pen, the Justice Department's Bureau of Investigation (which had been operating with discretionary funds and without congressional authorization since 1908) was founded, despite considerable public opposition.[13]

During its first decade, the Bureau of Investigation did everything possible to justify public concerns about its potential for corruption and the arbitrary exercise of power. According to historian Richard Gid Powers, the Bureau of Investigation veered from investigating major crimes against the nation "to a new role as the nation's agent of vengeance against whoever might be the public enemy of the day."[14] The Bureau could not seem to get out of its own way.

The Palmer Raids of 1919 and 1920 confirmed public fears of the frightening potential of a federal police force. The raids, named after Attorney General A. Mitchell Palmer, targeted anarchists and communists. Thousands of alleged radicals were rounded up, and most were later released. In the months after the raids, critics in the press and Congress highlighted the hearsay nature of much of the evidence against some of those arrested and the complete lack of evidence against others. In addition, the Bureau failed to obtain legitimate arrest warrants in many instances. In short, the Palmer Raids confirmed the potential for federal law enforcement to place itself above the law.

At first, the raids were portrayed as an appropriate response to a legitimate threat. The appeal of anarchism in the late nineteenth and early twentieth centuries as a solution to perceived injustices lay in its obliteration of centralized authority, which adherents believed would spark the restoration of economic and social fairness. Anarchy, colorfully described by one historian as one of the "great dumb forces loosed upon the world," advocated an end to all governmental institutions and the ascendancy of individual liberties.[15] Anarchism was a reaction to the massive and expanding gap between rich and poor in America. Workers were driven to be more productive, but when their increased productivity was not rewarded with wage hikes, corporate wealth and power and the perceived greed of individual barons of industry stoked widespread frustration beginning in the 1870s. Industrial workers felt trapped in the vortex of capitalism out of control.

The first wave of the anarchist movement in the United States, led by journalist Albert R. Parsons, was crushed in the wake of the Haymarket tragedy in 1886. The movement had been growing rapidly thanks to the mushrooming inequity created by the Industrial Revolution, along with the hardship of the economic depression of the 1880s. On May 4, 1886, Parsons and several others spoke at a rally in Haymarket Square in Chicago. After they left, a bomb was thrown at police, and in the ensuing melee, seven police officers and at least four civilians were killed. A nationwide, media-fanned, anti-red hysteria followed. Chicago officials, under tremendous pressure to punish the anarchists for the violence, indicted Parsons and seven others and charged them with murdering the police officers. Not surprisingly, given the media frenzy surrounding the case, the anarchists were found guilty of conspiring to incite the bombing, even though they had not been present at the time of the confrontation. Four of those convicted, including Parsons, were hanged, and the anarchist movement withered until it was revived in the late 1890s. In 1901, President William McKinley was murdered by a presumed anarchist, cementing the violent and revolutionary reputation of the movement.[16] Russia's Bolshevik Revolution in 1917 added a new set of "red" radicals—socialists and communists—to the mix. A series of anarchist bombings in 1917 aroused widespread fear of a growing and threatening radical subversive movement in America.

As exemplified by the anarchists, a frightening tradition of radical violence was already well established as an enemy within when America's entry into the Great War in 1917 formalized the enemy abroad. The war effort included a dramatic expansion of federal power and a corresponding crackdown on dissent. The United States was hardly united in its certainty that entering the war was a necessary and wise decision. In 1916, President Woodrow Wilson won reelection based on a campaign slogan that stated, "He kept us out of war." One of the first executive orders Wilson signed after U.S. entry into the war created the Committee on Public Information (CPI), a government publicity agency charged with fostering national unity, encouraging support of the war, and, importantly, encouraging citizens to purchase war bonds to finance expensive overseas combat operations.

Even as the CPI was created to encourage national unity, Wilson took steps to crush dissent within the United States. In an address to Congress on April 2, 1917, Wilson evangelized suspicion of dissenters when he declared that overseas enemies had "filled our unsuspecting communities and even our offices of government with spies and set criminal intrigues everywhere afoot against our national unity of counsel, our peace within and without, our industries and our commerce."[17] To address that threat, Wilson authorized the Department of Justice to investigate, arrest, and imprison any noncitizen found to be disloyal.

John Edgar Hoover came of age during an era of growing radicalism in America. Hoover was born in 1895 and lived all his life in Washington, D.C. His father and grandfather worked for the federal government. Hoover's father, Dickerson Hoover, suffered from depression and ultimately lost his job as a federal cartographer and was institutionalized. As a child and a teenager, Hoover leaned on his mother, Annie, for support. He lived with her in his childhood home six blocks southeast of the Capitol until she died in 1938,

J. Edgar Hoover at his Justice Department desk, December 22, 1924. (Library of Congress, National Photo Company Collection, LOT 12362, J. Edgar Hoover)

when Edgar was forty-three years old. In high school, Hoover led his school's cadet corps and debating squad. While studying law at George Washington University, he began his career in the federal government as a clerk at the Library of Congress, where he gained an appreciation for the institution's intricate system of indexing its holdings. After earning his law degree, Hoover joined the Department of Justice in July 1917, three months after the United States entered the Great War. A few months later, the twenty-three-year-old, newly credentialed Justice Department attorney became head of the Enemy Alien Registration Section. Throughout the war, Hoover led his section in compiling an extensive index of individuals deemed to be threats to national security.[18]

Labor and social unrest characterized the years after the Great War, as 4 million U.S. soldiers and 9 million war production workers competed for jobs in a faltering economy. The majority of U.S. workers labored twelve hours a day, six days a week, earning just pennies per hour. Anarchists, their ranks revived by the economic turmoil of the postwar era, turned to violence, hoping to ignite a workers' revolution to overthrow the U.S. government. Members of the anarchist movement punctuated those desires with a series of sensational bombings, including an attack on Palmer's home.

At about 11:15 p.m. on June 2, 1919, a man carrying a suitcase ran toward the front of Palmer's house on R Street in Washington, D.C. He tripped and fell, setting off a massive explosion that shattered the front of the house and obliterated the bomber. Palmer and his family escaped unharmed, except for ringing ears and a lost sense of security. Eight other bombs exploded around the country that night, all aimed at men who had urged or led crackdowns on alleged radicals. Two people died. Prior to the bombings, Palmer, an avowed progressive believer in Wilson's New Democracy programs, had eased the Justice Department's campaign against radicals, releasing enemy aliens and even suggesting that Socialist Party presidential candidate Eugene B. Debs be granted clemency (he was not). During his first three months in office, some members of Congress condemned Palmer for failing to address the radical threat. After the attack on his home and family, though, Palmer joined the growing antiradical backlash.[19] He turned to the bright, young, ambitious Hoover to lead the Justice Department's expanded antiradical efforts.

On January 2, 1920, Bureau raids directed by Hoover resulted in the arrest of approximately 10,000 alleged communists, anarchists, pacifists, socialists, and labor activists across the country. Agents in the field were instructed to coordinate their work with Hoover and were forbidden to notify local authorities. Two-thirds of those detained were immediately released, with the remaining 3,500 held for deportation hearings. In the end, only 556 were deported.[20] Among the foreign-born American citizens deported in the wake of the raids were famed anarchist Emma Goldman and her lover Alexander Berkman. Wisconsin congressman Victor Berger, reelected as a socialist in 1918, was convicted of sedition and sent to prison.

The brutal tactics and the nationwide extent of the raids, punctuated by the few prosecutions that resulted, raised questions in Congress and the press about whether a federal law enforcement agency could remain uncorrupted in nature and restrained in its practices. Congressional hearings were called, and the Senate Judiciary Committee denounced the performance of the Bureau of Investigation and the Justice Department as "the lawless acts of a mob."[21] Editors of *The New Republic* described the raids as "probably the most violent, lawless and inhumane proceeding which any department of the federal government has committed since the founding of the Republic."[22] In his 1958 article, Cook referred to the raids as an indiscriminate "dragnet."[23]

As details of the raids emerged and public sentiment turned against him, Palmer was called before the Senate Judiciary Committee on January 19, 1921, to explain the necessity of the arrests and defend the tactics employed. When asked for specific information about the number of search warrants issued, Palmer deferred to his General Intelligence Division chief, Hoover, who was seated beside him at the hearing: "If you would like to ask Mr. Hoover, who was in charge of this matter, he can tell you."[24] It was one of the few times that Hoover's involvement in leading the investigations that led to the creation of 450,000 security index cards on alleged radicals, directing the production of arrest and search warrants, and directing the raids themselves was publicly acknowledged. Those facts would later be added to the long list of inconvenient facts Hoover erased from his FBI and personal histories.

By 1923, the Justice Department and its Bureau of Investigation, tarnished by the fallout from the Palmer Raids and by ongoing allegations of corruption, were referred to in the media as "The Department of Easy Virtue" and "The Department of Hysteria and Intolerance."[25] The *New York Times* recalled that controversy in a 1940 article, citing it as a source of the mounting criticism of the pre–World War II FBI: "There have been times in years past when the practices of the FBI have been attacked. Twenty years ago, for instance, before the bureau assumed its present status, it was denounced by many prominent officials and attorneys including the present Chief Justice [Charles Evans] Hughes and Justice [Felix] Frankfurter, as well as by the Senate Judiciary Committees for the so-called Palmer Raids of 1920."[26]

The Bureau of Investigation's involvement in scandals did not end with the Palmer Raids. In 1923, Montana's Democratic senators Burton Wheeler and Thomas Walsh initiated an investigation of Interior Secretary Albert Fall's decision to forgo bidding and to issue leases for oil reserves in Teapot Dome, Wyoming, and Elk Hills, California, to two prominent businessmen. In response to the Senate investigation, the director of the Bureau of Investigation, William J. Burns, secretly ordered his agents to uncover damaging information about Wheeler. In the course of their investigation of Senator Wheeler, agents tapped phones, opened mail, and broke into offices and homes. When a congressional committee learned of the investigation and its

Harlan Fiske Stone on April 2, 1924, a few days before being appointed attorney general by President Calvin Coolidge. Stone's surprising choice of J. Edgar Hoover to lead the Bureau of Investigation later that year was the start of Hoover's nearly half-century directorship. (Library of Congress, National Photo Company Collection, call number LC-F8-29811; digital reproduction LC-DIG-npcc-10905)

tactics, and found evidence of other investigations of members of Congress, President Calvin Coolidge ordered Burns and his boss, Attorney General Harry M. Daugherty, to resign.[27] Critics' fears that the Bureau would inevitably transform into a secret police force had been confirmed, and the agency's reputation for overreaching and corruption was further established.

The Bureau of Investigation needed new leadership. In a May 1924 statement, Attorney General Harlan Fiske Stone issued what a 1976 congressional committee investigating FBI excesses labeled the "Stone Standard." In his statement, Stone warned of the dangers of a secret police system. "The Bureau of Investigation is not concerned with political or other opinions of individuals," Stone wrote. "It is only concerned with their conduct and then only with such conduct as is forbidden by the laws of the United States. When a police system passes beyond those limits, it is dangerous to the proper institution of justice and to human liberty, which should be our first concern to cherish. Within them it should rightly be a terror to the wrongdoer."[28] According to the Stone Standard, the corruption and political spying of the early Bureau of Investigation raised clear questions about the agency's legitimacy, which could be restored only through new leadership and a new direction.

The next day, in what now appears to be a confounding move, the newly appointed Stone, an outspoken critic of the Palmer Raids a few years earlier, addressed those questions of legitimacy by naming twenty-nine-year-old Hoover—one of the engineers of the Justice Department's campaign against radicalism—to lead the entire Bureau of Investigation.[29] Hoover's appointment as interim director was accompanied by the attorney general's statement reinforcing the Stone Standard and assuring the public that the Bureau's power would be held in check and the agency's integrity would be a top priority. Under its new leadership, Stone reiterated, the Bureau would not be "concerned with political or other opinions of individuals, only with their conduct and only with such conduct as is forbidden by the laws of the United States."[30]

The story of Hoover's appointment as interim director was captured in the agency's history, retold in countless media reports, and even taught as part of the curriculum at the FBI's police academies. According to Whitehead's authorized history, Hoover entered Stone's office and was told, "Young man, I want you to be Acting Director of the Bureau of Investigation." According to Whitehead, Hoover "knew that Stone did not hold him responsible for the policies, mistakes and corrupt actions of those who had directed the Department of Justice and the Bureau of Investigation in the past."[31] Hoover's role in leading the Palmer Raids apparently did not come up.

According to Hoover's version of events, he then issued a series of conditions for Stone to agree to, including isolating the Bureau from politics and establishing a system of merit-based appointments and promotions. According to Kenneth Ackerman, a biographer of Hoover's early career, the FBI version of Hoover's appointment was a lie. "In fact, it was Edgar's favorite kind of lie, the elegant silence of a kept secret," Ackerman wrote. "The conception was not immaculate at all. In convincing Harlan Stone to give him the acting job that day in 1924, bright, fresh-faced, earnest young J. Edgar Hoover had cheated the older man."[32] In fact, Ackerman stated that, as Palmer had suggested in his congressional testimony about the raids, Hoover had "argued the most strident views; demanding more arrests, higher bail, fewer rights for detainees, and a tougher line against anyone who stood in his way."[33] Yet somehow, Stone labored under the impression that Hoover had played a minor role in the raids. The symbolism of Hoover's entry into the directorship, under conditions that emphasized responsibility and incorruptibility, became an oft-repeated fable in the director's legend.

During Hoover's short tenure as interim director, the American Civil Liberties Union (ACLU) issued a report challenging the legitimacy of the Bureau of Investigation, which, it charged, had become a "secret police system of a political character." The fifteen-page ACLU pamphlet, titled *The Nation-Wide Spy System Centering in the Department of Justice*, accused the Bureau of a wide variety of excesses ranging from burglary to political blacklisting.[34] Stone forwarded the pamphlet to Hoover for comment. Hoover issued what eventually became a boilerplate reply to such criticism, a staple in asserting the Bureau's legitimacy. The Bureau only investigated violations of federal laws, Hoover said. He denied all charges of burglary and wiretapping and accused the ACLU of acting out of communist influence.[35] This pattern of claiming limited jurisdiction, denying charges outright, and ascribing subversive motives to accusers would be heard again and again throughout Hoover's forty-eight-year tenure.

Having prepared his boss, Hoover, Stone, and ACLU founder and executive director Roger Baldwin met. At their meeting, Hoover denied responsibility for the Palmer Raids and pledged to shut down the General Intelligence Division (GID). The first claim was a lie. The second became one when Hoover removed the GID from his organizational chart but kept its files and indices and continued to add individuals and information to them.[36] Nonetheless, both Stone and Baldwin believed him, and four months later, on December 10, 1924, the attorney general removed Hoover's "interim" label.[37]

To his credit, Hoover, the consummate bureaucrat, spent his early tenure adjusting the agency's bureaucratic structure and steering it clear of the temptation to enforce Prohibition.[38] He established the executive conference, initially made up of division chiefs, as a policy advisory group. He made the special agents in charge (SACs) around the country, who had enjoyed tremendous autonomy under prior directors, answerable directly to Washington. He initiated inspection teams to monitor compliance with his new rules. And he standardized a new filing and indexing system. He also established dress and personal conduct codes. Hoover created a set of standards and procedures—reflecting his own work habits and personal principles—where none had existed before.[39] The Bureau was no longer corrupt, but it remained a bureaucratic backwater, a little-known investigative agency with a small force of agents who did not carry weapons or make arrests.

The Great Depression and the election of President Franklin Delano Roosevelt promised a new deal for the American people and a new role for

Hoover's FBI. Beginning in 1933, Roosevelt's New Deal programs centralized economic power within the federal government, as well as emphasizing centralized federal law enforcement and public relations.[40] At about the same time, a number of midwestern outlaws began a crime spree throughout the middle third of the United States. Out-of-the-way places suddenly became household names. Crown Point, Indiana, site of John Dillinger's jailbreak, and Manitowosh Waters, Wisconsin, site of the Little Bohemia resort where Dillinger's gang shot it out with FBI agents, captured headlines as the war on crime began. Dillinger's fame became Hoover's after FBI agents, led by SAC Melvin Purvis, gunned the outlaw down outside the Biograph Theater in Chicago in July 1934. The FBI's pursuit of midwestern outlaws displayed its strengths, providing a clearinghouse of information that enabled a more strategic and nationwide approach to law enforcement. As the bodies of outlaws and FBI agents began to pile up, however, some critical voices again began to warn of corruption and lack of accountability. In November 1934, for example, *Harper's* published an article by attorney William Seagle headlined, "The American National Police: The Dangers of Federal Crime Control." Seagle, who also authored a book about ludicrous and outdated laws and went on to become a trial examiner for the National Labor Relations Board, decried the New Deal expansion of the Bureau of Investigation's jurisdiction in 1934.

The first expansion of the Bureau's limited jurisdiction had been passed by Congress in 1910, when the White Slave Traffic Act (the Mann Act) made prostitution a national crime. In 1919, Bureau of Investigation jurisdiction expanded again with passage of the Dyer Act, which outlawed the interstate transportation of stolen motor vehicles. Bureau jurisdiction remained static throughout the Harding and Coolidge administrations. Under Herbert Hoover, the Bureau gained responsibility for gathering crime statistics and maintaining a national fingerprint repository. The publicity surrounding the kidnapping of Charles Lindbergh's infant son in 1932 led Congress to extend the Bureau's authority to cover kidnapping with passage of the so-called Lindbergh Law.

Public fascination with outlaws such as Dillinger and the Barker-Karpis gang in 1933 and 1934, though, was the driving force behind a dramatic expansion of Bureau jurisdiction under Roosevelt. Attorney General Homer S. Cummings declared that the nation was "engaged in a war that threatens the safety of our country."[41] In May and June 1934, Congress passed nine bills dramatically expanding the Bureau's jurisdiction. Agents were authorized to carry firearms and make arrests. The Bureau became responsible for fugitive felons. The Lindbergh Law was expanded to automatically involve the Bureau in all kidnappings after seven days. The Dyer Act was expanded to involve the Bureau in any theft of property valued at more than $5,000. The robbery of any bank covered by the Federal Deposit Insurance Corporation became a federal crime.[42] Overnight, the Bureau was recast as a true police organization with broad jurisdiction. The legal authority for the Bureau's investigation of subversive activities was also enhanced in 1934 when Roosevelt ordered Hoover to investigate American fascism, an order he expanded to include communism and other subversive activities two years later.[43]

In his critique of the expansion of federal police power, Seagle opened with a simple question: "How many persons know that there is at this moment a national police force, or, if they know it, realize what this implies?"[44] He then alluded to the corruption of the Department of Easy Virtues before asserting that federal law enforcement placed basic civil liberties at risk. "Accompanying the unprecedented expansion of Federal power, and a Fascist spirit in the world at large, the assault upon local criminal jurisdiction betokens, to say the least, a danger of widespread assault upon civil liberties," Seagle wrote.[45] Near the end of his ten-page assault on federal law enforcement, Seagle reminded readers of Hoover's role in the Palmer Raids. "Indeed the present head of the Division of Investigations in the Department of Justice, J. Edgar Hoover, was an agent in the Department in the heyday of the Palmer red-baiting era, who, even after the Red scare had somewhat abated, devotedly spent a good deal of his time in shadowing harmless souls in the national capital."[46]

Meanwhile, Hoover was moving to counter challenges like those offered by Seagle. After the stories about Dillinger and the capture or killing of several other famed outlaws had faded, Hoover created a public relations–oriented Crime Records Section (later renamed the Crime Records Division) in 1935, and it handled public affairs for the Bureau throughout Hoover's tenure.[47] By doing so, however, Hoover opened himself up to further criticism from a key member of Congress: Tennessee senator Kenneth McKellar, who chaired the appropriations subcommittee responsible for the Department of Justice's budget. When Hoover appeared before McKellar's subcommittee in 1936 to request that his agency's budget be doubled to $5 million in the next fiscal year, McKellar pounced. (Hoover had also offended the senator by refusing to hire as special agents any of the men McKellar had recommended.) Senator McKellar criticized the Bureau's public relations efforts, noting that in the previous year, more than fifty feature articles on the FBI had appeared in magazines:

> Senator McKellar: Was anything appropriated to pay these writers?
> Hoover: No, sir; not a cent.
> Senator McKellar: Have you any writers in your Department or do you employ any writers?
> Hoover: Not in the Bureau of Investigation.
> Senator McKellar: No writers are employed?
> Hoover: Not in the Bureau of Investigation.[48]

This was not entirely true. The Crime Records Division employed a correspondence team and two or three key officials who shepherded journalists through the process of reporting on the FBI. They provided information, responded to queries, and even edited copy before publication. Crime Records officials also authored "Interesting Case" memoranda—dramatic retellings of Bureau exploits provided to the press. Hoover was splitting hairs. Was writing letters, including letters with a public relations intent, considered writing? Were those "Interesting Case" memoranda simply part of the normal record keeping of any government bureaucracy? Was editing and rewriting copy considered writing? Clearly, these activities fit the definition McKellar had in mind. But as Hoover and his aides frequently did in testimony to congressional committees—for example, answering "no" when asked if there were "secret files," because that was not the FBI's term for them—he prevaricated, defining writing and public relations narrowly.

As his chief "writer" in the Crime Records Section, Hoover had hired Louis B. Nichols, considered by some to be the second most influential person in the history of the FBI.[49] For more than twenty years, Nichols acted as the editor and protector of the FBI's public image. A Decatur, Illinois, native, Nichols earned his law degree from Hoover's alma mater, the George Washington University School of Law, in 1934. He entered the FBI shortly after graduation, bringing with him experience as a public relations officer for the Young Men's Christian Association, a job he had held during law school. Nichols's stunning rise coincided with Hoover's need for public relations advice. According to historian Athan Theoharis, Nichols "personally was responsible for developing the Bureau's policies regarding the press, radio, films, and eventually, television."[50] Nichols held other titles during his twenty-three years in the FBI, including assistant to the director, but he re-

In 1935, Hoover hired Louis B. Nichols to be his chief liaison with the press. Nichols was responsible for developing Bureau policies on the press, radio, films, and television. (National Archives at College Park, Record Group 65, Series F, Box 1, Folder 13, #6)

mained the most important public relations adviser in the Bureau's executive leadership.

Review any FBI file produced during Nichols's tenure, and you will find that his comments and suggestions with regard to public relations carried tremendous weight with Hoover and with associate director Clyde Tolson. Nichols organized the Crime Records Section as a clearinghouse for all media information coming into the Bureau. News clippings were reviewed, and any items of interest to the FBI were summarized. A correspondence team authored tens of thousands of letters that were sent out over Hoover's signature over the decades. High-level administrators in Crime Records edited and rewrote news, feature, and magazine stories produced by cooperative reporters. Crime Records staff rewrote scripts for radio, television, and film. In short, Crime Records was responsible for authoring and enforcing the FBI's preferred image of itself. Any reports in the news or entertainment media that were off message might create public concern over the Bureau's power or jurisdiction. Thus, it was up to Crime Records, and often to Nichols himself, to deal with off-message reporters and to stroke and flatter the Bureau's news-gathering friends.

Under Nichols, FBI public relations was a hugely successful combination of salient stories and rigid messaging discipline. The Bureau's growth in public relations acumen mirrored (and helped drive) the overall growth of the Bureau. By 1936, the FBI had grown from fewer than 100 agents in 1930 to nearly 900 agents stationed in the "Seat of Government," as FBI headquarters in Washington was called, and in fifty-two field offices nationwide.[51] Despite the ongoing crisis of legitimacy fanned by critics on the Left, the once unknown Hoover and his FBI had become "reassuring symbol[s] of security and stability for most Americans."[52] That same year, Secretary of State Cordell Hull gave the FBI oral authorization to investigate alleged subversion; this was strengthened by a presidential directive in 1939. With the 1940 passage of the Smith Act, outlawing advocacy of the violent overthrow of the government, and the Hatch Act, outlawing federal employment for any member of an allegedly subversive organization, Hoover had all the authorization he needed to become the American secret police that critics feared.

Even as he ramped up the investigation of subversives (very broadly defined in Hoover's narrow worldview), the director succeeded in addressing the Bureau's ongoing crisis of legitimacy by proffering his FBI as an all-American scientific agency fighting evil wherever it appeared and weaving together the patchwork of local law enforcement. Nichols and the Crime Records Section worked with reporters to amplify that message and drown out critics. The restrained but efficient FBI and the dogged and careful Hoover were images that Americans were, by and large, happy to accept. But there remained significant opposition to the idea of federal law enforcement in general and the Bureau of Investigation in particular. According to historian Powers, "After the Palmer Raids and the FBI's antiunion campaigns of the early twenties, the left's hatred of the Bureau had hardened into a basic fact of American political life."[53]

One place where Hoover monitored the potential for the Left to raise uncomfortable questions about the FBI was America's newsrooms. In the introduction to his "Molders of Public Opinion" report, Sullivan captured Hoover's belief that so-called subversive journalists were not simply dissenters but were active and conspiratorial agents of evil:

> The ability of the press or other media of public information to work for good or evil is dependent upon those who comprise its ranks. The views

of those within its ranks will inevitably be a reflection of some of their activities and personal beliefs. . . . Looking at the following representative segment of those molding public opinion today, we can raise the question as to whether or not many have made themselves worthy of American ideals so that they may be entrusted with carrying forward human progress and dignity.[54]

Sullivan's 1959 case study demonstrated the single-minded nature of the FBI that Hoover had built. It was a narrow and conspiratorial worldview that Sullivan completely internalized.

A Boston native, Sullivan joined the FBI in 1941 at an annual salary of $3,800. He was quickly promoted because of what a supervisor called a "particularly deep and thoughtful approach to his work."[55] He was also described as being "somewhat small," but with a "mature outlook."[56] (Nearly every performance review in Sullivan's more than 1,000-page personnel file mentioned his diminutive stature.) During the 1940s, Sullivan moved from the San Antonio office to the so-called Seat of Government in Washington, where he worked as a supervisor in the Strategic Intelligence Service (SIS), the Bureau's overseas spying operation. Sullivan was responsible for supervising SIS operations in Venezuela, British Guiana, Suriname, French Guiana, Aruba, Curaçao, and the Caribbean, with the exception of Cuba.[57] During this time, Sullivan began communicating directly with Hoover, for example, suggesting a special contact the Bureau could use to try to convince FDR to put the FBI in charge of overseas spying after World War II.[58]

Throughout the 1940s, Sullivan's ambition was on display. He was praised for volunteering for Christmas duty, pitching in on special assignments without being asked, and deferring his vacation to cover for colleagues. Supervisors described him as "unusually conscientious and hard-working," with "an unusual aptitude for research and writing."[59] Marksmanship was the only recurring negative on his annual reviews. In 1946, Sullivan moved from SIS and became a supervisor in the FBI's Atomic Energy Section; then, in 1947, he moved from the periphery to the center of Hoover's interest, supervising the Communist Research Desk of the Internal Security Section, where he created an index of alleged communist front organizations for the attorney general. About the same time, Sullivan earned his master's degree in education from George Washington University.

In 1948, Sullivan continued his campaign to catch Hoover's attention, thanking the director for a promotion and pledging his loyalty in a personal

Hoover congratulates assistant director William C. Sullivan for twenty years of service on July 24, 1961. Sullivan's rise to power in the FBI was followed by a swift fall from grace, resulting in his firing in 1971. (National Archives at College Park, Record Group 65, Series H, Box 31, #1697)

letter. He vowed to demonstrate that Hoover's confidence in him was justified and wrote, "in this time of crisis and of rapidly mounting threats to our country, our ideals, and our faith, I want you to know that I am immediately ready and most willing to serve the Bureau either inside or outside of this country in any capacity at all, irrespective of the rigors, privations, and dangers of the assignment."[60] Hoover wrote back that he appreciated the expression of loyalty.[61] Hoover next made note of Sullivan in a handwritten comment on a memorandum informing the director that Sullivan's premature son had died. "Keep [Sullivan] in mind," Hoover wrote. "He looks as if he has possibilities."[62]

Sullivan continued his rise within the Bureau, taking the initiative to write a number of summaries, including "Glossary of Marxist Terms," "Definitions of Socialism," "The Communist Party's Position on Fascism," and "Eight Points of Communist Philosophy." Sullivan began lecturing on the communist threat at FBI in-service training sessions. He was angling to become the Bureau's point man on communism and was getting noticed.[63] Upon his next promotion, he wrote another fawning letter to Hoover, exclaiming that "work done for the Bureau is not work at all. On the contrary it is a privilege freely given to a free person to use freely whatever talents he may have in the behalf of his deepest convictions—convictions which give meaning and purpose to life."[64] After another pay raise prompted by an eighty-three-day marathon during which Sullivan worked an average of three hours a day of "voluntary overtime," he was again promoted.[65]

In 1950, Sullivan was offered, and turned down, an executive position outside the FBI. An avid self-promoter, he provided Hoover with a copy of the letter he sent to railroad owner Frederick C. Dumaine Jr., rejecting the job offer. Clearly aiming to demonstrate his loyalty to Hoover, Sullivan told Dumaine that he could not take the position because he was completely satisfied at the FBI and cited four reasons, including Hoover's leadership. "While it is true I may be able to earn a larger salary outside of the government service," Sullivan wrote, "I do believe the four reasons given above adequately compensate for a larger salary."[66]

Upon his tenth anniversary at the FBI, Sullivan wrote to Hoover again, this time a florid, three-page tome expressing his feelings about the Bureau. "A man grows slowly into the FBI, absorbs its spirit and becomes a part of it as he becomes a part of his own family," Sullivan wrote. "It is both a pleasant and a painful process. The FBI, like one's family, has its ups and downs, its good days and bad days." Sullivan could not have chosen a more appealing theme. After all, Hoover had no family except for the FBI.[67] Hoover had the letter reprinted in *The Investigator*, the FBI's internal newsletter.[68] By 1953, Sullivan's pay had increased to more than $11,000 and he had been placed in charge of the Central Research Desk in the renamed Domestic Intelligence Division. He was the Bureau's top expert on communism and was responsible for giving lectures to other agents and to outside organizations.

Hoover's interest began to take on a paternal cast that same year when a serious viral infection put Sullivan in the hospital for several weeks and kept him away from his Washington office off and on for more than eighteen months. Hoover wrote a note on a memorandum updating him on Sullivan's condition: "Find out from Dr. Miller when he thinks Sullivan could safely return, add one week to it & I will order Sullivan not to return until then. He is one of our most conscientious & valuable men."[69] Upon Sullivan's return to work in late March 1953, Hoover noted: "He should take it easy."[70] Hoover sent Sullivan to the FBI office in Tucson, Arizona, on "special assignment" for several months, where he could recuperate in the dry conditions there.[71] During his time in Tucson, Sullivan continued his prolific writing, producing eleven new research studies on communism. The SAC in Tucson took advantage of Sullivan's presence by booking him to speak to local civic groups.

Thus Sullivan's focus on becoming the in-house expert on communism, along with his ability to coherently express the Bureau's (Hoover's) position in writing, had placed him on the director's radar as a rising star on the management team. In the ensuing years, Sullivan continued to show an uncanny ability to express positions that captured Hoover's imagination. He had become the golden boy among Hoover's cadre of anticommunist hawks and was positioned to continue his quick rise to the top in the Seat of Government. By 1954, Hoover was addressing Sullivan as "Bill" in correspondence and had promoted him to the rank of inspector.[72]

Between 1954 and 1963, Sullivan was the Bureau's go-to speaker on communism, addressing more than 200 government, military, and law enforcement groups. Sullivan's personnel file contains several hundred letters from those who sponsored or attended those talks, praising Hoover for sending such an expert and dynamic speaker. During that interval, Sullivan's health improved significantly, and he racked up an average of three hours of overtime per day. On October 25, 1957, Sullivan wrote another letter to Hoover in which he discussed "disturbing" events, including the launch of *Sputnik* by the Soviet Union, and praised the director for maintaining his focus on internal security. "In the light of these recent events, will these powerful opponents of internal security remove their ostrich-like heads from the sand to recognize the reality of the situation which you have been forcefully and clearly describing?" Sullivan wrote. "We must wait and observe, knowing only too well that 'there are none so blind as those who will not see.'"[73] During that same period, Sullivan began the odd practice of referring to himself in the third person in his memoranda: "Sullivan is of the opinion that next fall his lectures should be highly selective," Sullivan wrote.[74]

In 1957 and 1958, Sullivan, along with sixteen other FBI personnel, contributed to the production of a book, *Masters of Deceit: The Story of Communism and How to Fight It*, which was published by Henry Holt and listed

Hoover as the author. Crime Records chief Nichols cited Sullivan as the second most important contributor to the project, which was based largely on the studies Sullivan had produced in the General Research Section.[75]

On June 2, 1961, Sullivan's efforts were rewarded when he became assistant director in charge of the Domestic Intelligence Division. In 1963, his leadership of Domestic Intelligence was questioned in the wake of the assassination of President Kennedy. Lee Harvey Oswald was not included in the Bureau's extensive security index, and Sullivan was officially censured. Only a few months later, though, Sullivan earned an outstanding performance rating for his work in 1963 and 1964.[76] Clearly, he remained a Hoover favorite.

As assistant director in the Domestic Intelligence Division, Sullivan supervised the FBI's counterintelligence program, COINTELPRO, which was charged with disrupting and undermining, through various and often questionable means, groups considered to be threats to national security. Based on Sullivan's suggestion, the investigation of "racial matters," including coverage of hate groups such as the Ku Klux Klan and civil rights groups as well, was transferred to the Domestic Intelligence Division in August 1964.[77] Under that mandate, Sullivan approved (and may have authored) an anonymous letter to Dr. Martin Luther King that threatened to expose King's alleged extramarital affairs. This letter, according to historian Athan Theoharis, is "often interpreted as an effort to induce the civil rights activist to commit suicide."[78] In 1970, Sullivan was elevated to the number-three position in the Bureau, assistant to the director, behind Hoover and Tolson. Sullivan was the ideal FBI official, having adopted a perfect facsimile of Hoover's xenophobic and conspiratorial worldview. He was also a perfect example of how quickly Hoover could sour on an agent who had ideas of his own.

In 1971, the former golden child publicly criticized Hoover, who had refused to accept proposals by the Nixon administration that would have expanded the Bureau's powers. Fearing that Hoover would use the existence of White House–ordered wiretaps of members of the news media against the Nixon administration, Sullivan turned the material over to White House officials without informing the Bureau. Sullivan hoped Nixon would protect him and might even force Hoover out and elevate him to the director's office. Instead, Hoover forced Sullivan to retire because of what the director called his "insolence and insubordination."[79] Sullivan's final FBI performance rating from early 1971 was "outstanding."

When members of the media contacted the FBI and asked for a recent photo of Sullivan, their requests were denied.[80] When Sullivan, who had served in the FBI for more than thirty years, asked to retain his badge for sentimental reasons, Hoover denied the request.[81] Former *New York Post* editor and longtime Hoover critic James A. Wechsler observed that Sullivan "had been declared a non-person."[82] Others compared Sullivan's erasure from the Bureau to Hoover's rewriting of FBI history to remove Chicago SAC Melvin Purvis from the Dillinger case nearly four decades earlier. Washington columnists Rowland Evans and Robert Novak captured the lesson of Sullivan's firing in two sentences: "In frustration, some of the FBI's top officials began dealing, behind Hoover's back, directly with the highly conservative chiefs of the Nixon Justice Department. Furious, Hoover struck back with his reign of terror."[83]

Perhaps Hoover saw elements of himself in Sullivan. After all, Hoover had been Palmer's ambitious young aide and had made himself indispensable by becoming the Justice Department's top authority on radical anarchists and communists in 1919 and 1920. The lesson in Sullivan's steady rise and precipitous fall was this: the way to get to the top of the FBI (and stay there) was to adopt Hoover's narrow worldview and his simple, black-and-white ethical system while simultaneously flattering the director, who would designate as his golden children those who stood above criticism within the bureaucracy. Hoover was the Sun King of the FBI and expected all his employees to adopt his worldview, maintain it over time, and provide an endless stream of praise.

Sullivan's 1959 memorandum summarizing more than 4,000 cross-references in the files the FBI had compiled on journalists was based on reports authored over time by single-minded FBI agents who shared the director's distrust of the press; thus, it may be seen as reflective of Hoover's own views on the media and the political Left, which remained very consistent over time. Sullivan's 1959 review was based, in part, on a memorandum produced more than twenty years prior, in 1938, at the request of *Reader's Digest* editor Fulton Oursler. Oursler was a pen pal of Hoover's and an avowed friend of the Bureau, and he asked the director to provide material for a story about how "newspapers have interfered with crime."[84] *Reader's Digest* was, at the time, the most widely read periodical in the United States. Within a week, Hoover's public relations staff responded to Oursler with two lengthy memoranda. "Of course the material I am sending you will be more than you will want to use, but I wanted you to have a rather complete picture of some of the things with which we have been confronted during the past few years," Hoover's ghostwriter informed Oursler.[85] The letter writer even offered to check Oursler's article when it was done, "in order that there will absolutely be no comeback whatsoever from any representative of the press who might be involved in the instances mentioned."[86]

One of the attachments was a twelve-page review of situations in which the press had aided the FBI in its law enforcement duties. In a breathless, oddly punctuated, run-on, stream-of-consciousness sentence, the FBI of 1938 offered its view of the role of the press:

> Successful law enforcement is dependent upon a close friendly relationship with the press and other great molders of public opinion for these mediums have a public duty and a public obligation similar to that of the Federal Bureau of Investigation or any other law enforcement agency, and its ideals should never be prostituted for the sole purpose of building circulation through sensational articles which fail to treat crime subjects in the proper manner or through an unholy alliance with crime.[87]

In a nod to the fear-mongering notion that a massive criminal population was hidden in our midst—as asserted by Courtney Ryley Cooper's Bureau-authorized 1935 book *Ten Thousand Public Enemies*—the memorandum suggested that an apathetic citizenry allowed hordes of criminals to thrive in secrecy. The role of the press, the memorandum suggested, was to publicize crime only by reprinting law enforcement notices and photographs when asked to do so. Premature reporting on crime tipped off criminals "before the investigating officials have had ample time to complete their inquiries" and drove those 10,000 public enemies into hiding.[88] That sort of premature publicity emanated, according to the memo, from "the small percentage of the press totally devoid of ethics and civic responsibility."[89] The memorandum cited the Lindbergh kidnapping case and the shooting of John Dillinger as instances in which the press had aided the FBI's work by withholding information from the public and later printing the Bureau's accounting of events without question.

The second memorandum, titled "Press Interference and Successful Law Enforcement," ran fifty-four pages. In the introduction, the author asserted that, more often than not, "the press has fallen far short of discharging its public duty when it fails to serve as the active ally of law enforcement agen-

Columnist and broadcaster Walter Winchell was one of Hoover's closest friends in the media. Winchell presented this 1935 photo to Hoover, inscribed: "To John Edgar Hoover and Clyde Tolson—the 'Double G-Men' (Grand Guys). Faithfully, Walter Winchell." (National Archives at College Park, Record Group 65, Series HN, Folder 8-8, #2)

cies and officers seeking to further law and order." The remainder of the memorandum cited examples of the press hampering the FBI's work through premature publicity, unethical tactics, the "physical hindering of investigative activities and unwarranted attacks," distortion of facts, press alliances with the underworld, and glorification of the criminal.[90]

Considering Hoover's own attitude toward the press, the vituperative tone of these two memoranda is not surprising. The FBI was a patrimonial organization. Sitting at his desk in the Justice Department building, Hoover rarely spoke to his underlings; instead, he wielded his blue pen on memoranda to set the tone and shape the policies of his Bureau. His contempt for many members of the press was no secret either inside or outside the FBI. In 1936, for example, Hoover addressed the American Society of Newspaper

Editors (ASNE) in Washington, D.C. In an off-the-record speech, Hoover lauded columnist Walter Winchell for agreeing to withhold information about the Lindbergh kidnapping case. He told Winchell in a letter, "I thought the editors should know that there was at least one columnist who put patriotism and the safety of society above any mercenary attitude in his profession."[91] As a result of Hoover's ASNE presentation, the gathered editors pledged "to cooperate with all law enforcement agencies in guarding against the premature publication of information harmful to the successful completion of criminal investigations."[92]

Hoover's narrow, instrumental conceptualization of the Fourth Estate as a convenient megaphone for law enforcement was evident time and again throughout his tenure as director. In 1936, for example, Hoover claimed the Charles Weyerhauser kidnapping would be the nation's last such case. One month later, ten-year-old Charles Mattson, son of a prominent surgeon, was kidnapped from the same neighborhood as Weyerhauser. Mattson's lifeless body was later found, but the crime was never solved.[93] Defended by Winchell, Hoover declared that press criticism had undermined the FBI and thus caused the Mattson kidnapping:

> This crime can be traced directly to certain activities and forces which have been at work for some time in trying to belittle, ridicule and sneer at the "G-Men." There are certain writers of slime columns suffering from mental halitosis and certain editorial writers who have an aggravated case of mental diarrhea that regurgitate their own filth and must tear down something which was gradually growing to be a restraining influence on the criminal of the underworld.[94]

When challenged by critics, Hoover attacked, usually labeling those critics un-American and, at several key moments, declaring that a coordinated "smear campaign" was under way with the goal of overthrowing the government, starting with the FBI.

In requesting a review of journalists' files in 1959, Hoover was gathering intelligence in preparation to launch an attack on his critics. Less than two weeks after Hoover's request, assistant director William C. Sullivan forwarded his memorandum to the director. Sullivan and his staff had painstakingly combed through the FBI files of 100 reporters, editors, and publishers (Cook, a writer for *The Nation*, did not represent the mainstream media and was not included). In his memorandum—which was given the file index of 100, signifying a domestic intelligence investigation—Sullivan reported that twelve of the journalists had no subversive connections, many had subversive connections but had not acted on them in their publications, and forty had "pertinent factors in their backgrounds" that led them to produce stories that, in Sullivan's opinion, discredited the American way of life.[95]

Written in the style of an academic paper, Sullivan's introduction portrayed the press as a key battleground for the "minds and souls of men." He wrote, "There is growing concern among many in the United States today that some elements of our media of communication are either wittingly or unwittingly using their power to support the communist struggle for men's minds."[96]

In his eighty-page report, which moved through the executive team to Hoover, Sullivan boiled down tens of thousands of pages of FBI files into a series of so-called blind memoranda to "conceal the Bureau as the source," Sullivan wrote. "This was done in the event the Director should desire to make available to appropriate persons some of the information on an informal and confidential basis."[97] Blind memoranda were commonly used by the FBI and were, essentially, anonymous news releases shared with accommodating reporters, editors, broadcasters, publishers, and other opinion shapers. The documents were typically summaries of investigative material and analysis, some of it confirmed and some not. Blind memoranda ensured plausible deniability, in that there was no indication that the FBI was the source of the material. Of course, recipients who were friends of the Bureau knew the source, but they could be counted on not to cite the FBI in their reports or in their whispers to other influential stakeholders. The FBI hoped that by providing reporters with this first- or secondhand information, those who were loyal to Hoover would produce news stories and columns that undermined the director's critics.

In his preamble to the "Molders" memorandum, Sullivan quoted author and moralist J. G. Holland: "The mind grows by what it feeds on." And he noted that journalism "exerts a tremendous power upon the minds of men." Sullivan continued: "A vast segment of the representatives of the varied media of communication in this country advocate a deviation from strict adherence to right principles. Whether their efforts stem from naivete, poor judgment, misunderstanding, ignorance, or from calculated efforts to support communist objectives, the cumulative effect constitutes what amounts to psychological pressure on the American people."[98]

In its details, Sullivan's memorandum read like a modern supermarket tabloid. *New York Herald-Tribune* columnist Joseph Alsop Jr. was outed as a homosexual.[99] It revealed that *Pittsburgh Courier* reporter Horace Roscoe Cayton had told a church group in 1946 that communism offered a possible solution to racism.[100] *New York Post* columnist Murray Kempton and editor James A. Wechsler were identified as members of the Young Communist League in their college days during the 1930s—affiliations they had both publicly admitted and renounced.[101] The fact that Wechsler was, by 1958, an ardent anticommunist did not eliminate him from suspicion.[102] Everything from a fleeting association with an organization labeled "subversive" by the House Un-American Activities Committee to the publication of stories critical of the FBI was cited to suggest that the forty reporters, broadcasters, and editors were anti-American.

"In no other realm is the power of the press as important today as in the struggle between the Free World and the onrushing forces of world communism," Sullivan wrote. "This is particularly true in the sense that the primary purpose of journalism is communication of thought, while a basic tactic of communism is to utilize every media of communication to advance communist objectives."[103]

The "Molders of Public Opinion" memorandum is an interesting example of the FBI's extensive domestic intelligence operations. It demonstrates the voluminous details gathered over several decades through both passive monitoring and active investigation and stored in the FBI files of hundreds of American journalists.[104] By the late 1950s, the Bureau had systematically monitored influential journalists for nearly thirty years, categorizing them as friend or foe based on the information in their files.[105]

It also demonstrates the importance the FBI placed on its own public relations practices. Faced with an ongoing crisis of legitimacy, Hoover created a counternarrative in which his agency touted its undeniable utility, claimed restraint in its law enforcement efforts, and suggested that dispassionate science, not human foibles, set its investigative agenda. Most important, though, Hoover's story of the FBI cast himself as its careful, reluctant, but decisive leader. Americans could trust the scientific, responsible FBI because it was led by the ultimate American patriot, J. Edgar Hoover. Hoover spent thirty of his forty-eight years as director trying to "utilize every media of communication" to advance his own FBI narrative through public relations. News stories, magazine articles, radio broadcasts, motion pictures, and, ultimately, television carried that narrative. Just in case anyone stepped out of line or went off message, Hoover had his blind memoranda, which he shared with friendly journalists who used it to marginalize critics, trumpet the Bureau's successes, or simply retell the FBI narrative.

Hoover's files provide insight into newsrooms and show that for many reporters and editors, including several Pulitzer Prize winners, a desire to gain Hoover's favor won out over truth, democracy, objectivity, and other vaunted elements of journalistic canon. Reporters and editors were all too willing to sell out their watchdog status for bylines, headlines, and personal acclaim. They watched as the Bureau marginalized its critics and realized that their access to dramatic and salient FBI stories, and to Hoover himself, required them to check any critical impulses at the door. The FBI allowed almost any reporter one opportunity to access Bureau information. But continued access depended on a willingness to at least give the FBI the benefit of the doubt, and it might require that they become active, "objective" public defenders of the Bureau.

The story of Hoover's public relations, then, is a story of a government law enforcement agency that used its special powers to adjust reality and, as a result, placed journalists on one side or the other of a bright line that separated FBI friends and FBI enemies. It is also the story of the alleged watchdogs of the Fourth Estate—molders of public opinion—who, because of some combination of personal politics and ambition, chose to close their eyes to the Bureau's excesses, toe the FBI public relations line, and uncritically amplify Hoover's FBI myth, thus enabling the Bureau's transgressions of civil liberties. Beginning in the mid-1930s, the director began constructing the public relations machinery that allowed the FBI to exert power over its friends in the press, who in turn helped create and maintain the Bureau's cloak of legitimacy—a facade that hid the extent of Hoover's illegal political surveillance for nearly four decades.

Chapter 2

A Bureau Built for Public Relations

NBC radio listeners tuning in at 9:30 p.m. EST on Wednesday, July 17, 1935, were greeted by the chattering and clicking sounds of a busy communications room, the buzz of a telephone line, and the voice of an operator: "National 7117—Federal Bureau of Investigation. Just a moment, Seattle, I'll connect you with the Director's office." As people around the country gathered in their living rooms in front of their radios, they heard J. Edgar Hoover's staccato voice thanking NBC for introducing his Bureau to the audience:

> We like to feel that this Bureau is an agency built by the people of America, for America's protection, through its cooperation with the law enforcement agencies of the nation, state, county and municipality. . . . Tonight, inasmuch as I must stay at my desk I am turning over the tour of the vast mechanism, human and technical, of the Federal Bureau of Investigation, to my good friend and associate of many years—Courtney Ryley Cooper. I consider him one of the best informed men on this subject in America.[1]

The twelve months preceding the NBC broadcast had already been quite an introduction. Hoover's G-men shot John Dillinger in front of the Biograph Theater in Chicago on July 22, 1934. They killed Charles "Pretty Boy" Floyd in an Ohio apple orchard on October 22, 1934. In November of that year, two FBI agents died in a gunfight that also killed the bloodthirsty Lester Gillis, better known as "Baby Face" Nelson. A few days after the shoot-out, Gillis's body was found wrapped in a blanket and dumped in a ditch near Skokie, Illinois. In January 1935, FBI agents arrested Arthur "Doc" Barker in Chicago; a week later, they killed Ma Barker and her son Freddie in a Florida gunfight. Those and other high-profile outlaw cases made Hoover and his

Bureau household names. Cooper, meanwhile, had been one of Hoover's most important public relations advisers. A relatively unknown writer, journalist, and self-promoter, Cooper had become famous earlier that year as the author of the best-selling *Ten Thousand Public Enemies,* an FBI-authorized and -edited evangelism of suspicion that cast Americans as passive and thoughtless enablers of crime.

After leaving Hoover's office, Cooper's radio tour moved to the exhibits in the anteroom outside, a display showcasing guns, bullets, and other reminders of the Bureau's utility and its many dramatic victories in the war on crime. Next, Cooper described the FBI fingerprint repository, where white-coated technicians meticulously identified criminals by the unique whorls and loops they inevitably left behind. The FBI's remarkable ability to use science to identify criminals was on display. "Names mean nothing to us," inspector Hugh Clegg told Cooper, "but this one happens to be Robert Barrett. . . . All we care about are the deltas, whorls, ridges and other markings of his ten fingers." Fingerprinting science, Clegg said, was infallible. Next up on the tour was a visit to the FBI laboratory, where fluoroscopes could identify bombs in packages, an "ultraviolet ray" could make invisible ink visible, and bullets were matched to guns through ballistics. Cooper's role was Everyman, asking questions and facilitating the tour.

The thirty-minute national broadcast was an FBI public relations coup. The Bureau could catch criminals using clinical, dispassionate science so infallible that the criminals' names were irrelevant. Hoover was depicted as engaged from moment to moment in managing the vast human and technical "mechanism" of the FBI. It was as if the FBI had developed a story line designed specifically to ease public fears of its growing power and to promote the Bureau as America's indispensable agency.

In fact, that is exactly what the FBI did. The author of Hoover's comments and the rest of the script for the radio tour was none other than that most knowledgeable of all crime reporters, Cooper himself. Cooper, along with Washington newspaperman Rex Collier and Hoover's public relations team in the Crime Records Division, developed a formula—a flexible and reproducible narrative and a set of compelling themes—that shaped public perceptions of the FBI for decades. By 1935, the FBI and its director had, through its outlaw exploits and a diligent application of the Cooper-Collier narrative, become cultural icons and a government success story (rare during the Great Depression).

The transformation of Hoover and the Bureau could not have been scripted. Everything about Hoover's early life suggests he was bred to be a narrow and limited thinker with little tolerance for disorder, difference, or dissidence. Perhaps most tellingly, Hoover lived a sheltered existence with his beloved mother in the house where he grew up, blocks from the Justice Department, until she died in 1938.

Hoover presumed that his ability to see the clear, bright line between order and disorder was universal. An intolerance of dissidence, a burning ambition to be more than a night-school lawyer, and a penchant for secrecy fueled Hoover's work in the early years. These traits powered his dogged work on the Palmer Raids, during which he manned the phones at all hours and personally oversaw the activities of far-flung agents, attorneys, and police officers as they rounded up 10,000 alleged radicals. Despite his inexperience and young age, Hoover found a way to make himself indispensable to Palmer, leapfrogging more experienced agents. An opportunist and a strict authoritarian, Hoover made himself the Justice Department's expert on radicals, demonstrating his bureaucratic talents by compiling 450,000 index cards on alleged anarchists and communists along the way.

There is no clear evidence that Hoover was a student of the emerging field of public relations in the 1920s and 1930s. Nor is there any evidence that Hoover had any particular affinity for the press. But he was clearly a dedicated opportunist. He somehow convinced Attorney General Harlan Fiske Stone, an avowed civil libertarian and critic of the Palmer Raids, that he had played little or no role in the radical roundup. Given the charge to reform the Bureau of Investigation, Hoover cleaned up what had been a corrupt agency. And in 1933, when his superiors in the Justice Department and the White House urged him to do a better job of public relations, Hoover characteristically moved quickly and well beyond the mandate he was given.

During his first six years as director, however, public relations was simply not on Hoover's daily agenda. Instead, the focus was on internal reform, banishing the "Department of Easy Virtues" and replacing it with a more professional organization. Much to his credit, Hoover succeeded in transforming the Bureau. He fired corrupt agents and other political hacks who had insinuated themselves into the Bureau through patronage and cronyism under prior regimes. In 1924, he closed five of the Bureau's fifty-three field offices and returned $300,000 of his $2.4 million budget to the Treasury. Between 1924 and 1933, he slashed employment rolls from more than 400 agents to just over 200. Support staff decreased by one-third during that same period. Hoover established stricter hiring procedures, created new policies for agents' dress and decorum, and initiated a set of rules for performance evaluations. A new law enforcement training school was established.[2] Thanks to Hoover's bureaucratic and administrative skill—along with a bit of ruthlessness and single-mindedness—the professionalized Bureau of 1929 bore little resemblance to the Department of Easy Virtues of the early 1920s.

In addition, Hoover moved to capitalize on advances in law enforcement science. The world's first criminal identification using fingerprints occurred in 1892, when Argentine police official Juan Vucetich identified a murderer who had left a bloody print on a doorpost after killing her two sons. That same year, Sir Francis Galton published a book outlining the first fingerprint categorization system. And in 1901, Scotland Yard became the first major police organization to establish a fingerprint identification branch. The first criminal identification using fingerprints in the United States came in 1910, during the trial of Thomas Jennings for the murder of Clarence Hiller. Most of the evidence in the case was circumstantial, except for the imprints of four fingers left on a newly painted porch railing. Four experts concluded that the fingerprints belonged to Jennings, who was convicted.[3] The science of fingerprint identification was quickly accepted as a valuable law enforcement tool.

In 1924, at Hoover' request, Congress established the Bureau of Investigation's Identification Division.[4] The division's fingerprint scientists were made available to local law enforcement organizations nationwide. Criminals came to understand that although cheap and fast automobiles could provide mobility, they could not ensure anonymity. Within a few years, Dillinger and other criminals underwent painful acid treatments in a futile attempt to eliminate or alter their fingerprints. The creation of the Identification Division's fingerprint repository stands as a truly revolutionary moment in American law enforcement. The division's founding was followed by the establishment of a formal training program in 1928 and the creation of the Bureau's vaunted laboratory in 1932.[5] Hoover deserves credit for his early work in establishing a professional and scientific law enforcement agency.

An obsessive organizer, Hoover also labored in those early years to enhance his Bureau's information-gathering and record-keeping systems. The Bureau of Investigation had, from its inception in 1908, an extensive record-keeping system, but its filing system merely numbered cases sequentially, from 1 to 42,975. In 1919, two new categories of files were added—a Mexican file and Hoover's radical file. Then in 1921, the filing system was re-vamped, borrowing a classification system that numbered types of federal crimes from 1 to 60. All kidnappings, for example, were designated by the number 7, followed by a numerical designation (e.g., 7-2561 for kidnapping case 2561). Hoover later expanded this numbering system—for example, adding category 62, administrative inquiry. Under Hoover, the Bureau also implemented an extensive series of indices. The most important one, the General Index, ultimately included more than 65 million three-by-five-inch cards arranged alphabetically. Using Hoover's enhanced system, Bureau clerks could locate with relative ease all files citing a particular individual or organization. This extensive and accessible record-keeping system was an-other key to the FBI's success under Hoover. The Bureau became an infor-mation clearinghouse, and the director had quick access to decades worth of information about anyone the Bureau had stumbled upon during its intelli-gence-gathering efforts and active investigations.[6] Ironically, these meticu-lously maintained files would assure the undoing of Hoover's reputation and legacy after his death.

In 1930, Hoover took a small step toward creating a higher public profile for the Bureau when he inaugurated the compilation and publication of an-nual uniform crime statistics, providing a measure of crime in the country. The FBI's crime statistics became an annual news story as reporters and edi-tors analyzed the results for trends. They also provided Hoover with a ready-made argument to Congress for additional resources. And the statistics gave critics an opportunity to complain that Hoover had cooked the books. Pub-lication of the uniform crime statistics provided the Bureau with contacts in newsrooms around the country, and the stories they generated communi-cated the agency's utility to the public.

Another key public relations audience, local law enforcement, was addressed through a magazine inaugurated in 1932, the *Law Enforcement Bulletin* (later known as the *FBI Law Enforcement Bulletin*). The *Law En-forcement Bulletin* was considered "confidential," and access to its contents was "restricted to law enforcement officers." The bulletin included stories about the Bureau's innovative crime-control and information-gathering techniques, profiles of wanted criminals, and, tellingly, advice from Hoover. The *Law Enforcement Bulletin* was clearly intended to establish the Bureau as a national clearinghouse for crime information, and Hoover was depicted as the benevolent uncle in Washington offering cogent guidance to local police forces across the country. The image presented in the bulletin was that of a responsible law enforcement agency that was reluctant to interfere with local police but ready to offer assistance when asked.

Other than annual crime reports and the monthly magazine, however, public relations was not an integral part of the Bureau during Hoover's early directorship. From time to time, a reporter would wander into the Bureau's suite of offices seeking help with a story. In 1929, for example, *American Magazine* writer Charles J. V. Murphy requested information about the National Division of Identification, the fingerprint repository. With no public relations staff in place, Hoover himself handled press inquiries. He met personally with Murphy and then compiled a stack of useful documents for him, including narratives of several cases and a few photos. As an employee of the Justice Department, Hoover was required to vet the request and the materials through an aide to the attorney general, and once he received approval from above, he handed the packet over to Murphy and hoped for the best.[7] During those first years, however, requests for information about the Bureau were few, and Hoover labored in relative obscurity. He was, after all, the chief of one tiny, little-known division of the Justice Department. Hoover oversaw not seasoned law enforcement officers but a team of lawyers and accountants, investigators who worked on a short list of federal crimes, could not make arrests, and did not carry weapons.

Economic disaster, a perceived crime wave, and a political revolution gave Hoover new opportunities to expand his power. The Great Depression convinced many Americans that what had not blown away in a dust storm or vanished in the stock market crash was in danger of being carried off by thieves. Several factors combined in the 1930s to make stories of crime, criminals, and law enforcement particularly salient. The Progressive Era, with its central notion that society was perfectible and that government was responsible for stimulating reform, had changed the way Americans thought about government. The laissez-faire government of the late 1800s had given way to a more active one, leading to the Pure Food and Drug Act of 1906 and Herbert Hoover's Reconstruction Finance Corporation by the early 1930s. The Great Depression produced an American populace that was skeptical of federal power yet yearned for government to do something—anything—to improve society. In the first years of his presidency, Roosevelt's New Deal provided that action through an alphabet soup of new agencies, the centralization of power, and a willingness to experiment with new roles for government. An emphasis on expanding federal law enforcement was part of Roosevelt's approach.

President Franklin Delano Roosevelt signs into law the Twelve Point Crime Control Program proposed by Attorney General Homer S. Cummings (standing, far left). The law made bank robbery and interstate flight federal crimes and authorized FBI agents to make arrests and carry weapons. The public profile of J. Edgar Hoover (standing, second from left) benefited the most from these changes. Also pictured are (left to right) Senator Henry F. Ashurst (D-Ariz.) and Assistant Attorney General Joseph B. Keenan. (National Archives at College Park, Record Group 65, Box 4, Folder 206, #1)

Another factor, no doubt, played a role in the public's growing interest in stories of crime and law enforcement. The social contract, the nature of which had been subtly renegotiated after World War I, had broken down. The ordering forces of American society that had proved self-righting through previous panics seemed unable to change the direction of the economy. At a time when individual initiative and hard work no longer ensured success, dramatic stories of charismatic outlaws seemed particularly compelling. The assurances that America was an ever-expanding, opportunity-driven society were lost. Whether such a nostalgic ideal had ever existed was not the point. What mattered was that many people's everyday reality did not match up with the promises they had absorbed (as if through osmosis) by growing up American.

One can discern what was lost, and why heroic stories of criminals and law enforcement might be compelling, by examining the "Middletown" of Muncie, Indiana. Scholars Robert and Helen Lynd observed Muncie in 1935 and published *Middletown in Transition: A Study in Cultural Conflicts* two years later. By the time of their study, General Motors had closed and then reopened a plant in town. As one might expect, the Lynds found that the loss of a vital employer had a profound psychological impact on Muncie residents, undermining their belief that individual initiative could ensure success in America. A town of "individual strivers" became disillusioned when a huge corporation, itself at the mercy of larger economic factors, simply vanished overnight. Ironically, GM's later return only accentuated individuals' feeling of powerlessness. When it reopened the Muncie plant, GM demonstrated that it was a high-level business decision, not any idealistic notion of the American Dream or individual initiative, that determined success or failure.[8] This perceived loss of community and loss of individual agency helps explain why people in "Middletowns" across the United States were attracted to crime stories in which individuals—whether criminals or cops—demonstrated that individual agency and initiative still existed.

Crime narratives, however, emphasized the power and authority (and, in the case of the FBI, the centralized federal authority) that people feared. Why were people willing to relinquish their fear of centralized federal crime control, a previously taboo concept in libertarian America? The answer lies in the nature of Hoover's messages. "In short, the FBI is a very human organization," Hoover later wrote in the foreword to Don Whitehead's FBI-authorized history. "It is never very far from the crossroads of America, either spiritually or physically."[9] Hoover understood Americans' feelings of loss of agency and community, and in the stories they helped create, his FBI, rather than imposing its authority, was simply restoring order to small-town America, responsibly and through the application of scientific law enforcement.

The logical order of American society had been upset by forces beyond individual control. In that context, the midwestern outlaws' crime wave of high-profile kidnappings and daring bank robberies in the early 1930s captured the public imagination. Charismatic murderer and bank robber John Dillinger became the most intriguing of the motley crew of wandering outlaws that included Pretty Boy Floyd, Baby Face Nelson, and members of the Barker-Karpis gang. Dillinger and his ilk quickly become media darlings, offering an entertaining diversion from the grim social and economic realities of the day. With unemployment rates topping 25 percent, deflation and price declines slowly eating away wealth, and banks closing across the country, figures like Dillinger inspired ambivalent feelings in many Americans. Trapped in a moral panic exacerbated by the worsening economic situation, Americans teetered between admiration for the outlaws and disgust at their violent sprees. Colorful and entertaining exploits, like Dillinger's escape from a Crown Point, Indiana, jail using a wooden "gun," were juxtaposed with shocking violence, like his cold-blooded murder of a police officer during a bank robbery in East Chicago, Indiana. Was Dillinger a daring, handsome thief who returned money Robin Hood style, or was he a ruthless murderer of law enforcement officers?[10]

Whatever individuals thought of the midwestern outlaws, their border-crossing escapes from justice led to a dramatic expansion of federal law enforcement jurisdiction and, with it, a relentless public relations campaign touting the government's success in the war on crime. Despite fears of a centralized police authority, the argument that America needed an expanded federal law enforcement presence to stitch together the patchwork of local law enforcement agencies into an effective dragnet against mobile criminals carried the day.

In 1933, FDR tasked Attorney General Homer S. Cummings with expanding Bureau power and jurisdiction as an element of the New Deal, and Cummings responded with a "war on crime" metaphor. In 1934 and 1935, however, that war was waged against relatively unimportant but symbolic outlaws like Dillinger, who were embarrassing local law enforcement agencies with their ability to flee across state lines. With the ready availability of fast cars and access to fairly good roads, outlaws could commit a crime in one state and then flee to a neighboring state, where pursuing law enforcement officials had no jurisdication. Historically, law enforcement had been a local concern, recognizing the notion that each community should be able to set its own law enforcement priorities. The kidnappers and bank robbers of the early 1930s made a mockery of that assumption. Americans were ready to accept the expansion of federal power and authority across the board.

Hoover's Bureau, with its national jurisdiction, had a unique ability to fill the gaps between local law enforcement jurisdictions, and it ultimately became a focal point in the war on crime. At first, however, Hoover remained relatively anonymous, and Cummings occupied center stage. As late as 1934, Hoover was misidentified in news articles as the "Head of the Secret Service," according to historian Richard Gid Powers. "When Homer Cummings finally ended the bureau's nine-year exile from the spotlight in July, 1933, by naming Hoover to lead the government's new 'super police,' the press wrote him up as a new name and a fresh face."[11] In fact, creation of the new "super police"— ostensibly a merger of the nearly defunct Prohibition Bureau, the Bureau of Identification, and the Bureau of Investigation—was nothing but a paper-shuffling and public relations exercise. As director of the merged agencies, renamed the Division of Investigation, Hoover quietly dispatched the new agents thrust upon him and went to work with the same 225 agents he had supervised before the merger.[12]

Hoover's emergence from Cummings's shadow really occurred in the wake of the shooting of John Dillinger, America's most charismatic criminal, on July 22, 1934. The high-profile killing of "Public Enemy Number 1" simultaneously boosted Cummings's war on crime and threatened Hoover's status. Dragged into the Dillinger case relatively late in the game, after the outlaw had driven his kidnapping victims across the state line, Hoover's division found itself playing catch-up, and its seemingly haphazard conduct hardly inspired confidence. Hoover's agents, led by Chicago SAC Melvin Purvis, badly botched a raid at the Little Bohemia resort in rural Wisconsin. Purvis's agents ended up killing a civilian and suffering three casualties of their own when Baby Face Nelson severely injured two agents and killed special agent W. Carter Baum. Dillinger's entire gang, including Nelson, escaped. Purvis ostensibly continued to lead the investigation, but his inexperience led Hoover to dispatch inspector Samuel Cowley to assist. Cowley was later killed by Nelson, who was fatally wounded himself in the exchange. The Dillinger pursuit captured the public's imagination, and as Americans became more intrigued, Hoover and his Division of Investigation gradually emerged from obscurity.

Dillinger's death was a coup for the Division of Investigation and for Cummings, who, up to that point, had been the public face of the war on crime. At the same time, the public face of the division changed overnight, with Purvis threatening to displace Hoover as America's top cop. "Hoover

Hoover speaks with unidentified reporters on July 23, 1934, the day after fugitive John Dillinger was shot and killed by agents in Chicago. (National Archives at College Park, Record Group 65, Series H, Box 2, Folder 98, #6)

awoke the following day," biographer Curt Gentry wrote, "to find that he had been replaced by Public Hero Number One, Melvin 'Little Mel' Purvis."[13] Moreover, the vaunted science of law enforcement and the nationwide dragnet of agents had not yielded Dillinger's location. Dillinger died on the sidewalk near the Biograph Theater because an informer, Ana Sage, gave him up in the hope of halting her deportation and netting some reward money. Neither Hoover nor Cummings was prepared for the public hand-wringing that occurred after the shooting, with some critics suggesting that Dillinger should have been captured rather than killed. Americans still had ambivalent feelings about Dillinger, despite his gang's murderous crime spree, and those feelings lingered after the outlaw's death.

Concerned that public opinion about his war on crime needed to be altered, Cummings set out to change the perception of federal law enforcement. After consulting with columnists Drew Pearson and Robert

Allen, Cummings hired *Brooklyn Eagle* reporter Henry Suydam as his new press aide. Suydam would be the Department of Justice's lead public relations contact. Thus, in addition to Cummings and Purvis, Hoover now had someone else standing between him and the media.[14] Suydam was affable, well liked, and a respected figure in the newspaper business. He had worked for the government's publicity agency, the Committee for Public Information, during World War I and had served as a press aide to Secretary of State Charles Evans Hughes before joining the *Eagle* in 1922. Most recently, Suydam had been the *Eagle*'s Washington correspondent. His 1955 obituary noted that he was a "man of many talents, not the least of which was his ability to repartee with the press."[15]

As Cummings's press adviser, Suydam was in a position to approve or disapprove all of Hoover's press contacts, press releases, and potential collaborations with journalists. When one of Cooper's ghostwritten interviews with Hoover was presented to Suydam soon after he started at Justice, he worried that Hoover might be opening himself up to a flood of similar requests. Suydam was also concerned that there could be charges of favoritism when some requests for interviews were granted and others declined. Hoover downplayed these concerns in a memorandum to Tolson, and the interview was published as written by Cooper.[16]

Famed columnist Drew Pearson came to believe that Suydam deserved some of the responsibility for the dramatic growth in the FBI's cultural footprint. "He really went to town with Hollywood, the radio industry and everyone else to make the FBI invincible."[17] Hoover did not see it that way. Upon Suydam's death, the FBI circulated his *Washington Post* obituary throughout the Seat of Government. One passage was highlighted: "As special press assistant to the U.S. Attorney General . . . he worked with FBI Director J. Edgar Hoover in a campaign to strip the glamour from public enemies such as John Dillinger and Babyface Floyd [*sic*]." In the margin, Hoover's chief public relations aide, Louis Nichols, wrote: "It was also a campaign of obstruction."[18] In fact, Suydam gave his approval to most of the FBI's media relations efforts. In many cases, he raised questions and requried explanations, but he was far from an obstructionist.

Ever the opportunist, Hoover sensed the value of his agency's growing iconic public image in the wake of the Dillinger shooting. Purvis's fame demonstrated the public interest in Hoover's G-men. It also demonstrated to Hoover the difficulty of controlling a media message from his office. For Hoover, the key was to find a way to shift that public sentiment away from any individual agent and toward the Division of Investigation and Hoover himself. Hoover had the dramatic crime stories generated by his agents' work. He had the backing of the Roosevelt administration, which saw value in promoting government success stories wherever they might be found. What Hoover lacked in 1934 was an in-house public relations staff along with a simple, coherent story that would allow his agency to continue to grow while simultaneously calming latent public fears about a federal police force.

Public relations is a widely misunderstood practice. Stereotypical notions of public relations as merely "spin" or the glad-handing courtship of the media fail to capture the often tedious nature of the work. Scholarly definitions of public relations focus on its strategic nature and audience-centric approach to message creation and delivery. According to scholars, public relations is public communication that seeks to build and maintain communities of meaning made up of individuals who share an organization's preferred image of itself. The stated goal of public relations is to build and maintain relationships with key individuals and organizations. These relationships may be seen as a source of cultural capital, or nonmonetary value, for the organization. In the case of most public relations efforts, that cultural capital can be converted into action on behalf of the communicator. Politicians use public relations to build relationships with individual voters, creating cultural capital that can be cashed in at the ballot box. Organizations like the FBI may use public relations to essentially draw lines, with individuals staking out their positions as supporters or opponents of the organization. The effective use of public relations with a key demographic such as members of Congress or prominent journalists may provide an organization with cultural capital that can be cashed in later to alter policy, protect sinecures, or maintain public support. Those supporters who make an organization's public relations message part of their own meaning system may come to that organization's defense, and in a time of crisis, they might be more willing to accept the organization's version of events or the self-image the organization promotes. Public relations seeks to create common understandings that in turn create an atmosphere conducive to change that is in the organization's interest.[19]

Public relations historians disagree on the essential indicators used to trace the origins of the practice, with some historians viewing public relations as a progression of "firsts" leading to a series of clarifying epiphanies in the early to mid-twentieth century. In a 1947 essay, for example, public relations pioneer Edward Bernays described one of those epiphanies when he wrote of a two-way communication process between an organization and its strategic publics as the "engineering of consent."[20] Bernays and his wife, Doris Fleischman, coined the term *public relations* in the early 1920s, taught the first class in public relations, and are credited with recognizing the power of messages crafted to persuade based on insight into the understandings and beliefs of the audience, as determined through application of "the modern social and psychological sciences."[21] More simply put, Bernays and Fleischman talked to people, figured out what they thought about an issue, and then created public relations messages crafted specifically to persuade those people.

It is a simple idea, and many historians of public relations highlight the notion of insight into the public mind as a key idea separating Bernays's public relations from other activities, such as the unstrategic publicity practiced by Ivy Lee, who is often cited as a twentieth-century pioneer of public relations as well.[22] Lee was a publicity agent in the early 1900s, and his work focused on defending big business, which was then under attack by muckrakers and reformers. Lee felt no compulsion to be truthful, other than to pass on to the press the information provided by his client. In 1915, for example, Lee was called before a government commission to explain his work on behalf of the Rockefeller family in the wake of the slaughter of fourteen striking miners, miners' wives, and children by agents working for the Rockefellers. Lee was asked if he was there to give the facts, to tell the truth about the strike. "Yes," Lee answered, "the truth as the operators saw it."[23] Oddly enough, Lee's place as an icon of early public relations is largely based on his assertion that truth is an essential element in successful publicity. Lee's epiphany came in the form of his 1906 Declaration of Principles, and their emphasis on truth and accuracy has convinced some historians that he deserves mention as a pioneer of public relations.[24] Lee, however, practiced press agentry, a relatively unstrategic brand of communication often aimed at diverting attention or confusing the public.

At no point did Lee link the practice of publicity to social science, as Bernays did. Bernays's 1923 book *Crystallizing Public Opinion* set out the parameters of public relations practice in substantial detail for any organization that wished to change public opinion by creating messages based on an understanding of its public. "How does the public relations counsel approach any particular problem?" Bernays asked. "First he must analyze his client's problem and his client's objective. Then he must analyze the public he is trying to reach. . . . How will his client's case strike the public mind?"[25]

Thus, public relations in the twentieth century evolved into a strategic communication practice based on understanding an audience and then sending messages devised to motivate that audience to see things in a particular way. Nongeographic groups of like-thinking people might be aggregated, for example, by placing persuasive messages in the news. Public relations, often in collaboration with the news media, provided the public with what journalist and intellectual Walter Lippmann famously called "the pictures in our heads."[26] According to the dogma of public relations history, Lee and especially Bernays provided a revelation, in that they understood the importance of understanding the audience when crafting persuasive messages to build those pictures in people's heads.

Recent scholarship based on a thorough review of existing studies in public relations history has offered a framework that rejects the prevailing view of Bernays and Lee as parents of the practice. Instead, Margot Opdycke Lamme and Karen Miller Russell have categorized the pioneers of public relations based on the "scale at which tactics were employed."[27] In other words, the types of communication people choose and the messages they craft may be strategic, even in the absence of corresponding research into their audiences. The nature of the tactics, they suggested, indicates informal strategic intent and at least an anecdotal insight into the motivations of the intended audience. They found that, based on the literature, informal insight into an audience's motivations, loosely defined as any effort to seek feedback, was first used by a handful of nineteenth-century politicians and businesses.[28] Finally, Lamme and Russell identified the establishment of legitimacy, whereby an organization's actions match public expectations, as a motivation that has prompted the use of public relations techniques going back hundreds of years.[29] Utilizing the application of tactics as an indicator of strategic intent, rather than requiring some social scientific bent as a litmus test, leads to a much longer trail of public relations pioneers—a trail that, beginning in 1934, clearly included Hoover's Division of Investigation.

Beginning with his early collaboration with two key writers, Hoover appears to have stumbled upon a narrative template that humanized his organization and lessened concerns about its power and jurisdiction. Roland Marchand has described a process by which corporations began to recast their images in the 1930s, a process he called "creating a corporate soul." Essentially, Marchand was describing a process whereby corporations (and other large organizations) humanized themselves through storytelling in advertising and public relations, a technique that modern communications scholars might relate to branding.

In the 1920s and 1930s, vast corporations such as General Motors and AT&T found that a coherent story, well told, could naturalize a notion that seemed to be in opposition to the values of an ordinary person. Investigations of scandalous corporate behavior during World War I, along with the huge house of cards built by the hated trusts that contributed to the stock market crash and the Great Depression, had dramatically increased Americans' skepticism of corporate motives. Advertising and public relations campaigns transformed those faceless corporate entities, previously perceived as monoliths interested only in the contents of their customers' wallets, into human beings working side by side with their neighbors in the community. AT&T was no longer personified by a logo on a monthly bill; it was associated with friendly chats with distant relatives. The public's perception of the corporate logic of shareholder returns and bottom-line profits was replaced with a view of the corporation as an innovative, job-creating entity that made lives better through science and the miracles of consumer products. Hoover's Federal Bureau of Investigation (as it was renamed in 1935) was not the first to incorporate science into a persuasive communication program. Corporations had used the notion of science to demonstrate their future-mindedness beginning in the 1920s. General Electric and Western Electric focused advertising campaigns around their laboratories to demonstrate that they were forward-thinking and competent.[30] The FBI also capitalized on the public's appreciation for science, and that focus helped blunt criticism of potential pre-Hoover-style corruption or cronyism.

The campaign to create a corporate soul showed that such a narrative needed to be timely, simple, and compelling. If it could humanize General Motors, President Roosevelt's advisers surmised, surely public relations could ease public fears about the power of a federal police force and bolster positive feelings about government. In 1934, FDR signed the Omnibus Crime Control Act, which expanded FBI jurisdiction and authority.

The elements of the FBI's defensive narrative were in place by 1930 and included a professional team of agents in the field, the application of science (fingerprinting), and the incorruptible leadership of a steady and trustwor-

Washington Star *reporter and editor Neil "Rex" Collier fingerprints Hoover on September 30, 1935, as part of a campaign to encourage Americans to be fingerprinted. Collier was one of Hoover's earliest "friends" in the press. (National Archives at College Park, Record Group 65, Box 2, Folder 125, #5)*

thy "top cop"—Hoover. But the pieces were not assembled into a coherent narrative and peddled to the public until 1934. It took two writers, one a journalist and the other an odd combination of promoter and author, to create an enduring FBI story that could be retold endlessly: a story of responsibility, science, and leadership, themes that, not coincidentally, undermined critics' concerns about unchecked federal police power. *Washington Star* reporter and editor Neil "Rex" Collier and Courtney Ryley Cooper were the original authors of the Bureau narrative. This Collier-Cooper narrative became the Bureau's dogma for the next three decades, the corporate soul of the FBI.

In early 1936, Collier delivered the first six weeks of his *War on Crime* comic strip to the FBI for prepublication review. *War on Crime* was among the Bureau's first forays into entertainment media. The first six weekly strips expressed elements of the FBI's preferred narrative about itself, developed over the prior two years. During the frenzy surrounding the shooting of Dillinger, Hoover had discovered that he and his Bureau had to control publicity by being storytellers and peddling a strategically created story line emphasizing science, responsibility, and his own steady leadership.

The narrative themes came from the information provided by Hoover's public relations team and were no doubt chosen to counter critics' questions about the FBI's legitimacy. When citizens fearful of centralized government authority complained about the Bureau's potential to become an American secret police, the Bureau could point to a counternarrative that emphasized the clinical, careful nature of its work. Collier's comic strip, for example, which ran for two years in eighty newspapers across the country, succinctly captured those themes in an entertaining format.

When New York printer George Janosik initially proposed the creation of an FBI comic strip, Suydam turned down the request.[31] Six weeks later, Hoover agreed to meet with Janosik, who had brought Collier in on the project.[32] Hoover must have prevailed on Suydam to reconsider, because one day after the director met with Janosik and Collier, Suydam gave his blessing to the project, although he demanded that it be made clear that the Department of Justice and the FBI were not sponsoring the strip.[33] Despite that edict, promotional materials blurred the lines, declaring that *War on Crime* had been created "with the cooperation of the Federal Bureau of Investigation."[34]

Week one of *War on Crime* focused on Hoover, who, Collier wrote in the comic strip's text, "had the vision of a man twice his age." Hoover had cleaned up the Bureau, and "now he had men of unassailable integrity" in the field. Weeks two and three emphasized agents' extensive training regimen, reinforcing the theme of responsibility and integrity. Weeks four and five touted the work of the FBI laboratory and the Bureau's implementation of fingerprint identification science. Week six reminded readers of the FBI's utility, focusing on its success in capturing criminals: "In the Morgue of the Fingerprint Division are the cancelled records of criminals 'removed from circulation' such as Dillinger, Floyd and Nelson."

Bureau officials suggested edits that honed the themes of the narrative and eliminated any potential challenges to their preferred symbolism of science, responsibility, and Hoover. One caption was changed because it suggested recklessness and "might convey the impression that we shoot people down just because they do not voluntarily surrender and plead guilty." In another caption, the same agent recommended that handwriting recognition "be referred to as a science, and not as a trick, to safeguard any impression of the use of trickery on the part of Agents."[35] The Dillinger case occupied several weeks of the comic strip and provided Hoover with a welcome opportunity to write Melvin Purvis out of the story. Purvis was mentioned only in passing as an anonymous agent who lit a cigar as Dillinger exited the Biograph Theater.[36]

War on Crime was not the first collaboration between Hoover and Collier. They had first met in 1929, when Collier led a group of Justice Department reporters into Hoover's office to complain that they had been misled by a Bureau spokesman regarding a local murder case. Historian Richard Gid Powers spoke to Collier in the mid-1970s and reported that "Collier told Hoover that by helping reporters write their stories instead of making problems for them, he could ensure favorable treatment of the Bureau."[37] Beginning in February 1934, Collier delivered a series of favorable articles based on his work with Hoover. The articles covered topics ranging from the "super police" merger to the legislative restrictions and "inadequate facilities" handicapping the Division of Investigation as it battled heavily armed outlaws.[38] Hoover and his division were the centerpieces of Collier's stories. Cummings was rarely mentioned and never quoted. About a month before Dillinger was shot, Collier requested information about the division's work in the war on crime. The resulting article, which appeared in the *Washington Star* on June 19, 1934, and in papers across the country in the days following, included photos of agents undergoing firearms training in preparation for fighting the war on crime.[39] So pleased was Hoover that he had the article reprinted as a pamphlet and forwarded copies to hundreds of sheriffs, police chiefs, ministers, lawyers, and members of Congress around the country.[40] The pamphlet, authored by an "objective" journalist, allowed Hoover to trumpet his division to a number of key public relations constituencies: local law enforcement, Congress, and community leaders.

A syndicated story written by Collier appeared in the *New York Times Magazine* in August 1934 and focused entirely on Hoover's leadership. The lead made it clear who the public should be paying attention to in the war on crime:

"There's no mystery about it—just hard work and common sense."
J. Edgar Hoover, director of the Division of Investigation of the
Department of Justice, smiled at the query put to him by his interviewer.
. . . His black eyes sparkled as he laughed off the suggestion that there is

anything uncanny or mysterious about the achievements of the "G" men—those close-mouthed federal detectives designated as special agents of the Department of Justice.[41]

The author went on to describe Hoover's office and lay out his history as director of the Bureau and then the Division of Investigation. Scientific law enforcement was a prominent theme: "He trains all of his agents in the latest scientific methods of investigation," Collier wrote. "The value of this training has been proved time and time again." The division's responsibility was illustrated by the observation that dispassionate science can prove someone guilty *or* innocent.[42] Collier's story is one of the first fully realized examples of what became the FBI's public relations narrative: the stolid, careful Hoover (according to Collier, he liked to fish and filled his modest house with antiques) leading his responsible, businesslike team of scientific investigators. Copies of this story were also forwarded to key constituencies, including SACs in Bureau offices around the country.

Later in October, a multipart series about the Division of Investigation appeared in the *St. Louis Post-Dispatch Sunday Magazine.* And in early 1935, a Collier article on the renamed FBI's training regimen was reprinted as a pamphlet and mailed to hundreds of opinion shapers. Later stories by Collier completely erased Purvis from the Dillinger story, replacing him with Cowley. Collier referred to Purvis only as "Agent A," who was "loitering" in the vestibule of the Biograph Theater. Cowley, Collier asserted, was the leader of the division's efforts in Chicago, the hero of the day.[43] Despite being elevated to hero status, Cowley posed no threat to Hoover's prominence: Cowley was a martyred hero, killed in a gunfight with Baby Face Nelson in 1934.

Collier's contribution of a framework for the FBI narrative was in place by early 1935. His journalistic work, however, appeared only in newspapers and newspaper supplements. Written in the standard, conservative style of news features, the stories lacked the drama that could be provided only by a creative nonfiction writer. By 1935, Courtney Ryley Cooper had already begun polishing the FBI narrative in what became a remarkably prolific, seven-year collaboration with Hoover.

Born in Kansas City in 1886, Cooper was an unlikely partner for the straitlaced FBI director. Cooper ran away from home at age sixteen and became a circus clown and then a publicist for Sells-Floto Circus. From there, Cooper moved into circus management and publicity before leaving to be-

Author Courtney Ryley Cooper, one of Hoover's early public relations advisers, fingerprints the director in an undated photograph, circa September 1935. (National Archives at College Park, Record Group 65, Box 2, Folder 125, #6)

come a newspaper reporter. He was a feature writer for the *Kansas City Star, New York World, Denver Post,* and *Chicago Tribune.* He was also a creative writer, authoring more than 750 circus-themed short stories and winning an O. Henry Award in 1930 for the trite morality tale "The Elephant Forgets."[44]

Like Collier, Cooper became an important public relations adviser to the FBI, honing Collier's basic story line into a set of narrative themes that characterized FBI public relations messages for decades.[45] Cooper and Hoover first became acquainted in April 1933 when *American Magazine* editor Sumner Blossom assigned Cooper to rewrite a story authored by Charles J. V. Murphy. Cooper, who had been chosen because of his experience covering crime stories, wrote to Hoover and explained that Murphy's article required "human touches and high-lighting by which you and your work can be brought more clearly before the reader."[46] Hoover's response suggests how tentative Bureau press relations were at the time. He replied that he was surprised Murphy's article had not been submitted to the Bureau for editing and vetting by the press relations staff in the Department of Justice. Such an oversight by a journalist would later be grounds for banishment to the Bureau's "do not contact" list. However, Hoover invited Cooper to visit his office a few days later, and Cooper agreed to do so and explain the situation.[47] There is no record of the explanation, but it must have been satisfactory.

A few weeks after their first meeting, Cooper sent Hoover a telegram proposing that they collaborate on a multipart series "articulating the workings of the bureau under your signature."[48] After clearing the idea with his superiors in the Justice Department, Hoover began to supply information to Cooper in May, and the writer delivered his first two articles to the Bureau for editing on June 10, 1933. Science was front and center in the first article, titled "The Biggest Jail on Earth" (later renamed "Crime Trap"); it focused on fingerprint identification and was published in November 1933.[49] The second article, "How Smart Is a Crook?" was more of a morality tale, emphasizing the craven nature of criminals and the hopelessness of a life of crime, particularly when Hoover's special agents were on the case.[50] The title was changed to "How Wise Is a Crook?" before publication in December 1933. Two weeks later, "Purpose: Adventure," the dramatic retelling of a Texas arson and murder case, arrived at the Bureau. That article became "Brains against Bullets," published in February 1934. Hoover and his Department of Justice handlers quickly approved all three articles. Cooper then wrote that his editor, Sumner Blossom, had asked that Cooper's name be removed from the bylines.[51] The articles would no longer be "as told to" Cooper; they would be presented in *American Magazine* as Hoover's own work. Hoover quickly agreed.[52] Thus, Cooper became Hoover's most important ghostwriter of the 1930s.

In 1934, Cooper worked on articles about the Dillinger case and produced an "interview" with Hoover for the *Saturday Evening Post*. The interview was really just another "as told to" story in which Cooper, writing in Hoover's "voice," warned that too many Americans were complicit in the "roots of crime": "They are the crooked doctors, lawyers, nurses, beauty shop operators, fences, merchants, hideout owners and a dozen other forms of sub-criminality upon which major criminality depends for safety."[53] That statement foreshadowed another theme of Cooper's FBI collaborations: the evangelism of suspicion. Cooper was buttressing the FBI's utility and responsibility, and in the case of the "interview," he was simultaneously promoting Hoover as the agenda setter for the war on crime.

Throughout their collaboration, Cooper dutifully submitted his articles, even those that were only peripherally related to the Bureau, for editing prior to publication, and he accepted every change made by Hoover's public relations staff. Cooper's fawning nature and willingness to adhere to the strictures of FBI editors won him Hoover's attention and confidence. Cooper lived most of the year in New York hotel suites, spent his winters in Sebring, Florida, and was known to send Hoover and Cummings boxes of fruit or pecans.[54] In one magazine article, Cooper described Hoover in surprising and intimate terms, calling him "as complex as any woman, yet as masculinely translucent as a strong man. . . . I never saw a man more self contained, more courteous, more sophisticated."[55] In his 1937 book *Here's to Crime*, Cooper recalled the first time he saw the FBI Crime Laboratory and quoted Hoover as saying, "[the lab] is going to wipe out the crooked expert witness, it is going to make even the smallest police department in America as powerful as the biggest."[56]

During their collaboration, Cooper authored or ghostwrote twenty-four magazine articles, a half dozen movie and radio scripts, and four books, all sharing the themes that came to define the FBI public relations narrative. So prolific was their collaboration that people began to suspect that Cooper was a paid employee of the FBI. On August 3, 1936, Cooper wrote to Hoover and reported on a party he had attended at the home of public relations pioneer Edward Bernays. Bernays, Cooper noted, greatly admired Hoover and the FBI. But during a conversation with freelance journalist Forrest Wilson, Wilson suggested that Hoover was merely a well-funded publicity hound and that Cooper himself was a sellout "being paid secretly" by Hoover's press bureau.[57] Cooper may not have been paid by Hoover, but his journalistic success was enabled by the Bureau, which provided the raw information he used to create the heroic crime stories published in *Cosmopolitan, American Magazine*, and many others. Notations on Cooper's FBI file suggest that Wilson's utterance led the Bureau to investigate his background.

The effects of the Collier-Cooper narrative were apparent in a 1937 study of crime control by the federal government. The report by analyst Arthur C. Millspaugh can be seen as an authoritative statement of the progressive desire for order and as a call for political action to further centralize law enforcement. It should also be viewed through the lens of a dramatically changed public perception of federal crime control, brought about by

popular reports of FBI exploits. The assumptions of Millspaugh's study—
that crime was out of control and increased federal police action was
necessary—would have been unthinkable as a mainstream idea a decade or
two earlier.[58] Whereas the Bureau of Investigation had been little known in
1930, the FBI and its director had become iconic figures in American society
by 1937. Critics remained, but the Collier-Cooper narrative had become
accepted fact. The FBI was a responsible agency that employed science to
solve crimes. No one needed to worry about corruption or cronyism, went
the popular refrain, because of Hoover's steady and apolitical leadership.

The Collier-Cooper narrative provided evocative themes through which
the FBI's preferred self-image was, over time, constructed in the heads of
millions of Americans and key opinion leaders. The basic Collier-Cooper
narrative created an FBI "soul" and addressed concerns about the Bureau's
legitimacy by reshaping the notion of federalized law enforcement as a com-
monsense solution to problems that would otherwise be unsolvable. The existence of investigative files on untold numbers of Americans, many of
whom had committed only the "crime" of political dissent, was unknown at
the time. The existence of those files, of course, unmasks the Cooper thesis,
with its emphasis on restraint, as little more than a convenient allegory.

It was, however, a simple, effective, and enduring public relations template. A 1935 *New York Times* review of Cooper's xenophobic evangelism of
suspicion, *Ten Thousand Public Enemies*, breathlessly reported the themes of
the Collier-Cooper narrative, describing Hoover as the top G-man and highlighting the use of scientific law enforcement techniques. "One murderer
was identified by comparison of his teeth marks with those left in an apple
found at the scene of the crime," reviewer Robert Van Gelder wrote. "There
is a newly devised 'frequency table' for the decoding of cipher messages in
use by the division. . . . Use is made of the fact that unreadable writing on
charred paper can be transferred in readable form by use of fast photo-
graphic plates. Ultraviolet rays bring out writings in secret inks."[59]

Cooper helpfully authored a foreword for Hoover to contribute to the
book:

> Beyond all else, it must be understood that the work of this Division
> does not signify an attempt to usurp the law enforcement powers of
> state, county, or city. . . . There is nothing which can take the place of
> local forces properly equipped to deal with local crime. However, day by
> day, crime is laughing at localities. I have in mind an instance in the life

of the unlamented John Dillinger who left a hideout in Florida one day, robbed a bank in Indiana the next afternoon, tucked a wounded comrade away in a hideout apartment in Chicago the day following and within twenty four hours was carousing with his gang in Arizona.[60]

Hoover's "authorship" of a foreword for Cooper's book was controversial. Inspector W. H. Drane Lester believed it was unseemly for Hoover to contribute a prologue to a book that was "so extremely lavish—though deservedly so—in its praise of the Division and the Director." In addition, Lester said, local law enforcement agencies might be upset by the implied criticism of their work contained in Hoover's statement and throughout the book.[61] Clyde Tolson advised Hoover to go ahead with the foreword, although he cautioned that agents should check the piece carefully to avoid criticizing local law enforcement.[62] Tolson also required Cooper to remove a section of the book that was critical of parole boards and the Bureau of Prisons.[63]

Upon the book's release in March 1935, however, Sanford Bates, director of the Bureau of Prisons, attacked Hoover and the FBI for selling out to a novelist. Edward Tamm reported that Bates stated in a phone conversation: "Well, there are plenty of the confidential reports of the Division of Investigation in this book. . . . It has your Chief's picture on the front of it, and it has a foreword by him and it has a statement that this is absolutely the gospel truth because it was taken from the investigation records of the Department of Justice."[64] Ever attentive to criticism, Hoover claimed in a memorandum to an assistant attorney general that no confidential reports had been supplied to Cooper, who "drew upon sources other than those within the Bureau of Investigation for his information."[65] Bates was not the only one confused about the Bureau's role in the production of the book. The Library of Congress telephoned to ask whether *Ten Thousand Public Enemies* was an official publication of the FBI.[66] Cooper's book, every word of it meticulously edited and vetted by the FBI, was a best seller.

The Collier-Cooper narrative was fully formed by late 1935: Dispassionate clinical science, not politics, corruption, or cronyism, lay at the heart of the FBI, which was led by the careful and steady Hoover. The FBI was responsible to local law enforcement and essential to the safety of all Americans. The message reflected a careful, strategic response to public concerns about centralized police power and emphasized a heroic Hoover wielding the impartial and clinical magic of science to solve unsolvable crimes. It emphasized the FBI's central role in preserving democracy and protecting the American way of life from the enemies hidden among us. It was equally applicable whether the audience was a congressional committee considering FBI funding or Middle America desperate for a heroic tale in which the good guys win.

The Collier-Cooper narrative would serve the FBI well for decades, but only if Hoover could create a disciplined and single-minded public relations team to promote it. Late-twentieth-century studies of corporate public relations focus on the creation of an appropriate organizational structure and a disciplined internal culture as two keys to effective practice.[67] Including public relations experts in decision making at the highest levels is vital to building relationships with key audiences and thus promoting the organization's interests.[68] Effective public relations, as defined by Bernays, includes the systematic collection of information about key publics and audience reactions to an organization's messages. That insight is then carefully analyzed to craft better, more persuasive messages and more appealing tactics; identify potential crises; and persuade the public to share the organization's preferred meanings or public opinions about itself or other issues. Toward this end, Hoover structured his organization for effective public relations: bringing in talented individuals with an understanding of media; setting up a nationwide information-gathering system; convening an executive group in Washington responsible for plotting communication strategy; and taking advantage of new media such as radio, motion pictures, and television when they served his purposes.[69]

It was clear by 1935 that FBI public relations could not be handled in the casual, slipshod manner of the late 1920s and early 1930s. No longer could Hoover simply take the calls of reporters, hand them a stack of interesting case memoranda, and hope for the best. With agents spread out across the United States, mixed messages were being sent. For example, after Cowley was shot and lay dying in a hospital, Purvis spouted his frustration: "If it's the last thing I do, I'll get Baby Face Nelson—dead or alive," Purvis told *Chicago American* reporter Elgar Brown. "Nelson ought to know he hasn't a chance at eventual escape. . . . We aren't particular whether we get him alive or dead."[70] Purvis's understandably angry outburst violated the Collier-Cooper narrative by suggesting that the Bureau was driven by emotion rather than by clinical science. In addition, Purvis's personal fame had eclipsed that of Hoover, whose steady, unemotional hand was at the tiller of the increasingly powerful Bureau. Any violation of the notion of a responsible FBI driven by science and led by the steadfast J. Edgar Hoover provided a hook for naysayers. Thus, the lack of a disciplined public relations focus within the FBI contributed to public confusion about the agency's role and the scope of its powers. The Collier-Cooper narrative provided an effective defense, but it required a disciplined public relations bureaucracy to promote and enforce it.

As the leader of a large and fast-growing organization operating in an increasingly media-saturated environment, Hoover no doubt sensed the need for a bureaucratic solution to the problem. German sociologist Max Weber was among the first to carefully consider the nature of the bureaucracies that had become a central feature of society. Weber asserted that bureaucratic organization is characterized by the rational regulation of power relationships in society—specifically, the regulation of inferiors by superiors. According to Weber, the bureaucratic relationship is an impersonal one. The bureaucracy is shaped by rules and never sleeps. In an effective bureaucracy, each person knows the path between himself or herself and the top or bottom of the ladder.[71]

Hoover was the son and grandson of bureaucrats. Weber's list of bureaucratic attributes— including a belief in rules, the communication of policy through documents, obsessive record keeping, and clear organizational structures—was something Hoover had internalized early in his career. Hoover had shaped the Bureau of Investigation into a large and strictly hierarchical monolith that one former official described as the "FBI pyramid," with Hoover at the pinnacle overseeing every aspect of the operation.[72] In many ways, the FBI became an exact reflection of Hoover's bureaucratic personality, a patrimonial kingdom where subordinates who did not adhere to the director's rules were removed in favor of more compliant characters.[73] Hoover sat at the center of a feudal kingdom. Every employee answered directly to Hoover and was encouraged to report any violations of Bureau policy directly and even anonymously to the director. "Even stenographers were encouraged to report violations anonymously if they wished," William C. Sullivan wrote in his memoirs. "There was no appeal when Hoover decided that an agent should be demoted, exiled to an undesirable post, or summarily fired."[74]

Hoover surrounded himself with a small cadre of assistant directors, each responsible for one aspect of FBI work: one assistant director oversaw the Investigative Division; another supervised the administration of the FBI bureaucracy; another supervised the Bureau's public relations division, the Crime Records Section.[75] Titles and personnel changed over time, but the basic structure remained largely intact over Hoover's long tenure. The development of the Crime Records Section (later the Crime Records Division) in the mid-1930s demonstrates how quickly Hoover and the FBI adopted sophisticated public relations practices.

Shortly after beginning his collaboration with Cooper, Hoover hired Louis Nichols to head the Crime Records Section. Nichols had become interested in the FBI after hearing a radio dramatization.[76] Nichols; Edward A. Tamm, who oversaw the Investigative Division; and associate director Clyde Tolson became the key figures in FBI public relations and were members of the Bureau's Executive Conference for many years.[77] Tamm, who joined the Bureau in 1931, was a native of St. Paul, Minnesota, and a Georgetown Law School graduate. Quickly rising to a position of authority, Tamm resigned from the FBI in 1948 to become a federal judge and eventually served on the U.S. Circuit Court of Appeals. Even as a distinguished jurist, Tamm continued to advise Hoover on publicity matters, passing his suggestions along in short notes.

Nichols and Tamm were key figures in shaping FBI public relations policies, but it was Tolson who controlled the flow of information to Hoover and thus wielded tremendous power over all Bureau policies, including public relations. Born in Laredo, Missouri, Tolson moved to Cedar Rapids, Iowa, in 1917 and received a bachelor's degree from a business college there. He earned a law degree from George Washington University in 1927 and joined the Bureau the next year. No one rose more quickly or higher in the Bureau than Tolson. Only two years after joining the Bureau, Tolson became assistant director for personnel and administration. In 1936, a new position, assistant to the director, was created for him. His title was later changed to associate director, and upon Hoover's death in 1972, Tolson served as acting director of the FBI for one day. From 1930 to 1972, Tolson was Hoover's closest confidant. The two men rode to work together and even vacationed together. Their relationship was the subject of rumor and innuendo during their lifetimes and beyond. While it is impossible to say whether Hoover and Tolson were lovers, evidence—such as a photograph Hoover took of a sleeping Tolson—makes it clear that they were very close. In his will, Hoover left Tolson his home in Washington, D.C.[78]

Among other things, the Executive Conference discussed and set certain public relations policies and strategies for the FBI. Nichols often argued for relative tolerance of off-message stories by friendly reporters, and Tamm was a key evaluator of Nichols's suggestions. Tolson became an enforcer of the

Clyde Tolson was the second-highest-ranking official in the Bureau from 1928 until his retirement on May 16, 1972, two weeks after Hoover's death. (National Archives at College Park, Record Group 65, Series F, Box 1, Folder 3, #3)

Collier-Cooper narrative, stridently rejecting reporters' (and others') efforts to move beyond the confines of the narrative's themes. In fact, based on the many harsh handwritten comments and suggestions he left on memoranda, Tolson's view of the press was even more negative than Hoover's. Many times Tolson would reject Nichols's suggestion that the Bureau assist a reporter only to be overruled by Hoover. Whatever their affinity, or lack thereof, for journalists, the members of the executive team advised Hoover on public relations policies.

At a July 5, 1935, meeting of the Executive Conference, for example, the group discussed policies for withholding sensitive information from the news media.[79] In 1940, they ordered Nichols's staff to create a memorandum rebutting the charges in a series of critical *New Republic* articles.[80] The Executive Conference served as an advisory group for Hoover, but the director, using information provided by Nichols and influenced most strongly by Tolson, had the final word. Tolson's recommendations and Hoover's decisions on public relations matters were often communicated through handwritten notes on memoranda forwarded by the Crime Records staff. Once a decision was made, it was up to the SACs in offices across the country to carry out the order.

Beginning in 1927, the FBI's annual policy manuals outlined official policies on all manner of topics, including dealings with the news media. In addition to being the administrators of law enforcement activities in their offices, SACs were information gatherers and communicators; as such, they were evaluated in part based on their development of contacts among opinion shapers in their communities. Nevertheless, public relations decision making was totally centralized at the top in Washington.[81]

Scholars have identified several roles undertaken by public relations practitioners.[82] For instance, communication technicians handle the fieldwork of public relations, gathering information and producing written summaries and other materials for decision makers.[83] SACs played this role in the FBI. They were charged with maintaining ties to members of key local publics, including news reporters and editors, local law enforcement authorities, local government officials, U.S. attorneys, and any other contacts deemed useful. The goal of these relationship-building exercises was to cultivate supporters, defenders, and informants, who were sometimes formalized as SAC contacts. In his 1979 memoir, Sullivan explained:

> The real job of the special agent in charge of each of these field offices was public relations. The SAC was out of the office a lot, visiting the "right" people, those who molded public opinion in his territory: newspaper publishers and editors, owners and managers of radio and television stations, corporate executives, and church officials, to name a few. The SAC also plugged the Bureau line day in and day out at police headquarters, City Hall, Masonic Lodge meetings, Jaycee luncheons, even at the local college or university.[84]

Contact with newspaper editors was routine according to Cartha D. De-Loach, who ran the Crime Records Division after Nichols left the FBI: "As a matter of fact, at every field office I inspected, I was told to call upon newspapers and ascertain their relationship with the FBI. Was the FBI treating them right? We wouldn't have done that unless there was a conscious effort to cultivate the newspapers—we attempted to cultivate all communications media. The FBI was a little bit in awe of them."[85]

The Bureau's systematic, nationwide information-gathering effort focused on identifying potential public relations problems and evaluating the impact of press reports on opinion-shaping audiences. SACs were required to clip articles about the FBI's performance or related issues and forward them daily to Washington, along with memoranda analyzing the reports and relaying any other vital intelligence uncovered in the course of their work.[86] Failure to attend to news-monitoring duties would result in a letter from Hoover expressing his annoyance; if the failure continued, it could ultimately result in official censure. When the SAC in Boston failed to forward a review of *Ten Thousand Public Enemies* that appeared in the *Boston Herald*, he received a letter six days after the review was published, chiding him for being "lax in forwarding to the Bureau items appearing in newspapers and other publications of interest to the Bureau."[87]

Finally, SACs became an important conduit for delivering the Collier-Cooper narrative to local opinion shapers. Hoover frequently forwarded copies of interesting case memoranda, laudatory news articles, mentions in the *Congressional Record*, and other evidence of public praise to his army of SACs to share with mayors, newspaper publishers, sheriffs, members of the clergy, and other community leaders. At times, SACs were empowered to speak for the FBI in their communities, but only on a case-by-case basis, on limited topics, and typically using scripts provided by the Crime Records Division. Hoover reserved the role of primary Bureau spokesman for himself.

By the mid-1930s, Hoover had established the basic organizational structure and processes that would shape the Bureau's public relations strategies for nearly four decades. Nichols led the Bureau's public relations efforts for twenty years, giving way to DeLoach and then to Thomas Bishop, all of whom maintained the same disciplined focus on delivery and enforcement of the Collier-Cooper narrative. The fortuitous collaborations with Collier and Cooper provided the FBI with a coherent and compelling narrative structure and themes on which to base its public relations forays into newspapers and magazines, radio, comic books, motion pictures, and ultimately television. Cooper in particular fleshed out the themes and polished the narrative that was reified and defended obsessively through the FBI's public relations bureaucracy. He became a trusted public relations adviser, and his ghostwritten articles gave Hoover a combative voice that dramatically raised his public profile.

Hoover's collaboration with Cooper ended suddenly in 1940 when an article in *American Magazine* caused significant backlash and subjected the

Bureau to criticism from some of its most important supporters in Congress. Cooper's final ghostwritten article for Hoover, "Camps of Crime," continued Cooper's strategy of assessing blame and evangelizing suspicion. The subject of the article was tourist camps (early motels)—wide spots along the highway that often included small individual cabins where weary travelers could stop and rest as they toured the country. Cooper/Hoover portrayed the tourist camps that dotted the nation as hotbeds of criminal activity—safe, anonymous, and convenient stopovers for fugitives and staging areas for crime. The backlash from tourist camp owners and their representatives in Congress was immediate and voluminous. Complaints began arriving at the FBI within days of the article's publication. At first, Hoover's replies were defiant, pointing out sections of the article that qualified the criticism. But as the trickle of critical letters turned into a flood, Hoover began to forward copies of the letters, along with his more contrite form-letter response, to Cooper. Between February and September 1940, the previously frequent and very friendly correspondence between Hoover and Cooper ceased entirely.

On September 29, 1940, Cooper was found hanged in the closet of a New York hotel room, two FBI identification cards in his pockets. A note urged that the money he carried be used to settle his hotel bill.[88] Media reports speculated that Cooper's falling-out with Hoover drove him to despair, and the *Washington Times-Herald* headline mentioned an "FBI Spy Snub." The accompanying story quoted Cooper's widow, who claimed that her husband had become mentally unbalanced after Hoover showed no interest in Cooper's investigation of Nazi activities in Mexico.[89] In response, Hoover suddenly discounted his connection to the writer. "He had no FBI connection," Hoover wrote. "He had a building pass such as is issued to many. There could have been no snub as we didn't know he was back [from a trip to Mexico]."[90] In a letter to *Times-Herald* publisher Eleanor Patterson, Hoover distanced himself and the Bureau from his late ghostwriter. "Mr. Cooper was not in any way officially connected with the FBI," Hoover wrote.[91]

A few days later, Hoover struck Cooper's name from the faculty roles of the Bureau's National Police Academy and removed the author's fingerprints from the exhibit outside his office.[92] Cooper's fingerprints were replaced with those of Walt Disney.[93] Cooper's suicide had led to media coverage that embarrassed the FBI and undermined the narrative themes he and Collier had authored. As a result, Cooper, like Purvis before him, was erased from FBI history.

By the time Disney's fingerprints replaced Cooper's in the director's outer-office shrine, Hoover had an experienced and savvy team of public relations advisers in place, along with a clearly defined message template that advanced comforting, inoculating themes of responsibility and restraint. As Hoover and his Bureau became increasingly well known, the director found himself in a dominant position with the journalists who clamored to gain access to FBI stories. During the height of the outlaw era in the mid-1930s, few critics spoke up to challenge the Bureau's legitimacy. As the nation's focus began to shift from high-profile outlaws to fears of subversion and disloyalty, however, the FBI's increasingly intrusive and secretive tactics emboldened a new generation of critics inside and outside the news media to question the Bureau's legitimacy.

Chapter 3

Enforcing the Bureau's Image of Restraint

In 1936, when FBI director J. Edgar Hoover appeared before a U.S. Senate subcommittee, he was grilled by Tennessee senator Kenneth McKellar about the Bureau's reckless use of force. "How many people have been killed by your department since you have been allowed to use guns?" McKellar asked. Hoover responded that eight "desperadoes" had been killed, and four special agents had been killed by criminals. "In other words," McKellar summed up, "the net effect of turning guns over to your department has been the killing of eight desperadoes and four G-Men." McKellar listened as Hoover explained the Bureau's policy on the use of deadly force, then said:

> I doubt very much whether you ought to have a law that permits you to go around the country as an army would, and shoot down all the people that you suspect of being criminals, or such that you shoot down all the people you suspect of having guns, and having your men shot down. I am not blaming you for the enactment of these statutes, Mr. Hoover, because that is Congress' fault. If we turned guns over to you and told you to kill the people that you suspect of crime, why, that's our fault.[1]

Accusations that the FBI was reckless in its tactics and the use of deadly force struck at the very heart of the Collier-Cooper legitimacy narrative. Even if one accepted the notion that science, not human passion, fueled the Bureau's investigations, maintenance of the FBI's legitimacy relied on the public's confidence in agents' restraint and responsibility and in Hoover as the just and careful overseer of the agency's work. The very idea that FBI agents were trigger-happy cowboys could create doubt about the FBI's value as a federal crime-control force. During that 1936 hearing, McKellar may have been acting out of pique because Hoover had not appointed his con-

*Senator Kenneth McKellar
(D-Tenn.) was an
outspoken critic of Hoover
and the FBI. (Library of
Congress, Harris & Ewing
Collection, Call Number
LC-H25-134509,
Reproduction Number
LC-DIG-hec-21544)*

stituents as special agents, but he was expressing a real concern based on Americans' long-standing fear of the corrupting potential of centralized power. The same sort of concern had arisen in some quarters after the Dillinger shooting. Why hadn't agents simply tackled and arrested Dillinger instead of shooting him down on the street? Questions about the use of force and the tactics employed when making arrests lingered throughout Hoover's tenure and required careful attention from the Bureau's public relations and management team.

Two other cases from the late 1930s demonstrate how careful the FBI had become in striking down assertions that undermined its legitimacy. The first case involved the shooting of one of the last high-profile outlaws, Bennie Dickson, on a street in St. Louis. The second involved a firestorm of criticism after revelations about the FBI's use of wiretapping and the early-morning arrests of some alleged radicals, reminiscent of the Palmer Raids. In each case, the public relations staff in the Bureau's Crime Records Division

sprang into action, directly addressing the challenges to its message and using its position of power to encourage an army of compliant journalists to
join the defense of Hoover and the FBI.

When accused bank robber Bennie Dickson was shot and killed outside a
St. Louis hamburger shop on April 6, 1939, the FBI reported that the heavily
armed thief had pulled out a gun and threatened the four special agents on
the scene. The description was eerily similar to the circumstances of the
Dillinger shooting, right down to the location on a busy city street near an
alley and reports that a female informant had led agents to the scene. The
killing was justified, according to the Bureau, as an act of self-defense by federal agents in fear for their lives.[2] Ostensibly, the climax of the Dickson case
could have provided another exhibit for Hoover's outer-office shrine. His
highly trained investigators, the public was told, had applied all the Bureau's
powers to locate and eliminate a dangerous, violent criminal who was hiding
in plain sight, waiting for an opportunity to strike again. The Collier-Cooper
narrative was upheld, according to the FBI's version of events, and fears that
the Bureau might endanger civil liberties were unfounded.

Unfortunately for Hoover, though, some St. Louis newspapers directly
contradicted the FBI's account. A waitress at the Yankee System Hamburger
Shop, nineteen-year-old Gloria Cambron, offered a different story of reckless and careless agents who, with the help of a paid informant, arrived at the
last moment and shot Dickson in the back as he attempted to flee. According
to Cambron, who had watched through the window of the restaurant, Dickson left the shop and did not draw a gun when confronted by St. Louis SAC
Gerald B. Norris. In fact, according to Cambron, Dickson turned and ran toward a closed door that led to an upstairs apartment. As Dickson struggled
to open the locked door, his side and back to the special agents approaching
from his right, he was shot twice. Cambron also described a mysterious
"woman in brown" who had joined Dickson at the hamburger shop, a detail
reminiscent of Ana Sage, the "woman in red" who had led agents to
Dillinger.

Internal FBI documents corroborated Cambron's version of the story. In
a "personal and confidential" letter to Hoover, Norris described the wounds
Dickson received. "Agent [name withheld, but probably the inexperienced
John Bush] shot him twice in the body, one bullet entering his shoulder and
going down toward the front, and the other going from one side of his body
to the other."[3] If, as the FBI claimed, Dickson had been crouching directly in
front of the agents approaching on the sidewalk and drawing his weapon, it

seems highly unlikely that the bullets would have followed a back-to-front and side-to-side trajectory. If, however, Dickson had been struggling to open a locked door, as Cambron claimed, with the agents approaching from behind on his right side, the trajectories would make sense—one bullet striking his shoulder and proceeding from back to front, and another striking his side and moving across his torso.

The existence of a "woman in brown" likewise undermined parts of the FBI's preferred narrative. According to Cambron, it was a paid informant, not science or FBI sleuthing, that led agents to the hamburger shop that day. Until this woman contacted the Bureau, agents had no idea where Bennie and Stella Mae Dickson might be. In the weeks before the shooting, the FBI had issued thousands of press releases to newspapers from Maine to Los Angeles, suggesting that the fugitives had been sighted nearby. The papers responded with "the Dicksons might be hiding here" stories, and the subsequent flood of tips from all over the country was no help in locating the fugitives. In fact, Bennie and Stella Mae had fled to New Orleans and had been living there for weeks before traveling to St. Louis to visit the sister of one of Dickson's prison acquaintances, identified only as Naomi in FBI files. Naomi's brother had urged her to contact Dickson and ask for money so their mother could get the medical care she needed. So Dickson was in St. Louis to deliver aid to the family of a friend.

Naomi knew there was a reward for information leading to the capture of Bennie Dickson (she was later paid between $2,500 and $5,000). A few days before the shooting, Naomi contacted Norris and told him Dickson was on his way to St. Louis. On April 6 she phoned Norris again, fifteen minutes before the meeting was to take place. Coincidentally, Norris lived near the Yankee System Hamburger Shop, located in midtown near Forest Park. He hastily assembled a team of three agents and proceeded to 7 South Euclid Avenue, near the intersection with LaClede Street, where his team gathered in a barbershop across the street. Norris attempted, unsuccessfully at first, to identify Dickson by walking past the restaurant. He then entered the shop to get a closer look at the man sitting at the counter with Naomi. Once he was certain that it was Dickson, Norris gathered his agents in the alley next to the restaurant to wait for the fugitive bank robber to emerge. Within a few minutes, Dickson stepped onto the sidewalk and was shot to death. Agents quickly hustled Naomi from the scene.[4]

Based on the FBI's own accounts of the shooting, it seems likely that the incident occurred exactly as described by Cambron—the only witness who had nothing to lose by telling the truth. There were troubling clues in Norris's report and subsequent FBI summaries filed in the days after the shooting. If Dickson had drawn a gun, why did only one of the agents fire his weapon? At the coroner's inquest, why did Norris refuse to say how many agents had fired? Why had ambulance attendants found Dickson's weapon not in his hand but in the belt of his pants, under his coat? In the end, Cambron's story was the most credible.

Dickson and his young wife, Stella Mae, had robbed banks in Elkton and Brookings, South Dakota, in the fall of 1938. Both times they entered the bank early in the morning and waited for time-locked safes to open, detaining any customers who came in. In one case, in a Robin Hood–like gesture reminiscent of Dillinger, Dickson returned some cash to a farmer. The Dicksons escaped to a Lake Bennieton, Minnesota, cabin after each robbery and tallied about $20,000 in stolen cash and securities. The Dickson case is not remembered as a major case, and it stands apart from the highly publicized war on crime of the early 1930s that led to the creation of the Collier-Cooper narrative. But the two bullets that killed Dickson transformed the Topeka native from the complicated, confused young man he actually was into a violent character in a dramatic story patterned after Dillinger. The Dickson story was ultimately shoehorned into the narrative that characterized the FBI's public relations in the final three decades of Hoover's tenure as director. As reconfigured by Crime Records Division writers, Dickson became just one more symbol of the efficiency of the FBI, and his death was a morality tale of how crime doesn't pay.

Just as Hoover's Crime Records storytellers wrote Melvin Purvis out of the Dillinger story (and turned Ma Barker—by all accounts, a demented and lonely woman—into a criminal mastermind), Nichols's team transformed the bookish Bennie and the immature, sixteen-year-old Stella Mae into a pair of bloodthirsty, Bonnie and Clyde–style killers. Dickson was portrayed in FBI press releases before and after the shooting as a vicious, unpredictable threat to the American way of life. He was, like Dillinger, a good boy gone wrong.

The intensive nine-month investigation that led to Dickson's shooting resulted in hundreds of FBI press releases. In newsrooms across America, compliant reporters and editors—who were already predisposed to believe the FBI and were eager for the readership-boosting drama of a high-profile outlaw case—published and broadcast the Bureau's latest crime story. The massive publicity failed to turn Dickson into a Dillinger-like antihero, but tens of thousands of column inches of newsprint were devoted to the young couple's crime spree. And when Dickson was shot outside that hamburger shop in St. Louis, a questionable shooting was made heroic through a story line that falsely asserted the Bureau's responsibility and utility.

The news media, conditioned to value FBI outlaw stories, promoted the story of the husband and wife bank robbers, the fugitive pursuit, and the deadly shooting at the hands of FBI agents. It was told and retold for two decades and meshed perfectly with journalists' goals of informing and entertaining America and, of course, selling newspapers in the process. Bennie and Stella Mae Dickson fit perfectly into the Collier-Cooper narrative. Bennie Dickson was a charismatic figure with certain parallels to Dillinger. He was an intelligent young man from a good family who had turned away from a solid, Middle American future to pursue a life of crime. Together with his young wife (a gun moll, in FBI parlance), Dickson went on a midwestern crime spree, albeit a relatively tame one, consisting only of two robberies and a single, relatively innocent kidnapping (they stole a car with the owner still in it). So, with the exception of the lack of violence, there were parallels to the legendary Bonnie Parker and Clyde Barrow, which provided a hook for many news stories. Sixteen-year-old Stella Mae was considered stylish and pretty, and her marksmanship skills were alleged to be impressive.

In many ways, however, the Dicksons were very different from earlier outlaws. Public interest in outlaws had cooled dramatically after the Dillinger shooting, and the subsequent killings of "Machine Gun" Kelly and "Baby Face" Nelson and the capture of Alvin Karpis had drawn much less public attention. Several years had passed since the heyday of the outlaw era, and the United States was a very different place by the late 1930s. Most important, though, the Dicksons were not violent criminals. No one was injured during their bank robberies or their subsequent cross-country run from the law. And their "kidnap" victim escaped, unharmed, after a few miles. The Dicksons fired only two shots during their nine months on the run—when Stella Mae tried to disable a pursuing police car in Michigan. In contrast, police fired hundreds of shots at them on two occasions. Both Bennie and Stella Mae suffered minor gunshot wounds in those melees.

Back in St. Louis, in the hours following the shooting, Norris's handling of events demonstrated the FBI's single-mindedness when it came to protecting its carefully crafted and nurtured legitimacy narrative. St. Louis police officers actually arrested two of the FBI agents in the aftermath of the

Edward A. Tamm served in the FBI from 1930 to 1948 and was assistant director for investigations in 1939, when Bennie Dickson was shot in St. Louis. President Lyndon B. Johnson appointed Tamm to the U.S. District Court of Appeals in 1965. (National Archives at College Park, Record Group 56, Series H, Box 23, #1321)

shooting (assistant director Edward Tamm described it to Hoover as "technical arrest").[5] Alarmed by that development, Norris refused to answer police questions until he had spoken to Tamm. Clearly, Norris knew there was the possibility of negative publicity if the agents had inappropriately used deadly force.

Even after the Dillinger shooting, some media reports had raised questions about the Bureau's "shoot first, ask questions later" tendencies. As the outlaw body count rose (and as the FBI body count rose with it), more questions were asked. Indiscriminate or unjustifiable shootings, even those involving wanted fugitives, had the potential to strike at the heart of the FBI's legitimation strategies. The Collier-Cooper narrative described a responsible, careful FBI, not a Wild West outfit. At the very least, because only one, apparently inexperienced agent had fired at Dickson, the Bureau's training regimen—an important element of the responsibility theme—could be questioned.

With those implications in mind, Tamm and Norris carefully scripted the agents' stories and plotted strategy for the coroner's inquest. The day after the shooting, Tamm recounted his orders to Norris in a memorandum to Hoover:

> Each man should testify that he can not say as to who fired the fatal shots. . . . I requested Mr. Norris to be careful to make clear when the inquest is held at nine o'clock tomorrow morning that Dickson was recognized by all the agents when he came out of the hamburger stand, that he was called upon to surrender, . . . and was killed when he attempted to draw his pistol after refusing to give himself up.[6]

Tamm later reminded Norris not to disclose the name of the agent who had fired the shots. That order was not unusual for the FBI; a similar one had been issued after the Dillinger shooting. Hoover, perhaps not privy to the full circumstances of the Dickson shooting, added his handwritten comments to the bottom of Tamm's memorandum: "I see no reason for us to try to placate local authorities. Our men had a job to do, they did it, and a criminal was killed in the act of pulling a gun. Tell Norris to stand up and not be apologetic to anyone."[7]

Tamm and Norris, it appears, were less sanguine about the outcome of the inquest, since they took further steps to ensure a result that fit the FBI's public relations narrative. Norris told Hoover that he had enlisted the aid of a U.S. attorney, who then spoke to local prosecutors to "arrange" a favorable hearing in which certain questions would not be asked.[8] In addition, St. Louis police officers testified at the inquest that Dickson was a wanted "murderer." That was untrue. Dickson was wanted for bank robbery and had never even fired a weapon in the commission of his crimes. The St. Louis officers cited Norris as the source of the false accusation.[9]

There remained one significant threat to the legitimacy of the shooting: the story told by witness Gloria Cambron. Her unromantic, unheroic version of events undermined two themes of the FBI narrative: the Bureau's responsible execution of its duties, and its reliance on systematic, scientific law enforcement techniques. Cambron was scheduled to testify at the inquest, and Tamm had a simple remedy: threaten her. "I told Mr. Norris that this woman should be brought into the office and given a good scare and that . . . if we are going to have to prosecute her for perjury or something, we will do so."[10] As a result, Cambron stopped talking to reporters and did not repeat what she had witnessed at the coroner's inquest.

The FBI's actions in the wake of the shooting of Bennie Dickson were clearly intended to revise events to avoid embarrassment. The lengths to which the FBI went to hide what was, at the very least, a questionable use of deadly force demonstrated the importance of maintaining the integrity of the Collier-Cooper narrative. Tamm, an assistant director (and later a federal judge), coordinated the revision of events and ordered a credible witness, with no ulterior motives, to be threatened into silence. According to FBI reports, agents provided questionable information at the inquest and fed false information to others who testified. The FBI's heroism was reestablished through a single-minded campaign of revision orchestrated at the top levels of the Bureau.

As Norris stood over Dickson's body, a car sped away from the scene. In the rush to confront Bennie Dickson, it had not occurred to Norris that Stella Mae might be waiting nearby. In newspaper accounts of the shooting, Norris told reporters that Stella Mae was "just as tough a customer as Bennie" and was wanted just as badly.[11] In fact, Stella Mae was a scared child and immediately set out for her mother's home in Topeka. She was arrested by FBI agents as she stepped from a car in downtown Kansas City two days after her husband was shot. The driver had tipped off the FBI. "I knew the minute he stopped [the car] he was going to get a federal man," Stella Mae told reporters. "I didn't care. I just sat in the car. I knew if I got out and tried to get to Topeka by myself I wouldn't get there alive, and I wanted to see my mother."[12] Her mother, Hattie Redenbaugh, was not surprised that her daughter had been taken into custody without incident, despite FBI assertions that the sixteen-year-old was "extremely dangerous." "I knew Estelle would be taken, and I knew exactly the way she would act," Redenbaugh said. "By that I mean that I knew they would find Estelle unarmed and that she would offer no resistance to those who arrested her."[13] In her criminal defense, Stella Mae invoked the coverture rule, under which a woman (or child) could avoid prosecution if she was simply following the direction of an authority figure such as a husband or father.[14] Nonetheless, she was convicted of bank robbery in U.S. District Court in Sioux Falls, South Dakota. Hoover wrote to the judge urging a harsh sentence, and on August 21, 1939, Stella Mae, then seventeen years old, was sentenced to ten years in a federal penitentiary.

Cambron was not the only person who saw something other than a heroic tale in the shooting of Bennie Dickson. *Baltimore Sun* editor John W. Owens published an editorial headlined "Monotonous Tale," criticizing the FBI's continued reckless use of force to bring fugitives to justice:

Curiously enough, local policemen and detectives rarely find it necessary to shoot and kill the desperadoes with whom they frequently deal. Now and then they shoot down some fool who tries to escape. Usually, however, they bring in the prisoner intact. He is duly indicted, tried and, if found guilty, is sentenced to proper punishment. The ends of justice are thus served in an orderly and decent way. We don't pretend to know why the G-Men so frequently find it necessary to kill. In the case of Bennie Dickson, the man who they got yesterday, one G-Man at least was with him in the restaurant where he had his last mortal meal. One would think a tap with a blackjack might have been feasible. Or that a revolver leveled at him might have persuaded him that resistance was useless. As we say, we don't pretend to know. But we do know that a killing by G-Men, however quick, cheap, and effective, is not the method provided by law for disposing of criminals.[15]

It is easy to imagine alarms going off at FBI headquarters when Owens issued a direct and credible challenge to the legitimacy of the Bureau's conduct in the Dickson case. Nichols and his staff quickly produced a response—a five-page letter over Hoover's signature—that was published by the *Sun*. Typical of Bureau retorts to critical news reports, the letter countered the editorial sentence by sentence and word by word. Four times the letter restated the FBI assertion, now part of the record of the coroner's inquest, that Dickson had been killed while "resisting arrest." The letter even added one new detail not revealed at the inquest or in any FBI report: as he lay dying on the pavement, Dickson "endeavored to secure one of his weapons, but his failing strength was not sufficient to consummate the threat he had previously made."[16]

Crime Records staff forwarded copies of Owens's editorial, along with Hoover's response, to the Bureau's friends in the media. The FBI kept careful track of its media friends, even designating some "Special Service Contacts" or later "Special Agent Contacts" because of their willingness to perform certain services for the FBI, including gathering information and mounting a defense when the Bureau was attacked. One such contact, *Memphis Commercial Appeal* editor Jack Carley, eventually became one of Hoover's closest "friends" in the media. In 1939, even though that friendship had just begun, Carley was willing to publish a rebuttal of Owens's "Monotonous Tale." Carley's editorial, based on information provided by the FBI, clearly followed the Collier-Cooper narrative by casting Hoover as America's trustworthy top cop:

When the Federal Bureau of Investigation pins the label of public enemy on a man he can expect one of two things, imprisonment or death. With most of the major public enemies it has been the latter and usually because of their unwillingness to admit the Government has the drop. . . . If any citizen finds himself getting perturbed over what may seem to be the FBI's merciless manner in attending to the business at hand, he need but remind himself what little mercy he could face if he himself came face to face with one of Edgar Hoover's listed enemies.[17]

Hoover thanked Carley for the editorial, which, he wrote, "reflected the attitude of the outstanding editors and publishers throughout the nation."[18]

The Dickson story likewise became a positive assertion of the FBI narrative in the decades after the shooting. Within a few weeks of Stella Mae Dickson's conviction, the Crime Records Section produced a series of radio scripts and interesting case files detailing the heroic shooting of her husband, public enemy Dickson. The Bureau also collaborated on two books. In Frederick L. Collins's 1943 book *The FBI in Peace and War*, Dickson "went for" his guns before being shot.[19] *FBI Man: A Personal History* (1966), written by Louis B. Cochran, one of the agents on the scene, embellished the story even further. After being shot, according to Cochran, Dickson "lay on his back, his eyes closed tight, his hands on his weapons, one leg cramped under him, his hat by his side."[20] In fact, as noted earlier, ambulance personnel found Dickson's weapons in the waistband of his pants.[21]

With the help of some friendly journalists, the Dickson shooting was converted into a heroic triumph for the FBI. Less than a year later, though, the Bureau faced another crisis that led critics, such as Senator George W. Norris, to question the FBI's legitimacy. On February 3, 1940, FBI agents arrested a dozen American citizens in Detroit, charging them with recruiting Americans to fight on the side of Loyalists in the Spanish Civil War. Although such activities were technically a violation of federal law, the Spanish Civil War had ended in 1939, and Roosevelt's new attorney general, Robert H. Jackson, ordered all charges dropped on February 15.[22]

Ultimately, it was not just the filing of charges that riled Hoover's critics; it was the way the FBI carried out the raids. Agents arrived at 5:00 a.m., knocked down doors, and searched some homes without warrants. One of those arrested, Mary Paige, was forced to change out of her dressing gown in the hallway of her home with several FBI agents uncomfortably close by.[23] Agents lured Dr. Eugene H. Shafarman out of his home to be arrested using

Senator George W. Norris (D-Neb.) in Washington, circa 1940. (Library of Congress, Harris & Ewing Collection, Call Number LC-H22-D-8244)

the false claim that an injured man on the street needed his aid.[24] When Eugene S. Hartley refused to emerge from his home, agents broke down the door.[25] The activists were detained by the FBI and were not allowed to speak to their attorneys until minutes before their court appearances, nearly twelve hours later.[26] On the way to court, the accused were chained together and paraded before photographers.[27] The specter of a U.S. government agency using what critics called "third-degree" tactics to arrest Americans accused of nonviolent crimes confirmed for many their worst fears about federal law enforcement power. "If these charges are only partially true, it is a matter of taking the law into their own hands and punishing people who are not convicted of a crime, who are not charged with any malicious crime, who are not charged with anything which has attached to it any element of criminality," Senator Norris said in a much-publicized speech.[28]

The Detroit raids were not the only challenge to the Bureau's legitimacy in early 1940. The FBI was also under fire for its use of wiretapping, another activity that suggested the Bureau had become too powerful. In 1928, in *Olmstead v. United States*, the U.S. Supreme Court had legalized warrantless wiretapping as an evidence-gathering method. Wiretaps were not a violation of the Fourth Amendment, the majority ruled, because there was no search and seizure involved. Essentially, wiretaps were legal because they were secret. Six years later, the Communications Act of 1934 banned the interception and disclosure of the contents of telephone conversations. Hoover believed the law did not apply to the FBI because it had no intention of disclosing the information it gained. Hoover sought intelligence, not evidence to be disclosed and used in court.[29] In 1937, however, the Supreme Court ruled in *United States v. Nardone* that the ban included the activities of federal agents. The high court found that the intent of the Communications Act of 1934 was clear: all wiretapping was illegal, and "no person shall divulge or publish the [intercepted] message or its substance to any person."[30] When the government retried *Nardone* in 1939 using summaries of wiretap transcripts rather than the originals themselves, the Supreme Court struck the case down again, saying that the intent of the law was clear: the original wiretaps were illegal. President Roosevelt chose to ignore both the Communications Act and the Court's interpretation of it when, in 1940, he secretly authorized FBI wiretapping of persons suspected of subversive activities, freeing Hoover to wiretap without oversight.[31] For twenty-five years, Hoover used FDR's secret order to justify at least 6,769 warrantless wiretaps and 1,806 bugs.[32]

In November 1939, however, just a few months before the Detroit raids, Hoover was forced to admit in testimony before a House appropriations subcommittee that the FBI had been using wiretaps continually since 1931.[33] Once again, Hoover's FBI had been caught placing itself above the law—squarely in secret police territory—damaging its legitimacy in the process. "The wire-tapping incident illustrates the necessity of further inquiry into current FBI practices," editors of *The New Republic* wrote. "How long will Congress let Hoover run before it calls for a full disclosure of all the FBI lawlessness now hidden from its eyes."[34] Attorney General Jackson banned wiretapping on March 17, 1940, an action that the leftist magazine *New Masses* termed a "tacit admission of guilt."[35] Two weeks later, the controversy was still roiling. Hoover publicly renounced wiretapping and addressed the larger issue of centralized police power: "We are and have been thoroughly opposed to centralized or dictatorial police power, no matter under what name or guise it may be camouflaged."[36] Even as he made this statement, Hoover was working furiously to regain his ability to listen in on private conversations, justifying his goal by distinguishing between investigative activity and intelligence activity. Hoover went around the attorney general and met with Secretary of the Treasury Henry Morgenthau on May 20. Morgenthau pled Hoover's case to the president, and the next day, FDR sent a confidential memorandum to the attorney general in which he parsed his position carefully. FDR told Jackson that although he agreed with the Court's finding as it related to crime control, he was "convinced the Supreme Court never intended any dictum in the particular case which it decided to apply to grave matters involving the defense of the nation."[37] Thus FDR authorized wiretapping under the condition that its use be kept to a minimum.

So far as the public knew, Hoover opposed wiretapping. In secret, however, Hoover's intelligence gathering via wiretaps continued and expanded after only a brief hiatus. While wiretapping had been eliminated as a blot on the Bureau's public image, another threat immediately emerged. In a move that further enraged critics, Hoover announced in congressional testimony that the FBI had reformed its General Intelligence Division (GID) to maintain indices on allegedly subversive individuals and organizations.[38] The original GID of 1919 and 1920 had, of course, led the infamous Palmer Raids. Hoover added fuel to the fire when he and associate director Clyde Tolson visited Miami, ostensibly to supervise a series of vice raids, and were spotted by the media socializing in local nightclubs.[39]

Even before the controversies of 1939 and 1940, the dramatic growth of the Bureau's physical footprint and legal jurisdiction during the 1930s had already heightened concerns about the agency's power. With the addition of domestic intelligence and espionage investigations to its rubric (thanks to Roosevelt's 1936 and subsequent executive orders), critics were openly questioning the Bureau's power and legitimacy. In particular, the Detroit raids and wiretapping revelations galvanized resistance among some on the political Left. Editors of *The Nation* compared the FBI to notorious German and Soviet spy agencies: "Our G-Men, like those other G-Men of the Gestapo and GPU, are beginning to act on similar principles." They went on to note that Hoover's reorganized GID had compiled extensive indices on allegedly subversive groups and individuals in the United States. "What is the purpose of these 'extensive indices?'"[40]

The FBI's response to these serious challenges sheds additional light on its public relations strategies. Because of his iconic status in American society, Hoover was able to reach a generally supportive national audience when he went on the offensive, demonizing his enemies and suggesting an organized "smear campaign" in the wake of the Detroit raids. At the same time, he was defended by adjuncts in the press whose identities, politics, and access to information were wrapped up in their public support of Hoover and the FBI. The Bureau's response to what it labeled the "Smear Campaign of 1940" demonstrates how effectively it could control its public image, counter narratives that did not match its public relations template, and ultimately obscure the extent of its lack of restraint in political surveillance, which likely would have been unpalatable to large numbers of Americans.

One audience for Hoover's public relations efforts was his immediate supervisor, the attorney general. Relationships with key reporters, editors, and publishers in Washington and across the country were particularly prized by Hoover's public relations team. Journalists were central to the FBI's efforts to maintain its central position in American culture and government while legitimizing its existence through news columns produced by "objective" and authoritative reporters.[41] In many cases, those reporters, editors, and publishers provided Hoover with a megaphone for his message and a willing team of defenders against criticism of the FBI. In other cases, the relationships were merely a function of ongoing efforts to promote the Bureau's preferred self-image in the pages of local and national newspapers. As had been the case since the Bureau's cultural buildup in the 1930s, the FBI was working from a position of great strength and authority in its dealings with the news media.

On March 17, 1940, the *New York Times* published a wire service interview with Hoover headlined, "OGPU Unthinkable Here, Says Hoover." The FBI director dismissed allegations that his agency had become an organization of political repression similar to the Soviet OGPU, a precursor of the KGB. "In the first place, such an organization would be contrary to the principle of States' rights guaranteed under the Constitution," Hoover said. "Then, too, to centralize in one place law enforcement administration for the nation would weaken and devitalize local administration of justice."[42] In those two sentences, Hoover identified the primary public relations problem facing his organization and batted it down as a nonissue.

In the same issue of the *Times*, an article by Frederick R. Barkley expanded on the legitimacy issues facing the Bureau. Barkley noted that in prior weeks, "a number of newspapers and newspaper columnists began to attack Mr. Hoover as a 'night-club fly cop,' a seeker of personal publicity, and a potential secret police operator of the OGPU or Gestapo type."[43] These critics directly contradicted the Bureau's preferred message of dispassionate and scientific law enforcement led by a steady and trustworthy director.

In response to negative coverage of the Detroit raids, Hoover leveraged relationships with dozens of reporters and editors that had been built over the previous six years. This team of supporters in the media published dozens of favorable editorials and columns in the months that followed. Throughout this period, Crime Records staff closely monitored the public debate surrounding the raids and crafted responses that addressed the concerns of the FBI's most important stakeholders: members of Congress, the attorney general, and the public at large. Finally, Hoover leveraged his own iconic status and dominant position of power, embarking on a speaking tour, granting interviews, and generally designating the criticism a "smear campaign" designed to discredit the Bureau and undermine American society.

Immediately following the raids, *The New Republic* published the first national condemnation of the FBI in its February 19 issue. In an editorial headlined "American Ogpu," the editors decried the Bureau's tactics and warned Attorney General Robert Jackson that Hoover had become too powerful: "[Jackson] should study the whole record of the lawlessness of Hoover's bureau, and also the widespread salesmanship by which Hoover has made himself much too powerful to be easily curbed by a superior. In foreign countries people are forced by their governments to submit to their Gestapos. In this country, Hoover has the voluntary support of all who delight in gangster movies and ten-cent detective magazines."[44]

Two weeks later, the left-leaning editors of the more mainstream *St. Louis Post-Dispatch* complained that "something fishy" was going on and invoked the "American OGPU" label. "If Hoover really is bent on building up an American secret police, then it is high time to call a halt. Congress should brush aside the old argument that police activities must necessarily be secret, and turn an investigative searchlight on the FBI and its publicity-mad chief."[45] Hoover responded by removing all *Post-Dispatch* reporters and editors from FBI mailing lists.[46]

Attorney General Robert H. Jackson (right) playing horseshoes with his successor, Francis Biddle. Jackson only reluctantly came to Hoover's defense during the 1940 Detroit raids and wiretapping scandals. (National Archives at College Park, Record Group 65, Series H, Box 9, Folder 550, #1)

Even before the *Post-Dispatch*'s broadside, Jackson's deputies had become alarmed enough to summon assistant director Edward A. Tamm to the attorney general's office "to discuss the recent adverse publicity of the Director and the Bureau."[47] Following that meeting, the FBI created a detailed, twenty-two-page memorandum refuting some of the charges associated with the Detroit raids and confirming others: Doors had been broken down. The arrests had occurred at 5:00 a.m. to ensure that the accused would be at home. Some homes had been searched. The suspects had been chained together, but the U.S. marshal was responsible for that. Finally, the report confirmed that the accused had been kept from their attorneys until just before their initial court hearings. The overall tone of the memorandum was dismissive and defensive. "Every step in this case, taken by representatives of the FBI, was taken upon Departmental instructions and Court authority," wrote Tamm.[48]

After a four-hour speech on the Senate floor, Senator Norris picked up the themes and language of *The New Republic* editorial in a letter to Attorney General Jackson. "I cannot help but reach the conclusion that there is some well-grounded fear that the activities of this Bureau are overstepping and over-reaching the legitimate objects for which it was created," Norris wrote. "Certainly the Government of the United States cannot afford to be given to third-degree methods, inflicted upon men and women, known not to be criminals and, particularly, when they are charged with an offense which has no odium attached to it."[49] Norris ended by quoting Harlan Fiske Stone's statement of May 15, 1924, five days after Hoover was named director of the Bureau of Investigation: "There is always the possibility that a secret police system may become a menace to free government and free institutions because it carries with it the possibility of abuses of power which are not always quickly apprehended or understood."[50]

Jackson was slow to respond, and the tenor of his negotiations with FBI officials indicated his deep suspicion of Hoover. In a ten-page memorandum, Tamm recounted his four-day campaign to extract a defense of Hoover from the attorney general: "I endeavored to impress upon the Attorney General the fact that time was of the very essence of this situation and that if any action was to be taken, it would have to be taken promptly in order to preclude a widespread barrage of criticism upon the Bureau."[51] Two days later, a draft response had been written but not released. "I told the Attorney General that this situation was becoming increasingly agitating," Tamm wrote.[52] During their meeting, Jackson told Tamm that he had long been dubious of Hoover's policies and had been told by his predecessor that the FBI maintained a surveillance on White House aide Tommy Corcoran. Tamm said those charges were untrue.[53] "The Attorney General then stated that although he had considerable doubt in his mind concerning Mr. Hoover and the policies of the Bureau, his recent discussion with Mr. Hoover had considerably clarified this matter," Tamm wrote.[54] Finally, late in the afternoon on Friday, March 1, the Department of Justice released a tepid response to Norris, stating that Jackson had found "nothing to justify any charge of misconduct against the Federal Bureau of Investigation."[55] Norris was unimpressed: "Intimidation by third degree methods is indefensible and is illegal under our system of jurisprudence," he wrote.[56]

Two weeks later, with the controversy still percolating in the press, Jackson held a news conference to announce that, in response to Norris's charges, Henry Schweinhaut, chief of the department's Civil Liberties Unit, would conduct an investigation of the Detroit raids. Jackson said that Hoover had joined in the request for an investigation.[57] Meanwhile, Hoover's public relations team had mailed letters to dozens of influential Bureau supporters in the press and government, urging them to reject the charges on which the investigation would be based. Those letters quickly began paying dividends. Broadcaster Earl Godwin of NBC's Blue Network responded with a letter to Hoover on March 2. "May I say that you do not need to defend yourself with me," Godwin wrote. "I'm for you and what you represent as you know." Godwin added that he aired on sixty-five radio stations every morning and offered his services in defense of the FBI: "Sometimes it's more of a value to explain and interpret than to present a scoop."[58] Another NBC radio man, Frank Blair, had already come to Hoover's defense by attacking Norris in his March 1 broadcast.[59] Hoover's friend Walter Winchell broadcast a defense of the FBI to his thousands of loyal listeners on March 3 and then forwarded to the Bureau half a dozen supportive letters he had received.[60] Hoover's correspondence team sent each of the writers a thank-you letter, along with a copy of a newspaper article reporting Jackson's defense of the FBI.[61]

After a March 7 lunch with Nichols, influential conservative commentator Fulton Lewis Jr. weighed in on his 7:00 p.m. news and commentary program, carried on hundreds of radio stations nationwide.[62] On March 12, Lewis detailed critics' charges and told his listeners not to believe them. "Just to keep the record straight, don't believe a single word of it, because it isn't true," Lewis said. "It so happens that Mr. J. Edgar Hoover and the Federal Bureau of Investigation are quite unpopular with certain reporters and correspondents and columnists here." In his folksy style, Lewis then suggested that he was merely an objective observer of events, not a close friend of the FBI who had lunched with a top Bureau official five days earlier. "I don't mean to indulge in any defense of Mr. Hoover. It's not my job to defend him," Lewis said. "I'm merely trying to pass along to you the facts as I find them to be, on very careful investigation." Lewis spoke again in support of Hoover on his March 15 broadcast and thoughtfully sent the director a transcript and a personal letter. "To be entirely candid," Lewis wrote, "I am somewhat shocked at the apparent campaign among a few newspapermen in Washington to 'build a fire under you.'"[63] A few days later, Lewis declared victory. "From what I have heard around the Press Club, or rather from the lack of what I have heard, the 'smear' campaign seems to be definitely abated and I hope that we have managed to squelch it," he wrote to Hoover. Referring to his broadcasts in defense of the director, Lewis added, "I think you know how I stand on the matter."[64] Hoover sent a transcript of Lewis's March 12 broadcast to his fifty SACs at offices around the country, encouraging them to circulate the message to opinion leaders in their communities.[65]

Hoover could also count on his newspaper friends to join the defense. On February 24, editors of the *Flint (Mich.) Journal* lamented the "Attack on the FBI" and noted that Jackson had dropped the charges.[66] Again on March 28, *Journal* editors offered a defense of the FBI and restated the Bureau's ongoing public relations message of restraint: "Mr. Hoover has no ambition to become the kind of an ogre his critics might expect of a person in his unique position."[67]

Hoover knew his ally, *Washington Star* editor Rex Collier, would speak out on his behalf. Collier's editorial, titled "Attack by Innuendo," was published on March 13 and asserted that criticism of the Bureau was evidence of a "widespread and co-ordinated effort to undermine the Federal Bureau of Investigation." The FBI, Collier wrote, "should not be made the victim of a movement which has all the earmarks of a 'smear' campaign."[68] In a letter thanking Collier, Hoover called the attack one of the "most stinking and disgraceful episodes that I have ever come across in my life."[69] He picked up Collier's "smear campaign" label, with its suggestion of an organized conspiracy, and it became the Bureau's internal and external shorthand for the criticisms of early 1940.

New York Times columnist Arthur Krock, by 1940 a two-time Pulitzer Prize winner, weighed in on Hoover's behalf on March 25, dismissing charges that the director was an autocrat or a publicity seeker. Krock said the criticism of Hoover was ineffective because of the director's "useful record." "Despite the hopes of some of Mr. Hoover's critics . . . Attorney General Jackson stood firmly behind the chief of the G-Men."[70] Hearst columnist George Sokolsky also issued a defense of Hoover on March 25. "All this attack on J. Edgar Hoover as a civil liberties suppressor leaves me a bit aghast," Sokolsky wrote. Hoover "is not likely to break the law, much less the Constitution. He would know how to watch his step by intuition, training and experience."[71] And William Randolph Hearst himself, the owner of dozens of newspapers and radio stations across the country, defended the FBI on May 1, noting that although criticism was natural, "should it not be equally natural for all honest people to flock to [Hoover's] support and rout the criminals and rascally Red Radicals who are lending their discreditable support to the attempted 'smear'?"[72] Hearst's column, printed in all his newspapers and discussed on his radio stations, was particularly helpful to Hoover, who expressed his heartfelt thanks: "The editorial comments which have appeared in your various papers have been a real source of inspiration and encouragement and have served the very important purpose of not only calling public attention to the origin of the 'smear' campaign but have charged us with a new zeal to carry out our sworn duty regardless of the consequences."[73]

Nichols himself disarmed one potentially damaging story line from the raids—the fact that agents had forced Mary Paige to disrobe in a hallway while they stood nearby. In an interview with author Curt Gentry, Nichols bragged that he had undermined her character by telling newsmen that Paige, who was white, was living with a black taxicab driver.[74]

The Schweinhaut investigation was quickly concluded, but the results were not released for several weeks, even as the controversy continued in the press. When Norris delivered another blistering attack in a speech on April 25, Hoover pleaded with Jackson to release the findings of the investigation. "The original complaint by Senator Norris was made February 22, 1940," Hoover wrote. "I have no doubt that this speech of the Senator's will receive wide publication; certainly we can expect certain columnists and certain newspapers which are unfavorable to the Federal Bureau of Investigation to set upon this second outburst of the Senator's as occasion for further attack upon the Bureau."[75] Hoover was provided with a copy of the report on April 30 and quickly issued a nine-page rebuttal, concluding that Schweinhaut had not been forceful enough in his exoneration of the FBI.[76] Jackson waited until May 5 to announce that the Schweinhaut investigation had absolved the FBI of most of the criticisms related to its execution of the Detroit raids. Schweinhaut's report concluded that only two charges were valid: the chaining of the accused by the U.S. marshal, and the failure to provide access to attorneys.[77]

Senator Norris issued a quick denunciation of the report. The attorney general responded to Norris directly. "I am of course anxious, as you are, that in law enforcement we do no violence to our traditional civil liberties," Jackson said. "I am convinced that if those liberties are generally endangered in this country it is not by the FBI."[78]

The defense mounted by his media friends and the absolution by the Justice Department could have ended the Detroit and wiretapping controversies. Characteristically, though, Hoover used the criticism to whip up a frenzy of publicity, portraying the FBI as the victim of un-American radicals. Hoover went on the offensive, demonizing his enemies. In a series of speeches to conservative groups, Hoover drew a clear line between his critics and his supporters. In so doing, he emphasized the differences between those who adhered to the FBI's version of Americanism and those who did not. His critics were "international confidence men" or "conspiring Communists, their fellow travelers, mouthpieces and stooges," Hoover charged; they made up a "fifth column" bent on destroying the nation that Hoover's restrained agents and their dispassionate, scientific law enforcement techniques were protecting.[79]

On April 19, Hoover addressed the Washington, D.C., meeting of the Daughters of the American Revolution, asserting that all Americans should be on guard against those seeking the "professional destruction" of the nation's institutions, including the FBI.[80] On May 3, Hoover addressed the New York City Federation of Women's Clubs:

> I charge that the most vicious smear campaign which is being directed against the FBI is a part of the working program of various anti-American forces, the basis of which is to undermine public confidence in the law enforcement bodies of America, and thus weaken the defenses of our country. And I want to emphatically state that my remarks are not directed at any individual who sincerely criticizes the FBI from a constructive viewpoint.[81]

On April 26, a Hoover ally, Senator Alexander Wiley (R-Wis.), joined the offensive, telling his Senate colleagues that the criticisms of Hoover amounted to a "smearing attack from the left wing quarters."[82] Those left-wing critics, Wiley claimed, were both American communists and foreign agents.

Hoover's characterization of his critics as communists and fellow travel-ers caught the attention of editors at the *Des Moines Register* and the *Des Moines Tribune*. These publications had been reliable friends of the Bureau, but on April 20, 1940, the *Register* responded to Hoover's charges with an editorial headlined, "Whoa, Now, Edgar, Let's Clarify!" The editors unani-mously supported the FBI's work but suggested that Hoover was unfairly categorizing his critics:

> We hope J. Edgar isn't trying to convey the impression that *anybody* who at *anytime* criticizes something the FBI does, must therefore be "anti-American" or Communist. . . . We hardly think Senator Norris, for example, who was incensed by the high-handedness of the FBI's Detroit raids, is either a Communist or even "anti-American." No, we don't think the FBI wants to become an "Ogpu" or "Gestapo." But we certainly don't think it needs to be immune to debate and criticism, either. Just so we understand each other, Director![83]

The editorial directly undermined two elements of the FBI's public relations and legitimation campaigns, suggesting that agents conducting the Detroit raids had been overzealous and directly criticizing Hoover.

FBI officials responded by trying to arrange a meeting between Gardner (Mike) Cowles, president and publisher of the *Register* and *Tribune*, and Dr. Tom Denny, a prominent Des Moines citizen. Denny owned the Insurance Exchange Building that housed the FBI's local office and was a close friend of the Cowles family. FBI agent R. C. Hendon suggested that Denny and Cowles sit down for dinner, discuss the situation, and "try to straighten them [*sic*] out."[84] Hoover suggested sending a letter to Cowles because the editors "have distorted my speech & only read part of it."[85] On April 24, Hoover wrote to Cowles: "I want to reiterate to you that very definitely the recent campaign which has been directed against the Bureau was inspired by un-American forces and through the lies and misinformation which they distributed, well-meaning and otherwise sincere persons were victimized by their falsehoods." Hoover continued, "It is your duty to criticize freely when there is a need; it also is the American duty to stand by the brave, honest, efficient officers who give of their best for the communities they serve."[86] Hoover's staff did not believe Cowles was behind the attack, but just a few weeks earlier, on March 14, Cowles had raised concerns about the Detroit raids with Des Moines SAC E. R. Davis. "In this connection," Davis reported to Hoover, "Mr. Cowles stated that possibly the Bureau Agents were caught off first base at Detroit, Michigan."[87]

Two months later, *Des Moines Register* reporter Don Grant told SAC Davis that he believed the FBI had been irresponsible in the Detroit raids. Davis reported Grant's accusation to Hoover in a letter on June 4, 1940: "[Grant] believed some of the criticisms were well-taken. . . . Thereafter, he commented on the possibility of the F.B.I., becoming a Gestapo, etc." Davis advised Hoover that he had told Grant the FBI "was doing more to guard the civil liberties of this country than any other organization" and then reported the conversation to his superiors. When Hoover read the memorandum, he dismissed it as more evidence of the untrustworthiness of the *Register* and *Tribune*: "A typical newspaperman's viewpoint when it has been molded by Newspaper Guild propaganda."[88]

As a result of the "Whoa, Edgar," editorial, the FBI removed all *Register* and *Tribune* staffers, except for editorial cartoonist Jay N. "Ding" Darling, from its mailing list.[89] Although the newspapers' mailing list privileges were subsequently restored, the FBI continued to assert that the criticism had been part of an organized "smear campaign" by its enemies. The Bureau did not forget this anti-American attack by "Newspaper Guild" propagandists. It was a black mark that remained on the *Register* and *Tribune*'s FBI record, and it was brought up every time the newspapers were mentioned in Bureau reports, shaping the FBI's relationship with the publications for decades.

On August 1, 1940, FBI public relations officials tallied the supportive editorials and letters to the editor that had been published in newspapers nationwide during the prior seven months. The total exceeded 500—nearly as many as had been published in all of 1939. "It is felt that this is a fair criterion of the attitude of the press towards the Bureau," Hendon wrote.[90] A few brave critics remained, though. In 1941, independent journalist George Seldes wrote in his book *Witch Hunt*: "In Detroit the agents of the F.B.I. Chief J. Edgar Hoover, taking their lesson from the Hitler Gestapo treatment of Jews and non-Nazis, broke into bedrooms between four and five in the morning and took men and women, chained to each other, to jail."[91] In his newspaper *In Fact*, Seldes also referred to the FBI as a gestapo that has "attempted to suppress freedom of thought."[92]

A year later, Hoover received the news that his nemesis, Senator Norris, had been defeated after forty years of service to Nebraska. On a *Washington Times-Herald* news clipping, Hoover took credit for Norris's first electoral defeat: "It makes all the difference as to whose hide is stuck!"[93]

On October 21, 1955, FBI public relations official Milton A. Jones made a recommendation to his boss, assistant director Louis B. Nichols: Former Republican senator George W. Norris of Nebraska, a prominent Bureau critic, had died in 1944 and left his personal papers to the Library of Congress. Jones suggested that the FBI send an agent to the Library of Congress to review Norris's papers to determine "who had contacted Norris in connection with the Detroit case. If we can definitely show with whom he was in contact and then determine the background of these individuals, I believe it will be possible to show that 'Commies' had hoodwinked him."[94]

After first agreeing that the matter should be pursued, Hoover later canceled the operation when it was discovered that Norris's 100,000-item collection could not be "borrowed" from the Library of Congress.[95] Hoover's plan to smear a U.S. senator and FBI critic who had been dead for eleven years for his role in a fifteen-year-old incident did not come to fruition. The fact that it was even considered by top-level FBI administrators demonstrates the level of concern created by the events of 1939 and 1940.

Likewise, the events of 1939 and 1940 provide a convincing display of the FBI's position of power in reporter-source relationships. Using both public relations and brute authority to enforce its preferred public image among the mainstream media, the Bureau engaged an army of defenders to shout down critics. The "smear campaign" label was then employed to undermine the critics by characterizing them as anti-American. Although Hoover clearly prevailed in the challenges of 1939 and 1940, the Detroit raids unified dissident left-wing media to begin an impassioned critique of the FBI's power and legitimacy. One of the leading FBI critics to emerge in the early 1940s was a former mainstream journalist turned newsletter publisher: George Seldes.

Chapter 4

Silencing a "Useful Citizen"

On August 22, 1945, journalist George Seldes wrote to J. Edgar Hoover with a series of complaints. Seldes, a legendary foreign correspondent, avowed contrarian, alleged fellow traveler, and publisher of the progressive and often shrill *In Fact* newspaper, said he had documentary evidence that during a trip to Mexico, the FBI had shadowed the movements and searched the belongings of his wife, Helen Larkin Seldes. At the Fort Worth airport on her way to Mexico, Helen Seldes was interrogated by a man in uniform and an FBI agent. The uniformed man asked if she was "the wife of George Seldes, the notorious publisher of In Fact." She was also asked, "Who subsidizes In Fact?" The same man confiscated her papers, including her address book, and then returned them to her just before the plane took off. The official, according to Seldes, told her he had been waiting for the FBI to return the papers and added, "This has never happened before. You must be a dangerous person."[1] Furthermore, in a letter intended for the FBI but accidentally sent to Seldes, a postal official from Norwalk, Connecticut, had disclosed that Helen Seldes's mail was being read by the FBI. The postmaster's letter even included her "secret" FBI file number: 100-6956.

Seldes asked whether Hoover could shed any light on the situation. "Neither Mrs. Seldes nor myself have anything to hide," Seldes wrote. "We are running a weekly paper devoted to exposing the corrupt press (with the aid of hundreds of newspaper men across the country) and also exposing fascism. This weekly has been endorsed by at least twenty Senators and Representatives, Secy of the Interior Ickes, Senator Truman (now President of the United States) and other persons of importance. . . . There is nothing in my whole record which I would not tell you about openly."[2]

Hoover ordered his agents to report on Seldes's claims. A few days later, inspector D. Milton "Mickey" Ladd replied in an eight-page memorandum that all the claims were true. As Hoover knew, the FBI considered Seldes a

George Seldes, circa 1934.
(© Condé Nast
Archive/CORBIS)

"key figure" in the New York communist apparatus, despite the fact that numerous Bureau investigations had found no evidence linking him to the Communist Party, other than his leftist politics and leftist acquaintances. Likewise, Helen Larkin Seldes was considered a communist sympathizer (based on hearsay evidence) who might have influenced her husband's conversion from anticommunist to fellow traveler. Under the heading "Present Problem," Ladd acknowledged that agents had searched Mrs. Seldes's Fort Worth hotel room, where they found nothing but an empty rum bottle and three empty cigarette packages. Agents had arranged with Customs officials to search her luggage, and a detailed summary of her belongings, including the full contents of her address book, had been prepared. Two agents of the FBI's Special Intelligence Services (SIS) had indeed shadowed Mrs. Seldes in Mexico City. But as Ladd pointed out, plausible deniability existed because the surveillance team did not include anyone with the title "special agent" of the FBI. And yes, Ladd reported, Mrs. Seldes's mail had been opened and read by FBI agents for the past eight months.[3] Though George Seldes didn't ask about it, he probably suspected that the FBI had been reading summaries of his mail as well, and in fact, it had been doing so since 1942.[4]

The final page of Ladd's memorandum was devoted to how to respond to Seldes's inquiries. Ladd immediately canceled the mail cover, allowing the Bureau to deny it existed. Ladd expressed concern about the leak in the Norwalk post office, thus confirming that Seldes's letter from the postmaster was real. Regarding the other charges in Seldes's letter, the Bureau consulted a Justice Department lawyer. Special Assistant Attorney General Alexander Holtzoff (who later served more than twenty years as a federal judge) suggested a semantic, legalistic, and entirely misleading response. He told Ladd to deny any surveillance of Mrs. Seldes during her stay in Mexico; avoid any response to the issue of reading her mail, since there was independent proof of that; and assert that neither of the Seldeses was currently under surveillance.[5] In other words, the Bureau should simply lie.

Hoover's letter to Seldes displayed a combative and defiant tone: "Most travelers who found it necessary to leave the United State during the war were glad to submit to the slight necessary inconvenience encountered at the borders on the basis that this contribution on their part essentially worked to the benefit of the United States and protected this country against foreign agents, saboteurs and subverters."[6] Hoover went on to claim that there had been no surveillance in Mexico City and that Mrs. Seldes could not possibly hold the FBI responsible for the loitering of "native Mexicans." "I do wish to specifically advise you that Mrs. Seldes was not under surveillance by *Special Agents of this Bureau* [emphasis added] at any time while she was in Mexico," Hoover wrote, fudging the truth. Finally, the director promised to check on whether Mrs. Seldes's mail had been opened and read. He did not, however, promise to inform Seldes of his findings and never did so.[7]

An independent journalist operating squarely on the political Left, Seldes adhered to an ideology of criticism. The FBI perceived this as evidence of communist values at a minimum and even as plausible evidence of Communist Party membership. In the narrowly drawn black-and-white, good and evil political world of Hoover's FBI, there was little tolerance for shades of meaning. Criticism of any kind, adherence to progressive values, support of labor, and other sins of the Left were automatically interpreted as evidence that the critic was a communist, a fellow traveler, or, in unique Bureau parlance, a "near-communist." As even the FBI's own investigations had determined, the muckraking tradition of Seldes's hero Lincoln Steffens, along with his experiences as a foreign correspondent covering the rise of fascism in Europe, had shaped Seldes's philosophy of criticism. He took pride in illuminating overlooked stories, challenging corruption, and holding the press accountable. But that combination of progressive politics and muckraking journalism placed him in the same category as independent reporter I. F. Stone, strident FBI critic Fred J. Cook, and even conservative *New York Post* editor James A. Wechsler, who harbored an intense dislike for Seldes.

A New Jersey native, Seldes joined the staff of the *Pittsburgh Leader*, a pro-labor daily, in 1908 at the age of eighteen. His early perceptions of an overly compliant and often corrupt press were forged there. Seldes wrote a story about a rape complaint against the son of a Pittsburgh department store owner and *Leader* advertiser, but the paper's publisher spiked it. Rather than being printed, the article was handed over to the paper's advertising department, which used the threat of its publication to encourage the store owner to buy more advertising.[8] In 1935, Seldes wrote a book, *Freedom of the Press*, in which he warned that advertising pressure, not government control, was the primary cause of press censorship.[9] In his 1938 book *Lords of the Press*, Seldes cataloged the sins of the American Newspaper Publishers Association, concluding that "these human weaknesses eventually rob a nation of a free press as great editors will testify."[10] In that same volume, Seldes offered ten tests for a free press; these included telling the truth about cigarettes, rejecting organized pressure, publishing labor news, and ending the press's defense of child labor.[11]

Seldes covered World War I for a syndicate and stayed in Europe after the war as a correspondent for the conservative *Chicago Tribune*. There, according to his *New York Times* obituary, Seldes met the father of psychoanalysis, Sigmund Freud, fascist Italian prime minister Benito Mussolini, and Bolshevik leader Vladimir Ilyich Lenin.[12] After the Great War, Seldes was posted in Moscow with the *Chicago Tribune*, but he was expelled after being caught trying to avoid Soviet censors by sending uncensored reports in personal letters carried in U.S. diplomatic pouches. He moved on to Italy, where he documented the rise of Mussolini's Fascisti and reported honestly about the brutal tactics Il Duce employed to maintain and expand his grip on power. When Seldes reported on Mussolini's connection to the murder of opposition leader Giacomo Matteotti, he was expelled from Italy and narrowly escaped the wrath of the Fascisti, hiding among British officers when Mussolini loyalists stopped his train as he left the country. His first book, *You Can't Print That! The Truth behind the News 1918–1928*, cataloged his frustrations with censorship, corruption, and a lack of objectivity during his coverage of postwar Europe.[13] Seldes adhered to a contrarian view and saw himself as a critic whose purpose was to uphold the promise of social justice and watchdog journalism in a democratic society.

A single-minded devotion to facts and an unwillingness to bow to censorship had, by the late 1920s, made Seldes a legendary foreign correspondent. His boss, *Chicago Tribune* publisher Colonel Robert McCormick, was, like many leading American businessmen, an admirer of Mussolini. McCormick had backed Seldes in his dispute with the Bolsheviks but had not protested his ouster from Italy by the fascists. After Seldes returned from Europe, he wrote a series of stories juxtaposing U.S. and Mexican positions on south-of-the-border oil fields, but McCormick censored the reports, printing only the U.S. position. In protest, Seldes left the mainstream press for good. To Seldes, the failure to report all sides of an issue was the worst kind of censorship and smacked of fascism.

Freed from the constraints of the mainstream media, Seldes wrote a series of books critiquing the press and other centers of power and warning of the gathering storm of another world war. In *Lords of the Press* he warned of the concentration of power among a handful of publishers who conspired in secret to thwart labor and reformers. Rather than being driven by idealism or public service, these wealthy publishers routinely bowed to the human weaknesses "of egotism, of power seeking, of greed for profits, which men in other businesses often admit but which most publishers hide under beautiful words about public service."[14]

In the 1930s, Helen and George Seldes traveled to Spain, where the plight of the elected republican government, under siege by General Francisco Franco's fascist rebels, had become a cause célèbre among the American political Left. The Spanish Civil War, pitting the democratically elected left-wing government against Franco's nationalist insurgents, offered liberals, communists, and socialists all over the world a golden opportunity to act on their hatred of fascism. Thousands of soldiers flooded Spain, including nearly 3,000 Americans of the Abraham Lincoln Brigade. Likewise, many antifascist journalists gravitated to Spain to cover the action. Seldes's cheerleading and overly optimistic coverage of the republicans' efforts to repel the nationalists continued until Franco's forces won, a disillusioning defeat for the Left. Seldes returned to the United States without any clear prospects for his journalism career. In 1940, he published a book that predicted the web of loyalty inquisitions that would soon entangle many Americans on the Left.

In *Witch Hunt: The Techniques and Profits of Redbaiting*, Seldes predicted a period of escalating assaults on the political Left. "There are very few Communists, that is, real reds in America," he wrote, "but there are millions of Americans who are liberal, democratic, progressive—and it is among these that the reactionary forces often find their victims."[15]

Seldes was setting himself up to become an even more attractive target of the reactionaries. The same year *Witch Hunt* was published, Seldes partnered with an acquaintance, Bruce Minton, and founded *In Fact*, a four-page weekly newsletter. Referring to Seldes's work on *In Fact*, A. J. Liebling said:

> Seldes is strident, like a man shouting into a telephone in a dream, one of those dreams in which one simply can't raise the operator, although the house is on fire and a monstrous he-goat is about to thrust a red-hot poker in one's ear. He is about as subtle as a house falling in, and he makes too much of the failure of newspapers to print exactly what George Seldes would have printed if he had been managing editor. But he is a useful citizen.[16]

Seldes's critical sensibility appears to have failed him in his dealings with Minton, whose real name was Richard Bransten. Bransten was the son of MJB Coffee founder Morris Brandenstein of San Francisco. Bransten and his wife, *PM* writer Ruth McKenney, were members of the Communist Party. Partnering with Bransten was a pragmatic move for Seldes, but in Hoover's eyes, it was precisely the kind of conspiracy that epitomized the creeping communist menace. The connections between *In Fact* and the Communist Party were even more direct than Seldes knew. Bransten had borrowed the money for his investment in *In Fact* from Communist Party leader Earl Browder, and the party viewed this investment as an opportunity to establish a stealthy foothold in the "respectable" media. Seldes, who rarely failed to detect hypocrisy in others, always claimed that he was unaware of Minton/Bransten's Communist Party membership and the source of his partner's investment funds.

Marketed to progressives, labor activists, and other left-leaning groups, including socialists and communists, *In Fact* was filled with "insider" stories presented as straight news. There was no effort to feign objectivity, and *In Fact* staked out decidedly antifascist, pro-labor, and antiwar positions. Seldes, who relished mining government reports for news, was the first reporter to link tobacco and cancer. He highlighted the hypocrisy of the news media, which ignored government reports on the dangers of tobacco rather than jeopardize millions of dollars worth of tobacco advertisements. In addition, Seldes criticized the news media for ignoring the post–World War II emergence of government blacklists and loyalty investigations. *In Fact* was a weekly outlet for Seldes's seemingly bottomless well of outrage. The paper also included brilliant reporting and analysis, usually delivered with dramatic hyperbole. The newsletter billed itself as "An Antidote for Falsehood in the Daily Press" and declared that it was "for the millions who want a free press." Its headlines shouted the latest desecration of democracy that Seldes had uncovered: "1941 Censorship Like 1917."[17] "Hoover's FBI Repeats 1918 Wartime Terrorism; Attacks Opponents of Dictatorship and War."[18] "The FBI Replaces Labor Spy Agencies."[19]

Historian and press critic Ben Bagdikian observed that while Seldes no longer had access to the pages of the mainstream press, "he did . . . have access to a very important part of the journalistic community, of journalists who knew that there were flaws in the system."[20] Those flaws kept certain kinds of voices, particularly those that were critical of mainstream orthodoxy and media performance, out of the news. "I spoke up for making the weekly absolutely fair and factual, printing straight news, no slanted pro-labor news, just the facts," Seldes wrote in his memoirs. "Our subscription list approached 200,000—which we figured would be about one million readers; and we would have gone far beyond that had not almost every newspaper in the country and every crooked and prostituted journalist in the country united in red-baiting us—and finally destroying *In Fact*."[21]

Minton's determination to make *In Fact* toe the Communist Party line led to a rift with Seldes, who bought out his partner's share in the enterprise in 1941. The damage had already been done, however; by then, the FBI assumed that Seldes was a communist or at least a fellow traveler. But Seldes was no political ideologue. Although he approached public issues from a progressive perspective, his main focus, shaped by his experiences in Russia and Italy, was antifascism. Yet he did not adhere to a strict definition of fascism as a political ideology. For Seldes, "fascism" was synonymous with situations in which an imbalance of power led to injustice. The critique of tyrannical power as fascism, wherever it appeared—from Mussolini's Italy and Hitler's Germany to American newsrooms, corporate headquarters, federal government agencies, and the halls of Congress—was Seldes's chosen milieu. His devotion to empowerment and rejection of authority, of course, did not mesh with Hoover's narrow, simplistic, black-and-white worldview and his reverence for imposed order. Within Hoover's FBI, the continuum of liberal thought, politics, and culture was not carefully parsed. Instead, Hoover simply lumped all liberals together, as if the elusive Popular Front of allied liberal groups sought by some on the Left actually existed. As a leftist, antifascist cultural critic, Seldes clearly fell across the line of acceptable, mainstream orthodoxy as defined by Hoover and imposed downward through the FBI pyramid. Nor was the FBI tolerant of people who had acquaintances on the Far Left, even acquaintances with whom they disagreed. In the FBI's closed and paranoid worldview, acquaintance presumed agreement, and agreement with communists implied conspiracy. Seldes's partnership with an avowed communist, Minton, could mean only one thing to FBI analysts. In the simple, linear deliberations of Hoover's FBI, the evidence added up to only one conclusion. Because of his leftist politics and the politics of his friends and associates, Seldes must be a communist.

Ironically, Seldes began the J. Edgar Hoover chapter in his memoirs by declaring, "For many years, I thought J. Edgar Hoover was a friend. Our correspondence began shortly after *In Fact* was started and continued for five years."[22] As a shrill, combative, critical voice on the Left, Seldes should not have been surprised that he was a target of FBI investigations. The FBI's active investigation and monitoring of Seldes began six months after *In Fact* debuted in 1940, when President Roosevelt's secretary, Stephen Early, wrote to Hoover requesting an investigation of Seldes, who opposed FDR's steps toward U.S. involvement in World War II.[23] Two weeks later, Hoover sent Early and FDR memoranda summarizing the FBI files on both Seldes and *In Fact*. Of course, the investigation of the editor and his publication did not end there. As was often the case, Hoover's interpretation of Early's intent, and thus Roosevelt's, was that the Bureau should monitor Seldes indefinitely. That questionable interpretation resulted in a series of investigations that lasted more than ten years, long after both FDR and Early had died.

The information contained in Hoover's two memoranda expressed his immutable views about Seldes. The initial seven-page summary noted that Seldes had affiliated himself with what the FBI considered to be subversive groups, such as the International Committee for Political Prisoners, the National Committee for People's Rights, and the American Boycott against Aggressor Nations. Another red flag in Seldes's record was the fact that the editor's name had appeared in several *Daily Worker* articles, and his books had been reviewed in that publication. Alarmingly, according to the FBI, Seldes kept in touch with a German journalist friend he had met during his years in Europe.

One item highlighted by Hoover was that Seldes, along with two writers "who have communistic leanings," joined the Writers Emergency Committee to Save *New Masses*."[24] *New Masses*, a Marxist publication operating beyond the far left wing of American politics, had become of great interest to Hoover's communist sleuths. That Seldes, a determined advocate of a free press, might support a diversity of viewpoints in the media did not occur to Hoover's investigators. Nor did it occur to Bureau analysts that, unlike Hoover, Seldes could not control who published his name or reviewed his books.

Attached to the Seldes summary, a single-page memorandum on *In Fact* declared: "The viewpoint of 'In Fact' is simple: it is in favor of every idea, movement, and organization that is for what we carelessly call liberalism, democracy, progress, but it intends to follow up the frauds which hide behind these words; it is pro-labor and especially pro-progressive labor."[25] The conflation of liberalism, democracy, progress, and communism unmasked the FBI's interest in the political Left as little more than a vendetta against dissidence. It revealed the bright line separating us and them, good and evil, American and communist, as constructed by Hoover and internalized, as if by osmosis, among FBI investigators and analysts.

Immediately upon completing the memos for FDR, Hoover ordered the further investigation of *In Fact*. The special agent in charge in New York reported Minton's real name and affiliation with the Communist Party to Hoover.[26] Minton's involvement in the venture ultimately brought Seldes before Senator Joseph McCarthy's (R-Wis.) Permanent Subcommittee on Investigations in 1953; the senator was looking into U.S. Information Agency libraries, where Seldes's books had been found on the shelves. Undoubtedly, a key factor in the decision to call Seldes was the editor's past criticism of the committee and of its newly hired staff director J. B. Matthews, a former Hearst investigator.[27] James A. Wechsler, another McCarthy critic, was called before the committee on a similar pretense. According to transcripts of the hearings (which were not released until 2003), Roy Cohn, the committee's opportunistic and tendentious counsel, opened his questioning by asking Seldes about his alleged communist connections. The questioning displays Cohn's strategy of cornering witnesses within a maze of semantics, a method Wechsler later termed the "way to madness" as a society:

Mr. Cohn: Are you a member of the Communist party?
Mr. Seldes: No.
Mr. Cohn: That is very interesting.

Mr. Seldes: Who said I was?

Mr. Cohn: Who said you were? Has it ever been brought to your attention that anybody said you were?[28]

Within the McCarthy star chamber, merely asking the identity of one's accuser could be twisted into a tacit admission of guilt. Cohn continued by pressing Seldes to explain his connections to Minton:

Mr. Seldes: I started a weekly newsletter with another man. His name on the letterhead was Bruce Minton. I swear I had no idea he was a Communist. He was expelled from the Communist party, I think, 1945. Before that I want to say, after I started this newsletter, I said, "We will run news in this which is not in the newspapers." That was my only purpose in running it. I forgot—if I know any Communists? I know Bruce Minton.

Mr. Cohn: One you can name is Bruce Minton?

Mr. Seldes: Yes, I want to say how I happened to know that. I didn't know it until he had left my publication and was thrown out of the party.

Mr. Cohn: Your answer is that you know now that Bruce Minton was a Communist, but you didn't know it at the time he worked for your publication?

Mr. Seldes: No, I didn't know it.[29]

Cohn then quoted from a House Un-American Activities report, citing it as evidence of Seldes's communist sympathies. In the circular logic of McCarthyism, a prior congressional report based on anonymous sources and unverified, hearsay testimony could be presented as if it were damning, primary factual evidence of guilt. Cohn then read several paragraphs from Seldes's published writings:

Mr. Cohn: Do you consider these appropriate works, giving a true picture of the American-way-of-life fighting communism?

Mr. Seldes: I will answer that this way. I represented a certain view of life and think this ought to begin with other views. I am anti-Communist.[30]

The citations in Cohn's examination of Seldes closely match the information in FBI reports compiled between 1941 and 1944. While most scholars agree there is no credible evidence that Seldes was ever a communist, the authors of one modern study of communism in the United States claimed that Seldes lied to Congress when he denied he was a communist and denied that he knew about Minton's communist connections. In *Spies: The Rise and Fall of the KGB in America*, tenuously based on lost notebooks of secondhand transcriptions allegedly made from Stalin-era documents, the authors cited a communication from the KGB in New York that listed Seldes as a *potential* political contact. Based on that single reference, and despite the admission that "there was no further mention of recruiting Seldes," the authors concluded that Seldes was a hidden or near communist.[31]

Was Seldes a communist? Was he a leftist editor the KGB hoped to recruit? Or was he perhaps simply a contrarian leftist, a free press and organized labor advocate whose philosophy sometimes paralleled certain elements of the complex communist, socialist, liberal Left. It seems very unlikely that Seldes, a stridently independent advocate of press freedom and opponent of fascism and the concentration of power, would ever have a formal affiliation with a dogmatic political movement like the Communist Party. Not even Hoover's persistent FBI investigators could turn Seldes's relationship with Minton into a connection between Seldes and the Communist Party. Likewise, McCarthy and Cohn essentially cleared Seldes. Despite the accusatory tone of his interrogation, Cohn wrapped up his questioning quickly. Seldes was dismissed and was not recalled or even mentioned during the remainder of the 1953 McCarthy hearings.

Nevertheless, there was one person who forcefully and repeatedly asserted that there was a direct connection between Seldes and the Communist Party. This individual reiterated his charges to FBI agents multiple times, albeit without providing any factual evidence to back up his claims. "Seldes, though not a communist of his own admission, is regarded as a close follower of Communist doctrines," a New York FBI agent wrote.[32] The primary source substantiating this conclusion was Victor Riesel, an FBI confidential informant, strident pro-labor advocate, and outspoken critic of corruption and communist influence in unions. His anticommunist worldview clearly demonstrated the diverse opinions on the Left that the FBI was incapable of detecting.

In 1941, Riesel was managing editor of the socialist *New Leader*. He left the *New Leader* and joined the staff of the progressive *New York Post* in 1942 and then moved to Hearst's conservative *New York Daily Mirror* in 1948. Riesel became infamous when, at 3:00 a.m. on April 5, 1956, he was viciously assaulted as he left a restaurant in Midtown Manhattan. The assailant attacked Riesel with sulfuric acid, burning his face and eyes and ultimately leaving him sightless.[33] "As I turned to face him the deluge—it was more than a splash, it was a complete sudden burst of liquid—hit my face and for a moment I couldn't understand it," Riesel later testified. "I was surprised and shocked, then came the sharpest, most painful burning I ever felt."[34] After the attack, Riesel continued to write his crusading anticorruption and anticommunist column. Upon hearing of Riesel's blinding, Teamster leader Jimmy Hoffa reportedly complained, "He just had some acid thrown on him. It's too bad he didn't have it thrown on the goddamn hands he types with."[35] Riesel's attacker was later found dead, a bullet in his head. After a four-month investigation, the FBI arrested three apparently mob-connected men who had conspired to silence Riesel's criticism of union corruption.[36]

Despite their common cause in support of organized labor, Riesel was intolerant of Seldes's unwillingness to condemn communism and of his casual and not-so-casual associations with alleged communists like Minton and countless other fellow travelers. In an FBI interview, Riesel warned that *In Fact* was growing rapidly and proclaimed that the publication promoted communist ideals. Riesel told the FBI that despite Seldes's brilliance as a writer, "he has so discredited himself in the legitimate newspaper circles that it is impossible for him to obtain a position with any reliable newspaper."[37] Riesel also charged that the Communist Party provided financial support for *In Fact*.[38] Because of his status as an "objective" journalist and industry insider, Riesel was considered a reliable and credible source by Hoover's investigators. Solely based on Riesel's charges, Hoover wrote to Early and FDR: "It is reported that this publication is strongly backed by the Communist Party, and at various Communist Party meetings, the publication is frequently referred to by party members as being a good paper to read."[39] If "backing" can be defined by subscribers, that statement was true. *In Fact* was sent to all members of several CIO-affiliated labor unions, and among the 176,000 subscribers to *In Fact*, union members no doubt constituted a large majority.

Hoover's judgment that Seldes and his publication were affiliated with the Communist Party (based entirely on the interview with Riesel) was shared with others in government who were subjected to Seldes's outspoken attacks. Hoover responded when Brigadier General Sherman Miles, the chief of military intelligence, requested information on Seldes and *In Fact* after he was the subject of a critical article.[40] Hoover provided the same single-source memorandum to Attorney General Robert H. Jackson on March 27, 1941, after Jackson was targeted in a harsh front-page attack.[41] When members of Congress began receiving copies of *In Fact* from constituents concerned about its tone and content, Hoover passed along the FBI's single-source judgment to congressmen and senators as well.[42] Thus, a publication that became increasingly critical of the FBI over time was transformed into a public relations prop in the Bureau's ongoing campaign to establish its legitimacy.

Hoover himself developed an increasing interest in Seldes as criticism of the Bureau began to appear more frequently in the pages of *In Fact*. During the first half of 1941, Seldes often jabbed at Hoover and the FBI in his news columns. That criticism expanded over time. Seldes published a sharply critical commentary on May 12, attacking Hoover and the FBI for their conduct of several past and present cases, including the agency's approach to loyalty investigations. On June 2, *In Fact* struck at the legitimacy of Hoover's leadership and the FBI's power and jurisdiction. Seldes reminded his readers of Hoover's leadership role in the Palmer Raids and linked those raids to the FBI's FDR-authorized domestic intelligence and loyalty investigations. Seldes called the Bureau a fascist organization that was subverting democracy and chilling dissent. "The FBI is the agency today for nazifying America," Seldes wrote. "There are thousands of documented episodes to prove this." In the lengthy story, Seldes claimed that the FBI had become a "Gestapo," used illegal methods to suppress opposition to the war, compiled an index of 500,000 names, persecuted political minorities, and attempted to suppress freedom of thought. "Hoover's FBI today as in 1918 has two functions: to track down criminals, saboteurs, spies, agents of enemy governments," Seldes wrote. "No one can criticize this function. The other function is anti-labor, anti–civil liberties, illegal and terroristic."[43]

Not surprisingly, given Seldes's dismantling of the notion of a responsible, restrained FBI, a new round of investigations followed. Within a few weeks of the June 2 article, Hoover ordered a "complete, exhaustive report" on Seldes.[44] Agents in New York reviewed the credit records and checked the bank balances of Seldes and his employees. The balance in the publication's bank account, it was reported, stood in the low four figures. And credit records stated, "this magazine and its officers are left wing radicals."[45] A confidential source provided copies of an audit of *In Fact*'s finances, showing a net loss of $10,599 for 1940.[46] Another source provided a circulation figure of 96,000 and growing fast. In his interview with agents, Neil McNeil, managing editor of the *New York Times* and an ardent anticommunist, dismissed

In Fact as "just plain Communist propaganda stuff dressed up to suggest inside news."[47] An editor at *Liberty Magazine* (likely either Fulton Oursler or Frederick L. Collins) reported that *In Fact* was making considerable inroads on the Left.[48] Despite the details dug up by his agents, they had failed to find any overt links to communists, and Hoover pushed for more information.[49]

Though unaware that FBI agents were looking into his background, Seldes wrote a vituperative letter to his "friend" Hoover. Seldes reported that one of his subscribers had corresponded with columnist and broadcaster Walter Winchell, and the letter had somehow found its way to the FBI. Hoover's correspondence team had actually answered it, saying that an *In Fact* article referred to by the letter writer "contains a collection of lies and falsehoods." It was not unusual for Hoover's friends—and though his relationship with Hoover was complicated, Winchell was a friend—to send the director copies of correspondence relating to Bureau enemies. "It is my purpose to publish the facts, to get as near the truth as possible, and I have always kept my columns open to corrections of error," Seldes wrote. "If you will point out one statement or one word in IN FACT which is not true or honestly reported, I will print your correction." Seldes added a dig at Hoover's penchant for public relations: "Since you have time to answer individual letters on this subject you should have the time to keep the record straight and honest."[50]

Hoover immediately ordered his Crime Records Division to comb through the May 12 and June 2 issues of *In Fact* and craft a response. On July 23, Hoover's public relations staff—thorough as always—delivered a wordy and belabored seventy-page memorandum rebutting the 2,000 or so words Seldes had published on the FBI in May and June.[51] That protracted rebuttal was then reduced to a fifteen-page (but still long-winded) letter that was sent to Seldes with Hoover's signature. The letter, which focused entirely on reasserting the restrained FBI image of the Collier-Cooper legitimacy narrative, was likely intended to be distributed to the Bureau's friends to undermine Seldes and *In Fact*. The FBI could not have overstepped its authority, Hoover wrote, brushing off a few lines of venerable Bureau boilerplate, because it was a "fact finding organization which has for its objective the preservation of civil liberties." Other elements of the letter were similarly composed of tried-and-true Collier-Cooper standards. "No citizen has been harassed [or] intimidated by any Special Agent of the Federal Bureau of Investigation," Hoover wrote. Another charge was false, he stated, because, "activities of the FBI have always been open and above board." Seldes's charges regarding the arrests in Detroit in 1940 were untrue because "FBI agents at the time intimidated no one." The remainder of Hoover's letter to Seldes displayed similarly self-referential logic, along with a heavy dose of historical revisionism: "The facts are that fingerprints constitute an infallible means of identification." "The [Palmer] raids were conducted by the Bureau of Investigation, which at that time was under the direction of Mr. William J. Flynn. At the time I was a subordinate official in the Department of Justice assigned as a Special Assistant to the Attorney General." "At no time did FBI agents engage in anti-labor activities." Hoover closed by requesting that his entire letter be published in a future edition of *In Fact*.[52] Seldes refused to print it, in part because, at more than 3,000 words, it was far too long.

Hoover's campaign against Seldes and *In Fact* continued as he forwarded evidence, based on Riesel's claims and the New York financial investigation, to the Department of Justice and requested that Seldes be indicted for a violation of the Foreign Agents Registration Act (FARA). FARA, enacted in 1938, required that any person acting as an agent of foreign interests in a political capacity disclose those links to the government. The implication of Hoover's request was that the FBI believed Seldes was acting as an agent of the Soviet government. Of course, there was no evidence to support that claim, and the Bureau's request included none. Assistant Attorney General Wendell Berge reviewed the FBI's evidence and replied that he had found "nothing that indicates a probable violation of any Federal statute." Berge acknowledged Riesel's claim that *In Fact* was financed by the Communist Party but stated, "unless it can be shown that such funds might be coming from abroad, this probably would furnish no indication of a Federal violation."[53] Even though earlier investigations of *In Fact*'s finances had found no such link, Hoover used Berge's judgment to press for further investigation.

Meanwhile, the FBI's assistant director in charge of the National Defense Office in New York, Percy E. Foxworth, attempted to intervene. Foxworth contacted Hoover on September 12, urging that the investigation be held in abeyance because of the potential public relations problems it could cause. "It is entirely possible that Seldes will become aware of the fact that the Bureau is conducting an investigation of him," Foxworth wrote. "Should he become advised of the investigation, the possibility exists that in view of the temperament and disposition of the man he may publicize in print the fact that the Bureau on the same hand directed a letter to him offering cooperation in furnishing factual information concerning the Bureau's activity and at the same time instituted an investigation of him."[54] In other words, according to Foxworth, the FBI could not claim restraint and responsibility while concurrently conducting an intensive investigation of a well-known journalist based on flimsy hearsay. Apparently, Hoover was unmoved by Foxworth's argument. Assistant director Earl Connelly was ordered to continue to seek evidence that the Communist Party financed *In Fact*. On September 26, Connelly reported that his agents could find no such connection. "It is noted that at the present time, 'IN FACT' appears to have a large subscription list and in all probability is self-supporting," Connelly reported.[55] True to his stubborn, bulldog reputation, Hoover ordered that the investigation continue.

Seldes wrote to Hoover on September 29, thanking him for his response and explaining that it was too lengthy to reprint in *In Fact*. Seldes then asked Hoover if the FBI was gathering subscription lists of *In Fact*, *PM*, *The Nation*, *The New Republic*, or other liberal publications. Seldes speculated that post office clerks had been enlisted to gather names from address labels and submit them to the FBI. Seldes's belief that FBI agents, aided by postal employees, were gathering subscriber lists of leftist publications—a clear violation of civil liberties and of the law—appears to be supported by an October 1 memorandum from Nichols to Tolson in which Nichols reported on his own investigation of the matter. His entire discussion of the subscription list charge has been redacted in the FBI files under exemption 7(D), which protects records that would disclose the identity of a confidential source, such as a postal employee gathering subscription information.[56] Simple logic suggests that had there been no attempt to compile the subscription lists, there would be no Privacy Act exemption for a memorandum exploring whether such an attempt had occurred.

Meanwhile, Hoover continued his public relations offensive against Seldes, mailing copies of his fifteen-page refutation to a lengthy list of agenda-setting journalists and other friends. About forty opinion shapers, including journalists Jack Carley of the *Memphis Commercial Appeal*, Walter Winchell, Frank Waldrop of the *New York Times-Herald*, Collier, and syndicated broadcaster Fulton Lewis, along with approximately seventy other newsmen on the SAC contact list, received Hoover's letter. The friends list included several labor leaders, civil liberties advocates, and influential members of the clergy.[57] Hoover also forwarded copies of the letter to all his field offices, where the SACs presumably distributed them to local opinion leaders in their communities. Essentially, Hoover hoped to undermine Seldes among those in the mainstream media, journalists with the real power to set an agenda and rise to the director's defense. This tactic of circulating criticisms to friends to prompt them to jump to his aid was repeated over and over during the Hoover era. Critical challenges to the Collier-Cooper narrative were thus converted into opportunities to reinforce that narrative.

The oft-repeated strategy of drawing lines between "objective" friends and "bad" enemy journalists was extremely effective. Upon receiving Hoover's fifteen-page rebuttal of Seldes, a surprising individual responded with a defense of Hoover and the FBI. American Civil Liberties Union general counsel Morris Ernst had long been courted by Hoover's correspondence team and had come to believe that Hoover was a friend of civil libertarians. A cofounder of the ACLU's precursor organization, Ernst served as general counsel for the ACLU from 1929 to 1955. He served on the ACLU board of directors and became well known for his 1933 federal court victory that reversed the ban on James Joyce's *Ulysses*.[58] Ernst also argued successfully before the U.S. Supreme Court in 1937, when it upheld the federal Wagner Act codifying certain collective-bargaining rights.[59]

Ernst and Hoover exchanged hundreds of letters during their twenty-five-year relationship. Ernst addressed Hoover as "My Dear Edgar" and frequently provided the director with copies of his own correspondence with third parties on the Left. In addition, the two spoke on the phone hundreds of times and visited in person on many occasions. Hoover knew Ernst could be a valuable ally, a liberal defender providing cover on his left flank. The implication was that if the ACLU approved of the FBI's performance on issues of civil liberty, how could any reasonable (i.e., noncommunist) person see things otherwise? Over time, Hoover's charm worked, and Ernst became a believer in the FBI's preferred image. He became an outspoken defender of the Bureau, almost fanatical in his willingness to put his own credibility and that of the ACLU on the line for the FBI. It would be hard to imagine a more useful prop in an ongoing campaign to assert the FBI's devotion to civil liberties than the high-profile cofounder of and counsel for the ACLU.

In 1950, for example, the FBI successfully lobbied Hoover's pen pal, *Reader's Digest* editor Fulton Oursler, to publish Ernst's defense of the Bureau titled "Why I No Longer Fear the FBI." The article, which was cleared by the Bureau before its publication, was a response to Max Lowenthal's *The Federal Bureau of Investigation*, in which the author promoted an alternative vision of the FBI as, essentially, an American secret police force. In *Reader's Digest*, the most widely read periodical in the country, Ernst decried the "smear" campaigns against Hoover and the FBI. "The F.B.I. is unique in the history of national constabulary," Ernst wrote. "It has a magnificent record of respect for individual freedom. It invites documented complaints against its agents. It has done everything to prevent itself from violating the democratic process."[60] In his zeal to support Hoover's anticommunism, Ernst unwittingly provided cover for the Bureau's assault on civil liberties. For two decades, Hoover held up Ernst's 1950 article as credible, objective evidence of the FBI's civil liberties restraint.

In 1941, Ernst acted quickly to defend Hoover against the charges published by Seldes. Upon receiving a copy of Hoover's letter to *In Fact*, Ernst wrote to Bruce Bliven of *The New Republic* and urged him to publish a defense of Hoover. Ernst shared Hoover's rebuttal of Seldes with Bliven and helpfully forwarded copies of his correspondence with Bliven to Hoover. "Thank God he [Hoover] is not sophisticated, like more of our liberal friends," Ernst told Bliven. "He is no expert on the philosophy of factional isms, but I have yet to see a proven instance of the least violation of civil liberties."[61] *The New Republic*, a vocal and consistent critic of the FBI, did not rise to Hoover's defense.

On October 22, the New York bureau reported on its ongoing financial investigation in an effort to prove a FARA violation. In Hoover's view, unions were simply communist front organizations, and union members subscribed to *In Fact* in large numbers. However, a second, more thorough check of pertinent bank accounts, including those of individuals and companies that received money from *In Fact*, showed no sign of any communist or overseas contributions to the publication.[62] Based on leads developed in New York, agents in San Antonio and Los Angeles pressed the investigation in their localities but came up with no pertinent information. In early 1942, New York FBI agents undertook a third review of relevant bank accounts. All of Seldes's deposits and withdrawals in excess of $200 were examined in detail, going back to 1940. "The account reflected no deposits of any sizable amount from a foreign source or from known officials of a Communist Party," the investigating agent reported.[63] Withdrawals from the personal accounts of alleged Communist Party officials were compared to deposits in the *In Fact* accounts, with no similarities found.[64]

Nevertheless, in June 1942, a Custodial Detention Index card was created for Seldes, based on his alleged communist connections and because the "subject reached a large audience." Seldes was categorized in group A, meaning that if circumstances required the government to round up dangerous individuals, the editor of *In Fact* would be one of the first arrested and detained.[65] The Bureau's Custodial Detention Index (CDI) program, created by Hoover in 1939, was an effort to identify enemies of the state so that dangerous individuals could be rounded up and imprisoned in the event of a national emergency. FBI historian Athan Theoharis noted that Hoover initially created the CDI program to identify persons with German, Italian, or Communist sympathies—both citizens and aliens. Those deemed potential risks to the U.S. government were listed and ranked, based on the danger they posed. "The controlling criteria for these listings was not conduct, but *anticipated* conduct," according to Theoharis. "The listed individuals could not be detained, of course, since Hoover's unilateral action lacked statutory authority."[66] This index system was eerily similar to that employed by Hoover to round up anarchists in the controversial Palmer Raids.

Under the CDI program, foreigners on the list would be arrested immediately in the event of war; American citizens who were arrested would be subject to the adjudication not of a court of law but of a Justice Department committee. Ultimately, Attorney General Francis Biddle ordered the discontinuation of the CDI program in 1943. In a memo to Hoover, Biddle cited the lack of statutory authority for the creation of a detention list and noted that such a classification system was inherently unreliable: "The evidence used for the purpose of making the classifications was inadequate; the standards applied to the evidence for the purpose of making the classifications were defective; and finally, the notion that it is possible to make a valid determination as to how dangerous a person is in the abstract without reference to time, environment, and other circumstances is impractical, unwise, and dangerous."[67]

According to Theoharis, Hoover's response to Biddle's order "confirms how FBI secrecy and President Roosevelt's interest in having the FBI conduct noncriminal investigations undermined the attorney general's ability to oversee the Justice Department's investigative division." Hoover complied with the attorney general's order simply by renaming the Custodial Detention Index the Security Index, an internal list of subversives that could be shared if circumstances warranted.[68] Seldes's Security Index card was updated in June 1942, maintaining the editor's group A ranking and adding, "He has signed a number of Communist statements and if not a Party member is so close that a distinction is impossible in practical consideration."[69] That sort of soft and pliable definition of some watered-down but still dangerously subversive near communism could be easily expanded as needed. Analysts' crude judgments about individuals were recorded in the index as if they were based on documentary evidence. The production and maintenance of a catalog of subversion in preparation for some unnamed national crisis was precisely the kind of unchecked power critics like Seldes objected to.

The FBI continued to share its thinly sourced conclusions about Seldes with like-thinking people inside and outside of government. In August 1942, for example, Theodore Joslin, director of public relations for the DuPont company in Delaware, called on the FBI to inquire about Seldes. *In Fact* had published an article alleging that the DuPonts were fascists and were involved in smuggling arms to Hitler. Agent R. C. Hendon pointed out that Seldes had attacked the FBI and "advised [Joslin] confidentially, that information concerning Seldes' activities had been furnished to the Department for a decision as to prosecution."[70] The last statement was a white lie, of course; the Justice Department had ruled nearly a year earlier that there was no evidence that *In Fact* or Seldes had violated any laws.

When Seldes attacked the chemical giant again in his next issue, DuPont executive and former FBI special agent T. N. Stapleton contacted the Bureau and asked for any investigative information that might be useful in a lawsuit against Seldes. "After reviewing the file," the agent (whose name was redacted) wrote, "I suggested that he contact the Credit Bureau of Greater New York, the Congressional Record and the Library of Congress." Stapleton indicated that the DuPonts probably would not sue, because doing so would just give *In Fact* more notoriety.[71]

Hoover's fixation on finding Seldes's alleged connections to the Communist Party continued unabated through 1942, and the Bureau's investigations gradually expanded in scope and intrusiveness. In 1942, the Office of Censorship was asked to initiate a review of any mail addressed to or from *In Fact* or George Seldes.[72] Memphis agents tried to obtain an addressograph machine and a name-plate file formerly used by a bankrupt leftist magazine whose subscription list had been absorbed by *In Fact*.[73] Had they been successful, they would have had a new set of alleged subversives to investigate, identified by their subscriptions to *In Fact*.

When New York agents learned that Seldes's former partner, Minton, had reported the loss of a check payable to him in an amount exceeding $6,000, they labored to find the source of those funds, assuming it would link the Communist Party to *In Fact*.[74] Minton's partnership with Seldes had been dissolved nearly two years earlier, yet at some level of the FBI, the lead was deemed worthy of pursuing. After further investigation, it was determined that the money had come from a "reputable publishing company" as stipend for work completed by Minton.[75] "A review of the New York file at the present time reflects that all the leads outstanding have been covered," Foxworth reported, once again suggesting that the investigation be closed. "The results of this investigation do not indicate that this paper is operating as an agent of a foreign principal or that the paper's income is derived from any foreign source."[76] Hoover disagreed and asserted that three reviews of Seldes's personal finances were not enough. "The reports which have been submitted in this matter do not indicate that an exhaustive investigation has as yet been conducted covering the activities of Seldes," Hoover wrote. "It is further desired that an effort be made to effect appropriate arrangements whereby it will be possible to make an examination of the personal records of Seldes."[77]

The subsequent investigative summaries and reports suggest that Hoover's determination to find financial links between Seldes and the Communist Party led agents to revisit confidential sources. The result was another litany of unproved, hearsay claims, raising the question of whether informants were simply telling the agents what they wanted to hear. One confidential informant told the FBI: "Seldes is a well known literary prostitute who will print anything in his paper for a price and could be bought by anyone for $200." The same informant (probably Riesel) claimed, without evidence, that Seldes must have received financial support from communists. "However, he [the source] had no information of definite character which would show what his [Seldes's] source of income might be."[78]

The fourth review of Seldes's finances uncovered large expenditures that turned out to be for postage. *In Fact* was mailed to its more than 175,000 subscribers. Several large deposits were found to be aggregates of hundreds of small subscription payments. The investigating agent again recommended that the case be closed, but Hoover again pressed for further investigation.[79] The censorship of Seldes's mail continued, but postal censorship reports contained only routine acknowledgments of subscriptions, remissions of payment for subscriptions, and summaries of *In Fact* articles.[80]

Another investigative report highlighted the criticism of Seldes by another journalist, Eugene Lyons. Lyons's book *Red Decade*, about the Communist Party's impact on American media and culture, was published in 1941. A native of Russia, Lyons had immigrated to the United States with his family as a child. Though initially sympathetic to communism, he later became an outspoken anticommunist. Lyons worked for the Soviet press agency TASS until he was hired by United Press International and shipped to Moscow to cover the Soviet government. By 1941, Lyons was the New York editor for *American Mercury*, where he attacked liberals he considered insufficiently anti-Soviet, including Eleanor Roosevelt.[81] Seldes, whose time in the Soviet Union coincided with Lyons's, was targeted in a chapter of *Red Decade* titled "The Typewriter Front." Seldes had been expelled from Russia and spoke out against Stalin in the 1920s, but, Lyons wrote, "around 1937, George popped up far inside the communist orbit, a regular contributor to Stalin's American press, gunning for the hides of colleagues who were quoting his own stuff on Russia? . . . George, poor boy, had caught communism as one catches the flu in an epidemic."[82] Once again, hearsay became evidence in Seldes's FBI file, providing a rationale to keep on investigating.

In 1944, the New York office produced an updated seventeen-page summary report on Seldes. The Bureau's conclusions were again based on hearsay, other journalists' opinions, and the editor's own critical writings about the FBI and other government agencies. From that evidence, the New York SAC concluded that Seldes "consistently follows the Party line."[83] Specific evidence cited included Seldes's affiliation with multiple liberal, peace, and justice organizations; mentions of his name in the *Daily Worker*; Riesel's allegations; published criticism by other anticommunist journalists and authors; and the FBI's interpretation of the contents of *In Fact*. The Bureau's repeated and invasive reviews of Seldes's personal papers and financial records had failed to tie him to the Communist Party.

Yet the FBI continued to monitor Seldes and *In Fact*. In 1950, Seldes announced to his readers that *In Fact* was taking a hiatus, perhaps settling once and for all the question of secret Communist Party funding: "It is apparently impossible at this time to publish a newspaper, magazine, or even a newsletter, without financial help from outside—either advertising or a political party, or a liberal association, a labor union or a multi-millionaire sponsor," Seldes wrote in a front-page editorial on October 2, 1950. "Therefore In Fact is forced to announce it is suspending publication, temporarily."[84] Seldes further noted that both he and the publication had been labeled communist and that *In Fact* had "made enemies."[85] The chilling effect of the communist label had reduced subscriptions from a high of 176,000 to only 55,000. Americans on the Left had gotten the message that subscribing to a "communist" publication could expose them to charges of having communist sympathies. Other subscribers may have simply tired of the publication's shrill tone.

The FBI was built in the image of its director and had a strictly patriarchal management structure. Hoover's personal view thus became the point of view of his agents in the field. The director's hysterical anticommunism created a mind-set inside the Bureau whereby three or four investigations that failed to find a direct link between Seldes and communists meant nothing; in fact, the failure to find evidence was not considered exculpatory. Instead, the statements of confidential informants became "facts" that justified ongoing investigations and Seldes's inclusion in the FBI's Security Index. Foxworth tried to point out the danger of the FBI's investigation of Seldes, but still Hoover would not relent. Finally, when Seldes confronted Hoover with his suspicions about the surveillance of his wife, the FBI concocted a misleading response to protect its image.

The intrusive nature of the investigations of Seldes demonstrate an obvious lack of subtlety in the FBI's analysis of alleged communists and fellow travelers. The Bureau's conclusions about Seldes in the 1940s and the ability to conflate criticism and liberal politics into communist leanings presage the FBI's complicity in Senator Joseph McCarthy's anticommunist crusade of the early 1950s. In the eyes of FBI analysts, Seldes's antifascism, combined with his failure to advocate openly for the Communist Party, either constituted an elaborate ruse or suggested, given his obvious (to the Bureau) conversion to communism, a weakness of character. And of course, Hoover viewed weakness of character as a communist trait.

Hoover applied the same circular logic in his zealous investigations of other leftist opinion shapers who became FBI critics in the aftermath of the Detroit raids. Although *In Fact* had the largest circulation of any leftist publication of its time, *The Nation*, *The New Republic*, *PM*, and *I. F. Stone's Weekly* similarly focused on calling public attention to the Bureau's actions and its excesses. As a result, those publications were subjected to the same kind of political surveillance and intrusive investigations that characterized the Bureau's interest in George Seldes.

Chapter 5

Investigating Critics on the Left

On December 9, 1943, special agents from the FBI's Security Division delivered a 554-page study that Hoover had requested three months earlier, after a series of critical stories appeared in two liberal opinion journals. The study, titled "'The Nation,' 'The New Republic,' the Communist Party," reviewed the extensive FBI files on the two publications. It included sections on history, policies, and criticism of the FBI, along with personal biographies of key staff members of each publication since 1935. Although the title of the monograph, reflecting Bureau dogma, suggested that the two publications were synonymous with the Communist Party, the study found no direct connections. It acknowledged that "both journals have utilized the services of former Communists. . . . Admittedly both magazines have employed *near-communists* [emphasis added] concerning whom no specific proof of membership is available, but whose intellectual independence would seem to rule out the presumption of Party membership."[1]

The unidentified authors of the report, no doubt aware of the need to feed Hoover's expectations, noted that "neither journal is able to make a harmonious adjustment in a capitalist America" and that "both are interested in the establishment of socialism."[2] The authors asserted that the two publications were strong defenders of civil liberties "for the communists as well as for themselves, on the theory that once those fundamental rights have been abridged for Communists it is but a step to deprive other less obnoxious elements of the same rights."[3]

While the authors found no direct connection to the Communist Party, they uncovered extensive evidence that the two publications had sought to "smear" the FBI over the years. Within the paranoid culture of Hoover's FBI, ever vigilant for challenges to its power and legitimacy, any criticism of the Bureau and its leadership was seen as clear proof of communist conspiracy:

Both magazines have excelled in their disparaging remarks concerning the Director and the Bureau. It would seem particularly in the case of "The Nation" that hatred of the Bureau and the Director have been a phobia and a complex for some years. . . . It is noticeable that even the Bureau's accomplishments in cases which excite the fancy of the entire country are avoided. Even the news value of such cases is overlooked in an obvious effort to refrain from making favorable mention of the Federal Bureau of Investigation. . . . [*The New Republic*] too has often dipped its pen deep in venom and has, with apparent ill-will, attempted to stimulate popular distrust and contempt for the Bureau.[4]

The meticulously detailed, 554-page report had been ordered by Hoover after media critics in those publications and elsewhere began to raise questions about the FBI's investigations into Hatch Act violations and into federal employees accused of disloyalty by the House Committee on Un-American Activities. Criticism in *The Nation, The New Republic,* and *PM,* a new daily newspaper in New York, struck at the heart of the Bureau's responsibility narrative and raised the issue of its similarity to a secret police force or gestapo. Such comparisons could undermine the FBI's continued cultural, jurisdictional, and institutional growth, not to mention its ever-growing congressional appropriations. The Bureau's renewed and vastly expanded interest in internal spying during the 1940s and 1950s, following on the heels of the Detroit and wiretapping controversies, posed a significant challenge for Hoover's growing public relations team. The question for Americans on the Left was obvious: should a restrained and responsible government agency, interested only in violations of federal crimes, be investigating citizens' political ideology? The potential for a ripple effect of criticism after the close calls of 1940 led Hoover to urge his agents to refocus their attention on critical journalists and publications.

On April 30, 1941, for example, *The New Republic* published an editorial titled "What the FBI Is Doing," which compared the Bureau unfavorably to the secret police organizations of totalitarian regimes abroad. "When we challenge activities of the FBI, we do not in the least wish to interfere with its legitimate and proper functions," editor Bruce Bliven wrote. "We are only concerned that it not permit a repetition of that shameful spectacle of twenty years ago."[5] *The New Republic* had been founded in 1914 by Herbert

Croly, and he was its editor until his death in 1930; Bliven, a former journalism educator turned reporter, succeeded him.

Bliven was not the first writer in *The New Republic* to object to the expansion of FBI authority beyond criminal investigations and into intelligence gathering. On March 11, 1940, John T. Flynn raised questions about the FBI's interest in policing individuals' opinions. "It has introduced into its functions the investigation of what it calls subversive activities," Flynn wrote. "Now what are subversive activities? Communism is subversive, let us say. But what is communism? Who is a Communist? Who is to define a man's political views and activities and determine whether they are subversive or not?"[6]

At issue for Bliven, Flynn, and others was the creation and maintenance of security indices by the Bureau's General Intelligence Division (GID)—the reborn spy organization that, under Hoover's direction, had been responsible for the "shameful spectacle" of the Palmer Raids. *The New Republic*'s criticism was an unwelcome reminder (from the point of view of the FBI) that the GID had compiled an index of 450,000 individuals alleged to be security risks because of their anarchist or communist politics. That index had provided the source material for the Palmer Raids, during which thousands of alleged anarchists and communists had been arrested and then released without charges. Hoover had hidden the extent of his involvement in the raids back then, but Bliven's invocation of the Bureau's darkest days and Flynn's questions about the subjectivity of identifying subversives had the potential to tarnish Hoover's reputation and his agency's. Bliven wrote:

> We are not being alarmist about this. During the Great War and for several years after it ended, the Department of Justice, and the FBI in particular, was a disgrace to the United States government and to every decent American citizen. It made itself the tool of black reaction, it was strongly anti-labor, its agents broke the law repeatedly and outrageously. ... Every honest American citizen must be concerned that we should not repeat that shameful spectacle of twenty years ago.[7]

The re-formation of a domestic spying division came several years after President Franklin D. Roosevelt ordered the FBI to begin investigating domestic communism and fascism on a limited basis. For decades, Hoover referred to FDR's initial and limited verbal order in 1936 and to his 1939 written statement formalizing the Bureau's domestic intelligence role as the sources of his power to conduct intrusive intelligence investigations. In

1936, Roosevelt met with Hoover and Secretary of State Cordell Hull and authorized the FBI to undertake limited investigations of communist and fascist activities in the United States.[8] Hoover responded, according to historian Athan Theoharis, as if FDR had given him a blanket authorization for domestic intelligence: "For, having since 1924 disregarded former attorney general Stone's ban against political surveillance, Hoover now welcomed Roosevelt's initiative as providing formal presidential authorization for the broad-scale antisubversive investigations already being conducted by the FBI."[9] Similarly, Hoover interpreted FDR's 1939 directive authorizing investigations of espionage, counterespionage, and sabotage as formal written authorization for domestic political surveillance.[10] Whereas FDR had authorized the FBI to investigate potential violations of federal espionage, sabotage, and neutrality statutes, Hoover, as he often did, chose to construe the order as he saw fit. He perceived the order not as an expansion of the Bureau's jurisdiction under federal law but as a mandate to spy on Americans whose political leanings were outside the narrow mainstream—as defined not by law but by Hoover himself.

In the meantime, the escalation of the war caused the Bureau to redouble its efforts and expand its definition of subversion. Expanded responsibilities meant that, organizationally, the FBI needed to grow dramatically, and for that, it needed money and congressional approval. Hoover had announced the re-formation of the GID during testimony before the House Appropriations Committee in 1939. Apparently miscalculating the impact of his statement, he told Congress that the GID had already compiled "extensive indices" of individuals and groups engaged in subversive activities "or any activities that are possibly detrimental to the internal security of the United States."[11] In testimony a year later, Hoover expanded his description of the GID's activities: "We have a general index, arranged alphabetically and geographically, available at the Bureau, so that in the event of any greater emergency coming to our country we will be able immediately to locate those various persons who may need to be the subject of further investigation by the federal authorities."[12]

The broad power suggested by Hoover's unequivocal statement that the FBI would investigate any activities that might be detrimental to the internal security of the country alarmed critics on the Left. Hoover's re-formation of the hated GID followed passage of the 1939 Hatch Act, which banned federal employees' membership in "subversive" political organizations. In 1940, the act was expanded to include all state and local employees whose salaries included any federal dollars. The Hatch Act's presumption that dissidence could be interpreted as disloyalty alarmed civil libertarians, who rightly feared that the GID would become the political police, enforcing orthodoxy as defined by Hoover himself. The revelation that the GID had already created a security index showed that the FBI had secretly formalized its monitoring of dissent.

Bliven and his colleagues noted that many of those included in the security index had not violated any laws, and they wondered how the Bureau identified individuals worthy of investigation—the suggestion being that inclusion in the index implied some sort of accusation and a presumption of guilt. "Is it not evident that the duty of the FBI is to investigate crime, not vague actions loosely called 'subversive' or 'detrimental'—non-statutory words which can mean anything?"[13] The FBI would soon begin a $100,000 investigation of federal employees' loyalty, prompted by the work of the House Committee on Un-American Activities, chaired by Representative Martin Dies of Texas. "Under this proposal the FBI would get virtually the powers of a political police in a dictatorship," Bliven wrote.[14] The targets of those investigations, according to one historian, read "like a Who's Who of Popular Front Washington."[15]

By invoking the excesses of the Palmer Raids, Bliven challenged the basic tenets of Hoover's 1930s narrative, which claimed the Bureau had obliterated all connections to its corrupt history. Thanks to that blizzard of publicity in the 1930s, the irresponsible, corrupt Bureau of 1920 had been replaced in the public mind by the responsible, dispassionate, scientific FBI of the Collier-Cooper narrative. Bliven's editorial forced Hoover into crisis mode to protect the public image that his Crime Records staff had so carefully nurtured for almost a decade.

Within a few days of the publication of Bliven's editorial, Hoover sent a memorandum to his boss, Attorney General Francis Biddle. Hoover's defense is a prime example of the Bureau's penchant for revising inconvenient history. The rehash of the Palmer Raids, Hoover told Biddle, failed to recognize that the FBI was, back then, an entirely different agency. Hoover juxtaposed the "old" and "new" FBI by noting an administrative change, which, of course, was Hoover himself—even though he had been personally responsible for directing the Palmer Raids. Perhaps after nearly twenty years spent obscuring his role and rewriting the history of that ignominious event, Hoover had actually come to believe his own mythology. As he often did, Hoover played the misunderstood martyr, telling Biddle that he would not apologize for making a record of America's enemies. Hoover further claimed that the renewed internal security investigations were predicated not on political opinions but on actions, a fact belied by the content of Bliven's own FBI file, which called the editor a "liberal left-winger" who frequently launched vitriolic attacks on the FBI—*political opinions*—in print.[16] Clearly, Hoover's fraudulent and self-serving disconnection between opinions and actions does not reflect a reality where people, even leaders of law enforcement agencies, not only speak about their beliefs but also tend to act on them. The FBI, a patrimonial organization that purged dissenters, always acted on Hoover's beliefs and became a perfect reflection of the director's worldview.

The media were hardly bystanders, innocent or not, in the controversy over the loyalty investigations. Indeed, journalists and media organizations were subjected to the same loyalty tests being applied to federal employees. By the early 1940s, Hoover and his public relations team had mapped the landscape of the American media, drawing a clear border between two factions: friends and enemies of the FBI. Lists of these two groups were maintained, for the most part, in Hoover's head, and Louis Nichols's efforts to rehabilitate some publications or reporters frequently fell on deaf ears. The lists were also subject to Hoover's volatile whims and moods. He might place an organization or a journalist on his "do not contact" list one day, only to entertain inquiries from that same source the next day.

The Bureau soon formalized both lists. The FBI's closest and most useful friends in the media were designated special service contacts (SSCs), reinstating a program started just a few years earlier to identify individuals who had expressed a desire to "help" the FBI. Hoover told his SACs that these contacts were important "not only because of the assistance they may be able to offer but also so that their friendship for the Bureau may be developed."[17] Later, SSCs were added to the more informal special correspondents list, which contained the names of 350 people from across the nation, including 75 friendly newsmen in 1954.[18]

The Bureau's enemies in the media and elsewhere were relegated to the purgatory of a "do not contact" list. As enemies in the media made themselves known by their critical stories, Hoover, often in a fit of pique over a perceived slight, ordered them added to the list, making them persona non grata. Sometimes entire publications were blacklisted, as when Hoover rashly ordered the entire staff of the *Des Moines Register* and the *Des Moines Tribune*—with the exception of one of his favorite editorial cartoonists—

added to the list in 1940.[19] A few weeks later, they regained Hoover's favor and were removed from the no-contact list.

The same diligence the FBI applied to its investigative record keeping was applied to monitoring its friends and enemies in the press. Hoover might waver in his day-to-day designation of friends and enemies, but ultimately, the black-letter record of cooperation or criticism described in the Bureau's files determined the ongoing tenor of relationships with journalists. The Bureau's records of its dealings with reporters and media organizations were both comprehensive (like all FBI files) and meticulously indexed. At any given time, Hoover could request a historical review of the FBI's contacts with any given journalist or news organization and expect a comprehensive report within a few days.

Thus, the Bureau's relationships with journalists and news organizations often resembled a clique of teenagers falling in and out of favor with the popular crowd. With regard to some publications, though, the FBI made quick judgments and did not review those decisions. Three of the publications Hoover most despised in the early 1940s were the liberal icons *The New Republic, The Nation,* and the short-lived *PM.* Hoover rarely wavered in his hatred of those publications and their staffs, and the FBI's files on them grew into a mountain of information.

Former *Time* magazine editor Ralph Ingersoll's *PM* was among the most ardent critics of the FBI's loyalty investigations. *PM* stood for "Picture Magazine," indicating its founder's intent to publish a different kind of daily newspaper in New York. With *PM,* Ingersoll took a newsmagazine approach. *PM* accepted no advertising and would live or die on daily sales, a policy reflecting Ingersoll's belief that catering to advertisers would hamper his progressive approach to the news. To get the newspaper on street corners, Ingersoll turned to eccentric Chicago department store magnate Marshall Field III, whose more than $1 million investment funded a majority of *PM*'s startup costs and early operational expenses.

Many journalists found the idea of a new kind of newspaper appealing, and according to Ingersoll, 11,000 people applied for the 150 staff positions at *PM.* The makeup of its staff quickly became controversial, as critics complained that Ingersoll had assembled an overtly pro-communist staff. Based on information supplied by a frequent and "reliable" confidential informant, Victor Riesel, the FBI believed there were 30 communists on the original *PM* staff, if one included the 13 "communist sympathizers." When a blind memorandum of unknown origin began circulating among New York newsrooms, naming the alleged communists on *PM*'s staff, Ingersoll attempted to defuse the controversy: he published the list and photographs of the alleged communists on the editorial page under the headline "Volunteer Gestapo." In the accompanying editorial, Ingersoll mocked the FBI: "Despite the fact that the government agencies are very busy—and we hate to bother them— we are sending a copy of this slanderous document to the FBI, asking that as soon as they have hunted down all the Fifth Columnists and have some time, they come and investigate us. Or, if they wish, they could do it right away."[20]

Hoover chose the latter. Always prepared to believe in the existence of a communist conspiracy, he found the alleged communist influence at *PM* "very interesting" and urged the FBI to "bear down on it."[21] The implication was that FBI agents should investigate the staff, cultivate informants who could provide inside information, monitor the contents of the publication, and report their findings. It was ironic that the blind memorandum "outing" the communists at *PM* should circulate among New York newspapers, most of which had their own open and active communist cells. In the case of the *New York Times* and William Randolph Hearst's *New York Daily Mirror*, the cells were large enough that they had their own shop newspapers. At the *New York Times*, communist employees published *Better Times*, and at the staunchly anticommunist *Mirror*, communist employees published the *Hearst Worker*. According to *PM*'s Newspaper Guild vice president Amos Landman, there was no communist cell and no in-house communist newspaper at *PM*.[22]

Strident anticommunist labor columnist Victor Riesel was an outspoken critic of *PM* from the beginning. In a *New Leader* article headlined "Million-Dollar Daily Follows CP Line," Riesel detailed the existence of alleged communists among *PM*'s staff and investors. He asserted that anyone hoping *PM* would be a liberal voice for those "who had been pushed around" would likely be disillusioned by the paper's pro-communist bias.[23] As noted earlier, Riesel shared his judgments with the FBI. One FBI memo noted that *PM* "has been marked by a newspaper man [the redacted name is almost certainly Riesel] who is an avid reader of Communist publications to point out the 'Communist line' in its contents." Furthermore, according to FBI assistant director Edward A. Tamm, other newspapermen found significant similarities between the literary styles of *PM* and the *Daily Worker*.[24] Hoover found that pseudoacademic analysis "very significant."[25] The same amateur content analysis was repeated by Eugene Lyons in "The Strange Case of PM," which appeared in *American Mercury* in August 1940. After spending time in

Moscow and returning to the United States in 1934, Lyons had become increasingly critical of liberals who were, in his eyes, insufficiently anti-Soviet, so he possessed a certain credibility as a former communist who had recanted his red past and been cleared by the media and the FBI. The repetition of the literary similarity meme suggests that the FBI and Riesel were actively peddling their conspiracy theory.

Clearly, *PM* had been identified as an unfriendly publication, and its contents and staff were scrutinized and judged as enemies of the FBI (and, by implication, enemies of the United States). Being placed on the Bureau's no-contact list had real and serious consequences. For example, Custodial Detention cards (identifying individuals who should be monitored or jailed in the event of a national emergency) were updated for the thirty *PM* staffers accused of having communist sympathies.[26]

The FBI's careful monitoring of the media landscape included assessing potential threats even before they appeared. Shortly before *PM*'s inaugural issue in 1940, Crime Records chief Nichols reported to Clyde Tolson that one of Hoover's least favorite liberal reporters, Kenneth G. Crawford, would be on Ingersoll's staff. According to Nichols, Crawford's hiring by *PM* "does not look very good from the Bureau's standpoint in so far as this new paper is concerned."[27] Crawford had worked for United Press, the *Buffalo Times*, and the *New York Post*, and he had written a critical two-part profile of Hoover for *The Nation* in 1937. In addition, he had served as the second president of the Newspaper Guild in 1939, replacing Heywood Broun upon his death. Although Crawford had aligned himself with the anticommunists in the guild, the combination of union membership and criticism of Hoover and the FBI convinced the Bureau that Crawford was a communist sympathizer. In part one of his profile, Crawford had focused on Hoover himself, reminding readers of the Palmer Raids and portraying the director as a calculating politician.[28] Part two a week later began with a criticism of the director's "headline-stalking" and the Bureau's tendency to shoot rather than arrest criminals. "Hoover's flair for the dramatic shows itself in his shoot-to-kill orders," Crawford wrote. "He has no sympathy for the 'maudlin sentimentality' of those who would reform criminals or alter the conditions that produce them. . . . The science of criminology, so far as Hoover is concerned, begins and ends in his F.B.I. laboratory, where blood stains and locks of hair can be analyzed."[29] Indeed, the addition of Crawford to the staff of *PM* did not look good for the FBI. Within a few weeks of Nichols's initial judgment, the FBI initiated an investigation of *PM* that included searching Bureau files for all staff members and "discreet" sleuthing to determine the identities of the paper's financial backers.[30]

A reporter with whom Hoover had a friendly relationship, Ike McAnally, also joined the *PM* staff, prompting the director to lament, "PM is a bad outfit. I am sorry to see Ike mixed up with it."[31] McAnally soon became a key go-between for Ingersoll in his efforts to meet and establish a relationship with Hoover. Ingersoll, no doubt motivated by rumors of communist influence at his publication, sought anticommunist legitimacy by courting Hoover, the world's premier red hunter. In August 1940, McAnally had lunch with Nichols, who reported, "Ike said that if the Director met Ingersoll he would guarantee a friendship what would be lasting and one of value and that it would be a personal favor to him if the Director would drop Ingersoll a note stating he would like to meet him."[32] Five days later, McAnally tried again. "Mr. Ingersoll wants to sit down with Mr. Hoover, give him the facts and then take orders," Nichols reported.[33] A month later, Ingersoll contacted the Bureau himself. Agent R. C. Hendon reported that Ingersoll "wanted to contact Mr. Hoover at the earliest possible moment to talk to him about something which is 'going on' and stated that he could talk only to Mr. Hoover about it."[34] When nothing came of that request, McAnally wrote directly to Hoover. "I feel now that I can repeat the invitation to you to meet Ralph Ingersoll, the publisher of PM, on your next trip to New York." McAnally assured Hoover that "it would be purely a social meeting occasioned by his persistent desire to know you. I personally feel that such a meeting would bode well for both of you as you should become friends."[35] There is no evidence in the FBI files that the two men ever met.

The fact that Ingersoll was so determined to meet with Hoover demonstrates the value of a "friendship" with the director, whether to acquire access to FBI stories or obtain political shelter. At the same time, the normally solicitous Hoover (through his correspondence staff) rarely ignored the entreaties of influential editors seeking a meeting. If Hoover was unavailable, Nichols or another high-ranking official was offered as a proxy. But Nichols's initial view that *PM* looked "bad" had quickly ossified into a final judgment. The total absence of a response to Ingersoll's requests from Hoover's normally prolific public relations team can be viewed as a clear indicator that *PM* had been placed squarely and forever in the "enemies of the Bureau" column. Nichols speculated, no doubt rightly, that Ingersoll "has gotten out on a limb by hiring so many Communists and probably is trying to set himself straight."[36]

Interactions with publications that had achieved enemy status sometimes took on the tone of a bizarre, one-sided family feud as reporters, unaware of their censure, continued to try to work with FBI public relations officials. A simple request for information from a *PM* reporter was typically treated like a personal insult, as FBI officials parroted Hoover's pique. When a *PM* reporter requested statistics on car thefts, for example—information the FBI routinely released as part of its uniform crime reports—he was first ignored and then rudely rebuffed.[37] After the publication of a *PM* column only obliquely critical of the FBI, Hoover declared that the writer, Henry Paynter, was "a psychopathic liar."[38] Prompted by another critical article in *PM*, New York SAC Percy Foxworth suggested that the Bureau prepare a memorandum outlining its difficulties with the New York press. Such a memorandum would clarify for agents in the field which reporters and publications should and should not be given the benefit of Bureau cooperation.[39] Hoover liked the idea. "Yes, expedite," he wrote in the margin of the proposal, and a list of friends and enemies among the New York media was produced and distributed to SACs around the country. Meanwhile, the "enemy" reporters continued their work, unaware that they were considered heretics in the eyes of hundreds of FBI agents and officials.

In 1941, the House Committee on Un-American Activities (referred to from 1938 to 1945 as the Dies Committee after its chairman, Democrat Martin Dies of Texas) delivered to the Department of Justice a list of 1,121 alleged subversives working for the federal government. Congress quickly appropriated $100,000 for FBI and Civil Service investigations of these individuals. The investigations became controversial when journalists published details of the questions being asked of the accused. Later, when Attorney General Biddle submitted his preliminary report on the investigations to Congress, *PM* obtained a copy, no doubt from a liberal member of Congress. *PM* reported on August 31, 1942, that the investigations of more than 1,000 federal employees were, statistically speaking, a disaster. The dragnet produced only two forced resignations and six voluntary resignations. "The Dies red hunt was a wild goose chase that kept a considerable part of the FBI staff tied up when it should have been occupied with the important business of running down Axis spies, saboteurs, and propagandists," Crawford wrote.[40] In an editorial appearing elsewhere in the same edition of *PM*, Crawford blasted Dies while delivering a backhanded compliment to the FBI:

> As soon as Attorney General Francis Biddle submits his report to
> Congress showing that the Dies Committee forced the FBI to waste

$100,000 and the invaluable time of scores of trained agents making these investigations, Martin Dies will yell, "Whitewash." . . . He will say that he submitted to the Justice Dept. a list of 1121 dangerous Reds and that the Justice Dept. had only two of them fired. He might get away with such a defense except that the American people are not likely to believe that J. Edgar Hoover participated in a whitewashing operation.[41]

Biddle, who had planned to release his report to the public a few days later, wrote to Hoover and asked the director to find the source of the leak. He also noted that columnist and broadcaster Walter Winchell, a social friend of the director and frequent recipient of FBI leaks, had also obtained a pre-release copy of the report.[42] Hoover told Biddle an investigation was unlikely to disclose the source and proposed an extreme alternative that shows just how seriously he took media criticism of the Bureau: "I suggest that you give consideration to summoning before a grand jury Mr. Kenneth Crawford, over whose by-line the story appeared in PM magazine and such other officials of PM who are concerned with the daily printing of the paper," Hoover wrote. "I suggest further that you give consideration to subpoenaeing [sic] Mr. Walter Winchell before the same grand jury in view of the statement that he carried this information upon his broadcast of Sunday night.[43] No doubt the theatrical Winchell would have enjoyed the self-promotion afforded by a subpoena.

Biddle parried Hoover's suggestion and, through an aide, suggested again that the FBI initiate an investigation into the source of the leak. Hoover, ever concerned about his Bureau's public image, refused. "I still think such inquiries by FBI would be unproductive & create great hostility," he scrawled on a memorandum. "AG & [executive assistant to the attorney general Ugo] Carusi are always so solicitous about our not conducting subversive investigations because of ill will engendered against FBI. It seems strange they want this one which would turn loose on us the fury of a hundred wild cats."[44] For Hoover, the logic of convening a grand jury was simple: grand jury hearings are secret by nature. An investigation by his agents, in contrast, would quickly be detected and reported, further damaging his calculated image of restraint and responsibility.

By 1942, Ingersoll was frequently publishing articles critical of the FBI and, in particular, its conduct of loyalty investigations. The Bureau, *PM* asserted, had been insufficiently discreet in its investigation of alleged subversives. A series of articles described how liberal government employees were "lynched" by oafish FBI agents' investigative tactics. According to critics, the questions asked and the sources interviewed created doubt about these individuals' patriotism, regardless of the investigation's conclusions, and had serious consequences for loyal government workers. The FBI and Civil Service Commission asked questions about employees' family members and correspondents and about which periodicals they read. The implication of the questions, *PM* suggested, was that the employees had already been judged disloyal by someone, somewhere, and the investigations simply aimed to formalize that label. At the very least, according to *PM*, the investigations unduly damaged reputations and certainly chilled free speech. According to Ingersoll and his staff, the investigations were little more than political witch hunts, targeting liberals in government and conflating liberalism with disloyalty.

Yet like many critics of the FBI, *PM*'s editors remained supportive of the Bureau's work protecting the nation, even as they meted out criticism of the tactics employed. A June 1942 editorial, for example, heaped praise on the FBI's success in foiling a plot by saboteurs, but that praise was juxtaposed with criticism of the loyalty investigations: "The case against the FBI for its part in the witch-hunt in Washington has not been based on its zeal, but on the slovenliness of the investigations. The witch-hunters have been justly criticized for the stupid questions they've asked, for the hearsay evidence on which they've ruined men's usefulness, on the willingness of supposedly trained investigators to trust spiteful informers."[45]

As was always the case in such situations, Hoover and his team ignored the praise and focused on the public relations threat posed by the criticism. Hoover responded with a lengthy letter to Ingersoll, once again demonstrating his intolerance for public messages that undermined his Bureau's legitimacy. The allusion to the FBI as a secret police force, responsible for enforcing political orthodoxy, particularly galled Hoover. "I am very confidently convinced that you have been misinformed," Hoover wrote to Ingersoll. He pointed out that his agents were trained lawyers and accountants of good character, integrity, and ability. Hoover then pivoted to the Collier-Cooper narrative theme of reluctance and responsibility, telling Ingersoll, "the basic function of this Bureau was not to judge or determine a person's innocence or guilt but to obtain all the facts in a judicial, impartial and fair manner."[46]

After sending his letter to Ingersoll, Hoover attended to other public relations audiences whose confidence in the Bureau might be shaken by allegations that it abused its power. First, Hoover forwarded the *PM* editorial and his response to his boss, Attorney General Francis Biddle. In a memorandum to Biddle, Hoover essentially acknowledged the FBI's ongoing crisis of legitimacy: "This [abuse of power allegation] you will recognize as one of the long-standing criticisms against the FBI," he wrote. "And yet in every case which has come to my attention since this criticism has been developed . . . there has not been found a single case in which agents of this Bureau have been guilty of the allegations made."[47] With that blanket assertion of innocence, Hoover swept aside even the possibility of a mistake by one of his agents—a possibility he had admitted in his letter to Ingersoll and frequently used as a rhetorical device when responding to critics. The FBI was not infallible, Hoover often said, feeding the meme of his own steady hand engaged in ongoing quality control. According to the Collier-Cooper narrative, any excesses or mistakes by his agents were not the result of Bureau policy, would be taken seriously, and would have serious consequences for those involved.

Next, Hoover addressed another, more far-flung public relations audience, forwarding a copy of the letter and editorial to his front-line public relations team: the fifty-seven SACs stationed around the country. This time, Hoover tacitly admitted that improper questions had been asked by Civil Service agents but not by special agents of the FBI: "As you know, certain segments of the press have been quite vitriolic in their criticism of the Bureau as a result of our investigation of the Hatch Act violations and Government employees," Hoover told his SACs. "In every instance where the Bureau has had complaints as to the asking of improper questions, it has been ascertained that the investigation was conducted by some other Governmental agency."[48] Hoover knew his SACs would pass that message along to opinion shapers ranging from newspaper editors to local law enforcement officers in their communities. Thus, a public relations challenge also became an opportunity for Hoover to reinforce the themes of the FBI narrative to his core constituencies. Such challenges only proved to his supporters that Hoover's vigilance in monitoring subversives in society, including media critics, was justified. Mistakes by the FBI were turned into opportunities to strengthen the Collier-Cooper themes, buttressing the Bureau's armor against subsequent questions about its legitimacy.

Ingersoll replied to Hoover by forwarding another copy of the editorial, perhaps a snide suggestion that the director hadn't read it closely enough or hadn't understood it completely. Ingersoll reasserted his concerns about how the loyalty determinations were being made: "You were correct in assuming that I had been distressed by the reports [about the nature of the investigations] that have been brought to me—although as I wrote in another editorial, I am even more distressed by the misuse to which reports on the alleged subversive activities of liberals have been put."[49] Two weeks later, Nichols demonstrated how the director's umbrage had the force of law within the Bureau. Hoover's anger, communicated to his managers via handwritten comments on memoranda that crossed his desk, rippled through the Bureau and quickly became the party line. Nichols reported to Tolson that he had spoken informally to *PM* reporter Henry R. Lieberman, telling him:

> The Bureau did not want to have to be forced to make a public statement about the inaccuracies of *PM* but that unless *PM* produced the facts and made some sincere effort to print the truth that the day undoubtedly would come when in self-defense the Bureau would have to come out with the facts, that we were getting sick and tired of being kicked around by a bunch of scurrilous, prolific propagators of lies.[50]

It is interesting that Nichols, the author of many Hoover letters and speeches, used the phrase "prolific propagators of lies" to describe the press. Normally, such colorful, often alliterative phrases and staccato declarations were saved for Hoover's public pronouncements. Despite the veiled threat, those prolific propagators of lies were at it again just a month later, reporting some of the ugly statistics behind the loyalty investigations and, in effect, unmasking the political expediencies underlying the investigations and suggesting that the Bureau had become a tool of political enforcement.

Despite its premise and promise, *PM* never attained its circulation goal of 225,000 copies a day. After six consecutive years of losses, Marshall Field decreed in 1946 that the publication would begin accepting advertisements. Ingersoll resigned, but not even the change in advertising policy could save the newspaper.[51] *PM* folded in 1948.

Like Ingersoll at *PM* and Bliven at *The New Republic*, editors of *The Nation* strongly objected to federal loyalty investigations, which they viewed as witch hunts to drive progressives from government. In fact, *The Nation* was even more outspoken in its criticism of Hoover and the FBI than the others were. The liberal newspaper was described by *Time* magazine in 1943 as " a pulp-paper pinko weekly."[52] Founded by abolitionists in 1865, *The Nation* was a mere supplement to the *New York Evening Post* when Oswald Garrison Villard took over as publisher in 1900. The grandson of abolitionist William Lloyd Garrison and the son of journalist and railroad magnate Henry Villard, Oswald sold off the *Evening Post* in 1918 and remade *The Nation* into a

I. F. Stone seated at his desk, November 22, 1968. (© Bettman/CORBIS)

stand-alone liberal journal of current opinion. Progressive activist Frank P. Walsh once called *The Nation* the "greatest mystery in American journalism." Walsh had written articles about the railroads—one published in *The Nation,* which boasted a circulation of 27,000, and another that was syndicated in the Hearst newspapers, with a total circulation in the millions. But, as Walsh told Lewis Gannett in 1950, he "never . . . met a man who had read his articles in the Hearst press. But the day *The Nation* went on the Washington newsstands, Walsh's telephone began ringing."[53] Villard sold the magazine in 1935, and in 1943, *The Nation* became a nonprofit publication. Its outsized reputation as an influential voice on the Left has continued into the twenty-first century.

One of the most important journalists at *The Nation,* and one of the most iconoclastic journalists of the twentieth century, was I. F. Stone, who led the charge against the loyalty investigations of the 1940s. Born Isidor Feinstein (he changed his name in 1937), Stone was already a well-known reporter when the FBI took notice of him in the early 1940s. Before joining the staff of *The Nation* in 1939, Stone had worked for six years at the *New York Post* and had written a well-reviewed book about the Supreme Court. Stone became a confounding figure for Hoover and the FBI as they struggled to categorize him as friend or enemy. A 1941 memo recounting a statement from an informant noted that Stone "is not his correct name. He is of Jewish descent. [He] is very arrogant, very loud spoken, wears thick, heavy glasses and is most obnoxious personally."[54] Hoover scrawled two questions on the memo: "What have we on him? What is his name?"[55]

Over the years, Stone became very well known to Hoover. The tête-à-tête between Hoover's FBI and Stone over the course of two months in 1943 exemplifies their battles. The confrontation involved four articles published in *The Nation*: two articles by an anonymous author, "XXX," that attacked the FBI as a "Washington Gestapo"; a third article written by Stone that responded to Hoover's defense, mustered through two intermediaries; and a fourth article by *Nation* publisher and Hoover nemesis Freda Kirchwey (which ultimately prompted him to order the study linking *The Nation* and *The New Republic* to the Communist Party).

The first of the two "Washington Gestapo" articles by XXX appeared in *The Nation* on July 17, 1943. XXX, who identified himself or herself as a minor government executive, described the background of the government's "character investigations" of workers in war agencies. The investigations, XXX said, took valuable time away from the war effort and were often haphazardly performed by agents with little interest in the work. "What sort of people do investigators single out as victims?" XXX asked. "Ordinary, decent people like ourselves."[56] No employee, according to the author, was safe from an "obscene attack" that could result in dismissal over a disputed point of fact.[57] The second installment, published on July 24, 1943, described the anonymous author's encounter with a federal investigator who was probing a colleague's loyalty:

> The investigator asked me a number of routine questions about Smith.
> . . . Then a curiously fanatical look came into his eyes. Could I tell him
> why Bill Smith had grown a beard? What did he have to conceal? (He was

trying to hide a receding chin about which he is inordinately self-conscious.) Why did he sometimes use an alias instead of his real name? (When we were boys we nicknamed Bill "Hicky" after some now forgotten pitching hero, and the name has stuck.)[58]

The interrogation, according to XXX, continued with loaded questions about Bill's radio hobby and his love of Tchaikovsky, who was, after all, Russian. The questioner then asked XXX about Bill's interest in reading *The Nation*. "I said I did not regard *The Nation* as subversive," XXX wrote. "What made him think it was?"[59] That question summed up the loyalty program, XXX wrote. "'Subversive' is a vague word. But it is being used freely in Washington as a club with which to beat liberals out of town."[60] Bill Smith was using a radio to communicate with Moscow while he listened to Russian music. Combine that with a subscription to *The Nation*, and what other conclusion could the investigator draw?

The ridiculous implications of the questions and the overall nature of the investigation as portrayed in XXX's two articles again unmasked the FBI's preferred self-image of restraint, clinical science, and careful, thoughtful investigation. The oafish, uninformed investigator of the "Washington Gestapo" articles shattered that image. Moreover, the term "Gestapo" struck home by alluding to the Bureau's mysterious and all-encompassing power to police thought. The "Washington Gestapo" as described by XXX was, moreover, a brutish, uneducated, paranoid crew of bumblers.

The following week, Freda Kirchwey weighed in, calling for an end to the inquisition. Kirchwey began her long career at *The Nation* in 1919 as a reporter. She became chief executive editor in 1937, bought the journal from investment banker Maurice Wertheim, and later reincorporated *The Nation* as a nonprofit. Kirchwey was described as an "exuberant lady" in a *Saturday Evening Post* profile. "She goes merrily on her crusading way, smiting evildoers and letting the howls of pain rise where they may," the *Post* reported.[61] In 1944, columnist and radio commentator Dorothy Thompson praised Kirchwey for fighting "to throw light into dark places and to defend the people versus those interests that in our society have repeatedly striven to defeat the full realization of the promises of democracy."[62] From 1937 to 1955, Kirchwey led *The Nation* through the tumultuous period of war, loyalty investigations, and McCarthyism.

In her "End the Inquisition" editorial, Kirchwey told readers that hundreds of letters had come in recounting experiences similar to those of XXX. Kirchwey said she had discussed the excesses of the loyalty investigations with high-ranking officials in Washington, including one unnamed member of President Roosevelt's cabinet. "They all agreed that the inquisition was aimed at ridding the government service of as many New Dealers and other progressives as possible," she wrote. "One of the four thought the antagonism to Jews was equally strong. He also believed the situation would get worse."[63] Kirchwey did not blame the FBI or Civil Service agents who conducted the investigations; rather, she blamed the liberals in FDR's government who failed to stand up to the abuses of power. She complained that Attorney General Biddle, in particular, was too weak and dissembling to challenge the powerful Hoover. Men like Biddle, she said, "let men of will, the ruthless and unscrupulous men, ride over them and their decent convictions."[64]

Who better, then, to defend the FBI than two legendary civil liberties champions? Hoover counted American Civil Liberties Union cofounders Roger Baldwin and Morris Ernst among his friends. Both had been courted and charmed by Hoover, who managed to convince them that the FBI was not an enemy but a devoted protector of civil liberties. Baldwin and Ernst were enlisted to write to *The Nation* and defend the loyalty investigations and the Bureau. Both letters appeared in the September 25, 1943, edition of *The Nation.* Baldwin focused on the loyalty investigations themselves, writing that the government had chosen "a level-headed course in dealing with thousands of complaints of subversive activists." Ernst focused his defense squarely on his friend Hoover. Ernst claimed that he had carefully scrutinized the FBI's work and had never heard of a single proved case of the Bureau violating civil liberties. "This is close to a miracle," Ernst wrote. "I have been a pest to the FBI in picking them up on every possible complaint which has come to me. In the course of time these have run to a considerable number. I believe its protection of personal liberty is one of the outstanding contributions to the cause of civil liberties in my time in the United States."[65]

Another of Hoover's defenders came from within the Justice Department itself, where a former Washington correspondent for *The Nation* was serving as Biddle's director of public relations. Charles Malcolmson had worked at the *Philadelphia Record* before joining *The Nation* in 1939 and then moving to the Justice Department in 1940. On August 4, 1943, Malcolmson forwarded to Hoover a copy of a personal letter he had written in defense of the Bureau; Hoover read it, edited it, and returned it. Malcolmson then sent his letter, which he marked as not for publication, to Kirchwey. In it, Malcolmson pointed out that the Justice Department and the FBI had not been allowed to review *The Nation*'s articles prior to publication. He provided an exhaustive and petulant twenty-one-point refutation of claims made by XXX and complained that the accuser had hidden behind anonymity. XXX was, of course, of great interest to the FBI, which at first strategized how to determine XXX's identity. Hoover believed the author was attorney Max Lowenthal, head of the Re-Occupation Division of the Board of Economic Warfare and a former adviser to Senator Harry S. Truman. Indeed, Lowenthal later became an outspoken critic of the FBI, even authoring a high-profile book, *The Federal Bureau of Investigation*, in which he attacked the Bureau's political investigations.[66] Another theory at the time, based on a handwritten note on one of Stone's letters to Kirchwey, was that XXX was Edward F. Pritchard, an official in the Office of Economic Stabilization and former clerk for Supreme Court justice Felix Frankfurter.[67] Despite the FBI's efforts, XXX's identity remained a secret.

Stone, who as Washington editor had vetted the articles by XXX, responded to Baldwin, Ernst, and, without naming him, Malcolmson in his article "XXX and the FBI," which appeared in the September 25 edition of *The Nation*. Ernst felt the brunt of Stone's acid wit: "Morris Ernst says he has kept a 'rather close watch' on the FBI for 'close to ten years' and has 'yet to hear of a single proved case of violation of the most basic civil liberties. This is close to a miracle.'" Stone continued, "Like most miracles this does not stand up too well under examination."[68] He noted, for example, that the dismissal of charges against those arrested in Detroit in 1940 "serves to underscore the melodramatic lawlessness with which the FBI made the arrests."[69]

Malcolmson, referred to as an "off-the-record" correspondent from the Department of Justice, was next in Stone's sights. In his letter, Malcolmson claimed that Hoover had not, as XXX asserted, directed the infamous Palmer Raids. Stone refuted that point, citing a book by former attorney general Homer S. Cummings that specifically identified Hoover as being responsible for the administration of the raids. Stone, perhaps aware of the FBI's revision of history, noted that it was in Hoover's interest to downplay his participation in the Palmer Raids. "It may well be that Hoover has changed somewhat since those days," Stone wrote. "Under a progressive Administration, in a period when the labor movement is strong, the FBI could hardly operate Palmer fashion and survive. The strange thing is that even under these conditions, and during an anti-fascist war, anti-fascists should be as uncomfortable and as suspect as they often are in government service today."[70]

Hoover was livid. Once again, a liberal publication had highlighted a side of the Bureau that he would have preferred remain a secret. An influential if not widely read journal had portrayed the FBI as an American political secret police force. Moreover, first XXX and then Stone had repeated the truth of Hoover's culpability for the reviled Palmer Raids. Those two stories undermined both the responsibility theme of the Collier-Cooper narrative and Hoover's own credibility as the steady, careful leader of the FBI. "I would like a prompt analysis made of this article with specific documentary answer to each allegation as made against the FBI & as quickly as possible," Hoover wrote.[71] The analysis, produced by Nichols's Crime Records staff, was forwarded to Hoover on October 23. It began with a review of the Bureau's files on Stone and continued with a deconstruction of his two-page article in granular detail for twenty-four pages. In the memo, agent J. J. Starke of the Crime Records Division showed how completely FBI history had been sanitized. Starke wrote that attacking Hoover for his role in the Palmer Raids was "one of the most vicious smear attacks upon the FBI and its Director." Hoover's "alleged supervision" of the raids was a lie, Starke wrote. "The only assignment of the present Director of the FBI in regards to the raids was the correlation of evidence to be used in prosecuting the deportation cases."[72] Given a bureaucratic culture that allowed little or no dissent, there is no doubt that Starke believed what he wrote.

As a result of their critical articles, Hoover decreed that no Bureau employee was to speak to anyone from *The New Republic* or *The Nation*. Assistant director Edward Tamm worried that some FBI employee might inform journalists from these publications of the no-contact order, highlighting the Bureau's heavy-handedness and its extraordinary power to shape the public narrative.[73] Based on Tamm's suggestion, Hoover ordered his agents, specifically those in New York, not to speak to anyone from the offending publications and not to discuss the order of silence with anyone.[74] This double-secret silent treatment became a common tactic: any offending publication or journalist should be ignored entirely, like punishing a spoiled child.

Stone was not finished with the FBI. In fact, he became one of its most outspoken critics in a career that continued long after Hoover's death in 1972. Upon Stone's death in 1989, he was hailed as an "independent, radical pamphleteer of American journalism." Stone had begun his journalism career at age fourteen on a neighborhood monthly. Within a few years, he had moved to the *Camden (N.J.) Courier-Post* and then attended the University of Pennsylvania. He worked for the *Philadelphia Inquirer* and the *New York*

Post before joining *The Nation*. In his obituary, Stone was described as a "short, owlish maverick with dimpled cheeks and major handicaps in hearing and vision, [who] was a tough-minded but pacifist gadfly, a tireless examiner of public records, a hectoring critic of public officials, a persistent attacker of Government distortions and evasions and a pugnacious advocate of civil liberties, peace and truth."[75]

If one set out to create an anti-Hoover, it would be difficult not to come up with someone very much like I. F. Stone (or George Seldes before him). He was raised in Haddonfield, New Jersey, where Stone's father was a store owner and an unsuccessful real estate speculator. His mother suffered from bipolar syndrome and once tried to take her life by drinking Lysol. Stone, an awkward child, turned to books and was a voracious reader. An admirer of Hegel and Marx, he was briefly a member of the Norman Thomas–led Socialist Party but dropped out in 1932. The Thomas socialists, according to Stone's biographer D. D. Guttenplan, "owed far more to the Populists and other strands of indigenous American radicalism than to the lessons of Bolshevism."[76] Similar to Seldes, Stone's most ardent interest and the focus of his journalism career was, according to Guttenplan, the study of power.

Journalism came easy to the talented and bookish Stone. As a teenager, his intellect attracted the attention of the wife of J. David Stern, publisher of the *Camden Courier*, and Stone was given a job at the paper. When Stern purchased the *Philadelphia Record*, Stone moved there as a reporter and editorial writer. And when Stern became publisher of the *New York Post*, Stone immediately "high-tailed" it to the Big Apple and presented himself (without Stern's knowledge) as the paper's new editorial writer.[77] At the *Post* and later as a writer and editor at *The Nation*, the *New York Daily Compass*, and *PM*, Stone became a committed critic of the FBI. He poked at the FBI's use of wiretapping, for example, and, as exemplified by the "Washington Gestapo" series, frequently criticized the Bureau's conduct of the loyalty investigations.

The Bureau had been monitoring Stone for years, but only a handful of critical articles under his byline had been noted in his file before the "XXX" series. The first mention was in 1936, when an editorial he wrote in the *New York Post* accused the FBI of OGPU-like tactics and stated that Hoover was antilabor and antiunion.[78] In 1941, Stone wrote "A G-String Conspiracy" for *The Nation*, criticizing FBI tactics in investigating Trotskyites in Minnesota. Stone also authored two of *The Nation*'s critical reports on the FBI's conduct of the controversial Detroit raids.[79] A 1944 summary memorandum noted that a confidential informant, very likely Victor Riesel, had described Stone as a "fellow traveler," or a non–party member who sympathized with communism's aims. Also in 1944, Stone mocked a speech Hoover had delivered to the Daughters of the American Revolution. "We PMers had been hoping for some time that maybe J. Edgar Hoover was getting educated," Stone wrote. "We heard that he had some quiet talks with Attorney General Biddle and we noticed that for a good long time he hadn't been making any more of those G-Man speeches that sounded like William Randolph Hearst disguised as Dick Tracy."[80]

In a 1948 *PM* column, Stone objected to Tamm's appointment to the federal bench. "Eighteen years as a G-man do not constitute the best training for a judge," Stone wrote. "Many cases for which the FBI has laid the groundwork originate in the local, Federal District Court. Basic questions of civil liberty are often involved, for the FBI has become a secret political police, European style."[81] Proof of Stone's communist tendencies could be found, according to FBI reports, in his criticism of Hoover and the Bureau.[82] It was true that Stone did not trust Hoover or the FBI, particularly after the Bureau began to focus on investigating dissidence in the mid-1930s. The FBI's assertion that Stone was "Communist influenced," however, suggests that the Bureau was focused on monolithic communism and never grasped the nuanced continuum of liberal political thought and movements of the early to mid-twentieth century.

Although he often espoused socialist ideals, Stone, contrary to the reports of dozens of "reliable" FBI confidential informants, never joined any iteration of a communist party. The subtleties of Stone's complex political worldview eluded the FBI. In reality, though, the Bureau had a very simple test for communist influence: everyone on the political Left was suspect unless they publicly renounced communism. And in some cases, such as Bureau and McCarthy critic James Wechsler, anticommunism was viewed simply as a complex ruse. Guttenplan described Stone's politics as "movement" oriented. Stone was "trusted (if not liked) by Trotskyists, [and] sympathetic to (if no longer a member of) the Socialist Party, and with family ties to the CP, he was becoming [by 1936] a crucial intermediary among various elements of the American left, and more important, between the self-conscious radicals and the equally fractious but much broader elements of the body politic who answered to the label of 'liberal.'"[83]

Stone's tolerance for communists and his populist, liberal ideology, along with a tendency to criticize the Bureau, was enough for the FBI to label him at least a "near-communist." Later, based on the false testimony of an informant, it concluded he was a longtime Communist Party member. His liberal politics, in short, made it easy for Hoover's Bureau to presume that Stone—who generally eschewed party orthodoxy of any type—must be a communist. Stone was actually an organizing force at the center of another movement—the Popular Front of liberalism, socialism, and communism allied against fascism. Stone's role as a boundary spanner among groups generally aligned him on the left of politics and culture, but very different agendas led him to critique both Soviet-style communism and Roosevelt's New Deal "socialism." Often surrounded by ideologues of one stripe or another, Stone became an integrating force on the Left even as he confounded FBI efforts to pigeonhole him. For an FBI accustomed to making easy, permanent, black-and-white judgments of friends and enemies, the many gray areas of Stone's ideology and his wide range of acquaintances simply did not compute. Thus Stone continued to be of great interest to the FBI, which assumed he operated from revolutionary intent. The Bureau's interest culminated in two active investigations and the editor's placement on the Security Index.

According to a 1950 summary, the FBI searched its files for information on Stone under a bizarre series of spellings, ranging from "Isidore Finglestein" to "Isidor M. Feinstein."[84] The resulting updated summary memorandum was a typical example of FBI analysts taking unverified rumors and reports of confidential informants and turning them into proof of an individual's subversive or revolutionary intent. The summary included reports from confidential informants who claimed that Stone was a member of eighteen groups considered communist front organizations. The report detailed countless public presentations by Stone and noted that Stone, along with many others, had signed a letter published in the *Daily Worker* (without mentioning the subject matter of the letter). Other confidential informants claimed, again without evidence, that Stone actively advised the *Daily Worker*. In an instance of guilt by association, Stone's acquaintance with Wechsler, despite the *Post* editor's strident anticommunist writings, was cited as evidence of his communist ties. Within the upside-down world of the FBI's attempts to parse political ideology, a friendship with a former member of the Young Communist League who had very publicly renounced communism somehow meant that Stone must be a communist.

Several reporters provided information about Stone, including former colleagues from *PM* and the *New York Post*. One told an FBI investigator that

"Stone was not a Communist but was unusually brilliant and at times his ideas appeared radical."[85] That assessment, buried in the reports of other informants, was apparently ignored. When an antifascist Italian publication commented on an article by Stone, that was dutifully reported in the summary.[86] When Stone began writing for *PM* in 1941, the Bureau reviewed and summarized hundreds of his articles and editorials. Some of the unverified information in the summary was nonsensical to the point of being ridiculous: "The Congressional Record of February 1, 1943, contained on page 508 an allegation that I. F. Stone of 'P.M.' newspaper was a member of the Communist Party, *or contained a denial of such allegation* [emphasis added]."[87]

Stone's anti-Hoover rhetoric could be strident. After Hoover told a group of American Legion conventioneers in October 1946 that Americans should guard against "sly propaganda and false preachments on Civil Liberty," Stone responded with an editorial titled "Some Questions for J. Edgar Hoover." Labeling Hoover a "self-dramatizing dick," Stone downplayed the Communist Party's ability to mount any sort of coherent campaign for revolution. It was "hysterical nonsense to build up the Communist Party, which can't elect a dog catcher outside of New York City, into Public Enemy No. 1."[88]

Stone's appearances on radio programs in the late 1940s were summarized, and some were transcribed. He wrote another article about FBI wiretapping after moving to the *New York Daily Compass* in 1950, resulting in the preparation of a point-by-point rebuttal.[89] In 1949 and 1950, two more confidential informants claimed that Stone was "Pro-Soviet" and a communist.[90] The rabidly anticommunist newsletter *Counterattack* was cited as the source for several reports of Stone's public speeches. In a 1950 speech at a "rally against the H bomb" sponsored by the National Council of the Arts, Sciences, and Professions, Stone poked fun at the FBI. "Stone opened his speech with greetings to the FBI agents present," according to an informant. Stone then "said that perhaps he should address the audience as 'FBI Agents and fellow subversives.'"[91]

The 1950 summary of the information on Stone in FBI files ultimately ran more than 400 pages. During the course of compiling that summary, it was "discovered" that one confidential informant had identified Stone as a Communist Party member as late as 1945—the only person who ever definitively claimed that Stone was a "card-carrying" party member.[92] Based on that one informant's word, the Bureau initiated an active and highly intrusive investigation in August 1950 to determine whether Stone should be listed on the FBI's Security Index (a roster of individuals to be monitored or perhaps arrested should a national emergency arise). Stone's tax returns were scrutinized, and his bags were searched when he traveled.[93] Late in 1951, New York agents were instructed to surveil Stone at his home, follow him, and try to identify the people he met with and spoke to. The agents were warned to take special care to avoid detection: "The Bureau is aware of Stone's antagonistic attitude of long standing towards the FBI and his present employment as a newspaper columnist by the 'Daily Compass.' For this reason, surveillance of Stone must be conducted in an extremely discreet and cautious manner."[94]

With those instructions in mind, the New York SAC noted the difficulty of surveilling Stone at his apartment, located at the corner of Park Avenue and Ninety-First Street. With no safe haven to watch from, agents were forced to loiter on the street; as a result, they were authorized to undertake selective rather than around-the-clock surveillance to avoid being noticed.[95] The surveillance of Stone's New York home proved anything but revelatory: On September 14, 1951, at 10:30 a.m., he left the house and bought a pad of paper. On September 20 at 12:48 p.m., Stone was observed purchasing a Spanish-language dictionary. On September 26 at 10:05 a.m., he bought a newspaper at Max Schwartz's cigar store. Stone bought groceries at 11:00 a.m. on September 27. On October 30 at 1:17 p.m., he met two men on the street and talked to them. As they walked down Madison Avenue, three more people joined them, and they all went to lunch. Each person in the group was carefully described in surveillance reports. Several times in March 1952, Stone and a companion went to a luncheonette near the *Daily Compass* building, where they spent a few minutes, perhaps purchasing coffee. Stone's file contained more than 100 pages of handwritten surveillance logs beginning on August 21, 1951, and continuing until March 28, 1952. Hoover's agents watched Stone's home and monitored his comings and goings for more than 300 hours during that seven-month period—an enormous effort that amounted to precisely nothing.[96] A second round of surveillance was ordered and began immediately.

Notwithstanding the FBI's failure to catch Stone in the act of being a communist (whatever that might entail), the New York SAC recommended in October 1951 that a Security Index card be created for Stone. The agent placed an "X" on the line next to "COMMUNIST" on the form.[97] The Bureau agreed with the SAC's recommendation, with one caveat: "Inasmuch as

Stone has been only tentatively identified as [a] Soviet Agent, . . . the Bureau feels that his name should not be included in the Special Section [designated for Soviet agents engaged in espionage]."[98]

When the *Daily Compass* folded suddenly after its November 3, 1952, issue, Stone set out to start his own weekly newsletter and contacted George Seldes, former publisher of *In Fact*, for advice. "The Stones were friends of ours," Seldes told an interviewer, "and we told them exactly how we got started. . . . Start on a small scale, don't have investments, and don't risk everything on it." Seldes also provided Stone with a mailing list of more than 10,000 of his former *In Fact* subscribers.[99] In late 1952, *The Nation* carried a notice of the debut of *I. F. Stone's Weekly*. Before the first issue appeared, early promotional mailings had attracted more than 3,500 subscribers.[100] Stone also promoted his newsletter through ads in *The Nation* and other liberal publications. In a personal letter published in the December 7, 1952, issue of the *New York Post*, Stone laid out his plans for the *Weekly*:

> I am convinced there is no other way to go on doing the kind of newspaper work I have always done except by striking out on my own. . . . Emphasis will be on Washington coverage. From week to week I want to provide a vivid record of what the Republican Administration is doing, to portray its personnel and atmosphere, to supply information and sidelights you cannot obtain elsewhere, and to go on with the kind of campaigns waged in my column for justice and civil liberties. The next four years may be decisive for peace abroad and freedom at home. I want to stay in the fight for both.[101]

Stone certainly chose an auspicious time to publish a civil liberties newspaper. Seldes's *In Fact* had foundered three years earlier, with the editor declaring he could not go on in the face of his readers' intimidation by the FBI, not to mention a noteworthy lack of indignation and protest against the rising tide of fascism. Seldes believed that although indignation remained, the government's war on dissidence had succeeded in silencing protesters even before Wisconsin senator Joseph McCarthy appeared on the scene. "People are frightened to death," Seldes wrote in his farewell editorial in October 1950. The Emergency Detention Act, better known as the McCarran Act or the Internal Security Act of 1950, had been passed earlier that year over President Harry S. Truman's veto. The act required communist organizations to register with the attorney general and established the Subversive Activities

Control Board to investigate alleged subversives. Most chillingly, the act included an emergency detention clause, giving the president the power to detain anyone suspected of planning or conspiring to engage in espionage or sabotage. In his veto message, Truman said the act would provide communists with a propaganda victory "by discrediting as hypocrisy the efforts of the United States on behalf of freedom." Moreover, Truman called the act the greatest danger to freedom of speech, press, and assembly since the Alien and Sedition Laws of 1798. "This danger arises out of the criteria or standards to be applied in determining whether an organization is a communist-front organization."[102]

By the time *I. F. Stone's Weekly* debuted in 1953, Senator Joseph Mc-Carthy's shrill voice had heightened what some called the "American inquisition." Stone's biographer cataloged the foment of the times:

> The country was still at war in Korea. Republicans branded the New Deal "twenty years of treason" while Democrats and labor unions purged their ranks of Communists, former Communists, fellow travelers, and anyone unwilling to disavow previous sympathy for left-wing causes. At the annual Lincoln's Birthday luncheon of the American Civil Liberties Union, the ACLU cofounder Roger Baldwin was flanked on the dais by Robert Morris, counsel to the McCarran Committee, and Vincent Hartnett, coauthor of *Red Channels*, the broadcasting blacklisters' bible. Roy Cohn, the young prosecutor whose examination of David Greenglass sent the Rosenbergs to their deaths, sat among the honored guests. At J. Edgar Hoover's recommendation, Cohn had just been named counsel to Senator McCarthy.[103]

Stone charged $5 for a yearly subscription to the four-page weekly. By issue four, Stone reported that he had attracted 6,000 subscribers and offered the premium of a copy of his forthcoming book, *The Truman Era*, to anyone ordering two annual subscriptions.[104] The FBI, through one of its covers, was one of Stone's initial subscribers.[105] In April 1953, Hoover ordered his Washington field office to obtain its own subscription and review each issue for content of interest to the Bureau. "Since this publication consists almost entirely of editorials written by Stone, it may be desirable on occasions to include pertinent excerpts in an investigative report since in previous writings Stone has frequently indicated sympathy and support for certain policies of the Soviet Union, the Communist Party, and other subversive groups."[106]

Perhaps Hoover assigned that task to the Washington field office because his Central Research staff apparently missed Stone's first editorial mentioning the FBI. In the tenth issue, published on March 21, 1953, Stone refuted historian Douglas Southall Freeman's statement that "it is remarkable that the FBI, despite all the temptations, never became a secret police." Stone disagreed, noting that the FBI operated in secret and collected dossiers on private citizens, "including many of very moderate liberal views. It has the power to destroy reputation and livelihood in all those growing areas where 'loyalty' and 'security' clearance are now needed, from private business scientific laboratories to jobs on the waterfront." The FBI, Stone continued, preserved its informants' anonymity and did not disclose the results of its investigations to the private citizens being investigated. "This is certainly acting as a secret police, or what the Japanese called a 'thought police.'"[107]

Early 1953 saw the institutionalization of McCarthyism as Senate Republicans, who thought they were relegating their vituperative Wisconsin colleague to purgatory, made him chairman of the Senate Permanent Subcommittee on Investigations. McCarthy, of course, used his subcommittee to launch sweeping investigations of Voice of America, the International Information Agency, and the U.S. Army. Several journalists, including Wechsler (Stone's former colleague turned enemy), were subpoenaed to appear before the committee.

When Hoover, in a rare newspaper interview, said in August 1953 that he considered Senator McCarthy a friend and described him as "a vigorous figure who isn't going to be pushed around," Stone responded by devoting almost the entire September 5 issue of the *Weekly* to the topic.[108] He described "The J. Edgar Hoover–McCarthy Axis" as a fearful thought police with sweeping and unfettered powers. "McCarthy is America's most controversial figure. J. Edgar Hoover is its most feared," Stone wrote. "Hoover's closet is well stocked with skeletons. Many in the capital fear the stray bones he may rattle. A Hoover-McCarthy axis must also spike the feeble popguns of those faint-hearted liberals whose anti-McCarthy line has been 'let the FBI do it.' This *is* how the FBI does it."[109]

Stone evoked Hitler, declaring that McCarthy's friendship with Hoover gave the senator an advantage that Hitler lacked—"the advantage of close liaison and support from the secret police of the government he wants to take over."[110] The article deconstructed the Collier-Cooper narrative point by point. Rather than the trustworthy uncle, Hoover was portrayed as a feared secret policeman. The restrained, responsible FBI was, according to Stone, little more than the puppet master behind McCarthy's inquisition. Rather than relying on dispassionate science, the partisan Hoover twisted words and selectively released incriminating tidbits from his files to congressional witch hunters like McCarthy. And the Bureau's publicity efforts were unmasked. Stone identified Riesel as a reliable Hoover defender against "smears" from the Left.

Stone picked up his "axis" theme again on March 22, 1954, with an article headlined "The FBI, McCarthy and the Witch Hunt." In it, Stone portrayed Hoover and the FBI as the driving force behind government anticommunism all the way back to the mid-1930s. In fact, that was true, since FDR had engaged the FBI as a domestic spying agency. "The truth is catching up with McCarthy," Stone wrote. "And in the uproar, all too few will notice the key role the FBI has been playing in the witch hunt from J. Parnell Thomas to Joe McCarthy, and will continue to play behind the scenes as one adventurer succeeds another in the center of the stage."[111]

Even as Stone's anti-FBI rhetoric became more strident, the Bureau's investigation continued. If fact, it became an "espionage" investigation after it was discovered that a 1944 KGB communication had mentioned Stone's name. The communication was one of a massive cache of encrypted Soviet telegrams originating in the United States that had been captured by the Army's Signal Intelligence Service beginning in 1939 and kept until experts could break the codes and translate the contents. In 1948, with a significant number of decoded messages to be analyzed, FBI special agent Robert Lamphere became the Bureau's liaison to the project.[112] It was Lamphere who recommended that an espionage investigation be opened on Stone after a decoded telegram specifically mentioned that a KGB operative and TASS news agency correspondent had sought to make contact with Stone, who avoided him.[113] There was no evidence that Stone had either encouraged or discouraged the correspondent's overtures. Nonetheless, an espionage investigation was opened.[114]

Weekly reports from the Washington field office summarized prior reports, capsulized that week's *Weekly*, and added more reports of Stone's activities, including speeches, meetings, and affiliations. The reports averaged about twenty pages per week and were supplemented by investigative summaries covering the latest informant's report or results of the surveillance of Stone's movements. Hoover followed these reports closely. For instance, when a March 5, 1954, speech by Stone had not yet been summarized six weeks later, Hoover asked, "Why all the delay?"[115] Two weeks later, Hoover forwarded to Attorney General Herbert Brownell the summary of Stone's speech. "Stone charged that by slandering and lying, Attorney General Brownell is 'out McCarthying McCarthy,'" Hoover reported.[116]

The March 29, 1954, issue of *Stone's Weekly* reported that McCarthy committee member Karl Mundt (R-S.D.), in a speech to a Salt Lake City group, admitted that when the FBI could not indict a subversive, "it often . . . tips off a Congressional Committee." Mundt's statement, Stone said, proved his "axis" accusations and demonstrated the FBI's role as a primary driver behind the investigations of alleged communists. "Thus the FBI circumvents the grand jury system, and destroys in the public pillory those whom it cannot fairly indict and convict," Stone wrote. "They lost jobs and reputation and are effectively destroyed as if they had been sent to jail."[117] Mundt later denied making the quoted statement.

The FBI's active investigation of Stone was closed on December 16, 1954, after no evidence of either Communist Party membership or espionage activity had been found. The Bureau even passed on an opportunity to place an informant in Stone's office as a secretary.[118] However, the monitoring of *I. F. Stone's Weekly* continued, albeit without the production of twenty-page summaries.[119] Stone's name was removed from the Security Index in 1955.[120] In a bizarre twist, when Stone's May 28, 1956, issue criticized the Soviet Union, assistant director William C. Sullivan suggested that the FBI obtain 1,000 copies of it and distribute them to SACs, who would then circulate them among opinion leaders in their communities. "Here is a man known for his procommunism now doing a flip-flop," Sullivan wrote to his supervisor.[121] The FBI's top authority on communism thus failed to grasp the nuanced position of many American socialists who opposed Soviet-style communism. In fact, Stone had never been a supporter of what he saw as brutish, centralized Soviet communism. Ultimately, Sullivan's request was reduced to 300 copies because no distributor could supply 1,000 copies of the *Weekly*, other than I. F. Stone himself. For weeks, FBI agents were engaged in tracking down additional copies of the paper.

Despite closing its security and espionage investigations in 1954, the Bureau continued to monitor the newspaper and provide Hoover with summaries of pertinent articles. The Bureau took a renewed interest in the editor's activities in the early 1960s when Stone visited and then began writing and speaking about Cuba. Stone's Security Index entry was updated, and a new summary memorandum was produced in 1963.[122] Stone's outspoken opposition to U.S. involvement in Vietnam prompted the FBI's ongoing interest in *I. F. Stone's Weekly* until it ceased publication in 1971.

The FBI's scrutiny of I. F. Stone spanned thirty-five years. Ostensibly, Hoover's interest resulted from Stone's alleged connections to communism. What is clear from a review of the Bureau's actions with regard to Stone and other "near-communists," however, is that these individuals' ongoing campaign of criticizing the FBI was at least equally interesting to Hoover and his investigators. Stone's 1950s focus on an axis between congressional anticommunists and Hoover's FBI encapsulated the Left's discomfort with the Bureau, which could be traced back more than thirty years, all the way to the Palmer Raids.

Stone, Bliven, Crawford, Kirchwey, and others who filled the pages of *PM, The New Republic, The Nation,* and *I. F. Stone's Weekly* with critical assessments of Hoover's FBI drew a direct line connecting the Palmer Raids, the wiretapping controversies, the Detroit arrests, the loyalty investigations, and the ongoing communist witch hunt to latent American discomfort with centralized power. Rather than an incorruptible Bureau marked by Hoover's ascension to the directorship in 1924 and expressed through the science and responsibility themes of the Collier-Cooper narrative, the liberal critics of the 1940s and 1950s detected and protested an ongoing campaign to criminalize and silence left-wing thought and speech. The FBI's public relations image invited Americans to believe in Hoover's forbearance and in his ability to restrict his Bureau's scientific investigations to actions rather than thoughts. His critics portrayed a venal and judgmental Hoover capriciously unleashing his agents in an effort to mandate conformity and chill dissent. That secret police–OGPU–gestapo theme was perpetuated throughout the 1940s in *PM, The New Republic,* and *The Nation,* raising the vexing question of the FBI's legitimacy.

The anticommunist hysteria sparked by the vituperative statements of Senator Joseph McCarthy in the early 1950s provided critics with another opportunity to question the FBI's power and authority and add their voices to the critique. One of the most outspoken of McCarthy's opponents was *New York Post* editor James A. Wechsler.

Chapter 6

Dividing the Press

On May 6, 1959, *New York Post* publisher Dorothy Schiff had a telephone conversation with Joe Eckhouse, head of Gimbel's department store. A month earlier, Eckhouse had told Schiff that J. Edgar Hoover and Clyde Tolson had approached him in a New York restaurant, sat down at his table, and warned him that a planned *Post* series on the FBI was part of a communist-coordinated smear campaign. Eckhouse interpreted the surprise encounter as an effort to intimidate a major *Post* advertiser and, through him, send a message to Schiff that she should spike the series about the FBI. Eckhouse had naively suggested that he broker a meeting between Schiff and Hoover to defuse the situation. Clearly, he had no concept of Hoover's obsessive fear of negative publicity that might undermine the image of his agency. Schiff, who had tangled with Hoover before, knew there was little chance of a rapprochement between the progressive *Post* and the suspicious FBI director, so she could not have been surprised when Eckhouse reported that Hoover was not interested in a meeting. Eckhouse explained Hoover's reason for declining: "Apparently after a lot of talk . . . they are inclined to feel at this stage they are afraid a meeting with you and I and him would be misinterpreted on account of the pressure," he told Schiff.[1]

During that same discussion, Schiff inquired about another, more overt threat leveled by the FBI in an effort to prevent publication of the series. In a letter to Eckhouse, a Bureau official had claimed that *Post* editor James A. Wechsler's wife, attorney Nancy F. Wechsler, had been fired from her position as counsel to President Harry Truman's Committee on Civil Rights in 1948 because she was a communist. Her husband, according to the FBI, carried a grudge against the Bureau for identifying his wife's communism, and that grudge was the impetus for the proposed series. The implication was that Eckhouse should be careful not to associate himself or his company with known communists like the Wechslers and that he should share the information with Schiff so that she could perform her own due diligence. As was often the case when the FBI leaked information for its own purposes, it wanted Eckhouse to believe that the Bureau was doing him a favor, helping him protect his company from subversive associations. The FBI wanted recipients to believe that the Bureau was only reluctantly reporting whatever regrettable information it had gathered while doing its duty to protect the country from its enemies.

During their telephone conversation (which was transcribed for Schiff's records), Eckhouse told the publisher that the information didn't concern him. Schiff pressed the issue.

"Why wait twelve years to bring this up?" she asked.

"I wouldn't know. I am in a very embarrassing position," Eckhouse said.

"This is McCarthyism," Schiff replied. "What could be more damaging to the *Post* than saying this to important people in the community?"[2]

Schiff was an owner and then the publisher of the *New York Post* from 1939 to 1976, when she sold the paper to Rupert Murdoch for $31 million. Schiff was active in Democratic Party politics, and the *Post* was reliably liberal, supporting organized labor and social justice. It also became a strong voice against McCarthyism and against the tactics of Hoover's FBI. Wechsler, editor of the *New York Post* for more than three decades beginning in 1949, was an outspoken advocate for journalistic freedom and was among the most vocal critics of the FBI, relating Hoover's tactics to McCarthy by coining the term *Hooverism*. Upon his death in 1983, Wechsler was hailed as a "prominent voice of liberalism" and as one of the first, most dogged, and most prominent media critics of McCarthyism.[3] He was also criticized for naming names before the McCarthy committee in a questionable bargain that gave him access to a transcript of the secret hearings so that he could raise the alarm about the senator's tactics. Nancy Wechsler was a brilliant lawyer who graduated at the top of her class after being one of the first women admitted to Columbia Law School. She played a key role in the creation of a pioneering, 1947 civil rights report that, among other things, criticized the FBI.[4] Both Wechslers admitted to a youthful flirtation with communism and were members of the Young Communist League (YCL) during their college years in the 1930s. In 1937, after three years in the YCL, both left the group, citing an untenable incompatibility between classic liberalism and doctrinaire, Soviet-style communist orthodoxy.

James Wechsler had long been a journalist of interest to the FBI. He had first come to the Bureau's attention in 1940, when he and twenty-nine other staffers of the left-leaning New York newspaper *PM* were listed in an FBI memorandum, without any supporting evidence, as communists or communist sympathizers.[5] A Custodial Detention Index card was created for Wechsler at that time, identifying him as a potentially subversive radical. The FBI initiated its first active investigation of Wechsler, an internal security review, in 1941, and updated his CDI card. Wechsler, who was *PM*'s labor editor, was initially classified as B-1, meaning that in the case of a national emergency, his work would be monitored and his movements restricted. In 1942, however, Wechsler was recategorized as A-1, meaning that in a national emergency, he would be imprisoned without a hearing as a threat to the nation.[6] Wechsler's classification was maintained at A-1 after a second review of a summary report by the FBI.[7]

The primary reason for Wechsler's reclassification was the Bureau's discovery of his membership in the Young Communist League in the 1930s. Wechsler had joined the YCL under the pseudonym Arthur Lawson in April 1934, while he was a student at Columbia and editor of the *Columbia Spectator*. He later became director of publications for the American Student Union, a socialist and communist organization of college students founded in 1935. In that capacity, Wechsler organized a one-hour student strike at Columbia and was subsequently placed on the National Committee of the YCL.

Like many young liberals in the 1930s, James and Nancy Wechsler were idealists who quickly became disillusioned when confronted with the reality of Soviet communism. In 1937, the Wechslers led a student tour through Europe that included a two-week stint in the Soviet Union. Their close-up view of the dour, centrally controlled, authoritarian Soviet system soured them both on communism. "Upon our return we agreed that we no longer felt any genuine sympathy with the Communist movement," Wechsler later told the FBI. "From December 1937 until the present my wife and I have both refused to participate in any Communist activities and have worked in numerous organizations unequivocably opposed to Communists."[8] Nancy Wechsler admitted her involvement with the YCL in 1943. In his published writings that appeared in *The Nation*, *The Progressive*, *PM*, the *New York Post*, and many other liberal journals during his long career, James Wechsler demonstrated that he had become a strident anticommunist. He resigned his position at *PM* because of what he perceived as an excessive communist influence at the paper.[9] For a brief time, Wechsler's clear break with communism and his prolific, outspoken, and even combative anticommunist record caused the FBI to rethink its assessment. An unusually frank February 1945 FBI memorandum declared that Wechsler was "opposed to communism."[10] The security investigation of James Wechsler, ongoing for nearly five years, was closed a month later.[11]

Things changed in 1948 when Nancy Wechsler's work as counsel to Truman's Committee on Civil Rights caused both Wechslers to reappear on the FBI's radar. The committee had been established by executive order on December 5, 1946, to review civil rights statutes and recommend legislation to strengthen the federal government's hand in prosecuting racial violence. The *New York Times* reported that although Truman did not give details about the incidents that had prompted him to create the committee, "his language suggested such examples as the recent lynching of four Negroes in Walton County, Georgia; the resurgence of the Ku Klux Klan which wielded great power after the last war; the inception in Atlanta, Ga., of a hate organization called the 'Columbians'; the election riots last summer in Athens, Tenn. and current charges that Negroes were kept away from the polls in Mississippi by intimidation."[12] Truman named a fifteen-member committee that included ACLU counsel Morris Ernst, General Electric chairman and president Charles E. Wilson, and Franklin D. Roosevelt Jr., along with several clergymen and educators.[13] Wilson was named chair of the committee and was responsible for hiring and supervising staff through his executive secretary Robert Carr.

Prior to becoming counsel to the Civil Rights Committee in 1946, Nancy Wechsler worked, beginning in 1942, for the Board of Economic Warfare, the Office of Price Administration, the Office of Economic Stabilization, and the Department of Labor. Meanwhile, on March 21, 1947, Truman signed Executive Order 9835, establishing a Loyalty Review Board to oversee the nation's first general loyalty program, with the FBI providing investigative services. Loyalty Review Board inquiries were limited to investigating connections between federal employees and organizations included on the attorney general's list of subversive organizations. That list, created by Francis Biddle in 1947, initially contained eleven organizations believed to be subversive fronts. One of the organizations on the original list was the American Youth Congress; the Young Communist League was eventually added. Between 1947 and 1951, 3 million federal employees were investigated, a few thousand resigned, and 212 were dismissed over questions of loyalty. As the counsel to the Committee on Civil Rights, Nancy Wechsler was not subject to inquiry under Truman's executive order.

On September 29, 1947, however, Hoover wrote to Wilson, informing him that his committee's counsel had once been a member of the Young Communist League. Hoover noted that he had learned of Wechsler's YCL affiliation during the course of another investigation, probably that of her husband. Wilson told FBI officials that, when confronted, Nancy Wechsler confirmed her YCL membership, and Louis B. Nichols reported that, according to Wilson, "she had been dismissed from the committee."[14] Carr later denied that Wechsler had resigned or been fired. In fact, Carr told Schiff in a 1959 letter that Wechsler's appointment to the committee expired with the issuance of its report. She stayed on for an extra month at the request of the White House.[15] Carr's statement, of course, undermined Hoover's claim that the proposed *Post* series on the FBI was the result of a vendetta by James Wechsler. Why would he be angry with the FBI if his wife's appointment with the committee had simply run its course? Nancy Wechsler became the subject of a formal FBI loyalty investigation, initiated by Hoover, on April 13, 1948, six months after her committee appointment ended.[16]

A more likely explanation is that the entire incident was the result of Hoover's vendetta against both Wechslers. In particular, it may have been retribution for Nancy Wechsler's role in drafting the committee's civil rights report, issued in October 1947, that criticized the FBI. Nancy Wechsler had argued that the FBI's civil rights failings should be included in the report, whereas Morris Ernst, counsel for the ACLU and a close friend of Hoover's, disagreed. "The next thing we knew the FBI had sent a dossier on Nancy to Charles Wilson who was Chairman of the Committee," James Wechsler later wrote in a memorandum to Schiff.[17] Ernst, a longtime FBI apologist who fell for Hoover's claims of being a protector of civil liberties, likely informed Hoover of Nancy Wechsler's position. It is also likely that Hoover saw a draft of the report, in which Wechsler's position prevailed and questions were raised about the FBI's performance in civil rights matters. The Bureau was criticized for investigating too few civil rights complaints, for failing to make thorough investigations, and for working too closely with local officials, who in some cases impeded investigations.[18]

The timing and content of Hoover's letter undermining Nancy Wechsler prompted James Wechsler to write an article for *Harper's Magazine* titled "How to Rid the Government of Communists," in which he attacked the loyalty program because it failed to provide honest hearings for those accused of disloyalty.[19] Shortly after Hoover sent his letter to Wilson, James Wechsler visited Nichols at the FBI to protest, pointing out several errors of fact in the letter and asserting that it was a petulant response based on Hoover's dissatisfaction with the committee's report. Nichols claimed that the FBI had been asked to compile a summary report on all members of the committee's staff. No such request or FBI acknowledgment of such a request appears in the FBI files of James or Nancy Wechsler. Ultimately, the investigation of Nancy Wechsler was far more extensive than a simple summary report or loyalty check, as Nichols suggested. Instead, Hoover ordered his agents to undertake a "very thorough" investigation of her background, and he wanted the investigative reports forwarded to him personally.[20] FBI agents in New York, Boston, Chicago, Los Angeles, and Milwaukee were involved. Given that Hoover initiated the investigation after sending the letter to Wilson and long after Wechsler had left her job with the committee, it seems clear that this was simply a case of Hoover taking advantage of the situation to try to find compromising information about a critical journalist's wife.

After his tense meeting with James Wechsler in 1947, Nichols recommended that the FBI maintain contact with the editor, who had moved to a more prominent and thus more dangerous (for the Bureau) position as editor of the *New York Post*. Tolson included a comment on the memo: "OK, but this fellow is tricky." Hoover agreed: "Wechsler is a rat & is like a corkscrew—he can't be straightened."[21]

Nichols obtained a copy of the loyalty investigation of Nancy Wechsler that had been forwarded to the committee. "I have no doubt that eventually Nancy Wechsler will probably see the reports herself," Nichols wrote to assistant director D. Milton "Mickey" Ladd, who headed the Bureau's Domestic Intelligence Division. "I just wonder if it would not be a good idea for me to call [James] Wechsler and ask him about each of the organizations which according to the Un-American Activities Committee report he has associated with. This would give him an opportunity to say yes or no and we could include this in the reports and then Wechsler would be forced to admit the care with which the Bureau approaches these loyalty cases."[22]

Nichols's approach forced Wechsler to formally document his youthful flirtation with the YCL, something his wife had done five years earlier. On June 14, 1948, Wechsler met with Nichols and dictated a statement that summarized his and his wife's three-year affiliation with the organization, along with his subsequent break with communism.[23] Furthermore, Wechsler touted his extensive record as an anticommunist reporter and editor. "I believe that the first published article in which I attacked the Communists appeared immediately after the Nazi-Soviet Pact," Wechsler told Nichols.

"Since that time I have written innumerable articles in many publications, including PM, the New York Post, the LaFollette Progressive, Harper's, and others attacking the Communists."[24]

Wechsler thought that would be the end of it, but when the Bureau began exerting pressure on Schiff in 1959 to kill the proposed series about the FBI, James and Nancy Wechsler's YCL past was unearthed. Wechsler should have known better, because his one-time YCL membership had also caused controversy in 1952. "I thought that had resolved the matter as far as the FBI was concerned and I have never had any indication from the FBI that it did not," Wechsler wrote to Schiff, who knew all about his YCL membership. "The material I gave them was not particularly sensational, as I have indicated. It just happens that those of us in the youth group were not responsible for any more dramatic activities than anti-war meetings, academic freedom fights, etc."[25]

In 1952, the *Post* published a series on gadfly columnist and broadcaster Walter Winchell, including an article documenting Winchell's devotion to Hoover. The first article in the series appeared on January 7, 1952. By January 23, the FBI had prepared an updated blind memorandum on Wechsler, complete with attached news clippings from his YCL days.[26] Winchell himself remained uncharacteristically silent as the *Post* series was published.

Meanwhile, Winchell's home publication, the *New York Journal-American* (a Hearst newspaper), was battling Wechsler on a second front. Another series of articles in the *Post* had been critical of two Hearst writers, Lee Mortimer and Jack Lait, whose book *U.S.A. Confidential* alleged that a liberal conspiracy was unfolding throughout the United States. The authors sued the *Post*, Wechsler, Schiff, and columnist Murray Kempton for libel. "It is my judgment that this book is a compilation of big lies and half-truths and double talk," Wechsler stated on the New York television program *The Author Meets the Critics* on March 27, 1952.[27] The next day, Charles McCabe, publisher of Hearst's *New York Daily Mirror*, met with Schiff and asked her to withhold any further stories on Lait and Mortimer. "He said that experienced publishers knew that it never paid one newspaper to be critical of another," Schiff wrote in a memorandum for her files. "However, he warned that if we started anything about Lait and Mortimer he would no longer be able to control the people on his newspaper and he would go ahead and print stories about me."[28] Lait and Mortimer's attorneys ultimately deposed Wechsler for the libel case, and the day after that deposition, the *Journal-American* published its retribution: "Post Editor Admits He Was Young Red.

Wechsler Ties Bared." Wechsler had never hidden his YCL past, but the *Journal-American* article was controversial and led the Grand Union supermarket chain to pressure the producers of *Starring the Editors* to drop him from the program.

A few years later, after his continuing criticism of Hoover and later McCarthy, Wechsler's admission would provide the impetus for the Wisconsin senator to investigate the *New York Post* editor. On April 12, 1953, Winchell's evening broadcast was monitored by Alan H. Belmont of the FBI, and Belmont forwarded his report to his supervisor, Ladd, the next day. Among the items covered by Winchell were a wave of strikes "paralyzing Brazil," news of a "Red school for spies" near Crestline, California, and rumors of Wechsler's impending testimony before the McCarthy committee: "Washington, D.C. The United States Senate Committee investigating Commies and strange 'Red fellows' will subpoena former executives of the Young Communist League. First to be subpoenaed is James Wechsler, editor of the New York Post."[29] Belmont's contextual comments noted that "Wechsler has been the target of Winchell in many of his broadcasts and columns."[30] Winchell had a scoop, undoubtedly from his sources on the committee. Although Wechsler had heard the rumors, he was not actually subpoenaed until eighteen hours before the hearing was scheduled on April 24.[31]

Wechsler was called to testify after an "investigation" of the State Department's International Information Administration libraries. The mission to ideologically purify the libraries of alleged communist influences was undertaken by two McCarthy committee staff members: chief counsel Roy Cohn and chief consultant David Schine. They sought to identify books in the State Department's overseas libraries that carried communist messages, the logic being that taxpayers should not be funding the distribution of revolutionary propaganda. Cohn and Schine embarked in April 1953 on a whirlwind investigative tour of Europe. "Europe laughed its head off," journalist and author Richard Rovere later wrote of the tour.[32] Soon after their return, Wechsler was subpoenaed, ostensibly because several of his early books had been discovered in the libraries.

The hearings were characterized by a vituperative McCarthy and Cohn badgering a defiant but forthcoming Wechsler. Two themes related to the issue of freedom of the press defined the hearings. First, although the hearings were predicated on an investigation of books in the State Department's international libraries, the committee could not identify which of Wechsler's books were shelved in those depositories, and scant time was spent on the books themselves. Second, the majority of the hearings involved an inquiry into Wechsler's political beliefs, his newspaper's editorial policies, his alleged communist associates, and *Post* staff. Specific questions about editorial policy related to the *Post*'s criticism of McCarthy, other congressional committees, Hoover, and the FBI. Finally, McCarthy demanded, and Wechsler eventually provided, a list of former YCL associates.

The first session of the hearings convened on April 24, 1953, at 4:10 p.m. in room 357 of the Senate Office Building. Other than McCarthy, the only other senators present were Democrats John L. McLellan of Arkansas and Henry M. "Scoop" Jackson of Washington. The hearing was not open to the public. Within just a few minutes of beginning, McCarthy had turned his attention from Wechsler's books in the State Department's international libraries to the operations of the *New York Post*, interrupting Cohn's examination abruptly and asking, "Mr. Wechsler, do you have any other people who are members of the Young Communist League, who were or are members of the Young Communist League, working for you on your newspaper?" Wechsler agreed to answer the question because, he stated, "it is a citizen's responsibility to testify before a Senate committee whether he likes the committee or not" and "because I recognize your capacity for misstatement or misinterpretation of a failure to answer." He testified that there were no communists on the staff of the *Post* at that time, but that four members of the staff, including himself, were former YCL members.[33]

Wechsler continued by introducing evidence of his anticommunist stance, such as several *Daily Worker* editorials. He read a number of short passages into the record, including one strident attack that held him responsible for having "paralyzed independent political action (among Communists)." "I am rather fond of this tribute, and it may perhaps have some bearing on your comment that I have not been active in fighting communism," Wechsler concluded.[34] He also provided endorsements of his writings from Richard M. Nixon and Louis B. Nichols, among others. Yet Wechsler was unable to shake McCarthy's theory that he had renounced communism, as ordered by Soviet authorities, so that decades later he could lead the fight against anticommunists from an "objective" position. According to McCarthy:

I know if I were head of the Communist Party and I had Jim Wechsler come to Moscow and discovered this bright man, apparently a good writer, I would say: "Mr. Wechsler, when you go back to the United

States, you will break with the Communist Party, you will make general attacks against Communism, and then you will be our ring leader in trying to attack any man who tries to hurt and dig out the specific traitors who are hurting our country."[35]

Wechsler later noted the irony of McCarthy's position, particularly that an alleged communist was considered guilty until proved innocent: "But now I can personally report that [the McCarthy committee] is also a place where the existence of proof of innocence becomes damning evidence of guilt," Wechsler wrote. "This is the way, of course, to total madness for a nation as well as for individuals."[36]

The proceedings ignored the books that had supposedly prompted the hearings in the first place. McCarthy continued to probe the editorial workings of the *Post*, particularly objecting to the newspaper's criticism of anticommunist crusaders, including several members of Congress and Hoover's FBI. McCarthy presented the *Post*'s criticism as evidence of Wechsler's undercover communism:

> I know that you have never testified in a case against a Communist. I know that none of the men that you have named here as anti-Communists have ever testified in a case against Communists. I know that they and you have been consistently and viciously attacking anyone who does testify against Communists, anyone that exposes Communists. . . . So you cannot blame the average person who questions whether you ever did break with the party.[37]

Wechsler was defiant and entered thirty-four exhibits into the record, including examples of his anticommunist writings and negative comments leveled at him in print by communists. McCarthy also pressed the *Post*'s criticism of the FBI as evidence of Wechsler's undercover communism. The chairman asked repeatedly whether the *Post* had been critical of Hoover in its editorials and then whether the *Post* had ever published anything laudatory about the director or the FBI.[38] Wechsler noted that he had a sometimes contentious but friendly relationship with the Bureau.

In fact, the FBI considered Wechsler a radical and monitored the hearings and their aftermath closely after receiving transcripts from McCarthy on May 11.[39] On May 18, 1953, Alan H. Belmont, assistant director of the Domestic Intelligence Division, prepared a summary of Wechsler's May 5 testimony for assistant director Ladd, the third most senior administrator in the FBI.[40] The four-page summary confirmed that Wechsler had been forthcoming in his 1948 interview, when he had provided a statement outlining his YCL activities. A second memorandum, summarizing Wechsler's April 24, 1953, testimony, ran seven pages.[41] Hoover's view of Wechsler mirrored McCarthy's. Although Wechsler later became one of Hoover's most outspoken critics, at the time, the *Post*'s editorials had been relatively mild, and on occasion, Wechsler had even defended the Bureau. "We do not consider any Government agency as above criticism," Wechsler told McCarthy. "We have at the same time taken very strongly the position that the charge that the FBI is a Gestapo or Fascist agency was an unfounded, unwarranted charge."[42]

The May 5 hearing focused primarily on Wechsler's associates in the YCL from 1934 to 1937. His 1948 statement to the FBI had included the names of several YCL officials, but McCarthy wanted more:

> The Chairman: Do you know the names of any of those who were with you in the Young Communist League, or have you forgotten them? Do you know the names now of any of those fellow Young Communist Leaguers?
>
> Mr. Wechsler: Sure. Do you want a long list? A short list? How do you want this?[43]

Providing that list of YCL members from the 1930s became a condition for the release of the transcript of Wechsler's testimony. He needed that transcript because he intended to ask the American Society of Newspaper Editors (ASNE) to investigate the hearings. Wechsler had fallen into McCarthy's trap, but he managed to negotiate an agreement that the list he provided would not be made public; instead, it would be turned over to the FBI.

Wechsler was recalled to appear before the committee on May 5, 1953, at which time he would "complete" his testimony by providing the list of names. Then the transcript (minus the list) would be made public. In his opening statement, Wechsler explained that his decision to comply was related to his concerns that the proceedings posed a risk to freedom of the press:

> From the moment Senator McCarthy summoned me to Washington, it has been my conviction that he has raised grave questions of freedom of the press worthy of full investigation by the American Society of Newspaper Editors. I do not propose to allow anyone to cloud that issue.

. . . I believe Senator McCarthy instituted this whole proceeding as a reprisal against a newspaper and its editor for their opposition to the methods of this committee's chairman. In short, I believe I have been called here by Senator McCarthy not because of anything I wrote or did 15 or 18 years ago—none of which I ever concealed—but because of what my newspaper has said about the committee's chairman in very recent times.[44]

Wechsler repeated that he had never been told which of his books Cohn and Schine had found objectionable during their travels. According to Cohn, it was a "practical impossibility" to determine which books were being used to promote communism. "But that is a rather crucial question, Mr. Cohn," Wechsler replied. "Two of the books I wrote when I was an anti-Communist."[45] McCarthy denied that the hearings in any way infringed on freedom of the press. "It puts me in mind of so many people screaming that their right to scream has been denied," he said. "I have not found that your right to scream has been denied at all. I have not found that your right to distort and twist the news has been interfered with since you have been here."[46]

McCarthy had Cohn and committee consultant Howard Rushmore, a journalist and former communist, take a quick look at the names provided by Wechsler. "They tell me at this point that apparently there are no names on here except names of those who have been publicly known as Communists or Young Communist Leaguers."[47] The list was not released publicly, and there is no indication in Wechsler's FBI file that it was ever turned over to the Bureau.[48] It appears that neither McCarthy nor the FBI found the list to be a useful source to identify or investigate the communist infiltration of government and society. The remainder of the lengthy second hearing focused on Wechsler's political ideology and the operations of the *Post*.

Noting that McCarthy was positioned to make further inquiries into the press, Wechsler called for an investigation by the American Society of Newspaper Editors. "I believe such a committee [appointed by the ASNE] will agree that this hearing constitutes a clear and present danger to the freedom of the press. . . . I hope the ASNE will investigate this attack promptly and speak out eloquently."[49] The response of many newspaper editors and of the ASNE committee, however, demonstrated a clear ideological division among members of the journalistic community. They could not agree on whether the issue was freedom of the press or something less serious, such as mere intimidation. Some editors and reporters, including many who objected to

Wechsler's liberalism, found little to object to in the hearings. George W. Healey of the *New Orleans Times-Picayune* told McCarthy, "It was my feeling from the beginning that the controversy between you and Mr. Wechsler should have been confined to capitol hill and to the editorial pages of the *New York Post*."[50] Joseph Lee of the *Topeka State Journal* suggested that Wechsler was being childish by pushing the inquiry: "At certain times Editor Wechsler appears silly—should one say emotionally immature?—and Senator McCarthy shows at times that even he is capable of occasional lapses into the mood of courtesy. There is ambivalence here both of personalities and issues."[51]

Others felt, as Wechsler did, that the hearings were a clear and unacceptable challenge to the press's freedom. *Editor & Publisher* cited several newspapers that had expressed support for Wechsler's position and raised concerns about freedom of the press, including *Newsday*, the *Louisville Courier-Journal*, and the *Washington Post*. The *Washington Post* declared, "Senator McCarthy has now put editors and other newspapermen on notice that criticism of him in the press may subject the writer to a summons and a star chamber grilling by the Senator's private *auto de fe*."[52] C. P. Kimball, publisher of the Blackfoot, Idaho, *Daily Bulletin*, exemplified the politically conservative, mostly western editors who supported McCarthy and opposed Wechsler, regardless of his decades-long anticommunist record. Kimball wrote in a letter to *Editor & Publisher*: "Since when does a Senatorial Committee's questioning of an upstart editor constitute intimidation of the press? What a smoke screen! A typical Commie diversionary tactic. . . . We say more power to Senator McCarthy."[53] For their part, the editors of *Editor & Publisher* played both sides of the issue, reflecting the ideological division in the journalistic community. On May 16, they seemed to side with Wechsler:

> There is no doubt in our mind that Senator Joseph R. McCarthy's examination of *New York Post* Editor James A. Wechsler before the Senate Investigations Committee was an attempt to intimidate a newspaperman for expressing editorial views with which the Senator disagrees. That Senator McCarthy obviously failed in trying to intimidate Mr. Wechsler is beside the point. . . . We think it is an abuse of his [McCarthy's] position, and a dangerous precedent, for him to use the forum of his investigating committee to accuse an editor of subservience to the Communist cause because that editor's or newspaper's writings are not to his liking.[54]

One week later, however, the editors asserted that there had been no infringement of freedom of the press in the Wechsler hearings:

> Some people seem to see an outright infringement of freedom of the press in Senator McCarthy's investigation of James Wechsler, editor of the *New York Post.* We cannot agree. There has been no interference with the right of Mr. Wechsler nor of the *Post* to write or publish what they please. . . . The threat to freedom of the press was certainly implicit in Senator McCarthy's questioning, but there was and has been no direct infringement of that freedom.[55]

ASNE president Basil L. Walters, executive editor of Knight Newspapers, assigned the investigation to the organization's Freedom of Information Committee, chaired by James Russell (J. R.) Wiggins, managing editor of the *Washington Post and Times-Herald.*[56] The eleven-member committee examined the transcript and labored for several months in an attempt to agree on a response. In August, the committee produced two reports—a compromise report reflecting what all the members agreed on, and a minority report authored by four of them. The compromise report summarized the committee's differences of opinion:

> Indeed, the disagreement ranges from the opinion that Senator Joseph McCarthy, as committee chairman, infringed [on] freedom of the press with his questions about the editorial policies of The New York Post (an opinion held by the chairman of the committee), to the contrary viewpoint that the senator's inquiries did no damage to this freedom. In between are committee members who were disturbed by the tenor of the investigation, but do not feel that this single interchange constituted a clear and present danger to freedom of the press justifying a specific challenge.[57]

The bulk of the four-page report restated the circumstances and some of the exchanges of the hearings and concluded that editors should consult their attorneys if they are called to answer before Congress for their editorial judgments.[58] Each individual editor, the report suggested, should determine the implications of the hearings for himself.[59]

The minority report was submitted by Wiggins, *Hartford (Conn.) Courant* editor Herbert Brucker, *Eugene (Ore.) Register-Guard* editor William M.

Tugman, and Eugene Pulliam, managing editor of the *Indianapolis News.*
The dissidents' report objected to the hearings on the grounds that Wechsler
had been compelled to testify about his opinions and writings as a journalist, activities that are protected by the First Amendment to the U.S. Constitution:

> Freedom of the Press in these United States, as it has been understood
> since the adoption of the Constitution, could not long survive the
> repeated exercise by Congress of unlimited inquiry into the conduct of
> newspapers. . . . Congressional interrogation, such as occurred in the
> United States Senate committee on April 24 and May 5, if frequently
> repeated, would extinguish, without the passage of a single law, that free
> and unfettered reporting of events and comment thereon upon which
> the preservation of our liberties depends, for more is comprehended in
> the term "freedom of the press" than just immunity to punitive statutes,
> it having been the intent of the founding fathers to free the press from all
> restraints and harassment by government.[60]

Wechsler stated publicly that he hoped the "conscientious and extended"
inquiry would deter McCarthy's probing of the press. "As long as McCarthy's
activities are subjected to alert, vigorous and continuing scrutiny the chance
of a repetition of this episode is clearly diminished."[61] Privately, Wechsler
complained to his friend Arthur Schlesinger Jr. about the ASNE's failure to
condemn McCarthy's inquiries. "After the initial burst of solidarity, a lot of
editors now seem determined to avoid any action that might impair the traditional conviviality of the A.S.N.E. drinking party."[62] Writing in Wechsler's
New York Post, columnist Max Lerner declared victory, decrying the committee's "balancing act" but assessing a net gain for freedom of the press.
"Newspaper editors have had for the first time to face the meaning of Mc-
Carthyism to their own freedom," Lerner wrote. "And they have begun to sit
as a court on their own freedoms and survival. Even if they have started im-
perfectly, the fact that they have started at all is the important one."[63]

St. Louis Post-Dispatch editorial page editor Robert Lasch, writing in *The
Progressive*, opined that many editors could not see the challenge to freedom
of the press because of their sympathy for McCarthy's anticommunist crusade: "As I score it, McCarthy won this engagement on points. . . . The serious aspect of the episode is that if eleven distinguished leaders of the
nation's press do not know when their rights are being violated, who

does?"[64] Elmer Davis put his disapproval of the ASNE's failure to condemn McCarthy in more literary terms: "These gentlemen ask for whom the bell tolls, and when they hear it's only for somebody down the street, then they quit worrying."[65]

Having straddled the issue in previous editorials, on this occasion, *Editor & Publisher* sided with the committee's strongly worded minority report, reprinting it and concluding, "Those are our sentiments exactly."[66]

McCarthy called for an investigation of committee chairman Wiggins, alleging that he and the *Washington Post* had "prostituted and endangered freedom of the press by constant false, vicious, intemperate attacks upon anyone who dares expose any of the undercover Communists."[67] McCarthy once again denied that his hearings had infringed on freedom of the press: "When you dig out a crooked lawyer, other lawyers do not say you are impairing the freedom of the legal profession. When you dig out a dishonest banker, other bankers don't plead injury. It seems rather ridiculous to me that there are claims of infringement of freedom of the press whenever you attempt to dig out crooks or Communists in that profession."[68]

The issue was not put to rest with the release of the ASNE reports. Editors remained sharply divided. The Wechsler case was discussed at the 1954 and 1956 ASNE conventions in Washington, D.C. At the 1954 convention, *Trenton Times* editor James Kerney Jr. addressed the issue in a session entitled "Senator McCarthy in the News." Kerney began by calling McCarthy the "worst Senator in the entire history of the United States" and chastising his colleagues for failing to rally to Wechsler's defense. "I just can't get over the idea that this Society didn't rise wrathfully the moment an editor was attacked for his editorials," Kerney said. "It seems to me that this is one of the reasons we ought to have such a society, not for these clambakes in Washington, but because we ought to have a purpose."[69] Kerney took issue with those who claimed that no infringement of freedom of the press had occurred because Wechsler was not deterred in his campaign against McCarthy. "Jim Wechsler was intimidated," Kerney said. "Now it is a fact, thank goodness, that Jim Wechsler shows no effect of the intimidation. But the effort to intimidate him was made by a United States Senator. And the real point is that the effort was made, not whether or not he was intimidated."[70]

New York Journal-American managing editor Sam Day focused his rebuttal of Kerney on McCarthy, avoiding freedom of the press entirely. "I don't ask his critics to like Senator McCarthy," Day said, while asking his colleagues to join McCarthy's anticommunist crusade.[71]

The issue continued to divide the ASNE in 1956, when it devoted another session of its convention to a larger question: "Is Congressional Investigation of the Press a Threat to Freedom?" *St. Louis Post-Dispatch* editorial page editor Irving Dillard asserted that the press's relative silence when under investigation, including the Wechsler hearings, suggested that editors have failed to speak out to protect the fundamental rights guaranteed by the Constitution. "Liberty does not disappear overnight. History shows that it is crumbled away a little at a time," Dillard said. "The process is one of erosion and the time to stop that wearing away is when it makes its first beginnings."[72] Vermont C. Royster, senior associate editor of the *Wall Street Journal*, responded to Dillard, reiterating the position of those who believed that there was no infringement of freedom of the press because there was no proof that any editor had failed to state an opinion on McCarthy as a result of the hearings. "We have a tradition in this profession that we are not even intimidated by men who march into the city room with bull-whips in their hands," Royster said. "So I don't think that the intimidation question rests with the Committee as much as with ourselves."[73]

During a question-and-answer period, Wechsler commented that his unwillingness to demonstrate in some dramatic way that he had been intimidated might have weakened his case:

> I feel in a sense I am guilty of having confused the issue because it seems perfectly clear that if I had retired to Mexico or jumped off the 15th floor of the *Post* building at the end of the McCarthy inquiry, I would have established that this was a threat to freedom of the press, and that my physical survival has been cited since then as a rather dramatic evidence that this was an inconsequential episode.[74]

Far from being intimidated into silence, Wechsler continued to criticize Hoover and the FBI between 1953 and 1959. And the FBI continued to monitor the editor, periodically updating its summary and blind memoranda on both James and Nancy Wechsler. When Wechsler's political autobiography, *The Age of Suspicion*, was published in late 1953, the FBI produced a seven-page review, highlighting any mentions of the Bureau.[75]

An anonymous tip written on Washington Press Club stationery led the FBI to review Wechsler's December 15, 1953, appearance on *Junior Press Conference* on WFIL-TV in Philadelphia. That inquiry led the FBI to conduct a name check on the program's host, Ruth Geri Hagy.[76] A 1954 appearance on the TV program *The Author Meets the Critics* pitted Wechsler against conservative icon William Buckley, who called the *New York Post* the "dirtiest newspaper in America."[77] In 1955, Wechsler appeared on a New York television program and commented that he believed domestic communists presented no clear and present danger to the nation. And in 1958, the FBI reported, Wechsler participated in a debate on a radio program where he argued that the dangers to the United States lay outside its borders, not inside.[78]

Beginning with the publication of Fred J. Cook's anti-FBI piece in *The Nation* in October 1958, Hoover's publicity men had been on the offensive. They painstakingly cast the planned *New York Post* series on the FBI as part of a "smear" campaign by communists bent on destroying the Bureau. In fact, rather than being part of a coordinated effort, the *Post* series apparently just happened to be conceived around the same time Cook's article was published.

The *Post* had frequently chafed at Hoover's power. "Dolly [Schiff] and Jimmy [Wechsler] felt the director operated more like the head of the secret police in a totalitarian state than as a civil servant in democracy," Marilyn Nissenson wrote in a biography of Schiff. "They believed he ignored civil liberties and favored his conservative political positions over the impartial search for justice."[79]

On October 22, 1958, Hoover requested an updated summary memorandum on Wechsler. Tolson's handwritten notation outlined the Bureau's conflation of Cook's 1958 article and the *New York Post*'s planned series in 1959 as a coordinated "smear campaign." "Both James & Nancy Wechsler are radicals and leftists of the most dangerous type," Tolson wrote.[80]

The FBI was relentless in its pursuit of information about the *Post*'s planned series. Months before it ran, inspector William C. Sullivan (who would later lead the Bureau's counterintelligence programs investigating the New Left) had lunch with *New York Post* Washington correspondent William V. Shannon. When asked to explain the motivation for the series, Shannon offered several: the potential for increased circulation, Wechsler's dislike of the Bureau and Hoover, and the liberal worldview of the *Post* staff. The reporters, editors, and publisher of the *Post*, Shannon said, considered themselves iconoclastic liberals. "In short, they would destroy idols of the people," Sullivan said in his memo on the meeting. "Further, as 'iconoclastic liberals,' the owners, policy makers, and writers of the *New York Post* are in a sense opponents of the religious use of images and all cherished beliefs, seeking to reduce them to the level of myths." Sullivan further reported that Shannon knew of no connection between the Cook article in *The Nation* and the proposed *Post* series. "This, of course, is highly unlikely," Sullivan wrote, maintaining that a conspiracy had been hatched, even though no evidence of any coordinated attack could be found.[81] The FBI files on the *New York Post*, James Wechsler, Fred J. Cook, Dorothy Schiff, and others contain no evidence of any collaboration to undermine Hoover in 1958 and 1959.

There was, however, a coordinated campaign to undermine Wechsler and the *Post*. That effort included Hoover and Tolson's intimidation of Eckhouse and Schiff. It also included the use of Hoover's friends in an active effort to discredit his critics. Early in 1959, *NAM News*, the house publication of the National Association of Manufacturers, offered its critique of the as-yet unpublished *Post* series:

A New York newspaper long noted for its propensity to slant and distort information concerning law enforcement against subversive organizations and individuals also is joining in the attack on Mr. Hoover and the FBI. Under the guise of "objective reporting," this newspaper has announced it will publish a series of articles concerning the FBI and its director. It begins to look as if a concerted campaign is afoot among those who always seem to deplore efforts to deal effectively with subversion and subversives to get J. Edgar Hoover's scalp and curb the activities of the agency he heads.[82]

The FBI's interest in Wechsler extended from an internal security investigation in the 1940s until Hoover's death in 1972. Truncated summaries of the Bureau's investigations of Wechsler ran eighteen pages. A selectively edited version of that document became a three-page blind memorandum that was provided to the Bureau's friends to undermine Wechsler.

Faced with a critical threat from the media, it served Hoover's purpose to combine two isolated news reports—Cook's *Nation* article and the *Post*'s series—into a coordinated conspiracy to undermine the Bureau. Creating a vast conspiracy theory drew clear lines between friends and enemies and engaged the former in an active defense of the director and the Bureau. That defense, aided behind the scenes by blind memoranda and cozy personal relationships between Hoover or his staff and key reporters, seemed credible to the public, coming as it did from "objective" news reporters and trusted media organizations. The substance of the criticism of Cook, Wechsler, and others was rarely addressed, other than to be summarily dismissed or drowned in a muddy stream of allegedly subversive motives and tenuous connections.

Hoover's friend Walter Trohan, the *Chicago Tribune*'s Washington correspondent, epitomized the attitude of Hoover's "objective" friends in the media. (In their correspondence, Hoover and Trohan addressed each other sardonically as "comrade.") In 1960, the concocted smear campaign all but complete, Trohan sent the FBI a copy of a letter he had written to Wechsler. The letter was more of a prank between Hoover and Trohan than a substantive or meaningful criticism of Wechsler. "I am sending you a copy of the story I wrote on the FBI in last Saturday's *Tribune*," Trohan wrote to the *Post* editor. "I do not do so with any idea that you will be moved by facts or truth, but so that you and your boss can play parlor pink patty-cake, patty-cake with it, if you so desire."[83]

Despite the pressure from the FBI and its surrogates, Schiff printed the Hoover series, which ran from October 5 to October 20, 1959. The strident tone of the reporting prompted Cartha D. DeLoach, Nichols's replacement as Crime Records chief, to produce a twelve-page analysis of what he called the *Post*'s "smear series." The first inaccuracy claimed by DeLoach was the *Post*'s claim that the FBI had attempted to pressure Schiff into killing the series. As was often the case, FBI officials relied on semantics to prove a point. While the *Post* stated that Hoover had a "meeting" with a *Post* advertiser, DeLoach claimed that, in reality, Hoover had spoken to the advertiser "for a brief moment." Thus, in the tortured and legalistic logic of the FBI, no pressure had been exerted.[84] DeLoach pointed out eighty-five inaccuracies in the series. Several times in his documentation of these alleged errors, DeLoach relied on the "facts" contained in Don Whitehead's *The FBI Story*, which was based solely on information provided by the FBI's Crime Records staff. In effect, DeLoach was saying that most of the *Post*'s claims were false because the FBI said they were. DeLoach's analysis further identified eighteen themes in the *Post*'s "efforts to discredit the Director and the FBI."[85] Most of these themes were direct challenges to the legitimacy of the FBI, including charges that it was a secret police agency, that it was particularly adept at public relations, and that it was supported by "various writers who parrot the FBI 'line.'"[86]

The FBI's response to potential criticism in the *New York Post* demonstrates one way the Bureau differed from other public relations practitioners. Because it was both a public relations and a law enforcement organization, the FBI was able to bring to bear both the power of its friends in the press and the coercive power of the federal government in its efforts to silence a critic.

Chapter 7

Engaging Defenders in the Press

Although journalist and author Fred J. Cook was well known to the FBI as a longtime critic, the October 1958 special issue of *The Nation* containing his critique of Bureau history came as a surprise to the agency, which was accustomed to meticulously controlling its public image. Hoover expressed his frustration in a note scrawled at the bottom of a memorandum: "I can't understand with all our alleged contacts and informants we had no inkling of Cook's article in *The Nation*."[1] In 1957, Cook's article titled "Hiss: New Perspectives on the Strangest Case of Our Time" had been published in *The Nation*, followed by his book, *The Unfinished Story of Alger Hiss*, in 1958. Both publications included criticism of the FBI's role in the Hiss case. When Cook reviewed Hoover's anticommunist tome *Masters of Deceit* for *The Nation*, FBI public relations official Milton A. Jones wrote, "Cook does not attempt to attack the facts of the book, but rather asserts that Mr. Hoover is attempting to discourage original thinking in this country."[2] In 1964, Cook expanded his 1958 *Nation* piece into a book, *The FBI Nobody Knows*, published by Macmillan.

Cook began his journalism career as a reporter for the *Asbury Park (N.J.) Press* in 1932. From 1944 to 1959, he was a rewrite man for the *New York World Telegram and Sun*, taking raw information from reporters in the field and turning it into news stories. Throughout his career, Cook was also a freelancer, focusing on crime- and dissent-related investigative reporting. It was during his work on the Hiss case that he began to consider writing about the Bureau and its director. "I began to wonder: was the FBI becoming an American Gestapo," Cook wrote in his memoirs.[3]

By the late 1950s and early 1960s, Hoover, in his third decade as director, was at the height of his fame and acclaim. His legend had been secured years earlier through the disciplined application of the Bureau's public relations template. In 1949, for example, a *Time* magazine cover incorporated all the elements of the FBI's public relations message: Hoover was the centerpiece of the image. Behind him, a large fingerprint signified scientific law enforcement. A hand, representing the ubiquitous FBI, emerged from the background to "finger" a hapless crook in the lower left corner. The story inside portrayed Hoover as a dispassionate, careful manager who was monitoring the activities of the dangerous communists who lurked (according to the Bureau) in every corner of American society.[4] In 1964, *Newsweek* perfectly captured the director's preferred image of himself and his Bureau:

> This is J. Edgar Hoover, 69, top cop, nemesis of the wicked, spy catcher extraordinary, the Inspector Javert of meticulously counted legions of Commies, crooks, kooks, desperadoes, kidnappers, and other aromatic fauna of the nation's underworld. As director of the Federal Bureau of Investigation, he is custodian to the darkest secrets of millions of Americans, great and small. He is also, beyond the shadow of a doubt, an authentic folk hero—a fiercely dedicated public servant who in 40 years of service has transformed the FBI into the most respected, feared, and incorruptible police force in U.S. history.[5]

Editors of *The Nation* understood the ramifications of publishing Cook's harsh critique of such a vaunted agency. Four months later, when *Nation* editor Carey McWilliams, himself the subject of an FBI investigation, gave a speech titled "How Free Is the Press?" at a February 1959 meeting of the East Side chapter of the New York Americans for Democratic Action, an FBI agent attended and monitored the speech. According to a transcript provided to Hoover, McWilliams criticized the press for being "afraid to approach the powerful agencies of government." The agent also reported that McWilliams said, "No criticism can be made or published of the FBI or its Director, Mr. Hoover. If you do criticize Mr. Hoover, you will have to 'duck bullets' in the form of press releases that appear to suddenly flow from widespread sources. Whenever *The Nation* printed an article critical of the FBI, they readied for a sharp attack."[6]

Another critic of the Bureau, *New York Post* editor James A. Wechsler, put it more succinctly in a 1962 article in *Progressive Magazine*, stating that future Americans will wonder why so few critical voices were raised against Hoover and the Bureau during the director's tenure. "How has the Director beaten the rap so long?" Wechsler asked.[7] The Bureau's response to Cook's criticisms provides an instructive example of how Hoover managed to beat the rap, using his fame and leveraging the power he held over compliant news reporters.

Cook's 1958 article followed incendiary comments earlier that year by Cleveland industrialist Cyrus Eaton. Appearing on ABC's *The Mike Wallace Interview* on May 4, 1958, Eaton said the FBI's importance was greatly exaggerated and compared it to the German gestapo. The FBI had "sold itself in a marvelous way," Eaton told Wallace. "But I always worry when I see a nation feel that it is coming to greatness through the activities of its policemen."[8] Eaton's critique gained traction in the media because he was one of America's elite, a wealthy industrialist who could typically be expected to support the work of Hoover and the FBI. Instead, Eaton considered the government's attack on domestic communists to be a waste of time. He urged closer relations with the Soviet Union. "No man is less a communist than I," Eaton said. "My chief interest is working to help save capitalism and all mankind from nuclear annihilation."[9]

Eaton's 1958 condemnation of the FBI as a "gestapo" drew a swift response from Hoover's friend, reactionary columnist and broadcaster Fulton Lewis Jr. Lewis railed against Eaton on his radio broadcast and received a friendly thank-you letter from Hoover.[10] Lewis expanded his criticism of Eaton in the May 7 issue of his newsletter *Exclusive*, charging that Eaton was part of a communist-inspired drive to destroy Hoover, the FBI, and the congressional internal security committees. Lewis reported Hoover's response to Eaton, which had been provided by Nichols: "Mr. Eaton is running true to character."[11] Hoover again thanked Lewis in a "Dear Fulton" letter dated May 14: "Mr. Eaton's unwarranted attack upon the FBI, and his reckless comments regarding the menace of communism are indeed classic examples of distortion of facts."[12]

Cook's 1958 article followed in the turbulent wake of Eaton's critique. Cook's piece was a detailed rebuttal of the best-selling, FBI-authorized history *The FBI: A Report to the People*, written by Pulitzer Prize–winning journalist Don Whitehead and published in 1956. Whitehead's book, which glossed over Bureau failings and closely followed the FBI's preferred tale of science, responsibility, and the steady leadership of J. Edgar Hoover, was adapted into a movie, *The FBI Story* (1959), starring James Stewart.

Cook's 1958 rebuttal relied solely on public source information, including proceedings of congressional inquiries, and it painted a menacing portrait of Hoover and the Bureau. Cook's criticism was a shot to the heart of the FBI's nearly three decade–long public relations campaign. As justification for his piece, Cook cited the comments made by Eaton (who was subpoenaed by the House Un-American Activities Committee soon after his interview with Wallace).[13] Cook's theory was that Hoover stayed safely above the battle with Eaton, encouraging others to leap to his defense. As proof, Cook cited a letter Hoover wrote to the *Chicago Tribune*'s venerable Washington correspondent Walter Trohan, thanking him for defending the FBI against "wild and irresponsible" charges.[14] Referring to the Trohan letter specifically and to the Eaton imbroglio in general, Cook asked, "Does this letter strike one as lacking in the lofty and statesmanlike tone that would accord with the noble image painted through the years on the mental retina of most Americans? If it does, perhaps one is justified in inquiring further into the complex story of J. Edgar Hoover and the FBI."[15]

Cook highlighted the FBI's failures, particularly its failure to recognize and investigate the impact of organized crime, and he countered Hoover's oft-stated assertion that the Bureau would never stoop to involve itself in politics. Perhaps most galling to Hoover (who frequently encouraged the investigation of those who criticized his character), Cook portrayed the director as a vain, headline-seeking publicity hound. "Hoover's self-portrait of Hoover as a reluctant dragon, accepted at face value by Whitehead and [journalist Jack] Alexander, might carry greater conviction if, in the subsequent years, Hoover had not exhibited such a marked disposition to resent criticism and relish praise," Cook wrote.[16]

Despite its publication in a niche magazine with a relatively small circulation, FBI officials took Cook's criticism seriously. The New York office obtained an advance copy of the article on October 14, 1958. Hoover's top adviser, associate director Clyde Tolson, responded with a note at the bottom of the accompanying memorandum: "What do our files show re Fred Cook." Hoover replied with his own note: "Let me know."[17]

There were three immediate responses once the article was identified as critical and the Bureau began to prepare a defense. First, acting on orders from Hoover and Tolson, agents in the Crime Records Division began to contact friendly reporters and politicians to spur defenders into action. Second, FBI official Milton A. Jones prepared an initial ten-page summary of the article, the start of a coordinated and extensive effort to gather information to counter the damage.[18] Third, internal memoranda began to move through the FBI bureaucracy as special agents communicated their outrage to Hoover and proposed various courses of action.

Even before the FBI had determined how to respond to the article,

Hoover characterized the criticism as part of a larger plot to discredit the Bureau. "I think we should discreetly get a line on this man and his background," Hoover wrote, adding that the article "didn't [just] 'bloom'—it is a planned literary garbage barrage against the FBI by a dedicated Hiss apologist."[19] Taking the hint, a special agent quickly categorized the article as part of a "deliberate, planned scheme" paid for by a "financial angel," presumably referring to Eaton.[20] A week later, the subject line of an FBI administrative memorandum regarding the investigation of Cook had been changed to "Smear Campaign against Director—1958."[21] In the wake of Hoover's suggestion of a conspiracy, the Bureau uncovered evidence that the *New York Post* was making inquiries, suggesting that a critical story or series of stories was in the works.[22] Indeed, that was the *Post* series published a year later, appearing from October 5 to October 20, 1959, and prompting a detailed analysis and inquiry into members of the *Post* staff (see chapter 6).

Having declared that a smear was under way, Hoover's public relations team was quick to categorize any subsequent criticism as part of some grand conspiracy intended to undermine the FBI. In March 1959, occasional Hoover friend and journalist Victor Lasky provided the FBI with a copy of an article from January's *World Marxist Review*. The article was a critical review of Hoover's 1958 anticommunist tome *Masters of Deceit*—hardly a surprising or untimely topic. In light of the Cook and Eaton attacks, however, Hoover considered it proof of the conspiracy against him. The author, John Gibbons, termed Hoover a self-styled "guardian angel, whose sole concern is love for America and Americans." Hoover quoted scripture, Gibbons claimed, to assert that truth is a weapon of the FBI. "Yet truth is precisely the one element missing from the F.B.I. arsenal, and one would need a pretty powerful microscope to discover much of it in *Masters of Deceit*."[23] Hoover's correspondence team replied to Lasky on the director's behalf, ignoring the subject of the article and casting it as further proof of a massive conspiracy: "I am not, of course, surprised to find that the 'World Marxist Review' has concerned itself with the present smear campaign against the Bureau."[24]

In an organization unwilling to quietly accept public criticism, one industrialist critic, one published article, a single negative book review, and another possible series in the works were lumped together and interpreted as an organized, communist-inspired conspiracy to smear Hoover's reputation. In fact, the criticism was characterized as an organized conspiracy that sought the overthrow of the American government, starting with the director of the FBI. George A. Nease, whose memorandum kicked off the conspiracy theory inside the Bureau, offered the opinion that any attack on Hoover was, in fact, "an attack on the country."[25]

The Bureau's public relations staff was quick to answer Cook's broadside. Three days before the article was published, assistant director Alan H. Belmont urged Hoover to direct his Crime Records staff to contact reporters and "suggest that they take it upon themselves to challenge Cook publicly."[26] Hoover noted, "This would be good."[27] The first journalist contacted was the Bureau's authorized biographer, Don Whitehead, who received a copy of Cook's article along with a letter warning of the coordinated smear campaign. "If I can help to scotch any such campaign of slander—please let me know," Whitehead wrote.[28] Hoover's response to Whitehead suggests the level of alarm and paranoia at the FBI's Washington headquarters: "In your typical manner you lost no time in rallying to our support. . . . As you surmised, this attack by 'The Nation' is obviously the opening burst of a well-planned smear campaign against the FBI," Hoover wrote (apparently forgetting that his own people had planted the idea of a smear campaign; Whitehead hadn't "surmised" it himself). "Apparently, left-wing apologists who have realized some advances on other levels in recent months have chosen us as their next objective. It reeks of innuendo and falsehoods . . . and there is more to come." Then Hoover made his personal pitch for the reporter to come to the Bureau's defense: "Our desire is that the American public may see this whole matter in its proper perspective without being duped by these malicious forays by Cook and others of his ilk. I know we can rely on your assistance in this regard."[29]

Another reporter Hoover relied on to provide the public with the FBI's preferred perspective was *Chicago Tribune* Washington correspondent Walter Trohan. Despite authoring a slightly critical feature on Hoover in 1936, Trohan was one of Hoover's favorite and most trusted reporters, and he was one of the first people contacted after the FBI discovered that publication of Cook's article was imminent. "We have tried to get Walter Trohan but he is out of Washington but will be back later this week and I will follow on this matter," Nease wrote to Tolson.[30] Trohan, known as the "dean" of Washington reporters during his tenure, has characterized his relationship with Hoover and Nichols as very close. "He did some great things for newspapermen," Trohan said of Hoover in 2000. "He broke stories and gave them to them. He had kind of 'hired' some reporters to write good things about the FBI. He never offered me a dime, however. [But] I must say Lou Nichols fixed me up with information."[31] Trohan's description closely matches Leo

Rosten's 1937 portrayal of "news coloring and news suppression" based on personal relationships.[32] Trohan shared Hoover's worldview and thus became an uncritical yet, to the public, credible stenographer of FBI power.

By October 30, Nease had spoken to Trohan, who was traveling the country covering the 1960 presidential election campaign. According to Nease, "Trohan felt there definitely must be money being supplied for 'The Nation' to carry on an attack like the Cook article as the magazine has practically no advertising, and he feels that it could be financed by Cyrus Eaton if not by other communist apologists."[33] In fact, two weeks earlier, Hoover had urged Nease to explore the possibility that communists were financing *The Nation* and, in any case, to spread that rumor. "Innuendo of this type would completely destroy 'The Nation' as an allegedly independent and impartial publication," Hoover wrote.[34]

A *Washington Star* reporter (whose name was withheld in the files) agreed with Trohan and Hoover, claiming, "Cook is certainly following the Communist Party line."[35] A *New York Times* reporter (name withheld) speculated that Cook was a dupe employed by wily communists to further their cause. According to the reporter, Cook "is definitely not known as an outstanding crime reporter and, as a matter of fact, is not too well known in this particular field."[36] One of Cook's colleagues at the *New York World-Telegram* was contacted and described Cook as a "sensationalist," adding that he or she "could understand the way we [the Bureau] felt."[37]

Other reporters and editors offered more than mere opinions and advice. One editor, whose name was redacted in the FBI file, reported that his publication would "devote several pages to this article and Fred J. Cook."[38] A *San Francisco Chronicle* employee "volunteered that he would be very happy to use all the resources at his command to combat this attack on the FBI."[39] *The Tidings*, a Catholic newspaper based in Los Angeles, published a defense of the Bureau and Hoover on October 24, 1958, headlined "Ten-Part Smear Bespatters FBI." George N. Kramer's article described Cook's study as a "personal attack" on Hoover, "couched in distortion, innuendo, suggestion and half truth." Kramer further bemoaned the fact that "there is probably not one actionable libelous statement in the entire 60 pages."[40] In the reliably pro-Hoover *American Legion Firing Line*, editors likewise defended the Bureau: "A 'smear attack' reminiscent of the dastardly campaign waged in 1940 by the Communist Party, is once again being launched against J. Edgar Hoover. . . . Our thought is why not leave the hard-working, efficient FBI alone? The FBI is and always has been fully responsible to Congress and the people for its actions."[41] Nationally syndicated columnist George Sokolsky, another friend of the Bureau, devoted his radio broadcast and two columns (November 4 and November 20, 1958) to a vigorous defense of Hoover and the FBI. "The FBI is a subordinate organization of limited power," Sokolsky wrote, parroting a line favored by Hoover. "It is a division of the Department of Justice and takes its instructions from the Attorney General."[42] Hoover was sufficiently pleased with the column that he wrote to Sokolsky, "as long as there are thoughtful men such as you who are willing to keep the matter in perspective, we have no need for concern." He signed the letter "Edgar."[43]

In his November 20 column, Sokolsky linked Cook's article, a year-old report in the *Daily Worker*, and the in-the-works *New York Post* series into a coordinated effort to smear Hoover. "Certainly anyone may criticize any public official and many are deserving of criticism," Sokolsky wrote. "But the persistent attack upon J. Edgar Hoover and the FBI, emanating from the same quarters over a period of years, looks like revenge."[44] Hoover thanked Sokolsky for adding the communist newspaper the *Daily Worker* to the conspiracy: "Your devastating exposure will be a major setback to their efforts, and all of us are deeply grateful."[45]

Controversial conservative broadcaster John T. Flynn was more direct. In his November 30 nationally syndicated radio program, Flynn simply declared that Cook and the entire *Post* staff were communists.[46]

Nationally syndicated broadcaster and columnist Fulton Lewis Jr., one of the most influential journalists in the country, was among Hoover's most vocal defenders following the publication of Cook's article. FBI Crime Records staff worked with Lewis and his research assistant to produce a column that was published on December 13. Once again, in thanking his friend, Hoover linked the smear of the FBI and the overthrow of the U.S. government: "Anyone privileged to read your words should be convinced that the current smear campaign against us is nothing more than another effort by the enemies of democracy to destroy the faith and trust which American people have in this Bureau," Hoover wrote. "Your forceful column will contribute materially to spreading the truth which, after all, is the only defense we need against this smear attempt."[47]

Many of these defenders were simply fans of the FBI and Hoover, and some likely acted without any urging from the Bureau. Others were spurred to action by Nichols and the Crime Records staff. The FBI turned to two Pulitzer Prize winners for its active defense. As noted earlier, Whitehead (who won Pulitzers in 1951 and 1953) was sent a copy of Cook's article, and although he complained to Hoover about its "vicious distortion," he did not produce a nationally published response.[48] Edward J. Mowery, a 1953 Pulitzer honoree, was also sent a copy of Cook's article, along with information to produce a series of his own. With the help of Bureau publicists, Mowery authored a nine-part series rebutting Cook that was published in February 1959. Mowery's articles were entered into the *Congressional Record* and republished by the Government Printing Office as a brochure titled *Efforts of the Communist Conspiracy to Discredit the Federal Bureau of Investigation and Its Director*.[49] Editors of *The Nation* objected to the republication of Mowery's series at taxpayer expense. "It is not every day that a series of newspaper articles is reprinted as a pamphlet at public expense by a government agency," they wrote. "Frankly, it had never occurred to us to submit Mr. Cook's article to the Superintendent of Documents for publication; we are now happy to do so."[50] Ever vigilant, the FBI was prepared to respond if the superintendent of documents took the bait. "We will, of course, be on the lookout for any move by 'The Nation' to have the article made a Selected Publication," a Crime Records official wrote.[51]

The sweeping nature and sudden appearance of Mowery's rebuttal of Cook, along with its publication by the government, demonstrate how far Hoover's friends in the media and Congress would go to provide the FBI with an authoritative, "objective" defense. On October 27, an aide to Senator Charles Potter (R-Mich.) pledged, in the context of a discussion of the Cook article, that his boss "would render any service to the Bureau."[52] Senator John Butler (R-Md.) stated publicly that he intended to convene hearings to investigate *The Nation*.[53] Two congressmen offered remarks on the floor of the House of Representatives defending the Bureau. On January 15, 1959, Gordon H. Scherer (R-Ohio) spoke of a "communist-inspired smear campaign" and "patterned campaign of vilification" against Hoover. Scherer's remarks mirrored (in some cases word for word) the Bureau's internal discussions and blind memoranda on *The Nation*'s staff members. Scherer mentioned the in-the-works *New York Post* series as well as similar plans by the Emergency Civil Liberties Committee, an allegedly subversive group much discussed in the FBI's file on *The Nation*.[54] One week later, Prince H. Preston Jr. (D-Ga.) spoke in startlingly similar terms of the smear campaign and defended Hoover against Cook, the Emergency Civil Liberties Committee, and the editors of *The Nation*: "Now is the time for all of us to rally to the aid of a man, who thank God, has devoted his entire life to his country, and to an organization whose silent, efficient work allows us to sleep better at night—J. Edgar Hoover." Both Preston and Scherer quoted the American Legion's national commander Preston J. Moore, a longtime Hoover defender. A few weeks earlier, Moore had spoken in Hoover's defense: "We hope that the American press, which, with a few tragic exceptions, is commendably patriotic, will continue to give J. Edgar Hoover and the FBI their necessary and persuasive editorial vote of confidence."[55]

Hoover knew he could count on the Bureau's adjuncts in the press and in Congress to come to his aid. Trohan, Mowery, Scherer, Preston, and many others shared a common image of the FBI. They also profited professionally from their association with the Bureau, in the form of access to Hoover and authorized tales of his agency's popular exploits. These defenders provided Hoover with a public and objective defense against the criticisms in Cook's article. Behind the public response, however, the FBI continued its investigation of Cook.

In the weeks after the publication of Cook's article, special agents in Washington and around the country continued to investigate the author and *The Nation*. Within hours after the FBI received Cook's article, assistant director Quinn Tamm notified Hoover that all the supervisors in the Training and Inspection Division had been instructed to read and review the article for errors.[56] Tamm's group later offered a list of twelve charges made by Cook that they believed should be refuted, along with a series of questions reporters were likely to ask in relation to the article.[57] The New York office found a single typographical error and a series of "conclusions" drawn by Cook that the FBI disputed.[58] The fact-checking continued for more than two months, and on December 24, assistant director William C. Sullivan provided an interim report, followed by a more complete report on December 30.[59]

As the article was painstakingly deconstructed, the Bureau systematically monitored public feedback. No response was too insignificant to be cataloged, analyzed, and reported. Nease reported that a news vendor in New York was overheard berating a woman who had purchased a copy of *The Nation*. "It would appear that even the news vendors are very much unimpressed with *The Nation*," Nease observed.[60] Another agent reported a conversation between two men on a streetcar: "They were both of the opinion that the article is an attack upon the Bureau and that the Bureau is an effective and good organization."[61] Writers of letters to the editor supporting Cook's critique were name-checked by the FBI. On November 6, 1958, Jones provided Nease with a summary of the letters, along with brief biographies of the authors.[62]

As the FBI monitored responses to the article, Cook and *The Nation* were investigated most thoroughly and intrusively. On October 16, Nease reported to Tolson that the Bureau was looking into Cook's finances.[63] A few days later, an investigative summary, citing income figures obtained from the IRS, showed that Cook's work for *The Nation* had resulted in no notable increase in his annual income.[64] The same eight-page summary included a page of personal information about Cook, all of which was redacted under provisions of the Privacy Act. *The Nation* file included six such pages of personal information uncovered in the FBI's investigation of Cook. Cook later learned that the FBI had been working furiously to find communist connections in his background. A former assistant U.S. attorney later told Cook that FBI agents had interviewed him, and when he said he had no information, the agents "pounded their fists on the table and accused [the former U.S. attorney] of covering up" for Cook. "We know he's a communist. We know that," the agents reportedly said.[65] Actually, according to FBI records, the Bureau knew full well that Cook was not a communist. On October 27, 1958, Nease wrote to Tolson: "There is no indication that Cook personally has any political leaning himself."[66] The Bureau already had an extensive file covering *The Nation*, its editors, and its contributors. In 1943, for example, Bureau researchers had produced a 554-page report documenting the history of *The Nation* and *The New Republic* and both publications' staffs.[67]

The investigation quickly moved beyond *The Nation* and other similar publications. In response to Hoover's concerns about articles that were "severely and unfairly discrediting our American way of life," investigative staff produced the "Molders of Public Opinion" memorandum on March 18, 1959. Oddly enough, Cook didn't make the list of forty suspect journalists. Andrew Tully of Scripps-Howard's Washington bureau, who would later write an authorized book on the FBI, told special agent R. R. Roach that Cook was not a respected reporter.[68] William Shannon, a former *New York Post* reporter who then worked for the *New York Times*, told Sullivan that the critical articles were simply the products of iconoclastic liberals who had long before declared their opposition to the FBI.[69]

In his October 17, 1958, memorandum, Roach suggested an organized counterintelligence program to refute those iconoclasts by directly addressing the audience for their writings:

A program might be developed and aimed not at the man in the street, but to the intellectuals such as teachers, college professors, writers, etc. If we could get across to them the true picture of the Bureau, what its activities actually are, and the fact that the Bureau is not a threat to individual liberties, but is actually one of the last defenses left to personal liberties, articles such as the current one would have little, if any effect.[70]

Hoover's response chillingly foreshadowed the later excesses of the FBI's counterintelligence program (COINTELPRO) to infiltrate and sabotage the New Left. "Sullivan is already embarked on such a program," Hoover wrote. "It can be intensified."[71] With that line, Hoover revealed that within the FBI, there was no distinction between public relations, including the monitoring of negative stories, and the active sabotage of dissenting individuals and organizations that characterized COINTELPRO. Hoover's own teleological ethical code—that is, the end justifies the means—must have made it clear to his investigators and staff that the goal of muting criticism from the Left justified whatever efforts might be required.

The FBI's investigation of the 1958 Cook article concluded on April 15, 1959, with a meeting of Hoover's Executive Conference, chaired by Tolson. The Executive Conference often made policy and public relations recommendations to Hoover. At the April 15 meeting, Hoover's top aides reported that the analysis of Cook's article was voluminous, so its usefulness to a friendly reporter would be limited. Executives noted that the Mowery series, which answered major criticisms by presenting Bureau dogma, had become a U.S. Senate publication and was available as reference material should the smear continue. Finally, conferees questioned the wisdom of raising the issues in the article six months after the fact, giving new life to the allegations. "The conference unanimously felt that the disadvantages outweighed the advantage of having closer contact with some of our friendly news sources."[72]

Nonetheless, the monitoring of Cook continued and intensified a few years later when he turned his article into a book-length indictment of the FBI's legitimacy. By 1960, FBI summaries of Cook's background were referring to him as a "discredited" journalist and "unprincipled critic of the FBI."[73] Summarizing a thirteen-page review of "Gambling, Inc.," an article written by Cook that appeared in the October 22, 1960, issue of *The Nation*, Crime Records chief Cartha DeLoach told his superiors, "Cook's blatant disregard for truth and his animosity toward the FBI are well-documented and undeniable facts."[74] Whenever Cook published an article, DeLoach dutifully reviewed it for any mention of the FBI and did a Bureau-centric fact check.

In February 1964, though, DeLoach learned that Cook had a critical book about the FBI in the works. Jack Woolridge, managing editor of *Nation's Business*, met DeLoach for lunch and slipped him a copy of a Macmillan brochure listing upcoming books. Cook's book, *The FBI Nobody Knows*, was listed as a June 1964 release. DeLoach reported: "[Woolridge] said that at their editorial conference this morning Cook's new book came up and it was their unanimous opinion that they should immediately get in touch with the FBI and offer to do anything possible to make Cook's attack ineffective."[75] Woolridge and his colleagues planned to produce a lengthy, in-depth, positive article about the FBI and release it the same day as Cook's book. "They would not mention Cook or dignify his irresponsible allegations but would point out the Bureau's extensive accomplishments particularly in sensitive areas such as security and espionage investigations, civil rights matters, employment of minority group members, its historical record of running a 'tight business operation,' the Director's reluctance to take on any added powers, etc."[76]

A few days later, Macmillan wrote and asked for permission to reprint a 300-word quote from Don Whitehead's authorized FBI history in Cook's book.[77] That request, which was denied, led DeLoach to approach a longtime Bureau friend: former *Liberty* magazine editor Sumner "Blos" Blossom, then serving as president of Crowell-Collier Publishing, the parent company of Macmillan. Blossom spoke to his boss at Crowell-Collier, who promised to send page proofs to the FBI. Tolson thought "we should thank him when he sends the page proofs," but DeLoach disagreed and listed four reasons not to thank the sender.[78] First, Macmillan had "a lot of gall" to publish a book by Cook, "a journalistic prostitute," DeLoach wrote. Second, Macmillan had contracted for the book two years earlier and hadn't notified the Bureau. Third, it took a request from Blossom to get the proofs sent. Finally, the proofs weren't sent by the CEO himself but by "some underling." DeLoach ended with a recommendation: "After this book is fully reviewed, we might well want to 'blast' the publishing firm in addition to blasting Cook."[79]

Step one in responding to the book was a quick review by the Crime Records Division. Milton A. Jones provided that on April 24, terming the book "sewage" and promising a more thorough report. Generally, Jones highlighted Cook's claims that Hoover was contemptuous of the liberal press, that there was a dearth of African American and Jewish special agents in the Bureau, and that Hoover always accused his critics of being communists.[80] Within the self-reverential culture of Hoover's FBI, Cook's criticisms were considered extremely unfair. Any cursory review of FBI history today, of course, would find them all to be true.

Jones turned in his 101-page review of the 436-page book on June 11, 1964. "As a result of Cook's overeagerness to criticize, his ignorance of the truth, his ineptness or laziness as a researcher and his basic dishonesty, the book is largely a compilation of inaccuracies and distortions," Jones wrote.[81] Armed with a point-by-point refutation of the book, albeit based on the FBI's self-reverential logic, Jones called a Macmillan representative to apply pressure in the hope of delaying or scrapping the book.[82] The publisher's representative told Jones he would call an editors' conference to discuss the FBI's position. On July 23, Jones was informed that only two small changes would be made, and the book would be released, as scheduled, for mail-in sales on July 31, with copies in bookstores nationally on September 14. Jones reported that, according to Blossom, the decision to publish the book was based on Macmillan's investment, which would be lost if the book were withdrawn.[83]

Having failed to derail the publication of Cook's book, the FBI turned to its media friends to criticize it. According to the Miami SAC, a professor who reviewed books for the *Miami News* (his name was redacted from FBI files) promised to "blast" the book as soon as it became available in bookstores: "He said he wants the Bureau to know he is still loyal to the Bureau and the Director and that he's going to refute the allegations and put the Bureau's best foot forward."[84] *Washington Star* reporter Jerry O'Leary Jr. reported to DeLoach that *Star* editors planned to "give very little play to the book for the reason that any excessive comment would perhaps call attention to the book, increase sales and only whet readers' interests."[85] O'Leary's own review, headlined "Nobody Knows FBI Pictured in This Book," appeared two days later. "Nobody knows the FBI depicted in this attack on the motives and methods of J. Edgar Hoover and the employees of his efficient, dedicated bureau, because it doesn't exist that way at all," O'Leary wrote.[86] Bob Koenig of the *Deseret News and Telegram* in Salt Lake City wrote a straight review of the book, prompting the Bureau to conclude that Koenig had been "taken in" by Cook's lies.[87]

Cook's appearance on a New York radio program was monitored and summarized. The FBI official who authored a memo reviewing the broadcast pointed out, without noting the irony, that among the "lies" was Cook's charge that the FBI monitored and retaliated against critics.[88] In the days that followed, the FBI monitored or obtained tape recordings of Cook's radio appearances in Philadelphia and Boston and on the CBS radio network.[89]

Retaliation, though, was left to the news media itself, with FBI help. Miami radio host Alan Courtney, for example, broadcast a forty-five-minute diatribe against Cook on December 16, 1964. The Miami SAC reported that Courtney "obviously had performed a most thorough research job in preparing his monologue." Courtney told listeners, in language very similar to the FBI's blind memorandum, that Cook "was a good friend of Alger Hiss. Cook's latest vilification against the FBI in his book, 'The FBI Nobody Knows,' has relied heavily on other discredited sources."[90]

Not all "friends" turned out to be so friendly in their efforts to come to the Bureau's defense. On November 11, 1964, John McMullan, news director for Knight Newspapers in Detroit, Akron, Miami, and Charlotte, decried the "unfair" criticism leveled by Cook and asked Hoover for help with a series of articles countering the criticism. "The statements of people like Fred J. Cook in his book, 'The FBI Nobody Knows,' should not go unchallenged if they are untrue," McMullan wrote. "I am preparing a series of articles which I hope will put the situation in true perspective."[91] A review of the Bureau's files for information about McMullan, the *Miami Herald* (Hoover was on a first-name basis with the editor), and Knight newspapers concluded, "It would appear this would be a splendid opportunity to bring some of the Bureau's accomplishments to the attention of a large number of individuals through the media of the Knight chain and also combat some of the unfair criticism the FBI has recently received."[92]

When McMullan was not given an opportunity to interview Hoover, however, he forwarded a series of critical questions. McMullan also complained that whereas he had been allowed to interview the director as a high school editor in 1937, he was not given the same opportunity as a Washington correspondent. "The eight questions submitted by McMullan indicate that he has taken a hostile attitude toward the Bureau," Jones reported to DeLoach. "His questions are based on false assumptions and are replete with snide innuendos and criticism of the Director and the Bureau."[93] McMullan asked whether, given the Bureau's immense growth over the decades, standards for selecting agents had been lowered. He also mentioned that the FBI had been accused of leaking confidential information. Jones reported that one question was particularly "vicious," noting that some critics were worried that Hoover had become involved in politics. "McMullan's questions are insolent and loaded to place the Bureau in the worst light possible," Jones reported. In a handwritten note, Hoover added: "Cook couldn't have done a better smear on us."[94]

Typically, the FBI could expect friendly coverage from Armed Forces Radio, but when Cook's book was positively reviewed on the radio service, the Bureau was blindsided. The military leaders of Armed Forces Radio were apologetic and promised never to allow criticism of the FBI on the airwaves again. "They must be a pretty sloppy outfit," Hoover wrote, "with too much overhead & too many super executives who don't know what goes on."[95]

The Bureau continued to monitor Cook. In 1965, Jones reviewed Cook's article "The FBI and Organized Crime," which appeared in the alternative newsmagazine *Ramparts*. The article was a "typical Cook production," Jones wrote, "full of snide innuendoes, distortions and outright lies." The magazine included a "snide caricature" of Hoover on the cover, and the article was illustrated with photographs of old movies, including the Keystone Kops.[96] That same year, Jones reviewed another Cook article on the IRS and the Post Office Department that appeared in *The Nation*.

When it pressed every angle to investigate and discredit Cook (a relatively little-known journalist), the FBI demonstrated its increasing alarm over challenges to its legitimacy. Hoover had removed nearly all pockets of dissent within his own organization, creating an FBI that in most ways mirrored his own paranoia. The Bureau's response was calculated not only to discredit Cook and *The Nation* but also to engage its defenders in the reification of the FBI's preferred self-image. By declaring a "smear campaign" based on the statements and writings of a handful of marginal critics, the FBI challenged its defenders to act on the Bureau's behalf. The Bureau's public relations strategy was to engage its friends as adjunct agents, leveraging the surfeit of power the FBI held in the reporter-source relationship. Cook's attack on Hoover and the FBI became a personal attack on those journalists who were friends of the Bureau. The FBI's media friends had become, in the 1940s and 1950s, potent allies who willingly attacked Bureau critics and peddled the Collier-Cooper narrative to massive audiences. The FBI controlled its friends by providing them access to information and to "personal" relationships with Hoover, maintained through volumes of correspondence.

Chapter 8

Corresponding with Friends in the Press

The January 1955 edition of the *American Magazine* included a series of letters to the editor commenting on an October 1954 article, "The Communists Are after Our Minds." One of those letters caught the eye of an FBI public relations official, Milton A. Jones, in Washington. "Thank God that a man like J. Edgar Hoover is the head of the FBI," John P. Foster of Topeka, Kansas, wrote. "He is our greatest bulwark against the insidious Communist menace that is casting a shadow over this great land of ours."[1]

Ever watchful for published opinions about the FBI, Jones highlighted Foster's comments in a memorandum to his boss, Louis B. Nichols, head of the FBI's Crime Records Division and its top public relations official. "It is believed that Foster's letter is the only one which would merit a letter from the Director thanking him for commendatory remarks," Jones wrote. "We have no address for Foster—the current Topeka, Kansas, directory reflects no listing of his name—however it is believed that an address could be obtained through Sumner Blossom, editor of *American Magazine*."[2]

Blossom was a friend of the FBI, included on its "special correspondents" list. In addition, Blossom was described in Bureau documents as a "close personal friend" of Hoover. Nichols contacted the editor, addressed in FBI correspondence as "Blos," and requested Foster's mailing address. Blossom replied:

Now and then in the Letters column, when we want to make a specific point in connection with a published article which no one of our correspondents has made as directly or pointedly as we like, I drag out old "John P." and let him say his say. So I guess you will have to tell Edgar that I am "John P." or at least that the sentiments which "John P." expressed are mine.[3]

American Magazine *editor Sumner Blossom (center) with Hoover (left) and Courtney Ryley Cooper (right). (National Archives at College Park, Record Group 65, Series H, Box 2, Folder 125, #2)*

Nichols enjoyed Blossom's breach of journalistic ethics, replying over Hoover's signature that he could fully appreciate the excellence of the letter from the "old master." Blossom could be comfortable knowing, the letter said, that "there will be no investigation of John P. Foster."[4]

In an era before e-mail existed and when fax machines were uncommon, it is not surprising that a nationwide organization like the FBI would employ correspondence as a tool of public relations. The use of personal letters that correspondents were often led to believe had been authored by Hoover himself, though, demonstrates the agency's understanding and strategic application of its iconic power. Throughout Hoover's tenure, both personal letters and more institutional mailings became a primary public relations tactic employed to build and maintain relationships with key opinion shapers inside and outside the news media. Inclusion on the FBI's mailing lists and on Hoover's short list of "personal" correspondents identified recipients as friends of the Bureau.

The typical journalist-friend of the FBI was a reporter or editor of significance in his or her community or region or, better yet, nationally. Hoover's friends in the media were likely to be in sync with the director on issues such as communism and wiretapping, and they shared the presumption that the FBI and America could do no wrong. Many journalists with whom the FBI maintained friendships over time were willing to compromise their journalistic ethics on behalf of the Bureau. For example, many of Hoover's friends in the news media were willing to have their stories about the FBI edited by Crime Records staff before publication. Others, like labor reporter Victor Riesel, became confidential informants, naming their allegedly subversive colleagues. Still others essentially became adjunct FBI agents, providing special services for the Bureau and using their status as journalists to gather information in situations in which special agents could not make inquiries.

The director knew he could count on his friends in the media to provide an "objective" defense against his critics, just as they could be relied on to trumpet the Bureau's preferred narrative of science, responsibility, and Hoover in their broadcasts and news columns. The journalists chosen for special status knew, of course, that they could lose their access in an instant if they published a single word the Bureau found objectionable. Just as Hoover did not tolerate dissent within the Bureau, his journalist-friends were expected to adhere to the FBI line.

Two sets of FBI friends are easily identifiable in the files. First, there are those who, though reliable supporters of the Bureau, were not singled out as Hoover's friends. At any given time, the Bureau's public relations mailing lists contained hundreds of names of supporters across the country who received frequent FBI mailings. For instance, Hoover forwarded the annual uniform crime reports, crime bulletins, and other reports to people and institutions included on that list. Their letters to the FBI often prompted a polite but businesslike response from the Bureau over Hoover's signature.

A second group, however, was more carefully cultivated. Their "personal" relationships were built and maintained largely through friendly correspondence with Hoover that was actually authored by the Crime Records correspondence team. Mountains of personal letters poured forth from Hoover's staff, bearing the director's signature; the actual author was identified by his initials on the original, filed copy. The files of journalists favored as friends are filled with letters covering everything from congratulations on awards to condolences after losses, from gossipy and friendly chatter to confidential information about their organizations. Now and then, the reclusive Hoover would agree to meet with one of his media friends for a photograph or a brief chat, but for the most part, their relationships were created and maintained through the personal correspondence produced by the Bureau's letter writers.

Beginning in the 1930s, Crime Records included a five-agent Correspondence Unit that churned out thousands of such letters.[5] In his memoirs, disgruntled former assistant director William C. Sullivan derisively labeled the FBI the "greatest letter writing bureau in the history of the United States. Letters went by the thousands to the Jaycees, the newspaper editors, the movers and shakers so carefully cultivated as FBI contacts by our agents in the field."[6]

Hoover's closest correspondents were carefully selected from individuals who initiated contact with the FBI, held influential positions, and were considered "friendly." Correspondents were typically placed on one or more mailing lists: the special correspondents list included seventy-five journalists in 1954; a special service contacts list included a few journalists willing to surreptitiously gather information for the Bureau; and the SAC contact list contained the names of prominent individuals, including journalists, with whom the SACs in offices around the country were instructed to maintain frequent contact.[7] In addition, the FBI maintained its "do not contact" list of critical journalists and those thought to have subversive connections.[8] As documented earlier, those journalists considered most dangerous were included on various custodial detention lists maintained by the Bureau beginning in the 1930s.

Hoover rarely met with journalists. So seldom did he host reporters in his office that when he did, it was usually front-page news around the country. That limited personal contact with journalists held true even with his "friends" in the media. Although he carried on faux personal correspondences with dozens of reporters, editors, and publishers, including many pen-pal relationships that lasted for years, in most cases, Hoover met them in person only briefly and only a handful of times, if at all. However, those correspondents who were favored with FBI "interesting case" files and with personal attention from other Bureau officials came to believe that they were very much a part of Hoover's inner circle. In exchange for Hoover's interest in them, his pen pals rendered a variety of services to the FBI, publishing laudatory articles, providing access to information, and staging a spirited defense of the Bureau when asked to do so—and sometimes before being asked.[9] Some journalists even became quasi–undercover FBI agents, obtaining information in situations in which Bureau personnel could devise no suitable pretext to do so. In general, the media friends Hoover cultivated through correspondence provide an instructive example of how the FBI's position of power in reporter-source relationships could ultimately result in laudatory and even defensive coverage of the Bureau.

Several of the FBI's friends in the media stand out as particularly noteworthy. *Reader's Digest* editor Fulton Oursler provided the FBI with access to the pages of the most widely read periodical of the mid-twentieth century in the 1940s and 1950s. Memphis newsman Jack Carley became an important southern source of information and a defender of the FBI during the turbulent 1950s and 1960s. Scripps-Howard publisher Roy Wilson Howard enjoyed a cordial correspondence with Hoover. *Chicago Tribune* Washington bureau chief Walter Trohan so completely internalized the FBI's public relations narrative that he rarely had to be asked to defend Hoover and the Bureau against critics during their more than thirty-year relationship.

Hoover's first friend in the news media was also the cocreator of the Bureau's preferred narrative about itself. Between 1933 and 1940, Hoover developed a working relationship with journalist and author Courtney Ryley Cooper that resulted in two dozen magazine articles, three books, and four motion pictures.[10] Cooper's FBI file, totaling more than 4,000 pages, chronicles the development of that relationship and exemplifies the early stages of the FBI's use of personal correspondence to build beneficial relationships with strategically important individuals.

Cooper's correspondence with Hoover was informal and chatty, featuring unpretentious phrasing and always ending with, "Samezever [same as ever], Ryley." Hoover's early letters to Cooper were businesslike, even brusque, beginning with "Dear Mr. Cooper" and ending with "Cordially yours." By September 1933, Hoover's letter-writing crew, led in those early days by his top assistant Clyde Tolson, was greeting Cooper as "Ryley" and including more

*Cooper sent this personal photograph of himself with his dogs, "The 4 Barx Brothers,"
to Hoover and Tolson in 1938, indicating the friendly nature of their relationship.
(National Archives at College Park, Record Group 65, Series H, Box 7, Folder 9, #37)*

personal and contextual details.[11] A year later, Hoover's letters (authored by
Tolson) addressed Cooper as "My dear Ryley."[12] By October 1934, the correspondence became even more personal: one of Hoover's ghostwritten letters
included a health update on his close confidant Tolson (the letter's author):
"Clyde has returned to the office and is feeling much better."[13]

As Hoover's collaboration with Cooper became more substantive, the FBI
provided its "dear Ryley" with more and more material, edited his stories before publication, and gave him several tours of the Bureau.[14] Tolson's letters,
signed by Hoover, began asking about Cooper's wife, Gen, and, on behalf of
Hoover, declined invitations to visit the Coopers at their vacation home.[15]
Gen Cooper even struck up her own correspondence with Hoover.[16] For his
part, Cooper began referring to Hoover as "Edgar," and in one very informal
letter, he casually described renovations at his Florida home: "by about June
we should have a place to lure the Gstring men for some feeshin.'"[17]

The character of Hoover's letters to Cooper became dramatically more intimate when Nichols took over authorship of the correspondence. On October 31, 1938, for example, Cooper wrote that he and his wife had added three puppies to their household, bringing their total to four.[18] "I enjoyed very much reading of the birthday presents which Gen and you bought yourselves and undoubtedly the name 'Four Barx Brothers,' is quite appropriate," Nichols wrote on Hoover's behalf.[19] Throughout the 1930s, Hoover's correspondence with Cooper reflected the success of their collaboration. Cooper's value to Hoover as a coauthor, ghostwriter, and public relations adviser grew throughout the decade, mirroring Hoover's rise to public prominence.[20] Their exchanges were always cheerful and businesslike. They corresponded as close friends, although Cooper's file indicates that he and Hoover met in person only a dozen times or so, and always in carefully controlled situations. It wasn't until their *American Magazine* story about tourist camps created controversy that their relationship cooled.

Before his suicide in 1940, Cooper, the beneficiary of Hoover's ghostwritten friendship, provided a bit of correspondence advice to Nichols. Letters from Hoover to Sumner Blossom had been going out with a "Dear Sumner" salutation, and one letter slipped out with a "Dear Sir" greeting. "Ryley suggested that sometime in the future the Director write Blossom a letter and sign it 'Edgar,'" Nichols told Tolson in a memo. "He also suggested that you address Blossom as 'Dear Bloss' [*sic*]."[21]

As Cooper's relationship with Hoover was winding down, another journalist, Fulton Oursler, began a collaboration with the FBI that continued for fifteen years. A Baltimore native, Oursler became the editor of *Liberty* magazine in 1931. In 1942, he moved to *Reader's Digest* as a senior editor and began a very successful career as an author and freelance writer, penning news and feature stories and writing thirty-two books, including the 1949 religious best seller *The Greatest Story Ever Told*, which ultimately sold 1.5 million copies.[22] Oursler was invited to speak several times at FBI National Police Academy graduation ceremonies on the topic of public relations, and he lunched with Hoover on at least two occasions. But other than a few short visits to FBI headquarters, Oursler's relationship with Hoover, whom he considered an intimate friend, was conducted primarily through their letters.

Oursler's written exchanges with Hoover were frequent, highly personal, and authored primarily by Nichols. As he did with Gen Cooper, Hoover became a frequent correspondent with Oursler's wife, Grace. Oursler's correspondence with Hoover led him to be a prolific advocate for and defender of the FBI. Within months of their initial contact, Oursler had become "Fulton" and Hoover had become "Edgar" in their written salutations. In August 1938, Oursler invited Hoover to his Massachusetts home, Sandalwood.[23] Hoover, in a letter written by Nichols, declined the invitation but replied that the Ourslers' friendship was an inspiration to him; he later wrote, "You may rest assured that if I am not the victim of circumstances and continued overwhelming pressure, I am certainly contemplating a visit sometime in the near future."[24] Of course, he was not. It is doubtful that Hoover was even aware of Oursler's offer of a weekend at Sandalwood.

In November 1938, in a letter marked "read to Director" (indicating that Hoover was made aware of its contents), Oursler reported that he had assigned *Liberty* reporter Frederick L. Collins to do a series on the FBI.[25] Even before Collins visited the FBI for his story, Oursler forwarded an article of his own titled "Inked Out," in which he urged reporters to defer to police on matters of crime. "Newspaper men must come to realize that crime means that our society is engaged in a civil war," Oursler wrote. "In that war there can be no neutrality."[26] His letter to Hoover noted, "You promised to check it over for me, and I shall appreciate any time you can give to it."[27] Hoover replied with a two-page letter detailing a number of edits he (actually, Nichols) suggested.[28]

That exchange was typical of Hoover's correspondence with reporters.[29] The personal touch often led to laudatory coverage for the Bureau, and more often than not, the reporter-friend allowed the FBI to edit the final version of the story. After Collins visited the FBI on February 6, Oursler wrote, "Thank you for your kind offer to review the articles when they are ready. I was hoping you would be willing to do this, both from a factual standpoint and for any other suggestions you might care to make."[30] When the edited articles appeared in *Liberty*, Hoover thanked Oursler, prompting an emotional reply from the editor: "My admiration for you is so deep, my enthusiasm for the work you are doing so profound, that I have to restrain myself from expressing my full thoughts for fear of seeming a sentimentalist."[31]

In subsequent correspondence, Oursler forwarded a letter he had received from H. L. Mencken in which the muckraking "Sage of Baltimore" expressed his admiration for Hoover.[32] In a telegram sent in September 1939, Hoover expressed his condolences upon the death of Oursler's mother.[33] A month later, Hoover (through his ghostwriters) struck up a correspondence with Oursler's young son Fulton Jr. (Tony), which lasted for decades.[34]

Meanwhile, *Liberty* continued to publish articles promoting the Bureau's preferred Collier-Cooper narrative. Oursler's "Every Sheriff a Sherlock Homes," which touted the value of the FBI's National Police Academy, was edited by the FBI in late 1950.[35] The story's focus on training and science promoted the notion of the FBI as a responsible agency. The FBI also reviewed and edited a lecture Oursler gave in New York in 1941.[36] When Oursler left *Liberty* in 1942 to become *Reader's Digest*'s top editor, their collaboration and correspondence continued unabated.

As in all "friendships," the relationship sometimes became strained. In December 1945, Oursler complained "that he had not had a chance to sit down with the Director for over three years and that while he could get information from me [Nichols], he had to see the Director to get a little of his personality."[37] Oursler pleaded for an opportunity to collaborate with the Bureau: "He stated that we could absolutely control anything he wrote and it would be handled in any way we desired," Nichols told Tolson.[38] Citing *Reader's Digest*'s circulation of 11 million, Nichols arranged an in-person meeting between Oursler and Hoover. Once again, the quid pro quo of a carefully cultivated friendship was access to the pages of a publication where Bureau editors could mold a story to emphasize the FBI's science, responsibility, and Hoover memes.

With the publication of Oursler's best-selling novel, the relationship lapsed temporarily. In 1950, though, when Max Lowenthal published a book criticizing the centralization of police power in the FBI, Hoover turned to his "special correspondents" for an "objective" defense by unbiased journalists seeking the "truth" of the situation. Nichols convinced Oursler to publish "Why I No Longer Fear the FBI," by ACLU general counsel Morris Ernst, in *Reader's Digest*. Ernst's article was the culmination of years of being courted by the FBI through infrequent personal meetings and voluminous personal correspondence from Hoover's Crime Records letter writers.[39] The article's publication provided Hoover with political cover from the Left, and the Bureau cited it for decades as evidence of its restraint in civil liberties matters. As a reward for publishing the article, Oursler was invited to return for a second time to speak at the FBI's National Police Academy graduation ceremony in September 1950.[40]

The final exchange of correspondence occurred just days before Oursler's death. Oursler forwarded some letters to Hoover, and on May 2, 1952, Hoover thanked him for making those letters available.[41] Oursler died of a heart attack on May 25, and Hoover sent a letter to his widow, Grace, on May 27. "His friendship over the years has meant more than words can express," Nichols wrote for Hoover. "While in recent years we did not have the privilege of being together as much as I would have liked, I always knew he was as close as the nearest telephone and he, I am sure, felt the same as far as I was concerned."[42] There is no indication in Oursler's detailed and comprehensive FBI file that any telephone conversations between Oursler and Hoover ever occurred. Nichols also penned a tribute to Oursler that was published under Hoover's byline in the July 1952 issue of the Bureau's internal publication, *The Investigator*. "His friends in the FBI mourn his passing. The FBI has lost a great friend and a staunch booster."[43]

Beginning with a trickle of letters between 1939 and 1942, Hoover struck up a friendship with another journalist, *Memphis Commercial Appeal* associate editor Jack Carley. That trickle became a flood by the late 1940s, and their correspondence lasted into the 1960s. In contrast with Cooper, Oursler, and many of Hoover's other correspondents, the director himself authored two or three of the thousands of letters to Carley, and their friendship seems to have been something valued by both men, albeit not equally.

John Ogden Carley joined the *Commercial Appeal* staff in 1923 and served as editorial page editor as well as associate editor for more than twenty-five years. Carley's obituary described Hoover as "a close friend of many years" and noted that friends referred to Carley as "The Inspector" in honor of his relationship with the FBI.[44] Carley's nearly 1,000-page FBI file chronicles a relationship based almost entirely on correspondence. As with Oursler, Hoover's letter writers flattered and promoted Carley's interests, inviting him nearly every year to succeed Oursler as public relations lecturer at the FBI's National Police Academy. In exchange, Carley provided a running commentary on events in the South, defended the FBI against critics in his publication, and ultimately became an important covert source for the FBI.

It was Carley's work as a so-called special service contact (SSC) for the FBI that distinguished his friendship with Hoover. SSCs were formally identified as helpful amateur sleuths who could obtain information too sensitive for FBI agents to request. As early as 1943, Hoover considered Carley an important resource for the FBI.[45]

For his service to the Bureau during World War II, Carley was presented with an FBI Meritorious Service Award. In his nomination letter, the SAC in Memphis described Carley's contributions: "On numerous occasions during the war period, he discreetly secured information which this office desired and would have experienced great difficulty obtaining but for his assistance."[46]

Jack Carley, associate editor of the Memphis Commercial Appeal, *meets with Hoover after delivering the keynote address at the FBI's National Police Academy on October 26, 1959. (National Archives at College Park, Record Group 65, Series H, Box 29, #1591)*

Carley's assistance continued in the postwar years, as he published two anticommunist booklets with testimonials from Hoover, authored dozens of supportive editorials, and spoke at fifteen National Police Academy graduation ceremonies. Carley met briefly with Hoover seven times during those years, but their primary contact was through the mail. By 1945, Nichols had taken on the majority of Hoover's side of the written conversation.

In exchange for his favored status, Carley provided assistance whenever asked. In 1950, for example, several U.S. senators were holding up the FBI's appropriation in committee. "Try & have Jack help us on our appropriation problems," Hoover instructed Nichols.[47] Carley immediately called the powerful Senate Appropriations Committee chairman Kenneth McKellar of Tennessee, and the hold on the appropriations was lifted. Tolson wrote a thank-you letter to Carley that was signed by Hoover.[48]

Also in 1950, SACs were asked to provide memoranda justifying their local stables of SSCs. The Memphis SAC, D. S. Hostettler, clarified the services provided by Carley, designated "Special Service Contact Memphis #1":

> He has access to much information which is not ordinarily available to Special Agents. Bureau records will also reflect that he has access to certain Congressional leaders at Washington. On a daily basis, he immediately evaluates all local, state-wide, national, and international news which appear to be pertinent to our work. I am sure that he will make an effort to secure any information which the Bureau might desire in connection with National Security.[49]

In 1951, Carley wielded his influence again, advocating (at Nichols's request) for an executive salary increase for FBI administrators. "These men are not only my warm personal friends of many years," Carley wrote to Senator McKellar, "but they are richly deserving of every consideration that Congress can give them."[50]

The warm correspondence between Hoover and Carley, punctuated by in-person meetings from time to time, continued into 1954. In a memorandum to Nichols, an aide summarized the strategic, bureaucratic nature of the relationship between the two men and instructed inexperienced letter writers on the nature and content of Hoover's "friendship" with Carley: "Correspondence with Carley has been most cordial and he addresses his letter to the Director with the salutations 'Dear Edgar' or 'Dear Director' while correspondence to him always uses the salutation, 'Dear Jack.' On October 4, 1954, we wrote a most cordial letter to him in remembrance of his birthday, which was October 6, 1954."[51]

That same year, SSCs were redesignated as SAC contacts, and Hostettler nominated Carley for that status, noting that "he supports the Bureau against all attacks of every description. He is a personal friend of the Director and many others at the Bureau. . . . He has performed the above services and many special favors for the Bureau."[52]

Between 1954 and Carley's death in 1962, Hoover continued to rely on his friend for information about the burgeoning civil rights movement. Hoover praised Carley for his "objective analysis of the problem," and Carley relied on Hoover for guidance as to "what he should do" about civil rights.[53] In 1956, when the Mississippi legislature passed a bill that would prevent the FBI from investigating civil rights matters in the state, Carley was called on to help. First, he published a strong editorial asking "Does He Want Amateurs?" suggesting that Mississippi would get amateur investigators if it barred the FBI from the state. Next, Carley traveled to Jackson, Mississippi, to meet with Governor James P. Coleman and argue the FBI's case. "It appears now that it is up to Carley to convince Governor Coleman not to sign the bill," Nichols reported.[54] Apparently, Carley's intervention was persuasive. Coleman vetoed the bill.[55]

Beginning in the early 1950s, Carley's health began to fail. On eight occasions, he canceled planned appearances at academy graduation ceremonies. Still, he continued to defend the FBI from his base in Memphis. When journalist Fred J. Cook published his blistering 1958 critique of the FBI in *The Nation*,[56] Hoover's public relations staff sprang into action. It quickly characterized Cook's piece as part of a coordinated "smear campaign" and engaged its army of pen pals in newsrooms around the country to attack the critics.[57] Carley was one of those friends, and he promised to draft an editorial "to have in readiness" if called on to attack Cook.[58]

Carley's health continued to decline in 1959 and 1960, and the pace of his correspondence with Hoover slowed. Carley's declarations of friendship became sentimental. "As long as I can write—and I hope to be doing that for a long time yet—I will count myself a member of the Bureau family, the Bureau team," Carley wrote to Hoover in 1959. "It just couldn't be otherwise. It never will be otherwise."[59] Hoover, who was one year older than Carley, took a special interest in his well-being. When Nichols invited Carley to speak at the academy's fall graduation ceremony, the Bureau had to ship oxygen canisters to stops along Carley's train route. "I think it is an imposition to have set this up," Hoover wrote on a memorandum detailing the arrangements for Carley's trip. "Carley is a very sick man & such an arduous trip & strain might well end his life."[60] Indeed, it was Carley's last visit to the academy. When Carley died on February 20, 1962, Hoover's public relations staff authored a statement for the *Commercial Appeal*: " Like others who had need of his services, we in law enforcement found him ready at all times to answer the call," Nichols wrote for Hoover. "It was an honor to be among Jack's close friends. I feel a deep personal loss at his passing."[61]

While Cooper, Oursler, and Carley were friends of strategic importance whose relationships with the FBI spanned decades, two other prominent journalists—one a publisher and the other a Washington correspondent—

were particularly important mainstream players in defending Hoover's FBI against alleged communist smears.

Roy Wilson Howard's rise to power in the newspaper industry is a classic rags-to-riches tale. The son of a railroad brakeman, Howard's first newspaper job was as a delivery boy for the *Indianapolis Star.* After reporting for Indianapolis newspapers for a few years, Howard moved to Ohio as assisting managing editor of the *Cincinnati Post.* In 1906, he became a New York correspondent for the Scripps-Rae group, which included newspapers in Cleveland, Columbus, Toledo, and Cincinnati. When E. W. Scripps merged several news-gathering groups to create the United Press, he tapped Howard as the syndicate's first general news manager. Six years later, at age twenty-nine, Howard became United Press's first president. By 1922, he was chairman of the board of Scripps-Howard newspapers. In 1931, while retaining the chairmanship, he named himself editor of the *New York World-Telegram,* a title he held until his death in 1964. By 1960, the Scripps-Howard chain included twenty daily newspapers and eight Sunday newspapers spanning the continental United States.

Politically, Howard's newspapers dropped their support for FDR and the Democratic Party in 1940 and endorsed only Republicans until 1960.[62] Hoover added Howard to the Bureau's mailing list in 1936, and the Scripps-Howard chain became a reliable defender of the FBI.[63] Howard's personal letters to Hoover began with the salutation "My dear Edgar." Their relationship was mutually beneficial: Howard's defense of the FBI in chain editorials was rewarded by special consideration from the Bureau. In 1941, for example, Howard asked the Bureau to intervene on behalf of two of his servants, a steward and a chef, both of whom were Japanese nationals. Their service on his boat, Howard reported to Hoover, had become "uncomfortable," and both wished to leave and take up residence with a friend in New York. In essence, Howard was asking Hoover to intervene with the Office of Naval Intelligence and the Immigration and Naturalization Service, both of which were pushing for the men to be arrested and detained. In exchange for Hoover's help in accommodating the men's plans, Howard offered his help: "If the exigencies of war make it necessary for you to do a little fighting at this [home] front at any time in the near future, I would be delighted to have you look me up."[64] Following a flurry of FBI inquiries, the two men were instructed to take their case to the Immigration and Naturalization Service.[65] By early January, when he was notified of the FBI's recommendation, Howard had apparently lost interest in the case. "Since these two men deliberately passed up well-paying positions—apparently on the theory that Uncle Sam would feed them if worst came to worst—my interest in their welfare has been somewhat lessened."[66]

It wasn't until after World War II that the relationship between Howard and Hoover became particularly close, as attention turned from enemies abroad to alleged communist enemies in the United States. "I have been trying for a couple of years to get time to talk to you about the magnificent job you have done and are doing on this Communist thing," Howard wrote to Hoover in 1947. "I want to make clear to you not only our great appreciation of the job you have done, but the sincerity of our desire to cooperate in any way possible."[67] Two weeks later, Howard was invited to address the graduating class at the FBI's National Police Academy, an honor reserved for Hoover's closest media friends.[68] Howard declined the invitation, noting that he was not a good public speaker and addressed only newspaper groups.[69]

In 1948, Howard's newspapers came to Hoover's defense when several Republican senators publicly urged Governor Thomas Dewey—who, they presumed, would defeat Truman in the presidential election that year—to fire Hoover. At issue was the FBI's perceived poor performance while investigating voting fraud in Kansas City. But the Scripps-Howard editorial saw red in the attack. "The FBI is not a partisan agency, and it must not be made a political football," Scripps-Howard editors wrote. "There isn't a man in America better informed on the Communist problem than J. Edgar Hoover. That is why he has been a continuing target for Communist attack."[70] Hoover wrote to Howard and thanked him for running the editorial in all the Scripps-Howard newspapers. "I wanted to write you direct to express personally my official as well as personal appreciation for the succinct manner in which your editorial writer brought out into the open the whispered smears that can only be coped with by the spotlight of publicity."[71] In 1949, Howard once again declined an offer to address the FBI's National Police Academy.[72] But to express his appreciation, Howard forwarded Hoover an advance copy of a Gallup poll on Americans' perceptions of the FBI headlined "Charges that Bureau Is 'American Gestapo' Seen Making Little Headway."[73] Gallup's nationwide survey, which was reported in Scripps-Howard newspapers the following week, found that only 3 percent of respondents disapproved of the FBI.[74]

A 1950 editorial defending the Bureau against critics prompted another thank-you letter from Hoover. The editorial, headlined "The FBI's Big Job," decried the attacks on the FBI as communist plots against America. "No one but a criminal or a traitor has anything to fear from a careful, honest investigation, just as no law abiding citizen has any reason to object to being fingerprinted," editors wrote. "We must guard against any attempt to cripple the FBI."[75] A 1954 editorial, "FBI and Commies," supported Hoover's testimony before a House appropriations subcommittee. "Mr. Hoover noted that 105 Communist leaders have been indicted and 61 of those convicted. That is not nearly as comforting as it sounds. Most of these are open leaders. It is the subterranean variety which is the most dangerous."[76]

By 1954, Howard had turned over the presidency of Scripps-Howard to his son, Jack, maintaining the chairmanship for himself. Through an informant, FBI Crime Records chief Louis Nichols learned that the Howards had disagreed over whether to publish an anti–Joseph McCarthy series. Roy Howard wanted the series killed, but Jack Howard prevailed. "Roy Howard sought to change his son's mind by argument and reason rather than by order," Nichols reported. "Apparently there was some bitterness that had developed as a result of this series."[77] Nichols offered the inside information in an attempt to convince Hoover to agree to meet with Roy Howard. The meeting did not take place.

Their relationship cooled as Howard's involvement in operating the Scripps-Howard chain passed increasingly to his son. Still, Hoover's correspondence team maintained frequent contact with Howard. In 1959, after the *New York Post* published a series of critical articles about Hoover, Howard wrote to "Dear Edgar" that he was "pleased to note that the FBI has not yet gone out of business as a result of the extensive consideration it recently received from one of our New York contemporaries."[78] In 1960, Howard retired as editor of the *New York World Telegram and Sun* but pledged that the Scripps-Howard chain would continue to support and defend the FBI. "There will be no lessening of support or of recognition of the tremendous job you have done and are doing," Howard wrote.[79]

Howard was an influential friend at the top of a large newspaper chain that wielded tremendous influence through its editorial pages, but *Chicago Tribune* reporter Walter Trohan was Hoover's most reliable friend among the Washington press corps. Trohan's friendship with Hoover spanned the 1930s to the 1970s. Whereas Cooper's collaboration with Hoover sparked a friendship of convenience, Oursler seemed to gain an emotional boost from his relationship with the director, and "Inspector" Carley relished his status as an adjunct cop, the source of Trohan's relationship with Hoover was clearly ideological. The two men saw the world in much the same way, and public fear of communism fueled both their careers.

"Dear Comrade," Hoover wrote on April 10, 1952. "We can all rest easier now that you are back in the city and have taken over your old assignments of protecting the flanks of those who are trying to do a job."[80] The recipient of that letter and the protector of government flanks was Trohan, who once referred to himself as a "Poor Man's J. Edgar Hoover."[81] Vacationing in Tucson, Trohan responded with his own "Dear Comrade" letter, praising the efficiency of the FBI's Tucson office—not the Tucson agents' efficiency as crime investigators but as tour guides. As a friend of the Bureau, Trohan had been afforded the courtesy of travel assistance. The Tucson agents upgraded Trohan's accommodations and even provided guided tours of the area. According to Trohan: "[Special agent Herman Tickel] took me in hand, even to getting me to church on weekdays, and to mountain tops and around the highways and byways of Tucson and Pima County. He and his staff engulfed and surrounded me with protection, affection, and education. Carol [Trohan's wife] and I are deeply grateful for the kindness and attention." Trohan ended his letter with a joke, comparing the FBI's "service" to the Soviet internal secret police, the MVD. "I have never known its equal, even by the MVD, and I must note that it was much friendlier."[82]

In 1953, Tickel again squired the Trohans around Tucson.[83] The FBI's travel assistance was not limited to U.S. destinations. When Trohan and his wife traveled to Mexico City en route to Oaxaca for a month's vacation in 1954, the FBI's legal attaché there took them to dinner at a fancy restaurant.[84] Trohan received similar courtesies during Mexican vacations in 1955, 1956, 1958, and 1966 and on trips to Europe in 1957, 1959, and nearly every year during the 1960s.[85] In a 1969 "Dear Comrade" letter, Trohan again expressed his appreciation. "I must confess I do like red carpet treatment," he wrote, "but from your men I get a gold carpet."[86]

Trohan's VIP treatment, which involved pulling professional investigators away from their duties to act as personal valets, was not uncommon for friends of the Bureau. Hoover's friends and defenders, particularly those in the news media, were often rewarded personally, with travel assistance and other perks, and professionally, with access to information. In return, they provided laudatory coverage of the FBI and, when asked, stepped in to attack critics, providing an "objective" assertion of the Bureau's legitimacy.

Trohan grew up in Chicago and was hired by the *Tribune* after he covered the St. Valentine's Day Massacre—a 1929 mob killing thought to be linked to

Al Capone—for the Chicago City News Bureau. After five years covering Cook County, Trohan was transferred to Washington, D.C., as an assistant correspondent. He became the *Tribune*'s bureau chief in 1949, shortly after the paper published the infamous "Dewey Defeats Truman" headline. In Washington, Trohan covered the federal government and Congress, wrote a column, and broadcast a weekly radio commentary over Chicago's WGN. Trohan and his wife had three children, and Walter Jr. served as an FBI file clerk in the 1950s and 1960s.[87] Trohan served as *Tribune* bureau chief until 1969 and retired in 1972. He died in 2003 at the age of 100.[88] For decades before and decades after Hoover's death, Trohan defended the director's actions in print, broadcast, and film.

While Trohan's conservative politics and rabid anticommunism ultimately made him a friend of the Bureau, his relationship with the FBI began on Sunday, June 21, 1936, when his profile of Hoover appeared in the *Chicago Tribune*. Headlined "Chief of the G-Men—Record of His Career," the article was critical of Hoover:

> In less than three years a tide of printer's ink, accompanied by a roar of sound films and radio programs has given heroic stature to a relatively obscure burocrat [*sic*], the son and grandson of undistinguished toilers in the federal red tape vineyards. Behind this precipitous rise were years of preparation, for Mr. Hoover, like the cautious conspirator, did not disclose himself to a startled public until he was certain he could command its attention.[89]

Trohan compared Hoover to Javert of Victor Hugo's *Les Miserables*. Though both were devoted to duty, "unlike Javert, Hoover is not a police officer in training or by instinct. It is gravely doubtful whether Hoover—and this is said without disrespect—could single-handedly track down the perpetrators of a crime in the scientific manner taught at his school."[90] Trohan even highlighted an embarrassing appearance before a U.S. Senate committee in 1936, when Hoover was forced to admit he had never made an arrest. As Trohan reported it, "Hoover even confessed he had never been to a crime school, not even to his own elaborate school."[91] By holding Hoover up to ridicule as a mere bureaucrat, Trohan undermined a key element of the FBI's public relations narrative. Hoover, the small, uncredentialed bureaucrat, could not be trusted to rein in the Bureau's power the way the iconic "top cop" version of him could.

But in 1936, the Bureau's public relations section had not yet established itself as the all-powerful defender of Hoover's honor. Instead of trying to counter the article's impact, the FBI attempted to uncover Trohan's sources. Assistant director Edward A. Tamm speculated that one source for the article was the Treasury Department, with which Hoover had an ongoing spat. Another possible (but seemingly unlikely) source, Tamm suggested, was Rex Collier, the Bureau's collaborator on the *War on Crime* radio program and coauthor of the emerging FBI public relations narrative.[92] Hoover, fearing that Trohan's story had damaged his standing with Attorney General Homer S. Cummings, wrote a long, "personal and confidential" memorandum to his boss. In it, Hoover speculated that in addition to Treasury, Trohan's sources included the Post Office Department and the Secret Service. "I feel that the patently obvious inaccuracies and misstatement of fact appearing in his article are sufficient to convince any intelligent reader of its worthlessness," Hoover wrote. "However, the reported fact that certain officials of the administration were contacted by him and allegedly furnished him with some of this misinformation does seem to me to be reprehensible."[93]

Years later, Trohan revealed his sources for that early story. The context of that admission (a violation of reporter-source confidentiality) was a 1955 discussion between Trohan and Nichols about Hoover's resiliency. "He [Trohan] made the point that he has marveled at how the Director has been able to protect himself from more critical newspaper stories than have already appeared," Nichols reported. When Nichols brought up Trohan's critical 1936 profile of Hoover, "Trohan stated that he, of course, would never write such a piece as this today." Trohan attributed Hoover's public relations success to the policy of centralizing all communications with the press in the FBI's Washington headquarters. Trohan then named his 1936 sources, which as Hoover believed, consisted of government officials, including Cummings. According to Nichols, "Homer Cummings told Walter on numerous occasions that one of the biggest mistakes he ever made was not to replace the Director when he became Attorney General as the Director was difficult to handle, could not be controlled and had the faculty of attracting attention to himself."[94]

In the two decades between Trohan's critical story and his admission of his sources, he and Hoover solidified their friendship largely through their cordial correspondence. By 1950, with their relationship well established, Hoover offered Trohan, a collector of military memorabilia, a gift of some captured Japanese medals from World War II. "In recognition of your valiant efforts on many fronts, I am bestowing upon you numerous medals of distinction and 'extinction,'" Hoover wrote. "I regret this is not a more propitious occasion. In due time, however, an opportunity will present itself for me to make some fitting and appropriate remarks."[95] The simple fact that the Bureau's letter writers knew about Trohan's interest in military artifacts demonstrates the granular detail contained in FBI files and used in Hoover's correspondence. A few months later, Trohan was able to repay the kindness when he published a blistering review of Max Lowenthal's anti-FBI book. Lowenthal, a former aide to Truman, deconstructed the Collier-Cooper narrative. "Lowenthal belabors the FBI as a menace to freedom of speech and freedom of thought," Trohan wrote. "The verdict of this reviewer on Lowenthal is 'not guilty' of conservatism and 'guilty' of objectivity 'against' the FBI."[96]

Both the closeness between Trohan and Hoover and the Bureau's low tolerance for criticism are evident in the handling of a 1953 incident in which the reporter published an innocuous anecdote about the FBI in his column. Tucked into the middle of Trohan's June 19, 1953, "Washington Scrapbook" was a two-sentence item included, no doubt, for its ironic value. "The federal bureau of investigation [*sic*], long established as a symbol of integrity and fair play is blushing these days," Trohan wrote. "The FBI sandlot baseball team recently drew a year's suspension for foul play."[97] FBI public relations officials, always on guard for any criticism of the Bureau, were not amused. "I think we should straighten Trohan out on this," Tolson wrote.[98] Trohan, as it turned out, was in the hospital following a car accident. Nichols recommended that they send an agent to check on Trohan and wait until the reporter had recovered before bringing the situation to his attention. A month later, Nichols reported that he had spoken to Trohan, who claimed he had not written the item; it had been added to his column by a copy editor.[99] That the Bureau would concern itself with such a minor item indicated its attention to detail when it came to public relations. That it would wait a month before raising the issue with a "friend" who was convalescing indicated the value it placed on beneficial relationships with influential reporters like Trohan.

Trohan had great value to the FBI as an "objective defender," frequently taunting Hoover's enemies in letters he shared with the director. In 1958, for example, Trohan sent a letter to industrialist Cyrus Eaton, an outspoken critic of the FBI's "gestapo" potential, and enclosed a critical column he had written about Eaton. "I was moved to write the piece because I found [a] considerable dossier of your playing footy, footy with the Communists,"

Trohan wrote.[100] Three weeks later, Trohan wrote to Eaton again and sent a copy of the letter to Hoover. In it, Trohan scolded Eaton for sharing their correspondence with a third party (even though Trohan was doing the same thing). "I suppose you are gratified with having turned my letter over to the *New York Evening Post*, which has often followed Soviet aims," Trohan wrote. "I should think that you might have had a twinge of conscience about turning over personal correspondence, but I guess your conscience has lost the facility of twinging."[101] In addition to sharing his correspondence, Trohan provided Nichols with a thorough debriefing on his dealings with Eaton. In 1959, Trohan shared with Hoover a letter he had written to *New York Post* publisher Dorothy Schiff in the wake of the *Post*'s critical series on the director. Trohan presented himself as an expert on all things FBI who should have been consulted before the series was published. "I presume you are not interested in the truth, or you would have questioned me in the preparation of your series on J. Edgar Hoover," Trohan wrote. "I must conclude your only interest is in carrying out a personal vendetta with Mr. Hoover, which is your privilege."[102]

For his willingness to shill for the FBI, Trohan, like Oursler and Carley, was rewarded with the honor of speaking to the graduating class of the FBI's National Police Academy. A memorandum suggesting Trohan as a replacement for Carley in 1960 unmasked the bureaucratic nature of Hoover's "personal" correspondence. "A letter has been prepared addressed to Trohan as Dear Comrade and making light reference to his recent trip to Europe," a member of Hoover's correspondence team wrote.[103] In his speech, Trohan's biting sarcasm was on display, and FBI officials worried that academy graduates—law enforcement officers from around the country—would not understand the humor. "I want it known I'm in favor of beating some hoodlums," Trohan said. "It brings them back to earth. Like the Russians, they only understand a sock on the jaw." Trohan also said it would be preferable for police officers to accept bribes than to become communists. And he disagreed with Hoover regarding the use of the word *cop*, a term the director banned. Hoover expressed his disapproval in a handwritten comment: "I wonder if Walter would walk up to a crossing officer & say 'cop' which way is the White House."[104] Trohan was not invited back to the academy, and instructors were told to remind students that the views of visiting speakers did not represent those of the FBI. Still, despite his gruff and sarcastic nature, Trohan, like many other reporters, remained "members of the family" who stood "ready, willing and able to be of assistance to us at any time."[105]

Trohan rendered assistance, for example, after the assassination of President John F. Kennedy, when the Warren Commission criticized the Bureau for failing to recognize assassin Lee Harvey Oswald as a potential threat to the president's safety. The Warren Commission report, released on September 27, 1964, cited the FBI's failure to provide information about Oswald to the Secret Service.[106] In defending Hoover and the Bureau, Trohan—hardly a civil liberties advocate—called any criticism of the FBI unfair and characterized the report as "hindsight of the highest order." He claimed, "The precautions the protective services were criticized for omitting couldn't have been performed, and if they could have been, Warren's Supreme court would have been quick to condemn them as interference with human rights." If the FBI had detained all individuals who were potential threats to the president, Left, Right, and center, "they would undoubtedly have screamed about interference with their rights—and justly so—and there would have been cries of 'police state.'"[107] Hoover himself repeated the charges of "Monday morning quarterbacking" and echoed Trohan's argument that adopting the commission's suggestions could result in "totalitarian security."[108]

A controversy occurring at about the same time temporarily derailed Hoover's relationship with Trohan. On October 7, 1964, President Lyndon B. Johnson's longtime aide Walter Jenkins was arrested in a Washington, D.C., YMCA on a morals charge. When his arrest made the news, Jenkins resigned his position as a special assistant to the president.[109] Upon learning of Jenkins's resignation and subsequent hospitalization, Hoover sent him a bouquet of flowers. Critics on the Right, who could usually be counted on to support the Bureau, attacked the FBI director. Representative Walter H. Judd (R-Minn.) asked whether the FBI or Hoover was somehow implicated in the Jenkins scandal and feared "being hurt by some revelation Jenkins could make."[110]

The FBI carefully logged editorial reactions to Hoover's gesture. Critical editorials appeared in such stalwart conservative publications as the *Manchester (N.H.) Union-Leader* and the *Charleston (S.C.) News and Courier*. Broadcaster Paul Harvey commented negatively on the situation. Even Trohan criticized his friend. Hoover's wrath was swift: "I want all persons on our mailing lists who have improperly construed the action I took in sending flowers to Jenkins removed," Hoover wrote. "This includes newspapers, magazines and persons such as [Paul] Harvey, [Charleston publisher Thomas] Waring, [*New York Daily News* reporter] Ted Lewis, Trohan, et al."[111] In a handwritten note, Tolson added: "The same applies to Xmas cards." As was frequently the case, Hoover's pique did not last long. Nine months later, Trohan and several others were restored to the special correspondents list as thanks for their "strong support of Mr. Hoover."[112]

In 1966, Trohan's strong support took the form of a column defending Hoover against charges of indiscriminate wiretapping under his tenure. Trohan even implicated one of Hoover's nemeses, former attorney general Robert F. Kennedy, as the culprit behind the bugging. "The FBI has a file bulging with Kennedy approvals of wire taps which could be disclosed one a day, for months," Trohan wrote.[113] Ongoing wiretapping controversies allowed Trohan to render another, more personal service for the FBI: reporting on his conversations with William Loeb, publisher of the *Manchester (N.H.) Guardian*. Loeb, described as "fervently conservative" in an obituary, was in many ways an ideal match for Hoover's political views. For example, in 1972, Loeb described Democratic presidential candidate Senator Edmund S. Muskie of Maine as "Moscow Muskie." Loeb considered President Richard M. Nixon a "stinking hypocrite" and once declared that Secretary of State Henry Kissinger was "a tool of the Communist conspiracy."[114] Not even the FBI escaped Loeb's criticism.

In 1967, FBI wiretapping again became an issue when Teamsters president James Hoffa appealed his conviction on jury tampering charges. In November of that year, Hoffa's attorneys filed an appeal with the U.S. Supreme Court, requesting that their client's conviction be set aside and citing the FBI's use of bugging and wiretapping in connection with the case. Hoffa's attorneys claimed "that the Federal Government for many years has been intruding on petitioner Hoffa's right to counsel and obtaining evidence against him by unlawful means."[115] Hoffa's lawyers included a 1966 affidavit from Loeb stating that FBI Crime Records Division chief Cartha DeLoach had confirmed the wiretapping and bugging allegations. DeLoach denied doing so, and Trohan backed him up. Bureau officials asked Trohan to write a letter stating that Loeb was lying. According to Trohan, Loeb met with DeLoach and was angry because the FBI official had *refused* to confirm the allegations. Trohan was also asked by an FBI official whether he had furnished any information to Loeb, and Trohan denied it. On December 31, 1966, Trohan wrote a "Dear Comrade" letter to Hoover, restating his denial of Loeb's story and noting that he had also written to Supreme Court justice Stewart.[116] Trohan also signed a sworn statement recounting his discussions with Loeb and wrote to the New Hampshire publisher: "Your passion for affidavits reminds me of the school of leads on news stories that have been described by the phrase, 'Christ how the wind blew,'" Trohan told Loeb. "Even if everything you say in the affidavit is true, it doesn't help your friend Mr. Hoffa in the slightest, because there is no evidence in it."[117]

As his career wound down, Trohan's contributions became less substantive and more valedictory. In 1969, he wrote a column congratulating Hoover on his seventy-fifth birthday. In it, he provided Hoover with a blanket of absolution for overstepping his authority. "Hoover has done some things he didn't like for various Presidents and attorneys general, including wire tapping, pressuring editors to vote for press service admission of a favored newspaper, and undertaking various investigations that belonged properly to other departments or other police units," Trohan wrote, blaming all of Hoover's excesses on others. Then he addressed the Bureau's primary public relations problem: legitimacy. "In his determination not to permit his unit to operate with police state tactics, he has let [criticism] flow like water off a duck's back."[118]

On July 2, 1971, Trohan published the last defense that appeared during the director's life—a column attacking Representative Hale Boggs (D-La.), who had accused Hoover of tapping congressional telephones. After batting down Boggs's charges, Trohan suggested that Hoover's critics were taking the wrong approach. "Hoover's foes found that their attacks will not force his resignation but are more likely to keep him in office longer, because he will not go under fire," Trohan wrote, no doubt accurately summarizing Hoover's attitude.[119] On July 12, Hoover responded with his final "Dear Comrade" letter, thanking Trohan for the column and for a lifetime of support. "I do want you to know how deeply I appreciate your comments," Hoover's correspondence team wrote on his behalf, "and you may be sure your continuing wholehearted support of my administration of the FBI is indeed a source of encouragement to me."[120] Hoover's death in 1972 did not end Trohan's support. As FBI records were opened up and scholars began dissecting Hoover's tenure, Trohan became a go-to source for interviews about his friend. Trohan's admiration for Hoover did not waver, even in the wake of revelations about FBI excesses that trickled out during the 1970s, 1980s, and 1990s.

Newspaper reporters were not the only ones who routinely defended Hoover and the FBI. Popular broadcasters such as Fulton Lewis Jr. and George Sokolsky also became important FBI surrogates.

Chapter 9

Managing Friends in the Broadcast Media

On January 30, 1956, a member of conservative broadcaster Fulton Lewis Jr.'s vast radio audience wrote to complain that he had received only one of two of Lewis's anticommunist books he had ordered. The listener enclosed his returned check for $2 as proof. "I have mailed 3 letters inquiring about the other book, but no answer from any body," the listener wrote. "What can be done about this matter? Please try to clear it up for me."[1] This plea for assistance was addressed not to Lewis or to the Mutual Broadcasting System, which carried his show, but to a man everyone knew was a close friend of Lewis: FBI director J. Edgar Hoover. Hoover immediately forwarded the letter to his friend "Fulton," accompanied by a note signed "Edgar."[2] The letter writer was undoubtedly not the only American to link Lewis and Hoover so closely that he assumed they worked together in the Justice Department.

Fulton Lewis Jr. was among the most influential conservative voices on radio from the 1930s to the 1960s. Lewis and fellow conservative columnist George Sokolsky shared the distinction of being targets of leftist journalist George Seldes. In the February 28, 1944, issue of Seldes's *In Fact*, he lumped Sokolsky, Lewis, and publisher William Randolph Hearst together as, respectively, a red-baiting anti-Semite, a stooge of big business, and an American "Nazi."[3] A former editor at the *Washington Herald*, Lewis wrote a syndicated column, "Washington Sideshow," from 1933 to 1936. In 1937, he took a break from newspapers and accepted a job as a vacation replacement for Mutual Broadcasting Company in Washington. Known as "the voice of the snarl," Lewis was a zealous conservative opponent of the New Deal who later turned his snarl against Truman's Fair Deal and anything else he considered "communistic" or "socialistic."[4] Lewis was added to the Bureau's mailing list in 1938 after he asked Hoover to fill in for him on his weekly radio program, broadcast coast-to-coast.[5] In a memorandum to Tolson, Hoover noted that Lewis suggested he cover three or four news items in his twelve-minute seg-

Conservative broadcaster Fulton Lewis Jr. was one of the most influential voices on radio from the 1930s to the 1960s. (Library of Congress, Harris & Ewing Collection, Call Number LC-H22-D-6463, Reproduction Number LC-DIG-hec-26581)

ment. "Mr. Lewis stated . . . that any humor that could be injected would be so much the better," Hoover told Tolson. "I stated that I would be very happy to make this broadcast."[6] Reading from a script, Hoover touted a program to encourage civilian fingerprinting and praised Lewis for his role in helping to solve a minor FBI case. Hoover's radio appearance kicked off a cordial, eighteen-year relationship between the two men, who shared strikingly similar views.

While Lewis ruled the right wing on the airwaves, Sokolsky, known as the "high priest of anti-Communism" by his friends, wrote a widely read conservative column, "These Days," that appeared in nearly 300 newspapers nationwide. The son of a Utica, New York, rabbi, Sokolsky spent ten years as a foreign correspondent in Russia and China before returning to the United States as a columnist for the *New York Herald-Tribune*. In 1940, his column was syndicated, and he began a second career as a radio broadcaster. Sokolsky reached truly national status as a commentator when Hearst's King Features Syndicate began distributing his columns in 1944. When Sokolsky died in 1962, former president Herbert Hoover called his death a great loss for the country. "Whether one disagreed with Mr. Sokolsky's views, every one of the tens of millions who read or listened to him respected his courage, his independence, his magnificent literary qualities, as complete devotion to the welfare of our country."[7]

Between the two of them, Sokolsky and Lewis reached homes in every corner of the United States with their reactionary views. Both were anticommunist stalwarts and protectors of a narrow conceptualization of what it meant to be an American. Their xenophobic politics made them eminently compatible with Hoover and, combined with their widespread influence, led the Bureau to judge them worthy of friendship. It is useful to note, however, that hard right politics did not ensure Hoover's friendship. Journalist Westbrook Pegler, the irascible John Birch Society right-winger whom Journalism Guild president Heywood Broun labeled "the light heavyweight champion of the upperdog" and President Harry S. Truman called a "guttersnipe," seemed to be a natural ally for Hoover.[8] Pegler was a labor critic who hated Eleanor Roosevelt and the New Deal. A Minneapolis native, he entered the newspaper business in 1910, working for the United Press in Chicago. After serving in the navy during World War I, Pegler became a *Chicago Tribune* columnist and ultimately joined the nationwide Hearst newspaper syndicate.[9] Pegler was a right-wing critic of power, an analogue to Seldes on the Left. It was likely his unpredictability, along with his unwillingness to become a fawning acolyte of Hoover, that led the FBI to hold Pegler at arm's length, despite his ideological compatibility with the Bureau. Hoover and Pegler rarely corresponded, and when they did, the director's letters were very formal, unlike his interactions with other journalists who shared the same views.

Even though Lewis and Sokolsky shared a similar tendency toward unpredictability and irascibility, their relationships with Hoover and the FBI were far more friendly than Pegler's, likely because they were willing to flatter the director. Like many of Hoover's "friendships," Lewis's relationship with the director was conducted largely through correspondence and surrogates. In 1940, for example, Crime Records chief Nichols reported that he had lunch with Lewis, who pledged his support and offered to give the Bureau script approval of any statements he made about the FBI or its cases. In a statement that must have appealed to Hoover when he read it, Nichols reported that Lewis criticized Washington newspaper reporters: "He made the observation that there is probably more arrogance among Washington correspondents than any other section of the country," Nichols reported. "They feel they are so important they can either make or break an individual."[10]

Lewis's critique of reporters came as the Bureau was undergoing a round of criticism for its handling of wiretapping, the Detroit raids against Spanish Civil War recruiters, and a raid of the New York office of the Christian Front. Supported by controversial radio host Father Coughlin, the Christian Front was suspected of plotting to overthrow the U.S. government. During his lunch with Lewis, Nichols had worked to gain his support for the raid: "I pointed out to him [Lewis] that the case did have serious implications and while we were not afraid of the seventeen people overthrowing the Government at that time, they could have caused a great deal of damage and all great revolutions have sprung from the minds of a few individuals who at the time had seemingly crackpot ideas."[11]

By September 1941, Hoover's correspondence with Lewis had become more personal. Several letters opened with "Dear Fulton" rather than "Mr. Lewis." Their pen-pal relationship progressed to the point that Lewis felt comfortable asking Hoover to publicly endorse a series of broadcasts sponsored by the National Association of Manufacturers promoting the defense industry.[12] Hoover's correspondence team politely denied the request and, to smooth out the relationship, invited Lewis and his wife to attend the opening exercises of the FBI's National Police Academy.[13]

During his August 10, 1942, broadcast, Lewis honored Hoover's twenty-fifth anniversary as a government employee. Lewis forwarded a transcript of the tribute to Hoover, which described the director as "a very brilliant—a very fine, clean person, with the burning devotion to his country, and a magnificently effective organization he has built up."[14] Lewis's defense of Hoover included not only public broadcasts but also private testimonials to influential people. For example, on March 9 and 19, 1943, Lewis visited the Dallas home of oil magnate Clint Murchison Sr. Hoover and Murchison were close friends, and the millionaire often covered the director's tabs at a hotel they both frequented. During a dinner party at Murchison's home attended by seventy-five bankers, reporters, and oil men, Lewis was invited to address the crowd, described as comprising "economic royalists" by Hoover's Dallas SAC, R. G. Danner. Following his remarks, Lewis took questions and was asked why some newspapermen criticized Hoover. Danner reported Lewis's response to Hoover: "Mr. Lewis advised that regardless of their stature or position all newspaper men are part police reporters and, as he expressed it, wanted to park their cars in no-parking zones and to demand favors not accorded the average person."[15]

In turn, Hoover played along with several of Lewis's self-promotion and publicity stunts. In late 1943, for example, Lewis announced on his broadcast that someone had intentionally set a fire in his Los Angeles hotel suite—in the bed where he was supposed to be sleeping. The story, as told by Lewis, played out as an apparent assassination attempt by someone who wanted to silence him. D. M. "Mickey" Ladd ordered agents in Los Angeles to look into the incident. "I told [Los Angeles SAC] Hood that he should not worry too much about the jurisdictional angle but to go into it far enough to keep Lewis satisfied and let him know we are doing something about it," Ladd told his supervisor.[16] Hood's investigation determined that the fire was not caused by arson and that Lewis had never intended to sleep in the bed. The fire was started when Lewis's assistant, returning to the room drunk, dropped a cigarette in a pile of newspapers next to the bed and then, attempting to flee, chose the wrong door and found himself in a closet.[17]

Despite the lack of evidence to support his story, Lewis insisted that an attempt had been made on his life. "I can't understand how the fire started," Lewis told the *Los Angeles Times*. "The circumstances look as if they might be suspicious, although I've never been the target for this sort of thing."[18] Lewis was less equivocal when he spoke to the *Los Angeles Daily News*, which reported that the broadcaster called the fire sabotage and claimed that "enemies" had tried to burn him and his assistant, Fred Morrison, to death.[19] In an interview with FBI agents, he refused to budge: "[Lewis] stated he realized the police and arson investigators handle these cases in a stereotype way, and while he is not a qualified investigator in this field, he personally was of the definite impression that the fire was intentionally set by someone."[20] Despite its lack of jurisdiction in the case, the FBI investigated Lewis's charges sufficiently to keep the columnist happy, even though he likely either overreacted or decided to turn a careless accident into a publicity stunt.

Lewis ran afoul of Hoover in 1945 when he reported that the FBI had refused to investigate an alleged case of bribery involving an Office of Price Administration (OPA) official in San Francisco. According to Lewis, an OPA official had offered to allow the St. Moritz restaurant to change its price schedule in exchange for a $3,000 payment. When the restaurateur reported the incident to the FBI in San Francisco, the Bureau chose not to pursue the matter. Lewis had questioned special agent William H. McAdam of the FBI's

San Francisco office, who told him that, with more than 4,000 investigators at its disposal, the OPA was handling the investigation itself.[21] Lewis's broadcast triggered a flurry of letters to the FBI from critical listeners. Many members of Lewis's audience, which skewed hard to the right, were outraged that Hoover was not on the case. Lewis's suggestion that the Bureau had made a political choice not to investigate threatened the FBI's image as a responsible agency. At the same time, the influx of complaints underlined Lewis's influential status as one of the nation's most listened-to radio commentators. Hoover's damage-control efforts offered standard FBI boilerplate about investigating only crimes that came under its jurisdiction (although that had not stopped the Bureau from investigating Lewis's hotel room fire). Crime Records officials churned out dozens of letters to citizens and met with members of Congress to explain the situation.

The FBI's response to Lewis was very gentle, no doubt because of the broadcaster's enormous influence. A midlevel Crime Records official contacted not Lewis but his assistant, Ed Roddan. The official read him several of the letters received in response to Lewis's broadcast and told Roddan, "We did not believe Mr. Lewis meant to be critical of the FBI and would want to know of this reaction on the part of some of his listeners." According to the agent's report of the conversation, "We were not sure that Mr. Lewis fully understood the situation. . . . I told Mr. Roddan in view of the interest and friendship with Mr. Lewis in the past the Director felt sure he did not intend a critical reaction as a result of his remarks."[22] Given the director's demonstrated sensitivity to news reports that generated public criticism of the FBI, the Bureau's response to Lewis was remarkably tame. But it worked. On May 30, 1945, Lewis went on the air and quoted a letter of clarification he had been sent by Hoover. He then offered his own endorsement of the FBI's responsibility. "I was delighted that Mr. Hoover wrote this letter," Lewis said, adding that it "clears the FBI completely of every responsibility in this case."[23] Several weeks later, Mutual Broadcasting distributed an ad promoting Lewis's program and noting that the commentator had been "cited by J. Edgar Hoover for work with the F.B.I."[24]

Clearly, though, damage had been done to the relationship between Hoover and Lewis. Hoover normally offered travel and other types of assistance to friendly journalists through the FBI's domestic and foreign offices, but that was not the case when Lewis traveled to Honolulu in November 1945 to investigate the 1941 Pearl Harbor attack. Hoover ordered his agents to "be very courteous to Mr. Lewis" but "furnish him no information." They were told to direct Lewis's questions to Washington officials.[25] From that point on, although they still used first-name salutations, their correspondence took on a more formal and routine tone. For example, when Lewis was again the victim of what he considered a suspicious fire—this time at his Maryland home—the FBI ignored his request to send investigators.[26] On another occasion, when Lewis invited Hoover and Tolson to visit his rebuilt home, Hoover declined, saying he had been away and "must dig in" over the weekend.[27]

Their monthly correspondence became more infrequent. Yet Lewis remained a devoted supporter of Hoover and the FBI. For example, in 1950, he stepped in to defend the director against critics of Bureau wiretapping. Lewis told his listeners he could not understand the controversy about the FBI's use of wiretaps, adding that he did not care if anyone listened in to his own conversations since he had no one to fear, particularly anyone as "honorable as the FBI."[28] In 1952, Lewis used his radio program to vilify lawyer and Truman confidant Max Lowenthal, author of a critical book about the FBI. Lewis described Lowenthal as a "red tinted," sinister influence behind the attacks on Hoover.[29] Also in 1952, Lewis parroted Hoover's opposition to the creation of an internal security commission that would have access to FBI files as part of its review of U.S. intelligence services.[30] He praised the FBI's performance in the Greenlease kidnapping case, in which a $600,000 ransom had been paid for the son of a millionaire auto dealer, but the boy was murdered anyway. The FBI's handling of the case had been criticized, but Lewis defended the Bureau, claiming that it had no jurisdiction to get involved. The logical fallacy of praising an agency's performance while simultaneously asserting its lack of jurisdiction apparently did not occur to Lewis.[31]

Despite keeping the commentator at arm's length, Hoover took advantage of an offer to write a guest column during Lewis's 1951 vacation.[32] Hoover and Tolson also accepted Lewis's invitation to attend the screening of a 1952 motion picture, *Walk East on Beacon*, a forgettable thriller in which a G-man tracks a communist cell. More than eighty guests, including many members of Congress and friends of the Bureau, such as journalist Rex Collier, attended the screening. Thus, Hoover's personal time with Lewis would be limited, but the director's staff provided him with a helpful, three-page primer of noncontroversial "personal" topics to raise with his "friend": "there are two or three items on which the Director might wish to make some observation. For the past several years, Fulton has devoted considerable time and energy to a children's choir at the little Methodist church in Hollywood, Maryland. . . . Mrs. Lewis is quite a gardener. They have a sun porch with radiant heat that must be 20 feet wide and about 60 feet long."[33] The creation of a detailed cheat sheet of personal topics was not unusual and unmasks the contrived and ghosted nature of Hoover's "friendship" with journalists like Lewis. While his correspondents might have imagined that the details of their lives they revealed in their letters were familiar to Hoover, the director actually knew very little about his "friends."

During the mid-1950s, Lewis frequently praised Hoover and the FBI, but he devoted his broadcasts—which now included television programs—primarily to attacks on liberal groups such as the Fund for the Republic and liberal journalists such as I. F. Stone and the *New York Times*'s Jack Gould. Lewis dutifully reported rumors of Hoover as a presidential candidate or a Supreme Court justice. He promoted Don Whitehead's authorized history, *The FBI Story*. He eulogized Senator Joseph McCarthy as the victim of a "journalistic lynching."[34] He had become a reliable mimic, spouting FBI public relations boilerplate in response to criticism of the Bureau's handling of the integration of the Little Rock, Arkansas, high school in 1957. Lewis pointed out that the FBI was not a police organization but an investigative one, and he asserted that the Bureau was reluctant to get involved in cases that were better handled by local law enforcement.[35] Those lines could have been written by the FBI's Crime Records staff and had frequently been uttered by Hoover himself.

As the 1950s wound down, so did Lewis's career. Television had supplanted radio as Americans' primary source of entertainment and information. Declining ratings led to the creation, in late 1957, of a "Friends of Fulton Lewis" group dedicated to keeping the commentator on the air.[36] Though Hoover and Lewis rarely corresponded, they saw each other at least twice as the commentator's career waned. In 1962, Lewis wrote to Hoover to thank him for an invitation to an event hosted by the director. "I consider you one of our very greatest all-time Americans," Lewis wrote.[37] Hoover contributed a testimonial that was read at a party honoring Lewis for his twenty-five years as a broadcaster. "I am proud to say that I have been one of your more consistent listeners throughout this quarter century," Hoover's staff wrote on his behalf. "I join your many friends in hoping that you will continue for years to come to broadcast your penetrating interpretation of the news. Our nation needs your voice and the experience behind it."[38] When Lewis died in 1966, Hoover sent a sympathy telegram to the family, noting that Lewis's passing "is a severe loss to the entire country, which can ill afford to lose such dedicated patriots."[39]

As Hoover's arm's-length relationship with Lewis was evolving, his relationship with one of the country's best-known conservative syndicated columnists and broadcasters was ongoing. In George Sokolsky, Hoover had found someone who, like Lewis, was ideologically compatible. Unlike Lewis, though, Sokolsky was less of an unpredictable and bombastic character. Sokolsky's relationship with Hoover began slowly, but ultimately, the two became very close. Sokolsky even became a Bureau informant when he worked as a "clearance man" for the motion picture industry in the 1950s.

The first exchange of letters between the two men occurred in 1944, when Hoover thanked Sokolsky for his positive public statements about the FBI. Sokolsky responded with a glowing endorsement of Hoover's work: "I must tell you that I enjoy the opportunity to speak well of your work which I find is of the highest order because you have not used great power for unworthy causes or to hurt innocent, even if mistaken individuals."[40] Subsequently, however, there was little contact between them. In 1946, Sokolsky wrote a column defending Hoover from attacks in the *Daily Worker*. Sokolsky decried the "systematic, insidious, undercover campaign" being waged against Hoover and closed with a flourish: "Is the FBI essential? It seems to me that the FBI should receive from Congress the largest appropriation in its history—so large that it can really serve America competently in this fight."[41]

A few days later, Sokolsky complained to *Liberty* magazine editor Fulton Oursler, a close friend of Hoover, that he had never met the director face-to-face. Oursler defended Hoover as "very busy" and then reported the conversation to Nichols, who authored a letter to Sokolsky for Hoover's signature.[42] The letter stated that there had been no intent to give Sokolsky the "cold shoulder." "If, perchance, such an impression has been deduced from some specific matter, I would appreciate your writing me in detail in order that I might make a check of the facts," Hoover wrote.[43] Sokolsky responded by suggesting that Oursler had overreacted. "I am quite sure that I have no complaints to make about you or about the FBI but I should very much like to come to know you personally," Sokolsky wrote. "As you can understand from the way I write, that I not only admire your work but have great respect for your courage and manhood and for your deep devotion to America."[44]

Sokolsky's extreme conservatism sometimes put him at odds with his new friend. In 1947, Sokolsky began a campaign urging Congress to investi-gate the FBI, albeit only to determine who was hindering the Bureau's work. Nichols called to dissuade him—an investigation, of course, might reveal the extent of the Bureau's domestic intelligence operations—and he had to work hard to convince Sokolsky to change his mind. "I went into detail with him, pointing out that such a move, while motivated by a good intention, for all practical purposes would cripple the Bureau and that to champion such a program would be to play into the enemy's hands," Nichols reported to Tol-son. "I told him this was the last thing he should do if he wanted to help the cause."[45] Sokolsky maintained that the Bureau "could not do much about" communism. But "I challenged him on this," Nichols told Tolson. "And he agreed that while we could handle overt acts and were equipped and pre-pared to do it, nevertheless to really get after the Communists it would be necessary to root out Communism in the schools, the churches, publications and thinking."[46] Hoover was pleased by the outcome of his aide's conversa-tion with Sokolsky. "This shows value of making such contact & clearing up misunderstandings," Hoover wrote.[47]

Sokolsky proved his value by repeatedly stepping forth to defend the FBI against challenges to its legitimacy. In 1948, for example, Sokolsky wrote a column defending Hoover when rumors circulated in Washington that if presidential front-runner Thomas Dewey were elected, he would fire Hoover. "Dewey is essentially an administrator and therefore seeks efficient men about him, not those who will 'yes' him and then pull the carpet from under him by their errors," Sokolsky wrote. "Therefore, I disbelieve the sto-ries of his 'hate' against J. Edgar Hoover and put them down to campaign twaddle."[48] That same day, Sokolsky spoke to a church congregation in New York, and Nichols was there. "Sokolsky, as could be expected, tore into Com-munism, but did it on the basis of morality," Nichols reported in a memo-randum to Tolson.[49] Nichols then penned a letter to Sokolsky (signed by Hoover) that praised both his column and his speech. "I do wish from the accounts that I have received that I would have heard you," Hoover's ghost-writer lamented. "I certainly think you pin-pointed the most important sin-gle fact in the world today when you observed that what is all-important are high moral principles and if we have these, other things will fall in line."[50]

In 1949, Sokolsky unknowingly stepped into a Bureau controversy over crime programs on the radio. Since 1945, the FBI had collaborated in the production of a radio program called *This Is Your FBI*. It had been created to counter another program that initially had Hoover's blessing but quickly fell out of favor because of its sensationalized portrayals of faux FBI cases and its emphasis on violence: Frederick L. Collins's *The FBI in Peace and War. This Is Your FBI* (which broadcast 409 shows before going off the air in 1953) dramatized FBI cases, with Stacy Harris playing the role of special agent Jim Taylor. With titles like "Death in the Tropics," "Communist Agent," and "The Phantom Hitchhiker," *This Is Your FBI* earned high ratings and ticked all the boxes of the Collier-Cooper narrative.

In 1947, the American Bar Association (ABA) engaged Arthur Freund to study depictions of criminal justice in news and entertainment media. The ABA's Committee on Motion Pictures, Radio Broadcasting, and Comics in Relation to the Administration of Justice began its work in June 1947 and quickly identified two major problems: the emphasis on crime stories, and the way lawyers, judges, and the processes of law were depicted.[51] Ultimately, the committee chose to focus on the second issue, and its report asserted that depictions of crime in news and entertainment media had a "profound impact upon the mind of the juvenile, adolescent, and impressionable, and that grave harm has already resulted thereby to uncounted and perhaps uncountable members of our society." Unless the abuses were stopped, Freund's committee reported, Congress would likely pass legislation prohibiting federal officials from supplying information for dramatic portrayals and restricting the availability of such materials.[52] Freund declared himself personally opposed to any such legislation, particularly since no scientific data existed to prove the link between portrayals of crime for entertainment purposes and immorality in society.[53]

Faced with the specter of congressional action that would limit his public relations efforts, Hoover responded to the committee's early reports with a strangely philosophical statement that seemed to connect the sensational crime stories of *This Is Your FBI* and the works of great authors and poets of antiquity. "The profession of the storyteller is almost as old as language itself, and his favorite theme throughout the ages, long predating radio or the printed word, has been the struggle between good and bad men," according to Hoover's Crime Records ghostwriters. "The Bible itself, the virile epics of the Roman poets, legends, fairy tales, the ballads of the troubadours and the romantic adventure novels of more recent vintage, all have portrayed some phase of the conflict between good and evil."[54] Hoover continued by claiming that, when done well, radio dramas depicting crime educated and protected the public. "Americans have been awakened by their press to protect themselves against the robber and the swindler; to stave off the racketeer and the chiseler; to know the venal politician and recognize his violation of public trust; to appreciate the need for effective law enforcement and for a positive campaign against lawlessness."[55]

On February 1, 1949, Sokolsky entered the controversy, parroting Hoover's position and quoting the Freund report: "The effect of crime movies and radio broadcasts comes from actual reports of the Federal Bureau of Investigation, the respective judges and prosecuting attorneys throughout the United States."[56] That oddly worded quote caught Hoover's eye. "What about this statement?" he scrawled in the margin of a copy that had reached his desk.[57] As a keeper of secrets, Hoover was sensitive to any media story suggesting that FBI reports were shared with those outside the Bureau. Such suggestions undermined the Bureau's image of responsibility and suggested the existence of political motives behind the sharing of information. It was left to Nichols to explain the context of Freund's quote. In a memorandum to Tolson, Nichols noted that Freund had repeatedly complained about the Bureau's role in producing *This Is Your FBI*.[58] In 1947, Hoover had written to Freund, noting that he publicly criticized the irresponsible portrayal of crime but defended "responsible" portrayals like those on *This Is Your FBI*.[59] "Old man Freund is stretching a point in the statement quoted by George Sokolsky," Nichols concluded, but he recommended that no action be taken.[60] Hoover agreed, and Sokolsky was not contacted. However, the criticism of media portrayals of crime, along with the suggestion that secret Bureau reports had been shared, presented a dual threat to the FBI's legitimacy.

Luckily for Hoover, Sokolsky stood ready to issue a defense, and on July 7, 1949, he published a column headlined simply "The FBI." In it, he reinforced all the themes of the Collier-Cooper narrative:

> In our country, it is difficult to do such work as is the duty of the FBI, for, while we desire safety, we eschew the police state. Public opinion would never tolerate such a police organization as the N.K.V.D. of Soviet Russia. We demand of the FBI that it produce all the results of police protection without interfering with those guaranties of rights provided by the Constitution. The American formula is correct and the FBI has not transgressed it.[61]

Sokolsky also asserted the Bureau's utility in combating communism. A "vast international conspiracy," he wrote, requires a large law enforcement agency with the resources and manpower to piece together that conspiracy. "There are about 70,000 Communist party members in the United States and ten times as many friends and sympathizers and innumerable innocents who, for one reason or another do phases of the party's work."[62] Such support from columnists like Sokolsky, who were prized by the FBI as "objective" observers, provided Hoover with a constant reification of his chosen narrative themes. "Very good," Hoover wrote in the margin of the column.[63]

In 1950, a credible Washington insider published a broadside that presaged Fred J. Cook's 1958 takedown of the FBI's authorized history. A Minneapolis native and Harvard Law School graduate, Max Lowenthal had served in many federal government and advisory positions, including secretary of the Wickersham Commission, which investigated enforcement of the Prohibition laws in the early 1930s, and counsel to congressional committees in the 1930s and 1940s. During World War II, Lowenthal had been legal adviser to General Lucius D. Clay, the high commissioner for Germany—an appointment Hoover had attempted to thwart.[64] After decades in Washington, D.C., Lowenthal was well connected: he was a friend of one of Hoover's least favorite members of Congress, Senator Burton K. Wheeler (D-Mont.), as well as a longtime friend and confidant of Harry Truman and Supreme Court justices Louis Brandeis and Felix Frankfurter.

Lowenthal's book, *The Federal Bureau of Investigation*, was published by William Sloane Associates in 1950. In more than 550 carefully documented pages, Lowenthal described the FBI as an effective law enforcement agency that had become entwined in domestic intelligence, passing judgment on individuals' loyalty based on tenuous affiliations and associations. He devoted nearly half the book to the Bureau's early history and role in the Palmer Raids. In the final chapter, "Investigation of Beliefs," Lowenthal questioned whether domestic spying by a large federal law enforcement agency was compatible with democracy. Not surprisingly, given his access to powerful people in Washington, Lowenthal's analysis of the Bureau's intelligence-gathering methods was accurate:

> In addition to building up FBI dossiers on persons attacked by neighbors or acquaintances as "subversive," the FBI has retained a vast number of other names mentioned incidentally in the complaints or acquired by its detectives in investigating the charges it receives. Once a name is brought into an inquiry, by whatever means, it becomes part of the FBI's permanent records, and information or charges against the person thus

included or mentioned in any investigation acquire the permanent status of "information . . . maintained in the files."[65]

Lowenthal's book was a direct challenge to the legitimacy of the FBI, undermining the responsibility meme of the Collier-Cooper narrative and suggesting that the Bureau had become an American secret police force. A *New York Times* reviewer noted that the book "pulled aside the self-righteous cloak in which the F.B.I. has wrapped itself."[66] Lowenthal portrayed the Bureau as an out-of-control agency investigating individuals' beliefs and led by a scheming spy rather than a benevolent sheriff.

In fact, Lowenthal had been sending that message in other venues for years, and the Bureau's interest in him predated Hoover's tenure as director. By 1950, the FBI had compiled an extensive file on Lowenthal, documenting investigations that included everything from reading his mail to active surveillance. The Bureau suspected that, despite being a prominent and well-connected attorney, Lowenthal was a communist. More important, Hoover viewed Lowenthal as a threat to the Bureau's legitimacy long before the publication of his book. A 1945 summary memorandum described Lowenthal as having "consistently and persistently engaged in a vilification campaign against the Federal Bureau of Investigation predicated on an aggravated distortion of facts."[67]

In his November 30, 1950, column, Sokolsky tore into Lowenthal, closely mirroring FBI assessments of the author. Sokolsky alluded to Lowenthal's testimony before the House Un-American Activities Committee (HUAC) that year. In several instances, Lowenthal had refused to answer questions about his government work or simply said he could not remember details of certain incidents. Sokolsky, a consummate red-baiter, observed, "Time after time, Mr. Lowenthal cannot remember dates, names, facts which no ordinary man could forget. It is difficult to help wondering how a man who forgets so much so easily could remember so much about the FBI."[68]

A televised challenge to the FBI's legitimacy in 1952 afforded Sokolsky another opportunity to promote Hoover's interests. On April 10, *New York Herald-Tribune* television critic John Crosby appeared on the WTTG-TV program *The Author Meets the Critics* in New York City. Actress Faye Emerson—famous for her high cheekbones and for being a former daughter-in-law of President Roosevelt—was the host. The format of the program permitted two journalists, one in support and one in opposition, to question an author about his or her work. On that evening, Merle Miller, author of

Undated photograph of attorney Max Lowenthal with then-Senator Harry S. Truman. When Lowenthal's critical book about the FBI was published in 1950, Hoover enlisted George Sokolsky and others to publicly undermine Lowenthal. (Library of Congress, Harris & Ewing Collection, Call Number LC-H22-D-4707, Reproduction Number LC-DIG-hec-25181)

The Judges and the Judged, faced off against Crosby and reactionary anticommunist evangelist and former FBI agent Theodore C. Kirkpatrick, publisher of the *Counterattack* newsletter and editor of a book titled *Red Channels: The Report of Communist Influence in Radio and Television,* which outed 151 alleged communists in the entertainment industry.

Kirkpatrick (known as "Mr. Counterattack") and two other former FBI agents, John G. Keenan and Kenneth M. Bierly, had founded *Counterattack* in 1947. It was a four-page weekly compendium of rumor and innuendo relating to alleged communists and fellow travelers. The publication used many of the same devices employed by Hoover's FBI, including the declaration of a smear campaign against it. In the April 11 issue of *Counterattack* (one day after Kirkpatrick's appearance on *The Author Meets the Critics*), the editors charged that Miller's book was "the culmination of the campaign spearheaded by the Communist Party (CP) to smear Counterattack."[69] One claim in Miller's book particularly irked the *Counterattack* editors: that Hoover disapproved of *Counterattack* and *Red Channels*. On April 1, Keenan wrote to Hoover and asked whether it was true. The nondenial in Hoover's response was telling. On April 4, he wrote: "While I do not know the basis upon which Mr. Miller has made this statement, I thought you might like to know that I have always refused to dignify with a denial anything which he has written or said."[70] Apparently failing to perceive the subtleties of Hoover's ambivalent response, Keenan called the FBI to ask whether Kirkpatrick could use the director's letter on *The Author Meets the Critics*. Not surprisingly, he was told that the correspondence was personal and could not be mentioned on the air.[71]

In fact, Miller's book criticized the entertainment industry's communist purges that authors like Kirkpatrick catalyzed through their vituperative publications. In Kirkpatrick, the producers of *The Author Meets the Critics* had chosen a provocative guest to interrogate Miller. And in Crosby, they had selected one of Kirkpatrick's most vocal critics. The year before, Crosby had called *Red Channels* "one of the dizziest phenomena of the postwar period. . . . Its chief editor, Theodore Kirkpatrick, is on the record as saying, 'We've never said the facts in "Red Channels" were correct or incorrect.'"[72]

Viewers hoping for a lively discussion were not disappointed. According to FBI Crime Records official Milton A. Jones, who watched and summarized the program for Nichols, Kirkpatrick termed Miller's book "dishonest and stupid" and claimed that its purpose, among other things, was to smear *Counterattack*.[73] Crosby defended Miller's book and charged that Kirkpatrick was interested only in "damaging people"; he also quoted Hoover as having said, "Don't call anyone a Communist unless you have the facts."[74]

During the rebuttal period, Emerson interrupted Kirkpatrick's rant and, according to Jones, "in a very high-handed manner demanded to know if he was accusing Crosby and Miller of being Communists." Kirkpatrick said he believed both were being used by communists.[75] Miller said his critique was based on the fact that few of those making accusations against supposed communists were trained investigators, noting that Kirkpatrick's FBI service was limited to just a few years during World War II. It was during the rebuttal that Crosby made a claim that angered Hoover, struck at the Bureau's legitimacy, and resulted in the FBI opening an investigation into his background. Crosby accused Kirkpatrick and his colleagues of exaggerating their service in the FBI. "Everybody was in the FBI during the War," Crosby said. "It was a way of getting out of the Army. We have copy boys on our paper who were in the FBI during the war." Jones noted that the studio audience could be heard booing Crosby at the end of his outburst.[76] In the margin of Jones's memo, Hoover wrote: "This is an outrageous allegation. We ought to nail this. What do our files show on Crosby?"[77] In his summary of the program, Jones agreed with Crosby's assertion that Kirkpatrick and his ilk were exaggerating their FBI service for effect. "[Kirkpatrick] attempted to rely to a great extent on the prestige of the Director and the fact that he was a former Agent of the Bureau."[78]

Of course, Crosby's assessment of the FBI as a clearinghouse for men seeking to avoid military service undermined the Bureau's legitimacy by suggesting that its personnel were neither professional nor capable. Hoover was livid and ordered New York SAC Edward Scheidt to confront Crosby. According to Scheidt, Crosby broke down in tears and pledged to write a letter of apology. "He said he was so mad at [Kirkpatrick] that he simply lost his head," Scheidt reported. "Crosby said he could kick himself all over for having made this mistake."[79] Nichols responded that a letter was not enough. "There were an estimated 500,000 listeners who heard Crosby's remarks," he wrote, and he told Scheidt that "nothing short of a correction of the record would satisfy us." Hoover added that the proper penance would be an apology at the beginning of the next episode of *The Author Meets the Critics*.[80]

Nichols authored Hoover's letter to Crosby. "Every man has a right to express himself as he desires," it stated. "He also has the responsibility, however, of truly relating facts." Hoover told Crosby that his statement was "maliciously false" and closed with a threat: "I do not intend to let this statement go unchallenged."[81] Crosby quickly responded. "I'm afraid it was a low blow and I deeply regret having made it," he wrote. He then turned his attention to former FBI agent Kirkpatrick, who had leveraged his Bureau connections to become an authority on communism. "I still think that [Kirkpatrick's] constant use of [his FBI service] is doing your organization more harm than anything I could have said," Crosby wrote. "I was furiously angry at a man who accused me of being a dupe of the Communist Party for which I have the utmost loathing. [Kirkpatrick] has smeared a great many innocent people. I regret having been induced by anger into emulating his own methods."[82]

After dismissing the idea of complaining to the program's sponsor, Pepsi-Cola, the Bureau turned its attention to determining a suitable medium for Crosby's public apology. Frantic negotiations followed. Hoover sent a telegram to officials of the DuMont Network. "Your vast TV audience has no way of knowing of Mr. Crosby's apology," Hoover said. "In fairness to thousands of loyal patriotic FBI agents who entered our service during war years, I feel they deserve to have the record set straight over the same medium used to cast reflection upon them last week."[83] Crosby, Scheidt, and DuMont Network officials quickly agreed to air the apology on the April 17 episode of *The Author Meets the Critics*. Reaching consensus on the contents of the apology was not so easy. Crosby asked for changes to the text that would be read by Faye Emerson. He wanted to emphasize his frustration with Kirkpatrick as the reason for his outburst. The FBI wanted a "clean cut" apology without any conditions or justifications. Nichols instructed Scheidt not to give in to Crosby and added, "if necessary, we will take the matter into our own hands."[84]

Bureau officials pressured Crosby's superiors at the *New York Herald-Tribune*. Specifically, they contacted one of the sons of publisher Helen Rogers Reid. Reid had inherited the publisher's chair when her husband, Ogden Mills Reid, died in 1947.[85] The couple had two sons, Whitelaw Reid II and Ogden R. Reid, both of whom held management positions at the newspaper. The name of the particular son contacted by the FBI has been redacted in its files. Nichols reported on his conversation with one of the Reid heirs, noting that he was "pretty low about the whole incident" and that he was "all for firing Crosby." Nichols also reported that, according to his inside source, the other brother "simply does not comprehend the situation" and that his mother, publisher Helen Rogers Reid, was angry but indecisive. Nichols reported that the publisher's son "let his hair down" and "was very bitter over some of the people in the Tribune who have been influencing his mother." Nichols then suggested that Crosby's statement was more than simply an expression of frustration over Kirkpatrick's claims:

> told [redacted, but either Whitelaw Reid II or Ogden R. Reid] that certainly it was a tragedy and especially in view of all of the good work and the efforts he had made to purge the Herald Tribune of the "pink tinge" for someone in his own shop to come right in behind him and undermine him. I told him as far as he and his mother were concerned, our feelings had not changed but we certainly could not afford to compromise with a scoundrel like Crosby. [Redacted] stated that Crosby is just one more name in his little black book and that in time he will find a way to deal with him.[86]

Hoover, as always, took the hardest line: "We must not yield an inch. This fellow Crosby is a rat," he wrote in the margin of Nichols's memorandum.[87]

The FBI, meanwhile, had begun an intensive review of Crosby's background, gathering information from its own carefully indexed files and adding new information from the reporter's military records. The review found no evidence of any subversive connections, and the FBI's judgment that Crosby was not a friend of the Bureau seems to have been based entirely on his disdain for the Hoover-authorized *This Is Your FBI* radio program, along with his criticism of Kirkpatrick and *Red Channels*.[88] As a result of the file review, FBI assistant director Alan H. Belmont ordered the New York office to conduct a "very discreet" inquiry into Crosby's background. As was typical during the Hoover era, Belmont jumped directly from Crosby's criticism of the FBI and blacklists to communism. "I pointed out that Crosby's zeal for civil liberties would seem to center on the alleged civil liberties of Communists or Communist fronters," he wrote.[89]

Despite the bluster of Hoover and Nichols, the apology read during the April 17 episode of *The Author Meets the Critics* was not the "clean cut" mea culpa they desired. Emerson reported that Crosby intended no reflection on the "patriotism and integrity of the splendid organization for which he has always had the utmost respect. He [Crosby] explained that the discussion was so surcharged [*sic*] with emotion that he lost his temper, and did not intend the implication against the FBI conveyed by the words used by him."[90]

On April 22, Sokolsky informed his readers—an audience vastly larger than the few who saw *The Author Meets the Critics* on April 10—of the incident. "John Crosby may not like Ted Kirkpatrick because of 'Counterattack' and 'Red Channels,' but to attack the FBI's war record, in the year 1952, is a dangerous support of men and women whom no American should regard as friends," Sokolsky wrote. "The FBI kept this country free of Hitler's agents during the war; the FBI can do the same in relation to Stalin's agents."[91] Thus, Sokolsky used a statement made on a low-rated program during the early days of television, when relatively few American homes had TV sets, as an opportunity to promote the FBI.

The next day, Sokolsky started working in another capacity for the FBI—as a confidential informant. The year 1950 had ushered in the golden age of blacklisting when the U.S. Supreme Court declined to hear the appeals of the so-called Hollywood Ten, who had been convicted of contempt of Congress for refusing to name names for the House Un-American Activities Committee. More than 300 Hollywood personalities were publicly named as communists by the HUAC and blacklisted. Several grassroots groups stepped up as enforcers of the blacklist. One of them, the American Legion, devised a system for "clearing" those individuals accused of being communists. According to historian Richard Gid Powers, the Legion engaged an expert on communism to handle these clearances:

> It [clearance] was a process that entailed a visit to local Legion officials to explain suspect affiliations. Those who refused to state whether they were Communists or refused to disavow past Communist associations became unemployable. Those who satisfied this initial scrutiny were asked to "write the letter" requesting clearance. The industry and Legion selected George Sokolsky as a kind of "pope" of the clearance process, to sit in judgment on the accuracy and sincerity of those letters.[92]

In addition to gaining Sokolsky's approval, blacklisted persons were required to provide the FBI with a statement and to volunteer to testify before HUAC before they could be considered employable in Hollywood.

Just to be sure no communists slipped through the dragnet, Sokolsky provided copies of the letters he received to the FBI, beginning with the first set of six letters mailed to Crime Records chief Nichols on April 23, 1952. "These letters are sent to you for your files and information," Sokolsky wrote. "They are to be treated confidentially. Similar letters will be sent to you from time to time addressed to officials of all companies."[93] Sokolsky forwarded another dozen letters to the FBI on May 8,[94] another eight letters followed on May 15,[95] and four more letters were shared with the FBI on May 26.[96] (All these letters have been withheld from public release via the Freedom of Information Act under a privacy exemption.) In many cases, the FBI forwarded the letters to the Los Angeles SAC as part of the Bureau's investigation of the motion picture industry (COMPIC).[97] Ironically, when a correspondent wrote to Sokolsky in 1957 and alleged that one in five Americans was included on some kind of FBI blacklist, the columnist was unequivocal: "No such blacklist exists."[98]

In ensuing years, Sokolsky remained a faithful defender of the FBI. In 1955, he was invited to speak to the graduating class of the FBI's National Police Academy.[99] In 1956, he wrote a column promoting Don Whitehead's authorized FBI history and contrasting it to Lowenthal's. Restating the Collier-Cooper thesis, Sokolsky wrote that Whitehead's book was valuable because "it gives much of the story of how this country evaded the dangers of establishing a national police force. . . . By avoiding the responsibility for prosecuting, the FBI avoided the possibility of becoming a national police force."[100] During Sokolsky's many years as a syndicated columnist, the FBI clipped and filed dozens of his columns that promoted the Bureau's position on one issue or another. Sokolsky's column was one of four read every day by Hoover.[101] No other nationally syndicated columnist of the era devoted more words to the defense and promotion of Hoover and the Bureau than Sokolsky did.

Sokolsky's work on Hoover's behalf continued until his death in December 1962. Two months before he died, Sokolsky's column offered Hoover as a model of respect for civil liberties:

> Government bureaus have a way of excusing excessive and improper harassment of citizens by explaining that the instructions came from those in authority, which is no explanation at all. Since the time when Harlan F. Stone was Attorney General, it was the pride of the nation that J. Edgar Hoover stood like Horatio, one man against all the forces of government to prevent his FBI from becoming a Federal Police and safeguarding his country from becoming either a police state or tolerating vigilante movements on the part of the citizens. This alone made J. Edgar Hoover a hero in the eyes of the American people and the FBI has been respected beyond any other similar organization.[102]

Ideologically, Sokolsky and Lewis hewed as far right as Hoover did—and in some instances, farther. The massive audiences for their syndicated columns and radio broadcasts made them both valuable collaborators for the FBI (Lewis's odd tendency toward self-promoting stunts notwithstanding). It is clear that Hoover understood the value of maintaining close ties to these two men. For their part, Sokolsky and Lewis gained credibility with their conservative followers through their association with Hoover and the FBI. Unlike others who made their careers based on their relationships with Hoover, Sokolsky and Lewis were already successful and famous on their own. Hoover's favor was not crucial to their audience appeal. Whereas *Reader's Digest* editor Fulton Oursler, *Chicago Tribune* reporter Walter Trohan, and *Memphis Commercial Appeal* associate editor Jack Carley were feted as "friends," Sokolsky and Lewis maintained a more distant connection to the FBI, based more on ideology and ambition than personal appeal.

Although influencing the news media was the day-to-day focus of the Crime Records staff, the FBI simultaneously worked to establish a more enduring record, a body of knowledge that emphasized its preferred themes in the more intellectually weighty genre of books. To do so, the FBI engaged friendly authors to reinterpret Bureau history to more closely match the Collier-Cooper themes.

Chapter 10

Renewing the FBI Story
in Bureau-Authorized Books

In early May 1957, award-winning reporter Don Whitehead was paid $1,000 to deliver the Don Mellett Memorial Lecture in Journalism at the University of Nebraska–Lincoln. Whitehead, a former Associated Press newsman and then a *New York Herald-Tribune* reporter, took the opportunity to lavish praise on an organization he called "the symbol of integrity and efficiency" in the federal government, J. Edgar Hoover's FBI.[1] In a speech meticulously vetted by FBI officials days earlier, Whitehead defended the Bureau against charges that it had become too powerful, a threat to fundamental freedoms of speech and thought. "There is no danger of 'gestapo' as long as our President is a man of honor, as long as our courts protect defendants' rights, as long as Congress is uncorrupted, as long as the press remains vigilant and exposes wrongdoing at all levels of government," Whitehead told his audience. "Today we have an FBI of which we can be proud—and let's insist it stay that way."[2]

On that evening, criticism of the Bureau's investigation of alleged communists—a "witch hunt," as many on the Left referred to it—was not on the agenda. It is likely that Whitehead's audience in Lincoln, smack in the middle of the country and essentially a world away from the ideological warfare in Washington, D.C., seldom encountered *I. F. Stone's Weekly* or the *New York Post*, with their tendentious coverage of the FBI. In a matchup based on journalistic credibility, FBI critics scarcely measured up. Stone, because of his leftist politics and unwillingness to condemn communism, had become a pariah. His *Weekly* was influential, but only among a small group of liberal elites. James A. Wechsler, despite his anticommunist credentials, was just another labor journalist to Nebraskans (those who had heard of him). George Seldes had long left the stage and entered oblivion. And Fred J. Cook was a mere rewrite man operating on the communism-tainted political Left. Whitehead, in contrast, was widely considered one of the nation's most im-

On July 25, 1956, Don Whitehead, two-time Pulitzer Prize–winning journalist and author of The FBI Story: A Report to the People, *was presented with a plaque bearing his FBI ID badge. (National Archives at College Park, Record Group 65, Series H, Box 22, #1321-2)*

portant, authoritative, and objective journalists. Whereas I. F. Stone was small, chubby, deaf, and invisible, Whitehead was imposing and famous, a macho war correspondent who had stormed beaches and risked his life in battle. His journalistic work as a correspondent for the Associated Press and then as Washington bureau chief for the *Herald-Tribune* was highly regarded.

Whitehead was also considered the nation's most authoritative voice (after Hoover) on the inner workings of the FBI, having authored a best-selling book, *The FBI Story: A Report to the People* (1956). Chosen for the job by Hoover himself, Whitehead demonstrated the ongoing salience of the science, responsibility, and Hoover memes of the Collier-Cooper narrative created in the 1930s. Whitehead's book seldom pushed beyond the well-known and well-loved heroic stories of FBI history. But what the leftist critics might see as just another public relations puff piece, the public saw as a famed, objective journalist's independent retelling of fabled truths. Promotional materials for Whitehead's book claimed that he had been given "unrestricted" access to Bureau files and personnel in order to tell the true story. Hoover, who wrote the book's foreword, stated: "The author was free to ask questions and we felt it was our duty to provide him with full facts so he could form his own independent judgment on our policies, procedures and performance. . . . This volume, then is Mr. Whitehead's report. He has selected the material which has been used and the facts reported are supported by the Bureau's record."[3]

Reviewers with their own impeccable leftist credentials helpfully reinforced the notion that the book represented an objective work of journalism. As Whitehead said in his preface, his goal was to "learn the facts so I could report the inside story of the FBI."[4] In *Commentary* magazine, book reviewer and six-time Socialist Party presidential candidate Norman Thomas reinforced the objective reporting theme. "It comes close to being a eulogy of the man and the institution," he wrote. "It would, however, be very unfair to dismiss the book with this statement. Unquestionably it is an honest piece of work."[5]

In a piece illustrated by a photograph of FBI agents firing tracer rounds from submachine guns, *New York Times* reviewer Cabell Phillips lavished praise on *The FBI Story*, highlighting Whitehead's trustworthiness and journalistic credentials. "This highly readable book of Don Whitehead's does nothing to destroy the aura or mystery and high adventure which surrounds the F.B.I., but it does offer a pleasing and reassuring change of pace in the literature about it," Phillips wrote. "It is the nearest thing extant to a sober and definitive history of probably the most efficient police and intelligence agency in the world. And while it is freighted with enough gunfire and derring-do to suit the most discriminating mystery fan, the book as a whole is written with the restraint and respect for facts which one expects of a first-class journalist like Mr. Whitehead."[6] Whitehead's effectiveness in capturing the FBI's preferred image of restraint was evident in Phillips's closing paragraph:

Mr. Whitehead, who heads *The New York Herald-Tribune*'s Washington bureau, makes it clear that the F.B.I. is a one-man organization, molded in the moral and administrative image of J. Edgar Hoover, its director for more than thirty-two years. Loyalty and discipline are the two prime requisites of a successful G-Man. If there are some dangers implicit in this authoritarian concept—as some contend—there is the compensating advantage that the F.B.I. has evolved into a strongly protective arm of Government and one whose integrity has not been successfully challenged.[7]

District of Columbia ACLU director Irving Ferman, who reviewed the book for *The New Republic*, agreed. Whitehead's book, he observed, made a solid case that the Bureau's investigations of suspected communists were restrained and careful and, most important, the result of orders from above. "Whitehead therefore makes it clear that the FBI has been delegated clear authority to perform its intelligence functions," Ferman wrote. "But has it acted, as FBI critics maintain, in Gestapo-like fashion? I would answer unequivocally in the negative."[8] Readers of *The New Republic* might not have been so sanguine about Ferman's positive review of *The FBI Story* had they known that, at the same time, he was writing to Nichols to warn the FBI about an ACLU member's plan to attack the House Un-American Activities Committee.[9] Ferman was one of those "reliable" informers the FBI used to monitor the Left. Acknowledging Hoover's letter thanking him for the positive review, Ferman gushed, "My only wish is to have a forum someday to express my feeling that the FBI has been the positive force, perhaps the strongest, for the preservation of our liberty during the cold war period."[10]

Whitehead's nearly 600-page FBI file and related files from other authors who worked with the Bureau suggest that the author's collaboration with the FBI was far from a work of honesty, openness, or independent judgment. Instead, Whitehead, like other friends of the Bureau lucky enough to collaborate with the FBI, allowed Hoover to control nearly every aspect of the project. In return for prior restraint, Whitehead and other friendly authors were granted highly selective and limited access to FBI public relations materials. They showed their gratitude by becoming "objective" public promoters and defenders of Hoover and the FBI. For some, like Whitehead, that adjunct status was formalized with designation as a "service contact," a title reserved only for those most discreet and useful friends who were willing to provide information to the FBI and to attack critics or otherwise defend the organization. "If I never have anything to do more difficult than tell people the facts of life about the FBI—then I'm loafing," Whitehead wrote in a letter to Hoover. "And I'm sure you know that whenever I can help the cause—you need only to call."[11]

When public relations pioneer Ivy Lee was asked in 1915 to explain his obligation as a publicity agent to confirm facts and adhere to standards of truth, he said, "I had no responsibility for the facts and no duty beyond compiling them and getting them into the best form for publicity work."[12] Despite his Pulitzer Prize pedigree, when it came to the FBI, Whitehead was little more than a publicity agent passing along the Bureau's facts; he did not undertake any independent verification or even discuss the concerns of critics, other than with his Bureau handlers. In his work with the FBI, Whitehead was as uncritical as former circus promoter Courtney Ryley Cooper had been in coauthoring the Collier-Cooper thesis in the 1930s.

Among the dozens of journalists and authors who vied for the opportunity to write an authorized history of the FBI, Whitehead was a savvy choice by Hoover. He brought impeccable journalistic credentials and credibility to the task. A Kentucky native, Whitehead had first won acclaim during World War II, reporting on Normandy, the liberation of Paris, the Allied invasion of Sicily, and Montgomery's North African campaign. He was the first American reporter to file a dispatch out of liberated Paris. In 1950, he covered the American landing at Inchon and the capture of Seoul. For that coverage, he won his first Pulitzer Prize in 1951. In 1953, Whitehead won his second Pulitzer for his story "The Great Deception," about a secret trip to Korea by President-elect Dwight Eisenhower. For that story he also won a George Polk Award and a Sigma Delta Chi Award. After World War II, he was one of sixteen correspondents to be awarded the Medal of Freedom by President Harry S. Truman.[13]

What Whitehead and other journalists came to defend and amplify was simply a retelling of the 1930s Collier-Cooper narrative that had morphed, twenty years later, into the dogma at the heart of the Bureau's news management strategy. The scientific, restrained FBI of legend was built and maintained through the Bureau's careful investigation of prospective collaborators' backgrounds, its tight management of information, and authors' willingness to cede all control over the finished product to FBI editors. Journalists who desired access to Hoover's cache of information and cultural cachet essentially became public relations adjuncts à la Ivy Lee, unquestioningly passing along the facts they were provided. Any effort to go beyond the Collier-Cooper constraints could result in being moved from the friends to the enemies column.

Thomas, for example, noted the lack of original reporting in Whitehead's book and pointed out a few glaring omissions, such as the fact that controversial, red-baiting Wisconsin senator Joseph McCarthy did not appear in the text. "We are left to guess Mr. Hoover's opinion of him," Thomas wrote. "There is no clear account of the degree to which the FBI was drawn into very dubious types of loyalty and security investigation."[14]

The nature of Whitehead's objectivity should have been more than a marketing question. Robert A. Hackett has described the central tenets of objectivity: detachment from sources, nonpartisanship, a reliance on facts and balance, and equal access for opposing sources.[15] Richard Hofstetter has identified several sources of bias in news reporting, including a structural bias in which certain political actors receive more coverage, or more positive coverage, because they position themselves as authoritative sources who provide timely, vivid, colorful information when needed.[16] The popular fiction of the dogged, independent reporter comes apart when the reality of the work is considered in context. News work falls in the gap between the principle of objectivity, as described by Hackett, and the reality of for-profit media organizations that rely on authoritative sources and seek out timely, colorful stories to attract readers. In that quest for access to authoritative sources who (like Hoover) control massive amounts of information that the public desires, reporters cannot apply strict notions of objectivity to their work. Objectivity could require a reporter to write a critical story, resulting in the loss of access to information and, as the dominoes fall, a perception that the reporter isn't professional or dogged enough to "get the story."

Many authors and journalists ceded their power to critically evaluate source material to the Bureau's public relations officials: journalist Frederick L. Collins, whose book about the FBI was published in 1943; journalist John Floherty, who collaborated with the FBI on a book for young people in 1942; author Carroll Burleigh Colby, who in 1953 received FBI assistance on a short book of photographs and captions; and Whitehead. A review of their work demonstrates the one-sided relationship between the Bureau and its authors, while also highlighting the benefits and dangers of becoming one of Hoover's favored collaborators.

The FBI received requests from journalists and authors seeking to collaborate every day. They pitched everything from radio and television programs to feature stories and, of course, books. Such requests, typically couched in flattering language intended to confirm the author's admiration for Hoover and the FBI, were strategically triaged. Many of the requests were denied, usually in language that emphasized Bureau staff members' busy schedules. In most cases, assistant director Nichols in the Crime Records Division assessed the worthiness of FBI cooperation, based on factors such as the character and loyalty of the author and the potential impact of the resulting report on strategically important audiences. Several rules appear to have guided Nichols's recommendations. One key factor in every case in which the FBI agreed to cooperate was the author's willingness to give the Bureau complete editorial control over the finished product. Prepublication control meant that if authors wanted to enjoy an ongoing relationship with the Bureau, they could not critically evaluate the information provided by the FBI. Nor could they do their own independent reporting, such as interviewing individuals with opposing points of view. Finally, authors who were unknown to Nichols were name-checked against the FBI's files, and any hint of a subversive connection or any critical writings or utterances were sufficient to flag the person as an enemy of the Bureau. Those individuals were sent a "too busy" response. If the FBI chose to collaborate, authors were deluged with information in the form of interesting case reports, news clippings, and other materials that had been carefully chosen and vetted for public consumption.

Frederick L. Collins was one of the first journalists to collaborate with the FBI on a book. Educated at Harvard, Collins was an experienced journalist who had been editor of *Woman's Home Magazine* from 1906 to 1910 before serving as president of McClure Publications from 1911 to 1920. During the last seven years of his tenure, he also acted as editor of *McClure's* magazine, a Progressive Era muckraking publication. After working in the War Department during World War I, Collins spent a year as president of the Periodical Publishers Association of America. He was a freelance writer until 1932, when he became the principal staff writer for *Liberty* magazine, a position he held until 1942, when he got involved in the radio industry.[17] In 1942, Collins contacted the FBI and proposed a collaboration on a book. *The FBI in Peace and War*, published in 1943, was the definitive FBI-authorized history until Whitehead's book came out thirteen years later.

Collins's approach to the task was identical to Whitehead's. *The FBI in Peace and War* was written with the assistance of Crime Records staff and included not a single word of criticism. As with Whitehead's book, an introduction by Hoover declared that in no sense was Collins's book a "controlled or censored account. Mr. Collins has scrupulously maintained his position as an independent outside observer entitled to his own interpretations and conclusions."[18] Hoover's declared belief in fostering the independence of his authors was simply a reinforcement of the Bureau's image of practicing restraint in all things. In reality, of course, Collins, Whitehead, and the other authors who collaborated with the Bureau in the 1940s and 1950s were anything but independent observers. They were forced to acquiesce to the FBI's constraints on their projects in order to maintain their access to inside information.

On August 24, 1942, *New York Herald-Tribune* reporter John Floherty contacted Nichols, requesting assistance on a book for teens about the FBI. Born of American parents in Ireland, Floherty moved to the United States at age twenty and became an artist, photographer, reporter, and publicist. Beginning in the 1930s, he realized that his teenage children and their friends were interested in the tales of his many different occupations. That observation developed into a thirty-year career as the author of youth-oriented books. Upon his death in 1964, Floherty was hailed as "a star reporter for American youth."[19]

In his 1942 request to Nichols, Floherty noted that he had written many other books for teens that could be found "in most of the schools and libraries of the United States."[20] Within three weeks, special agents in New York had completed a thorough investigation of Floherty's character and loyalty. Agents discovered that Floherty's home in New York was valued at $60,000, that there were no internal security flags in his record, and that he was well regarded in his field.[21] J. J. McGuire, a Crime Records staffer, spoke to Floherty by phone and then recommended to Nichols that the FBI cooperate on the book.[22] Nichols agreed, pointing out in his recommendation to Tolson, Hoover's top aide, that Floherty's previous books "have a rather widespread distribution particularly since they are placed in most of the high school and grade school libraries."[23]

The investigation proved that Floherty was potentially a reliable collaborator whose work could be of strategic value to the FBI. But in this and other cases, it was Floherty's willingness to cede control of the book's content that convinced FBI officials to work with him. After their telephone conversation, McGuire reported that Floherty "wants the Bureau to thoroughly check everything he writes in the interest of accuracy."[24] Bureau editors' meticulous control over how the FBI was portrayed was what gave the Collier-Cooper narrative its longevity.

In 1953, another writer of nonfiction for youth, Carroll Burleigh Colby, contacted Hoover and requested assistance on a book about the FBI. Colby had authored several pictorial books for children, such as *Submarine: Men and Ships of the U.S. Submarine Fleet* and *Ships of Our Navy: Carriers, Battle-*

ships, Destroyers, and Landing Craft. Through his public relations staff, Hoover replied that it would be impossible to help. "I regret that the volume of work confronting us here at the FBI at the present time makes it impossible for me to be of service."[25] But Colby did not give up.

A New Hampshire native, Colby had served in the U.S. Customs Service before selling his first story in 1939. He supported himself as an aviation writer, and during World War II, he served as a war correspondent with the U.S. Army in noncombat areas. In 1950, he published his first book, *Gabbit the Rabbit*, and in 1951, he published his first book of photographs for children, *Our Fighting Jets.* By the time of his death in 1977, Colby had published ninety-three books with titles ranging from *Earthmovers* to *Wild Dogs.* His most popular work, other than his book on the FBI, was an odd collection of UFO and other supernatural tales titled *Strangely Enough,* published in 1959. "I think the secret (if there is one), of successful writing for youngsters is first of all to like writing, youngsters, and what they like," Colby wrote in a family history. "To me, writing for youngsters is a wonderful 'racket.'"[26]

By 1942, Colby was already known to the FBI. That year, Colby informed the FBI that he suspected two Japanese agents were being sheltered at a Catholic parish near his upstate New York home, prompting the FBI to undertake an enemy alien investigation.[27] The "Japanese agents" turned out to be Korean immigrants who had sought shelter at the church.[28] The incident was mentioned in a memorandum attached to the draft of the response to Colby, but the conclusion was: "Files indicate nothing derogatory with correspondent [Colby]."[29]

Undaunted by the rejection of his proposal, Colby visited the New York FBI office and was directed to write a second letter, this time addressing his proposal to the person most qualified to assess the value of such a book: Nichols. "I assure you this would take a minimum of time and inconvenience from a Bureau member," Colby wrote. He also enclosed an outline but noted, "Undoubtedly you or your staff would have far better suggestions due to your close touch with the bureau and its activities."[30] Nichols recommended that the FBI consider Colby's request and start by investigating his background. On December 23, 1953, a two-page investigative summary was forwarded to Hoover by the New York office. Agents had reviewed Colby's credit and voting records and confirmed his address, marriage, and employment history, noting once again that "no derogatory information" was found.[31] Nichols's aide Milton A. Jones recommended on January 4, 1954, that the FBI extend its cooperation to Colby, "under the condition that the Bureau must give its absolute approval to all material in the book."[32] On January 19, Jones reported that Colby "was in absolute agreement that the Bureau would have complete control over the material used in his book."[33]

Another journalist and author of youth-oriented books, Quentin Reynolds, had also contacted the Bureau in 1953 with a proposal for a book about the FBI. Reynolds, a former war correspondent, was perhaps best known for having been the victim of a literary hoax. Reynolds's story of George Dupre first appeared in *Reader's Digest* and was later expanded into a book, *The Man Who Wouldn't Talk*, published by Random House. Dupre was a Canadian who claimed that, while participating in the French Resistance during World War II, he acted like the village idiot to avoid detection by the gestapo but was ultimately captured and tortured by the Germans. Dupre's story was discovered to be false when a Canadian Air Force officer reported that he had served with Dupre not in France but in Canada. As a result of the scandal, Random House simply changed the book's designation from nonfiction to fiction, and it sold well. "I would have bet my life on that man," Reynolds told the *New York Times*. "He didn't ask for money and was surprised when he was told he would share in the proceeds of the book's sale."[34]

Reynolds was known by the FBI for his work as a war correspondent. On October 17, 1947, Defense Secretary James V. Forrestal had requested information on Reynolds, and Hoover reported that he had known Reynolds for years and, while "he might properly be termed a confirmed liberal, he has said he 'despises Communism.'"[35] Hoover also attached a nine-page "blind memorandum" on Reynolds.[36] (Blind memoranda, which were typed on white paper with no marks indicating that the FBI was the source of the information, were commonly used to distribute information outside the Bureau.) Reynolds's literary disgrace was still a few months away when the FBI agreed to assist him with his book. As with Colby and Floherty, it was Reynolds's agreement to give the FBI control over the final product that ultimately convinced the Bureau to work with him. "I'll finish the book in a month or so, and will send it to Lou [Nichols]," Reynolds told Hoover. "I've asked him one favor—if after reading it he does not think it will be useful to the Department, to drop it into the nearest waste paper basket."[37]

Unlike the book projects of Collins, Colby, Floherty, and Reynolds, Whitehead's book on the FBI was initially conceived within the Crime Records Division, and Whitehead was selected to be the author by Bureau officials. Whitehead had worked frequently with the FBI on articles for the

Associated Press. He wrote a laudatory feature series on Hoover in 1954, and in 1955, he suggested to Nichols that "now would be a very good time to do an article which would recount what had been done in the fight against Communism and what the Communists are now doing."[38] Nichols recommended that the FBI assist Whitehead on the article because "Whitehead has certainly established his reliability."[39]

In September 1955, Hoover directed special agents in six states and the District of Columbia to conduct a thorough investigation of Whitehead's character, reputation, and loyalty. "The investigation must be handled by mature, experienced agents on a very discreet basis," Hoover wrote. Whitehead's "present employer, the Associated Press, under no circumstances should be contacted."[40] The resulting investigation involved thirty-five interviews, and the raw investigative data filled more than fifty pages of Whitehead's FBI file. In the course of the investigation, the FBI verified his birth, education, marital status, and employment history. Agents reviewed his credit and criminal records, finding only a $7 speeding violation in Virginia. Agents discovered that Whitehead's brother, Kyle, had at times been slow in repaying his debts. A summary of the investigation's findings described Whitehead as honest, hardworking, industrious, respected in his field, and reliably discreet.[41]

Prospective collaborators were carefully investigated and vetted, but choosing compliant authors did not necessarily guarantee that the resulting books would harmonize with the FBI's public relations message. To ensure that the publications matched the FBI's preferred image of responsibility and utility, the process of information gathering was entirely controlled by the Crime Records Division. Nichols's staff provided authors with carefully chosen documents and access to the data contained in the FBI's voluminous files.

On October 19, 1942, Floherty received a massive amount of information for his project. The package included half a dozen charts, volumes of crime statistics, 135 photographs, a series of newspaper stories and columns, the text of 62 speeches by Hoover, more than 100 reprints from the *FBI Law Enforcement Bulletin*, and more than 100 dramatic, four- to five-page summaries of investigations the FBI considered important, called "interesting case" memoranda.[42] Floherty was also given tours of FBI headquarters and the FBI training facility at Quantico, Virginia. Finally, he was permitted a brief audience with Hoover himself, although Nichols advised, "There is absolutely no need for Floherty to engage the Director in any extended interview."[43] The meeting resulted in little of substance, although the author was sent an autographed picture to commemorate the event. Floherty later requested and was provided with more information about the FBI laboratory.[44] It is interesting to note that although Floherty and Hoover apparently met only once, the author's obituary mentioned that he was a "friend of J. Edgar Hoover."[45]

Bureau control over Colby's book project was even more complete: Nichols and Jones essentially handed him a finished manuscript. Colby's books typically consisted of forty-eight pages of captioned photographs, preceded by a broadly drawn, one-page introduction to the subject matter. For his pictorial review of FBI procedures and practices, Colby proposed that the FBI choose the photos and write the captions as well. On February 12, 1954, Colby received ninety-seven photographs and sixty-eight captions from the Crime Records Division.[46] A review of the resulting book, *FBI: The G-Men's Weapons and Tactics for Combating Crime*, indicates that Colby exclusively used the FBI-authored captions in "his" book, each one reproduced nearly word for word.[47] Colby expressed his gratitude in a letter to Jones. "Bill Gunn [Jones's assistant] has done a magnificent job of not only selecting the best photos but in furnishing splendid caption material," Colby wrote. "Rest assured that you will see the captions when they are ready for publication."[48]

Likewise, Reynolds relied entirely on the information provided by the FBI for his book *The Story of the FBI*. Reynolds was given photographs, transcripts of speeches by Hoover, and more than a dozen "interesting case" memoranda—some involving well-known cases, and others selected for their emphasis on the Collier-Cooper themes of science, responsibility, and Hoover.[49] Reynolds received information, for example, on "Ma" Barker, John Dillinger, and several kidnapping, extortion, fraud, and theft cases.[50] Like Floherty, he toured FBI headquarters and the FBI training facility at Quantico. Reynolds, it was reported, was very enthusiastic about his guided tours of the FBI facilities and asked for additional case information focusing on the work of the FBI laboratory.[51]

Thoroughly investigated and vetted as a reliable chronicler of FBI history, Whitehead was set up with an office in the FBI's Justice Department building and began writing on November 1, 1955.[52] He worked there for weeks, with Crime Records staff delivering information and providing access as needed. Whitehead delivered the first four chapters of *The FBI Story* to Bureau editors on March 16, 1956.[53]

Providing authorized information to journalists and authors in the hope of influencing the content of their work is not unusual for any organization practicing strategic public relations. But Floherty, Colby, Reynolds, and Whitehead ceded editorial control of their projects, relying entirely on the FBI for their source material and choosing not to consult critical sources or question the information they were given. Importantly, all four were granted access to that information, essentially borrowing the FBI's valuable brand and image to sell their books, in exchange for a promise to give the Bureau final approval of their work.

Bureau editors' vetting of Floherty's work included a line-by-line, word-by-word review of the draft manuscript and FBI approval of the title, *Inside the FBI*.[54] On April 5, 1943, the Crime Records staff forwarded eleven typewritten pages of edits and a draft of Hoover's foreword to Floherty. Hoover's imprimatur became a potent tool to attract collaborators and justify extensive FBI editing. The Bureau's recommended revisions ranged from correcting simple spelling and typographical errors to creating fictitious names for key figures. The edits even included extensive and specific rewrites of key narrative passages.[55] Floherty made all the requested corrections, forwarded updated galleys to the FBI, and reported that, as a Junior Literary Guild selection, the book had been reviewed by First Lady Eleanor Roosevelt.[56] McGuire prepared a memorandum for Nichols, reviewing the changes and providing a detailed, chapter-by-chapter summary of the book. In a handwritten comment on the memo, Nichols noted that he had read the entire book, and "it is good."[57] And by "good," he no doubt meant it presented the FBI as it wished to be presented, promoting science, responsibility, and Hoover and thus buttressing the Bureau's image as a legitimate and restrained law enforcement agency.

As noted earlier, Crime Records staff essentially conceived and created Colby's pictorial review of the FBI. Nevertheless, the FBI was given a final opportunity to review the finished manuscript, and on April 22, 1954, it was delivered to Jones, reviewed, and quickly returned. "The material for the book has been thoroughly reviewed in the Crime Records Section and corrections and changes have been made on the manuscript itself," Jones told Nichols. "The book presents an exceedingly favorable picture of the Bureau."[58]

Reynolds provided a draft of his first three chapters to Nichols on August 29, 1953. Even then, before the humiliation of the Dupre hoax, Reynolds's reputation as a careless reporter was well known. "As you know, Quentin is a little careless with his facts and I am sure that while we are going to get a good product, there will be a lot of it we will have to do ourselves," Nichols reported to Tolson. "The book will probably be drafted three or four times."[59] Later that year, Reynolds submitted a full draft to Nichols, who assigned Jones to review it. Jones made his corrections directly on the manuscript in pencil, and "where a whole story or sequence of events was factually wrong this has been pointed out in a memorandum which sets forth the suggested revisions and in some instances additional research material for Mr. Reynolds."[60] The attached memorandum included twelve pages of detailed revisions, including wholesale rewrites of awkward passages.

There is little information available about the FBI's work with Collins and Whitehead. In fact, the Bureau was unable to locate Collins's FBI file. However, since Collins's book included a foreword by Hoover, it is likely that he too relied entirely on the Bureau for his information and allowed Crime Records staff to edit the final manuscript. Whitehead's FBI file contained little detailed information about the editing of his book. But given the fact that he submitted the first chapters in March 1956 for Nichols's review, combined with the inclusion of the FBI seal and a foreword by Hoover, it is safe to assume that the manuscript was meticulously edited by Bureau officials, just as Colby's and Reynolds's books were.[61] Whitehead's book, after all, was intended to be the definitive history of the FBI. As such, Nichols and Jones undoubtedly made whatever revisions were necessary to ensure that it was on message.

Collins's and Floherty's books were published in 1943, while the books by Colby, Reynolds, and Whitehead were published between 1954 and 1956. The FBI carefully monitored sales of the books and encouraged Bureau employees to buy their own copies at discounted prices. Collins's book received positive reviews that reinforced the Bureau's preferred themes. "The story of the F.B.I. is one of the marvels of our age," Redmond P. Gibbons wrote in the *Journal of Criminal Law and Criminology.* "Mr. Hoover has set a standard for every police executive—that is worthy of the name—to emulate."[62] *New York Times* reviewer Fowler Hill highlighted Collins's focus on science, responsibility, and Hoover, pointing out that the director's foreword assured readers that the book was not a "controlled or censored account."[63] In many ways, Collins's book was an interim report superseded by Whitehead's better-known authorized history of the FBI.

Bureau employees purchased more than 2,500 copies of Floherty's original book and a revised version released in 1951.[64] In September 1954, a letter sent to all field offices directed the SACs to canvass employees and forward orders for the Colby and Reynolds books.[65] It is hard to imagine any ambitious special agent rejecting a plea from Hoover to purchase a book. Nearly 2,000 copies of each book were sold as a result.[66] Reynolds's book ultimately sold more than 70,000 copies.[67]

Whitehead's *The FBI Story* was a smash hit, reaching number one on the *New York Times* nonfiction best-seller list on February 3, 1957. Whitehead had repackaged the 1930s-era Collier-Cooper narrative, with its familiar stories of outlaws and spies, for an audience of adults who had never known the corrupt Bureau of Investigation of the Palmer era. A movie based on the book was released in 1959: *The FBI Story*, starring James Stewart. Copies of Whitehead's book were also provided as resource material to the screenwriters for *The FBI* television series in 1965.[68] The message to the television production team was that Whitehead's work concisely captured the updated FBI narrative template and that Hoover expected them to follow it. The success of *The FBI Story: A Report to the People* allowed Whitehead to retire from daily journalism. In 1958, he resigned his position at the *Herald-Tribune* to become a full-time freelance writer.[69]

Collins, Floherty, Colby, Reynolds, and Whitehead all published successful FBI-authorized books. But their work with and on behalf of the Bureau had only just begun. In the course of promoting their books and for years afterward, the authors (with one exception) became reliable defenders of the FBI. Their promotional work for the FBI included making public and media appearances, directly advocating on the Bureau's behalf, and providing an "objective" defense against FBI critics when asked to do so. Floherty and Whitehead were sufficiently helpful over the years that they were designated special service contacts, discreet and reliable information gatherers and trustworthy defenders whose roles were formalized in the Bureau. SACs were expected to maintain contact with such individuals and, if needed, call on them to perform duties that necessity and discretion would not allow Bureau personnel to undertake.

After the publication of *The FBI in Peace and War*, Collins was approached by radio producers who wanted to create an entertainment program based on the book. Sponsors were offering Collins $1,000 a week to serve as a scriptwriter and consultant for the program, originally titled *This Is the FBI*. Hoover was not pleased that Collins had negotiated a radio deal and withheld Bureau cooperation. Collins put off signing the contract so that he could lobby the FBI for its blessing. On September 25, 1944, Nichols reported that he had told Collins the FBI's name could not be used because it would suggest official approval of the program.[70] It is likely that Bureau officials were worried that the public would resent the FBI's participation in an entertainment program during wartime. The initial scripts and audition recordings Collins provided raised other concerns, such as the violent content of the program. "I told him also that we did not like the whole idea, it had a gang-buster approach and we just could not go along with him in any respect or phase of approving or cooperating with the radio series," Nichols told Tolson.[71]

Desperate to gain Hoover's approval so he could sign his lucrative contract, Collins sent a letter to the director on September 28, 1944. "I am sorry that the first draft of the radio program did not please you—but I am not surprised," Collins wrote from the Hotel St. Regis in New York. "Your criticisms coincided with many of my own. I beg you to believe, however, that the very obvious flaws from your standpoint were not due to my lack of care or effort on the part of my associates."[72] Collins attached a revised script and a memorandum explaining its rationale. "My understanding—and again correct me if I am wrong—is that you do not wish to stand in the way of my making a considerable amount of money out of my book, and that, provided I make it clear to the radio audience that my dramas are written with the same regard for the Bureau's interests that the stories in the book were written, you will not place anything in the way of placing 'This Is the FBI' on the air."[73] Collins pledged to choose appropriate actors and to give the FBI the opportunity to edit the scripts and approve casting choices. The program's sponsor, Procter and Gamble, was offering twenty-five minutes at 10:30 p.m. on Saturdays, beginning November 26—a prime radio spot.

The same day he posted the letter and memorandum to Hoover, Collins wrote to Tolson with a similar plea. "A considerable amount of money for me personally is involved and I am under considerable pressure to sign a most favorable contract," Collins wrote. "But I do not wish to do so until I know that the Director, even if he cannot cooperate as I had hoped, is willing that I should go ahead."[74]

Collins eventually gave up on the original title for the radio show and decided to use the book's title instead. In subsequent discussions, he asked for permission to use Hoover's introduction to the book in the radio program. He was told no. He was also told that the Bureau objected to the reading of a list of wanted fugitives in the program's introduction, along with the offer of a $2,500 reward. Hoover's notation on Nichols's memorandum was unequivocal: "Definitely no."[75] In their next conversation, Nichols obliquely threatened Collins. "I told Collins that we want to put him on his guard and that I was going to call [redacted, but likely Procter and Gamble]."[76] Nichols again told Collins that the FBI would not provide any assistance in creating the scripts. Nichols thought Collins would regret not having access to material from the Crime Records Division, and he told Tolson, "There is not enough news on Collins' book to last for any long length of time, and he is really going to find himself out on a limb."[77]

Collins signed the contract, and *The FBI in Peace and War* aired on CBS radio from 1944 to 1958—nearly 700 half-hour episodes. Its presence on the air was a constant annoyance to Nichols and Hoover. After receiving what amounted to informal cease-and-desist letters from Nichols in early 1945, Collins—whose radio drama was a hit by then—grew increasingly upset. "Frankly, the tone of both letters puzzles me," Collins wrote to Nichols. "They would seem to be the letters of an angry and unreasonable man, which I know you, under normal circumstances, not to be."[78] Through his producers at Biow Company, Collins proposed several changes, including new language for the program's disclaimer. The original disclaimer, which read "based on actual cases now in the files of the F.B.I.—as recounted in the book 'The F.B.I. in Peace and War,'" would be changed to "adapted from cases as recounted in the book 'The F.B.I. in Peace and War.'"[79] Collins also disclosed that Procter and Gamble was urging him to allow the FBI to review his scripts, an offer Nichols resisted. "The very moment we started reviewing the scripts we would then be put in a position of approving the program," Nichols wrote in a memo to Tolson.[80]

For Collins, the breakdown in his relationship with the FBI, particularly the pressure Nichols was applying by complaining to Procter and Gamble, must have been difficult. Collins was very upset during a telephone conversation on February 2, 1945. "Collins then, in a very confidential-like manner, asked why couldn't we deal like we used to deal, and why couldn't I call him on the phone and tell him what to do and not to do in order to give him guidance," Nichols reported to Tolson. "I told him that what he did with his book, of course, was none of our business."[81] The message was that Collins had become more trouble than he was worth, and he shouldn't expect any assistance from the FBI in the future. Within days, the FBI had its own program, *This Is Your FBI*, in the works. "With reference to our new radio program," Nichols wrote to Tolson, "I anticipate within the next few days some rather violent repercussions from Fred Collins, [redacted], and possibly

Procter & Gamble."[82] *This Is Your FBI* aired on ABC radio for 409 episodes starting April 6, 1945.

In many ways, the FBI's radio program only confused the issue, and Collins's program remained a headache for Hoover. Complaints from listeners about the show's content arrived frequently. In 1947, for example, Walter Winchell pointed out in his column that the theme song for *The FBI in Peace and War* was taken from *L'amour des trois Oranges*, an opera written by Serge Prokofiev—"one of the world's leading communists," according to Winchell. When Nichols checked out the story, he discovered that Prokofiev's music was also the motif for the Bureau-sponsored *This Is Your FBI* on ABC radio.[83] The FBI searched its files for information on the Russian composer but could not trace his politics, other than membership in a Soviet musicians' organization. Nichols argued that the Bureau should request a retraction from Winchell since the program mentioned in his column was not an FBI production.[84] Hoover disagreed. "It looks as if W. W. has got us this time."[85]

At times, even FBI employees confused the two programs. In November 1947, the SAC in Los Angeles sent a telegram to Hoover, forwarding an inquiry from a Bakersfield radio station. The station, which had added *The FBI in Peace and War* to its programming, wondered whether the Bureau had any comment about plans to promote the program using advertising slogans such as "The FBI Is Coming" and "Watch Out for the FBI."[86] Hoover replied by telegram that the FBI was not involved in the production of Collins's program. "In fact Bureau has forced program to carry an official disclaimer. Under no consideration should we have anything to do with any advertising except to interpose objection to the use of name of FBI."[87]

In 1948, the *San Francisco Chronicle* published a tongue-in-cheek "open letter" to Hoover under the headline "Two Programs about FBI—Which Is the Official One?" "Both speak with authority," the writer observed. "Both seem to advance the views of your department with equal impunity. Both give evidence of ready access to your files. . . . One program is true to the FBI and one is not, or both are true, or neither is true."[88] Hoover responded with a letter to the editor that acknowledged the FBI's involvement with *This Is Your FBI*, but he had no sense of humor on the subject of Collins or his radio program.

In 1949, the FBI investigated American Legion reports that some of the actors on *The FBI in Peace and War* were communists, creating another headache for the Bureau.[89] Hoover was forced to send an agent to "see that Legion understands we have no connection with it."[90] In an effort to head off such criticisms, the FBI started monitoring Collins's program in 1949. At the bottom of a memo describing one episode of *The FBI in Peace and War*, Hoover wrote, "It is a shame that they use our name."[91] In the meantime, Hoover had cut off all contact with Collins, who never recovered his standing with the Bureau and died in 1950.

The other authors of FBI-authorized books remained in Hoover's good graces and even became informants for and active public defenders of the Bureau. In the weeks prior to the publication of his book on May 19, 1943, Floherty began a series of media appearances and then embarked on a promotional speaking tour. In most cases, he vetted his schedule with his contacts in the Crime Records Division and filed detailed reports from his tours. In March 1943, for example, Floherty was invited to appear on a New York radio program and asked the FBI for permission to speak about his upcoming book on the air. "It is felt that the broadcast will be satisfactory from the Bureau's standpoint and that Mr. Floherty will be most favorable in his remarks concerning the Bureau," J. J. McGuire reported.[92] The book was reprinted in several countries and then revised in 1951. Throughout, Floherty kept the FBI informed about his public appearances and speeches, in which he always praised and applauded the Bureau. In 1948, for example, he sent Hoover a list of fifty-five personal appearances he had made during a two-year period.[93] After Max Lowenthal's critical book about the FBI, *The Federal Bureau of Investigation*, was published in 1950, Floherty called to declare his very negative impression of the book and to offer his assistance in countering its negative message about the FBI.[94]

In 1955, Floherty was identified as a "SAC contact" by the special agent in charge of the New York office. From the 1930s to the 1950s, the Bureau's designation for its friends and adjuncts changed several times. During World War II, confidential informants were called special service contacts (SSCs). In 1946, the SSC program was discontinued, and individuals were reassigned to the Bureau's regular classifications as confidential informants, sources of information, or contacts.[95] In 1950, the SSC program was reinstated "in view of the present world situation," and SACs were urged to develop SSCs both for the assistance they could provide and for the opportunity to establish "their friendship for the Bureau." Importantly, Hoover told SACs in 1950 that SSCs should not be recruited. "It is preferred that an offer of assistance first be received before any effort is made to cultivate and encourage a potential Special Service Contact."[96] In 1954, the program was discontinued again, and the designees were moved to the SAC contact list of persons "who because of their positions, can and do render extraordinary service or provide unusual and highly valuable assistance to the FBI upon request of the SAC."[97]

Because their professions involved information gathering, journalists and authors had plausible reasons to ask sensitive questions, making them particularly valuable service contacts. In a recommendation to Hoover, the New York office noted that Floherty, "through his writings, can obtain considerable favorable publicity for the Bureau. He is also in a position to furnish information concerning other writers in this area and assist in Research Matters. He can on request conduct discreet inquiries."[98] Floherty continued working with the FBI until his death in 1964 at age eighty-seven.

Colby's ongoing assistance to the FBI included service both as a journalist and as an informer. Beginning in 1955, Colby authored a column, "Adventure Today," that appeared in a regional chain of Westchester County, New York, newspapers. The FBI was frequently featured in Colby's columns; when it was, the material was provided by the FBI, and the columns were edited by Jones in the Crime Records Division.[99] During the five-year run of "Adventure Today," the FBI provided information and editing services for more than forty Bureau-related columns.

More intriguing than his public work for the FBI was Colby's stint as an anticommunist informer in his Briarcliff Manor, New York, community. In 1956, Colby informed Jones of a "dangerous educational experiment" being undertaken in the Briarcliff school district. The program, an "Essential Ideas Seminar" for gifted high school seniors, would expose them to fifteen films produced by controversial educator and philosopher Mortimer Jerome Adler. Many conservatives saw Adler as a dangerously subversive character due to his efforts to bring philosophy to the masses and his alleged support of "world government." Colby reported that this film program had been suggested by Wilbur "Ping" Ferry, a member of the Briarcliff school board and vice president of the Fund for the Republic, a social justice and civil liberties organization bent on exposing the damage done by the communist inquisition of the 1940s and 1950s.

Upon receiving his report, the FBI provided Colby with a pair of blind memoranda summarizing the public source material on Adler and Ferry from Bureau files.[100] Colby, as the Bureau no doubt intended, shared the information with an editor at the local newspaper. "He is ready to go all out on this subject if we find that such action is warranted," Colby told Jones.[101]

Colby also enlisted the aid of the local chapter of the American Legion, and he kept the FBI informed at every stage of the process. On several occasions, he requested and received additional blind information from the Bureau.[102] With the help of his friends at the FBI, Colby battled the Briarcliff school board and other "subversives" in his community for more than two years.

In 1969, Colby and the FBI collaborated again on an updated version of his FBI picture book, retitled *FBI: How the G-Men Use Science as Well as Weapons to Combat Crime*. Once again, the Bureau provided the photographs and captions and did the final edit on the book.[103] The continued success of Colby's book earned him the reward of a personal visit and a photograph with Hoover.[104]

Reynolds also worked quietly on behalf of the FBI after the publication of his book. He offered intelligence from abroad during his overseas travels, requested assistance on multiple complimentary FBI articles, and repeatedly proposed the production of an FBI television program. As early as 1955, Reynolds approached the Bureau with the idea of a television series based on his book. "Does the Bureau have a definite policy on anything like this?" Reynolds asked. "If you say forget it—that's all right, of course I'll understand."[105] Nichols informed Reynolds that the FBI wasn't interested in a television series and would object if Reynolds went forward with such a project, so he dropped the idea.[106] In 1956, Reynolds, by then well known for his part in the Dupre hoax, proposed a series of *Reader's Digest* articles on the FBI, but he was told the Bureau was too busy to assist.[107]

Reynolds continued to defer to the FBI's judgment when he was approached to participate in two critical series on Hoover and the Bureau. In 1958, *New York Post* editor James A. Wechsler produced an extensive critical series on Hoover, and in October of that year, New York journalist Fred J. Cook published a highly critical article about the FBI in *The Nation*. When Reynolds was contacted by a *Post* reporter, he immediately notified the FBI of the impending series, offered to attempt to stop its publication, and assured Hoover that he would not cooperate with the *Post*.[108]

Whitehead, who was traveling in Italy at the time, was also apprised of the "smear campaign." Nichols's letter cast the Cook article as a "smear" not only on the Bureau but also on Whitehead personally. "Cook disparages your book, 'The FBI Story,'" Nichols wrote. "This, in itself, is enough to indicate the biased nature of the article."[109] Whitehead took the bait; he characterized the article as a "sideswipe" against him and a "vicious distortion," adding, "If

I can help scotch any such campaign of slander, let me know."[110] Whitehead's reaction demonstrated that, after a successful collaboration with the Bureau, reporters and authors had a personal interest in building and maintaining Hoover's iconic image. Authors like Whitehead stood to gain personally (through sales) and professionally (through reputation) if the FBI maintained its legitimacy. Likewise, they stood to lose face personally and professionally should Hoover be criticized.

Whitehead, Floherty, and Reynolds gave up their high-profile newspaper careers once their books were published. Whitehead, though, maintained ties to his profession, working as a freelance feature writer and a columnist for the *Knoxville News-Sentinel.* He also maintained a relationship with the Associated Press, covering events related to the civil rights movement from his home in Tennessee. These ties to national journalism circles, along with his status as the author of the Bureau's sanctioned history, meant that Whitehead's ongoing relationship with the FBI was the most extensive and substantive of the four authors, continuing after Hoover's death in 1972 and including his designation as a SAC contact.

Sometimes their collaboration was merely technical, as when Whitehead was provided with an FBI translator to help with a book on international police forces.[111] Hoover also made sure his international FBI legal attachés met Whitehead and his wife on their travels and provided them with logistical assistance—a common duty for Hoover's foreign staff.[112] Other times, Whitehead served by amplifying themes from his book in columns for the *News-Sentinel.*[113] Over a twelve-year period, Bureau officials authored twenty-seven letters over Hoover's signature thanking Whitehead for a complimentary column. In 1961, the SAC in the Knoxville office recommended that Whitehead be designated a SAC contact, noting that Whitehead "is extremely friendly to the Bureau and can be depended upon to comment favorably concerning the Bureau whenever the occasion arises."[114] In 1962, Whitehead's journalistic talents became useful when Hoover was publicly criticized by the Fund for the Republic's "Ping" Ferry (Colby's vexing neighbor in Briarcliff). When informed of the criticism, Whitehead pledged to "prepare a blast at that jerk, Ferry, and I'll send along a copy."[115]

In 1962, Whitehead requested FBI assistance in writing a youth-oriented version of *The FBI Story.* Assistant director Cartha DeLoach, one of Nichols's successors in the Crime Records Division, thought it would be a "good opportunity to enhance the prestige of the Bureau, particularly among youngsters below the age of 16."[116] The Crime Records Division reviewed and edited the manuscript in 1963, and the book was published later that year. Like *The FBI Story*, it sold well.

Whitehead's most useful moment as a SAC contact came in 1964, when the Associated Press assigned him to write a series of feature articles covering the civil rights movement. Whitehead called the FBI seeking data on civil rights enforcement and requested a rare, on-the-record interview with Hoover on the subject. Jones wrote to DeLoach: "This would, of course, be an excellent opportunity to bring to the public's attention our accomplishments in the civil rights field, particularly since it would be carried by the Associated Press and the series is being done by an individual who has been so favorable toward the Bureau. We have already sent him appropriate material on our civil rights work."[117]

DeLoach reported to his boss, John P. Mohr, that it was "obvious that the Associated Press series will be of great assistance to us . . . inasmuch as Whitehead is definitely attempting to be of service to us, it would be appreciated if the Director could just shake hands with him and chat for a moment or two."[118] What DeLoach intended to be a brief chat turned into a fifty-minute interview on a wide range of topics. Whitehead's coverage of the meeting received major play in newspapers and on news programs around the country. Jones's typed notes from the interview ran four single-spaced pages and revealed that the meeting covered everything from Hoover's diet to the Kennedy assassination. Hoover criticized Chief Justice Earl Warren as a judge who "interferes capriciously with efficient law enforcement through tricky decisions." On civil rights, Hoover reiterated his criticism of Martin Luther King as the "most notorious liar" in the country. Whitehead wrapped up the interview by stating that his "only desire was that of trying to be of assistance to Mr. Hoover and the Bureau with the articles he plans to write."[119] The headlines emerging from the interview no doubt pleased Hoover. Whitehead's story, published in newspapers nationwide on December 5, led with Hoover's intention to stay on the job and emphasized the director's denunciation of King and his defense of the FBI's role in the South.[120]

In 1965, Whitehead wrote a column outlining his view of the FBI's responsibility with regard to civil rights. "The FBI has no authority to act as bodyguards for any group," Whitehead wrote. "It is not empowered to act until a Federal law has been broken. . . . The wisdom of Mr. Hoover's position in this situation should be clear to everyone concerned with proper law enforcement—mainly because he has been hammering on this theme for 41 years."[121] A few days later, Hoover wrote to Whitehead to thank him for the column: "Your complimentary comments and staunch support of this Bureau mean a great deal to all of us in the FBI." He signed the letter "Edgar."[122]

The FBI-authorized books of Floherty, Colby, Reynolds, and Whitehead were commercially successful retellings of the theme cited in Whitehead's civil rights column: the FBI, according to its own responsibility narrative, could not intervene unless there was a violation of federal law. The Bureau, according to these four authors' books, would never involve itself in policing political philosophy, speech, or thought. The notion of the FBI as a "gestapo" was simply impossible. The FBI depicted in the authorized books was a scientific law enforcement agency that acted only in cases of clearly established authority, such as bank robbery, extortion, or espionage.[123] Special agents were the skilled practitioners of the G-man quick-draw, as depicted in Colby's book. They were the scientists in the FBI laboratory hunched over their microscopes or mixing chemicals in test tubes. Trained at the "West Point of Law Enforcement," FBI agents were ready to protect the nation whether the enemy was a small-time thug terrorizing the Midwest, a spy ring operating during wartime, or the red revolutionaries of a communist cell operating in someone's neighborhood. The responsible FBI would never abuse its power to investigate dissent, it was claimed.

Of course, history has shown that Norman Thomas was right to worry aloud about the FBI's role in McCarthyism and its overzealous loyalty investigations of ideologically liberal Americans. Books by ostensibly "objective" and reputable authors were one tool used by the FBI to maintain its legitimacy in the eyes of the public while obscuring its far-reaching investigations of dissent. The Bureau was extremely cautious in selecting authors and journalists as collaborators. Requests for assistance from Floherty, Colby, and Reynolds triggered careful investigations of their backgrounds. Once it was satisfied that they were ideologically acceptable partners, the FBI still required a pledge that it could edit the authors' finished products before publication.

The FBI's ability to control the flow of information from its voluminous investigative files, along with the value placed on that information by a public fascinated with crime stories, meant that authors had little choice but to accept whatever facts they were given. Colby, for example, pitched a concept to the Bureau, and the photographers and writers in the public relations–oriented Crime Records Division provided a finished book for him. Floherty received hundreds of pages of information, carefully selected to communicate the Bureau's preferred image of itself. Reynolds's drafts were rewritten and scrutinized in great detail by FBI editors who were worried that he might be careless with the facts. Working from a desk inside FBI headquarters, Whitehead relied solely on Bureau information, forgoing any outside research and not interviewing anyone outside the walls of his Justice Department work space.

Once their manuscripts were finished, FBI editors in the Crime Records Division pored over them in minute detail. Nichols, Jones, and McGuire provided line-by-line edits and even rewrote entire passages or removed sections that didn't fit the heroic, responsible meme so carefully created and maintained throughout the Hoover years. After the publication of their books, the authors became part of the FBI family. They were beholden to the Bureau for their commercial success, and their fates as journalists and authors were inextricably linked to the fortunes of Hoover's FBI. No doubt these men were ideologically predisposed to adhere to Hoover's narrow view of patriotism and Americanism, but their professional success was based on a tightly constrained collaboration with the FBI. Some, like Reynolds and Colby, performed minor services for the FBI, informing on neighbors or defending the Bureau against critics from time to time. Others, like Floherty and Whitehead, performed services that were considered sufficiently valuable to formalize the relationship by identifying them as SAC contacts.

Whitehead was particularly valuable in 1964 when the Associated Press assigned him to write a series of articles on civil rights, including the FBI's enforcement efforts. In that instance, he was seen as the ultimate "objective" voice—a two-time Pulitzer Prize winner and law enforcement expert—to assess the FBI's performance in a series that would run in hundreds of American newspapers. The FBI allowed him rare access to Hoover precisely because he was a SAC contact and because it knew the director and the Bureau would be happy with the results. Bureau officials knew that Whitehead, author of *The FBI Story*, had a personal stake in maintaining the agency's image. After all, he had helped maintain the public image of a "responsible" FBI in his books, columns, and news stories. FBI public relations officials were comfortable turning a national reporter loose in Hoover's own office— as long as that reporter was Whitehead, who had publicly praised the FBI for its "integrity" and would not ask any difficult questions or report any gaffes by Hoover. Along with Floherty, Colby, Reynolds, and many others who were considered friends of the Bureau, Whitehead was both an author and a defender of the FBI myth.

Whitehead's book and the movie based on it became the foundation of the Bureau's efforts to establish itself in the entertainment media. The result of those efforts was a prime-time television program that built on the Bureau's dominant cultural position and became the ultimate expression of FBI public relations.

Chapter 11

Building a Television Audience

On June 17, 1968, the *New York Times* published an article identifying a movement among Hollywood writers and directors who were upset by the level of violence in television and motion pictures. Many of them pledged to stop participating in television and motion picture productions showcasing "senseless violence for its own sake."[1] Luminaries such as Jack Lemmon, Dennis Weaver, Richard Boone, Tom Smothers, and Jack Valenti, president of the Motion Picture Association of America, signed the pledge. The group's spokesman, Screen Actors Guild and Directors Guild member Jerry Paris, explained the group's message to the *Times*: "We will no longer lend our talents in any way in the shaping of any entertainment that celebrates senseless brutality, aimless cruelty, pointless and violent death."[2]

A few days later, the *Times* article reached J. Edgar Hoover's desk. Since 1965 the Bureau had been cooperating in the production of *The F.B.I.*, a one-hour ABC television series that was frequently criticized for its violent content. Hoover's handwritten note in the margin of the *Times* clipping that circulated among FBI executives carried the force of an edict: "We must carefully screen the scripts in our TV show so as to eliminate violence."[3]

Hoover's use of the phrase "our TV show" accurately describes the FBI's extraordinary level of control and sense of ownership of *The F.B.I.*, which was produced by Quinn Martin Productions and Warner Brothers Inc. The prime-time drama was the culmination of nearly forty years of comprehensive FBI public relations and branding efforts beginning with a few magazine articles in the mid-1930s. It was the final and by far the most widely seen public relations tactic of Hoover's forty-eight-year tenure as director. Prime-time television allowed the Bureau to reach millions of viewers each week with a dramatization of FBI cases that shaped the organization's brand and asserted its legitimacy by focusing on its utility and responsibility. Given its importance as a public relations tool, no element of the program was left to chance. An FBI agent worked on the set, supervising the production. FBI officials reviewed and rewrote scripts. All members of the production crew and every potential performer were carefully vetted by the FBI, and more than a few were blackballed because of alleged communist ties, past misdemeanors, or lifestyle choices the Bureau found objectionable. The FBI signed off on all sponsors for the show. Any detail, whether controversial or mundane, that might somehow undermine the FBI's message of responsible, effective law enforcement was carefully scrutinized.

The F.B.I. has obvious cultural importance as a highly rated network television program viewed by tens of millions of Americans each week for nine seasons. The extensive documentation contained in the show's more than 4,000-page file details the FBI's state-of-the-art public relations and brand management at the end of Hoover's tenure. The high-profile TV production, involving hundreds of people operating thousands of miles from Washington, engaged the top level of the FBI pyramid in a daily effort to shape the content of the weekly broadcasts. A review of the FBI's extensive efforts to control the production and to enforce its message of responsibility and utility—considered in the context of revelations about the Hoover-era FBI that have emerged in recent decades—raises the question of whether democracy is well served by government-authorized entertainment productions. Finally, *The F.B.I.* represented the culmination of more than three decades of public relations practiced by the FBI and showcased the ultimate expression of the Bureau's preferred self-image, shaping perceptions of the agency during a time of cultural upheaval in America. An analysis of these issues requires a review of the development of the FBI's public relations and branding template, consideration of the origins of the series itself, and an examination of how the messages of responsibility and utility were strictly enforced by FBI participation in the series.

The television series was the final Hoover-era expression of the Bureau's long-standing legitimation strategy. The origins of the series can be found in Pulitzer Prize–winning journalist Don Whitehead's 1956 best seller *The FBI Story: A Report to the People.* In 1959, Hollywood producer Mervyn LeRoy adapted Whitehead's book for the silver screen, casting the calm and familiar Jimmy Stewart in the lead role. Based on the success of the motion picture, Warner Brothers suggested a television series, and Hoover reluctantly agreed, with the caveat that the FBI would have total control over the production.[4]

In the 1950s and early 1960s, entertainment executives had tried more

Hoover meets with Warner Brothers president Jack Warner on January 22, 1957. (National Archives at College Park, Record Group 65, Series H, Box 23, #1355-1)

than 600 times to entice Hoover into cooperating with the production of a prime-time television program.[5] In 1953, for example, Gardner "Mike" Cowles of Cowles Media inquired about the Bureau's interest in television, sparking Hoover to ask his staff to look into it. "Yes, certainly there are being done now some excellent TV crime series such as Dragnet; Treasury Men in Action; the program on which Sean O'Connor is the narrator and others," Hoover scrawled on a memorandum.[6] Louis B. Nichols, head of the Crime Records Division, expressed his doubts: "I do not think we should ever go into television unless we can have the best television show on the air and this I know we cannot do unless we get into the field ourselves in order to give it character and authenticity."[7] When Hoover finally relented and signed a deal with Warner Brothers in 1964, he did so with the expectation that his public relations team would "get into the field" and control every aspect of the production.[8]

The original agreement for *The F.B.I.* consisted of a one-page letter from Warner Brothers' executive vice president Benjamin Kalmenson to FBI assistant director Cartha DeLoach. The letter spelled out the basic financial structure of the agreement, including a one-time payment of $75,000 for the rights to Hoover's anticommunist tome *Masters of Deceit,* plus $500 for each episode produced.[9] The funds were turned over to the FBI Recreation Association, a fund promoting employee activities that was also alleged to be a tax shelter and personal travel fund for Hoover and Tolson.[10] The letter further stated that the FBI and Warner Brothers "will mutually cooperate in the production of the series and in the publicity and advertising as pertains to all of its phases."[11]

A January 12, 1965, meeting in Washington was scheduled so the key players in the series could meet with Hoover. Attendees included ABC president Thomas W. Moore, Kalmenson, and Quinn Martin of QM Productions. According to notes taken by DeLoach, Moore promised that "all [ABC] personnel . . . will closely follow every instruction and bit of guidance given them by the FBI."[12] Hoover told Moore that the television show was needed not only to "straighten out misimpressions but to allow the public to know of the accomplishments of the FBI."[13] Martin told the director that he was "most anxious" to portray the FBI in a positive light.[14] As the meeting ended, the three TV executives "again offered their assurance of fully protecting the name of the FBI and producing a program that the Director and all FBI personnel could be proud of."[15]

Later that same day, Moore wrote Hoover a thank-you note reiterating his assurances: "We intend to reflect the high ideals of the Bureau and to acquaint the television audience with the real function of your great organization."[16] Martin wrote to Hoover two days later, pledging to "do the best show on the FBI that is in me."[17]

At no point during or after the meeting did the four men discuss the details of how their mutually pledged cooperation would unfold. Nor did they discuss the cross-purposes at play: Hoover had the long-established FBI brand to promote and enforce by emphasizing science, responsibility, and his own leadership. The entertainment executives served shareholders who no doubt expected a program that satisfied audience appetites for action, adventure, and violence. It is not surprising, then, that the creative team at QM Productions, which was spending between $175,000 and $450,000 per episode, found it difficult to produce entertaining television that lived up to audience expectations while adhering to the strict constraints of the FBI's extensive, highly detailed, and often last-minute script changes.[18] From Hoover's perspective, Warner Brothers and QM had ceded power over everything, including story lines, casting, hiring of the production crew, and even final script approval. With an ambiguous contract containing only a one-sentence statement defining control over the show's content, Hoover and the QM staff clashed immediately and repeatedly.

For the FBI, managing a television program produced across the continent in Los Angeles posed an extraordinary set of challenges. Some of the challenges resulted from the complex logistics of the production. Others threatened the FBI's brand and thus its image of legitimacy. Associations with certain advertisers had the potential to damage the FBI's image, as did the hiring of certain actors, directors, writers, producers, and other crew members. The story lines themselves carried the risk of harming the FBI brand by depicting irresponsible or violent acts by agents. An outside challenge involved the news media's scrutiny of the production. Journalists' questions about the appropriateness of FBI involvement in a TV drama dogged the show throughout its run.

Enforcing the FBI brand on the series required the combined efforts of dozens of Bureau agents and staff members. On the set, the cast and crew were advised and controlled by an FBI agent assigned full time to monitor the production. Inspector Ed Kemper was the on-location production adviser for the first two years; special agents Dick Douce and Dick Wolf oversaw the show for the remainder of its run. Kemper, Douce, and Wolf instructed the cast and crew on proper FBI procedures, ensuring that nothing detrimental to the Bureau's image was allowed to slip in and acting as liaison between QM Productions and the FBI's top administrators.[19]

In addition to an FBI presence on the set, agents in the Crime Records Division and upper-level managers in Washington edited scripts, reviewed story proposals, and otherwise monitored and shaped every aspect of the production from afar. Agents from the Investigative Division were involved in the hundreds of name checks and investigations required to vet actors, crew members, and advertisers. For more than nine years, a small army of FBI agents and staffers in Los Angeles and Washington labored to anticipate and correct any wayward public relations messages. The television team worked under the direct supervision of Clyde Tolson.[20]

Beginning in March 1965, the FBI began vetting writers, directors, crew members, and actors. Even the advertising agency employees responsible for producing the Ford commercials that ran during the program were checked out.[21] For weeks before production started, and throughout the show's nine-year run, the FBI did name checks on hundreds of people, filtering out anyone with criminal records or potentially subversive or compromising connections in their pasts. Actors Robert Duvall, Tom Bosley, and Sharon Tate were approved, while Bette Davis and others whose names are redacted in the files were rejected.[22] Davis was rejected due to unproven allegations that she had murdered her husband years before.[23] Nancy Sinatra was rejected because of her father's philandering reputation and alleged friendships with organized crime figures.[24] Helen Hayes was approved despite her one-time membership in "organizations ostensibly attempting to correct social abuses," such as the National Council for American-Soviet Friendship.[25] Hoover took the unusual step of preemptively banning Robert Blake after the actor was quoted in a news story empathizing with criminals. "See that Blake never appears on 'The F.B.I.,'" Hoover wrote.[26]

An unnamed actor that Kemper recommended for acceptance was rejected by Hoover for past membership in the Progressive Citizens of America. "No," Hoover wrote. "I do not want even a fellow traveler in the cast nor one who is stupidly naïve."[27] The series' lead actors were likewise checked out. Efrem Zimbalist Jr. was not the first choice to portray Inspector Erskine. Hoover and Moore preferred Dick Egan for the role, but he was unavailable.[28] John Wayne was rejected as a possible narrator for the show, in part because Tolson objected to his connections with the John Birch Society, and in part because Hoover simply didn't want a narrator: "If we can't put over the story by acting, then it can't be very good."[29] In season two, Jimmy Stewart was asked to narrate the show, but he declined, citing his respect for Zimbalist.[30]

No detail was too insignificant for the Bureau to consider. The FBI obtained photographs of the lead actors in the series to make sure they met with Hoover's approval.[31] The FBI provided a disabled Bureau handgun, a Smith and Wesson .38 Special, for Zimbalist to carry.[32] The FBI also supplied photographs so that a set showing Erskine's Justice Department office next door to Hoover's could be created.[33] The Bureau enforced strict rules for the display of law enforcement credentials by the actors. Likewise, there were rules regarding the use of the FBI seal in the title credits and promotions.[34] Scripts based on espionage cases were reviewed by the Domestic Intelligence Division to verify that no confidential investigative techniques were compromised.[35]

To ensure that Zimbalist understood the subject matter, he spent a week

Publicity handout from the television show The F.B.I., *starring Efrem Zimbalist Jr. as Inspector Lewis Erskine. (© Bettman/CORBIS)*

of what the Bureau called "indoctrination," touring FBI offices in Washington and its training division in Quantico, Virginia.[36] At the end of his visit, he met with the director, who regaled Zimbalist with tales of old Hollywood, lamented the cancellation of the *Alfred Hitchcock Hour*, and explained why the FBI was doing background checks on everyone affiliated with the program. According to DeLoach's notes from the meeting, Hoover told Zimbalist, "The communists constantly try to infiltrate the FBI. . . . The Director additionally stressed the necessity of the FBI checking scripts before the program was put on film or placed on the air."[37]

In the absence of any agreement spelling out the relationship between the FBI and the production team, the Bureau exerted absolute control over story lines, stage directions, and dialogue in the scripts. Every script submitted by

Martin's production company was edited line by line by an FBI agent in the Crime Records Division. The script for the series' first episode, "The Monster," focused on a fictional villain who strangled women with their own hair. But Hoover's closest confidant, associate director Tolson, rejected it: "This is a very bad script—Too many murders. I can't approve it."[38]

The FBI made it clear early in the first season that it was dissatisfied with the quality of the scripts provided by Warner Brothers' writers. "I told Kalmenson I realized the end product had to be one of entertainment rather than a dry documentary of institutionalization," DeLoach wrote in a memorandum to John P. Mohr. "However, despite this fact, the program should not be cheap and tawdry, neither should it confuse the American public as to the jurisdiction of the FBI."[39]

From episode 1 through episode 241 nine years later, FBI editors painstakingly rewrote scripts and created memoranda detailing the suggested changes. Often the changes were minor, such as removing references to ostensibly secret law enforcement techniques like black-bag jobs, wiretaps, and surreptitious electronic monitoring, which might suggest something other than a restrained, responsible FBI. Beyond that, though, FBI editors changed dialogue, altered plots, and sometimes speculated about the dramatic value of a given scene. FBI officials could not understand why writers and producers, who had been given copies of Whitehead's authorized FBI history as a reference, consistently added violence and other off-message elements to the scripts.[40]

Early in the first season, FBI script reviews generally ran two pages or less, provided a synopsis of the story, and dictated only a few minor changes per episode. For example, the script for "A Slow March up a Steep Hill" included a scene in which Erskine surprised another agent and his fiancée who were embracing in the office. "It is not felt proper that the Inspector should walk into Rhodes' office or any other Bureau office and find this romance taking place," Milton A. Jones, Crime Records' primary script editor, stated. The Bureau also asked that a scene in which an assistant director of the FBI apologized to Erskine be omitted. "It is not felt an apology is necessary and this statement should be deleted."[41]

As time passed, and as violent content became more of an issue, the FBI began a more thorough review of the scripts. Ten episodes into the first season, Hoover had seen enough violence. "Let me know how many have been killed in the first ten scripts," Hoover wrote on a memorandum.[42] Jones reported that the first ten episodes included ten killings, five by special agents and five by subjects. Jones noted that there were also numerous instances of "woundings," where agents, criminals, or citizens were shot or otherwise injured.[43]

By the beginning of season two in 1966, Tolson, too, had seen enough. "There are entirely too many killings in our TV scripts," Tolson wrote. "Please see that this is corrected." Hoover added his own note: "I certainly agree."[44] Thus began an escalation in the battle over violent content in the series. FBI officials began to reject most violent scenes, labeling excessive killings as "violence for violence sake."[45] In addition to limiting violence, the FBI objected to other portrayals that could indicate a lack of responsibility on the part of the Bureau. FBI reviewers rejected scripts that showed agents drinking alcohol, using diet pills to make weight requirements, exercising poor judgment, losing their composure, and, interestingly, demonstrating excessive compassion for criminals.[46]

Over time, script reviews became much longer and more detailed, and the FBI raised more objections to scenes depicting violence or law enforcement techniques that might damage its reputation. For a script entitled "The Defector—Part I," for example, Tolson required the deletion of a scene in which twenty-four people were killed in the fire-bombing of a small café. In the same script, Jones objected to a reference to wiretaps. "It is felt that this technique used by any Federal agency should not be openly admitted on a television program," Jones wrote. To show his agreement, Tolson double-underlined "not" in Jones's sentence.[47] Intrusive investigative techniques like wiretapping didn't fit the responsible, restrained FBI image.

The showdown with QM Productions over violent content came to a head in 1967. In January of that year, Hoover decided to end the series, saying that "two years is quite sufficient exposure."[48] He ordered DeLoach to call ABC president Moore and inform him that the Bureau was withdrawing its support for the series. "Moore was flabbergasted," DeLoach reported to Tolson. "He stated he was greatly shocked particularly inasmuch as the show had been doing so well and no doubt the ratings would continue going up for some time." In the margin of the memo, Hoover scrawled, "At least he didn't threaten 'legal recourse.'"[49] A few days later, Hoover relented and allowed the series to continue.

Two years later, however, Hoover issued a more detailed edict on violence after a script called for three killings:

I want to make it emphatically clear that I do not want any extreme acts of violence portrayed on our TV program. I have stated this previously but apparently it is not being given the attention it should. There is a nationwide feeling that TV presents entirely too much violence and various groups and organizations have publicly stated the same and testimony has been given before Congressional committees to that effect. I do not intend that the FBI's TV program be in that category and you must, therefore, give more attention to the review of these scripts.[50]

Two weeks after that edict, Hoover and Tolson refined their objections to violence on *The F.B.I.*, offering more specific guidelines about what would and would not be allowed. To the ban on "extreme violence," Hoover added that no "violence in any form directed toward a woman" would be tolerated. "I want no equivocation about this either here or at the studio," Hoover wrote at the bottom of the memorandum.[51] Martin called DeLoach in the wake of Hoover's order to ask if the director would object to "an occasional wounding" of a criminal in the show. He was told that would be acceptable. Hoover read DeLoach's report detailing the discussion and added a note to the memorandum: "I want no yielding in the instructions I have laid down."[52] On November 10, 1969, an episode entitled "Blood Tie" aired on ABC, depicting the final three killings allowed on *The F.B.I.* For the remainder of its run, the program would be free of extreme violence.[53]

The battle over scripts was taxing for the QM staff. The show's original producer, Charles Larson, left after four years of fighting with the FBI over its detailed script changes, according to his successor Philip Saltzman. "He [Larson] would send these finished scripts to the FBI in Washington," Saltzman recalled. "Then they'd jump all over them and say, 'This isn't right. This is how we do it. We didn't approve this,' and on and on and on. So at the last minute, when they were getting ready to shoot, he wouldn't have a script. He'd have to do massive rewrites to get their approval."[54]

Even the commercial breaks were subject to FBI approval, and many prospective sponsors failed to measure up to Hoover's standards. In particular, he had ordered that no tobacco or alcohol be advertised during the show. Prior to the airing of the first episode, ABC's Moore asked Hoover to reconsider the ban on tobacco ads. Hoover ultimately relented and allowed the American Tobacco Company to advertise on the series, but his disdain for Martin, Warner Brothers, and ABC television continued. Hoover wrote at the bottom of a memorandum: "We have for all practical purposes lost con-

Cartha (Deke) DeLoach joined the FBI in 1942 as a clerk in the Identification Division. He rose steadily through the ranks, becoming assistant director of the Crime Records Division before being appointed deputy associate director, the third ranking official in the FBI, in late 1965. (National Archives at College Park, Record Group 65, Series F, Box 1, Folder 9, #37)

trol of this project due to Martin mowing us down so I can't see any greater harm coming because of a sponsor who at least won't try to dictate the details of production as Martin has done with complete disregard of our wishes & combined with a boorish insolence."[55]

For the most part, though, Hoover and his successors got their way when it came to advertisers, and the FBI brand was spared any association with controversial products and companies. For the first several years, the series was sponsored mainly by the Aluminum Company of America (ALCOA) and Ford Motor Company, with several other minor sponsors (all acceptable to Hoover). Sponsorships totaled $12 million in the first year: ALCOA paid $4 million, Ford paid $6 million, and Mutual of Omaha picked up the remaining $2 million.[56] Although ALCOA dropped out after the first season, Ford continued to sponsor the show to some extent throughout its nine-year run. Hoover even appeared in a Ford promotion, an eighty-second clip of him receiving a Freedom Foundation award recognizing the contributions of *The F.B.I.*[57]

During the last five years of *The F.B.I.*, as ratings began to drop, large sponsors gave way to an array of individual commercial messages sponsored by a wide variety of companies, all of which were vetted by the FBI. An ad for Champale was rejected in 1970 because the malt liquor was "basically an alcohol product."[58] Ballantine Brewery was rejected in 1969 for the same reason.[59] The Pfizer Company was rejected in 1971, and the Food Equipment Corporation, a toaster manufacturer, was rejected in 1972, both because of alleged price fixing in the 1960s.[60] LaChoy Food Corporation was rejected in 1973, a year after Hoover's death, because it had admitted to price fixing and bid rigging in the 1960s.[61] That same year, Allied Van Lines was rejected as a sponsor because of its admission to a violation of the Sherman Antitrust Act in 1963.[62] Kentucky Fried Chicken was rejected in 1972 for reasons that were redacted by the FBI when the file was released under the Freedom of Information Act in 2004.[63]

Some FBI objections were as petty as Hoover's own personal entertainment preferences. In 1968, Tolson banned a Ford ad from future broadcasts because the singer had a "very abrasive voice."[64] When Colgate-Palmolive was proposed as a sponsor, both Hoover and Tolson objected because the company produced "toilet items." Although he approved the ad, Hoover expressed his disgust with the nature of the advertising: "Eventually the sponsors will be for cures of bad breath, B.O., & birth control pills."[65]

The battle for control over the content of the series extended throughout the show's life and beyond Hoover's tenure as director, requiring a large amount of time and attention on the part of the FBI. Although the Bureau was ultimately able to control the violent depictions and brand associations that threatened to devalue its image in the eyes of the audience, it could not control the news media, Congress, or the public's reactions to its participation in a television series.

Jack Gould of the *New York Times* was the first to question the FBI's approach to the series when he reported that the Screen Actors Guild had concerns about the investigations of actors and crew. Gould paraphrased an anonymous guild member who asked whether "a review of an actor's private life was not tantamount to introducing a 'blacklist.'" Hoover responded defiantly, writing, "We most certainly will check out any person connected with this show irrespective of Gould's peevishness or Screen Actors Guild's sensitivity."[66] Martin reported that he and Kemper had received many calls from guild members and suggested that the FBI plant an article with a friendly journalist to the effect that Zimbalist and the other principal actors had also been checked.[67] On June 3, the *New York Daily News* reported that Zimbalist did not object to having his background checked. "It seems perfectly logical that the FBI, one of whose duties is to be involved with subversives and the activities of Communists, would not want to be portrayed by one," Zimbalist told the paper.[68]

In the longer term, though, the FBI was frequently embroiled in controversy emanating from journalists, members of Congress, and interested citizens who questioned the Bureau's affiliation with a television program or criticized the program's content. In 1966, for example, a front-page story in the *Washington Post* reported that two men arrested for extortion and the attempted sabotage of the Boston and Maine Railroad claimed they had been inspired to commit the crime by an episode of *The F.B.I.*[69] The episode, entitled "How to Murder an Iron Horse," aired on December 12, 1965. Alarmed at the suggestion that its television series was inspiring copycat crimes, FBI agents in Washington and Boston reviewed the case and offered a detailed rebuttal of the charge for Hoover.[70]

Two first-season episodes that dealt with Japanese war criminals generated controversy among advertisers and among an important FBI constituency: members of Congress. The first, "Will the Real Traitor Please Stand Up," dramatized the FBI's arrest of a World War II Japanese prison guard who was found in the United States in 1947. The episode was ultimately shelved after a complaint from Senator Daniel Inouye of Hawaii. Hoover was not pleased with ABC-TV's capitulation to Inouye's demands: "It is a shame ABC didn't have the 'guts' to go through with it."[71] Another episode originally broadcast in1965, "To Free My Enemy," similarly explored the investigation of an alleged Japanese war criminal. When the program was scheduled to rerun in March 1966, Ford pushed ABC to substitute another episode, and ABC agreed. Once again, Hoover was disgusted: "This will be the last TV show we will do. I regret we ever agreed to do it for another year. Such sensitivity is asinine."[72]

At various times, episodes of the show generated conflict with the California Highway Patrol,[73] the aeronautics industry,[74] scientists expert in the field of radiation,[75] Italian Americans,[76] TV violence watchdog groups,[77] savings and loan executives,[78] and various other members of Congress.[79] The

FBI, however, was particularly concerned when such controversies became the subject of media coverage that could damage its brand on a mass scale with the general public.

In 1970, for example, ABC news correspondent Frank Reynolds commented about Hoover's strained relationship with former attorney general Ramsey Clark. Reynolds said that Clark had "dared to be critical of Hoover, which is apparently some sort of federal offense," and he labeled Hoover "the real untouchable in Washington." Reynolds went on to say, "Eliot Ness himself would not have dared pull the plug in the Hoover bathtub had it been found full of gin during the prohibition years."[80] Reynolds's critical comments, coming from a newsman who worked for the same network that carried *The F.B.I.*, prompted a petulant response from the Bureau.

Three days after Reynolds's report, an FBI official contacted ABC vice president I. Martin Pompadour at his home to notify him that Hoover was withdrawing his approval of a seventh season of *The F.B.I.*[81] Pompadour told Jones of the Crime Records Division that Reynolds was acting out because his contract had not been renewed, an explanation that did not change Hoover's mind. That same day, ABC vice president James C. Hagerty, former press secretary for President Dwight Eisenhower, flew to Washington to meet with Hoover in an attempt to save the series. It was an extraordinary meeting, with Hagerty begging Hoover's forgiveness multiple times. Jones's notes from the meeting indicate that Hagerty's stated purpose was to "apologize on behalf of all of the officials of the American Broadcasting Company for the maliciousness of Frank Reynolds." Hagerty continued, citing his "deep personal feeling for the Director and the Bureau, and his personal interest in the television series, 'The FBI.'"[82] Hagerty's apology convinced Hoover to rescind his order to cancel the show.[83]

Much of the media coverage of *The F.B.I.* questioned the fiscal responsibility of the Bureau's involvement in the series. Hoover's letter writers in the Crime Records Division routinely misrepresented the extent of the Bureau's participation in the series. For example, in 1967, when *Washington Post* reporter Julius Duscha implied extensive FBI involvement in the TV show, Hoover replied: "We do not have any personnel who are assigned solely to assist in the production of this series."[84]

Hoover responded to a citizen's 1969 complaint by asserting, "We have nothing to do with the dramatization and filming of the program."[85] In 1971, the Bureau responded to a series of written questions from *Los Angeles Times* reporter Jack Nelson, downplaying its investment in the program:

"Time commensurate to the service of two FBI employees is required in furnishing story ideas, reviewing and making suggestions regarding scripts, and furnishing technical assistance to the production staff."[86] In fact, dozens of FBI employees were routinely involved in shaping and vetting the production. SACs in dozens of offices promoted the series by visiting local television affiliates.[87] The FBI provided thousands of brochures and posters to local television stations that requested promotional materials.[88]

In March 1972, David W. Rintels, chairman of the Writers Guild Committee on Censorship, published an article in the *New York Times* questioning the truthfulness of *The F.B.I.*'s depiction of the Bureau. The *Times* opinion piece followed Rintels's testimony before the Senate Subcommittee on Constitutional Rights, which was conducting hearings about freedom of the press. Rintels testified, and then repeated in his op-ed piece, that although the stories on the series were said to be inspired by real cases, they were not: "I was offered a job writing on the series," Rintels wrote. "When I asked them which case they wanted me to adapt, they told me to come up with a story of my own invention—no case needed." Rintels added that when he was allowed to write about a real case—the bombing of a black church that killed four girls in Birmingham, Alabama—he was told to change the facts of the case: "The church must be in the north, there could be no Negroes involved, and the bombing could have nothing at all to do with civil rights." Rintels went on to note that the series showed no instances of bugging, phone tapping, or hiring of paid informants. "They're bad public relations," Rintels wrote. "The public can be spared these truths."[89] Rintels also objected to the vetting of actors, crew members, directors, writers, and sponsors by FBI investigators.[90] Rintels closed with a clear challenge to the FBI's brand as captured in the television series, but his conclusion could easily be applied to FBI public relations beyond the show: "By now the message should be clear. The American people are being force-fed a dishonest picture of the work of a Government agency and any writer who attempts to portray the real world, suggesting that white-collar or business crime exists or that crimes against people's rights are as much a source of national concern as crimes against their persons, is simply not allowed to do so."[91]

Rintels's direct challenge to the validity of the series and his overt suggestion that government involvement in TV was improper, along with his exposure of the FBI's public relations concerns, could not go unchallenged. Hoover requested his staff members' thoughts, and Jones wrote a six-page memorandum rebutting the thrust of Rintels's arguments and attacking the writer. Jones blamed the scriptwriters' ineptitude for the failure to produce shows about white-collar crime or civil rights violations. Although Jones admitted that wiretapping, bugging, and other "confidential investigative techniques" were not allowed in the series, other decisions about content were made by ABC, not the FBI, he claimed disingenuously. Finally, Jones said, Rintels was right: the FBI did approve everyone who participated in the production. "If Rintels thinks we are going to approve for our television series some of the drunkards, kooks, perverts, faggots, junkies, and others of this ilk, he is sadly mistaken," Jones wrote. "The indignation of right-thinking Americans would most certainly be justified if we permitted people like Jane Fonda and Dalton Trumbo (of the Hollywood Ten) to participate in our television series."[92]

A few weeks after Jones authored that memorandum and ghostwrote a *TV Guide* article for Hoover that rebutted Rintels's assertions, the director died in his sleep at age seventy-seven. In the *TV Guide* article, published a few weeks after Hoover's death, he justified his Bureau's interest in the program's authenticity, thus asserting the FBI's responsibility and utility while ducking charges that the TV show manipulated the public's understanding of a government agency. "So long as there is a television program which bears our name and seal," Hoover wrote, "we will view it with the same critical eye as applied to every other area of our work."[93]

When producer Quinn Martin told a newspaper reporter in 1965 that previous depictions of FBI personnel in entertainment programming "made them look like robots," Hoover scrawled, "We certainly are in 'quicksand' with this outfit," in the story's margin.[94] Another newspaper article that appeared before the first season sparked Hoover to write, "And I regret ever going into this. It has been a headache."[95] The process of negotiating Hoover's need for total control and Hollywood's desire to create entertaining, sometimes violent programming was a difficult one.

The program's prime-time success, however, eased those tensions somewhat. Frequently rated in the top twenty (and regularly finishing in the top ten during its first five years), the program ultimately aired in fifty-three countries and ran for years in syndication.[96] Despite Hoover's vituperative declarations on internal memoranda, the collaboration among the FBI, QM Productions, Warner Brothers, and ABC television lasted for nine seasons and 241 episodes, until *The F.B.I.* was finally canceled in 1975. Inspector Lew Erskine, portrayed by Efrem Zimbalist Jr., became a well-known television icon, the Ford Mustang he drove sold millions, and the series became Martin's biggest hit in a string of popular crime series.[97]

Bureau-approved story lines and Bureau-edited scripts countered questions about the legitimacy of federal law enforcement by depicting the FBI as a model of consistency, restraint, and effectiveness, neutralizing critics' concerns that the agency had become an out-of-control "American gestapo." Bureau-approved sponsors filled commercial breaks with messages that Hoover considered appropriate matches for his preferred, conservative image of the FBI. The FBI characters in the series showed steadiness, thoughtfulness, and competence. Criminals were depicted as stereotypical degenerates, lacking judgment and intelligence. And all the actors, directors, and crew members involved in these portrayals were cleared by FBI investigators.

Depictions that might raise questions about the FBI's role in society and challenge the Bureau's legitimacy—a subject of debate in many circles during the series' run—were simply banned from the broadcasts. By controlling the content of an hour of prime-time programming each week, the FBI was able to create an onscreen Bureau personified by Hoover and epitomizing utility and responsibility. By establishing those key values through its television series, Hoover's FBI was able to assert its legitimacy even as critics of the 1960s and early 1970s were questioning the actions and power of the FBI and the length of Hoover's tenure as director. The series clearly obscured the civil liberties excesses that were central to the FBI's work throughout the Hoover era. The criticism by screenwriter Rintels, who questioned the propriety of government involvement in entertainment television, was as true in its own way as was Hoover's assertion that the FBI was just doing business as it always had done.

The F.B.I., shaped by public relations staff in the Crime Records Division, presented a mythical Bureau brand to 40 million Americans each week. Questions about the propriety of a government law enforcement agency participating in a television program and criticisms of Hoover's Bureau itself were simply overwhelmed by the FBI-approved stories of Inspector Erskine and his iconic Ford Mustang that were beamed into tens of millions of American homes each week.

Conclusion

When Senator Kenneth McKellar asked J. Edgar Hoover in 1936 whether the FBI had spent any money on publicity or whether it employed any writers, the director's response was unequivocal. Not a penny was spent on publicity, Hoover said, and there were no writers employed by the FBI.[1] In 1971, when a newspaper reporter asked how much the FBI spent to support its eponymous television program, a Bureau spokesman declared that the agency's contribution amounted to merely a few hours per episode as part of two agents' larger duties.[2] During the intervening decades, the FBI's work was characterized by its own public relations efforts as tirelessly and relentlessly, yet dispassionately and responsibly focused on violations of federal law. Mainstream news organizations nearly always stuck to the FBI's preferred narrative about itself. In those instances when a mainstream writer or broadcaster strayed into even the mildest criticism, that message was dismissed as part of a biased "smear campaign" or simply drowned out by others reinforcing the honorable themes of the Collier-Cooper public relations template.

From its founding in 1908, the FBI and its precursors faced an ongoing crisis of legitimacy among those Americans who feared the agency would inevitably devolve into a corrupt and intrusive secret police force. During the late 1910s and early 1920s, those fears were realized as the Bureau of Investigation stumbled from the repressive mass arrests of the Palmer Raids into the corruption of the Teapot Dome scandal. To those members of the public who were predisposed to fear a loss of civil liberties and who shared a pessimistic view of the corrupting influence of power, those early missteps must have seemed obvious signs that the Bureau should be eliminated. J. Edgar Hoover, the young head of the General Intelligence Division who coordinated the Palmer Raids, learned his lesson well. What had begun as a triumph of good over evil in press accounts evolved into a travesty of justice that reinforced public concerns about the legitimacy of a federal law enforcement agency. The Palmer Raids no doubt opened Hoover's eyes to the power of the press to shape and reshape the meaning of events.

That moment in 1924 when Attorney General Harlan Fiske Stone determined that the young lawyer who had directed the controversial Palmer Raids was somehow the right man to reform the Bureau was a fateful one. Stone's decision put Hoover in a position of power, and he spent nearly five decades consolidating that power and using it to protect his own interests, whether by promoting his own xenophobic politics or preserving his reputation. Hoover's FBI was both a law enforcement innovator and a lawbreaker.

According to his Bureau-authored hagiography, Hoover agreed to take the directorship only if several conditions were met that would ensure the agency's incorruptibility. Given the consequences of Stone's decision over the next forty-eight years, the moment when the attorney general convinced himself that Hoover could clean up the Bureau stands as one of the most consequential in American civil liberties history. Having lived through the furor over the Palmer Raids, Hoover understood the power of public opinion and chose to regroup and wait for an opportunity to expand his power. To his credit, though, the young director did purge political hacks and corrupt officials from the Bureau. Hoover also instituted his first tentative public relations tactics and adopted the then-controversial science of fingerprint identification.

Yet the Bureau remained a little-known federal agency in 1932, when Franklin Delano Roosevelt was elected president. Even before Roosevelt took office, Hoover faced a crisis when FDR selected Montana senator Thomas Walsh as his nominee for attorney general. Walsh was an anticorruption crusader who, in the weeks following his selection and prior to the inauguration, pledged to reorganize the Department of Justice with "almost completely new personnel."[3] Walsh was among those who questioned the FBI's legitimacy and worried about its potential for corruption and overreach. Walsh died of a heart attack before he could be confirmed, but his intention to replace Hoover reinforced the director's view that he needed an alternative to the Palmer Raids and Teapot Dome narratives that were still percolating through American society.

Walsh's replacement, Homer S. Cummings, cared little about Hoover's past, and during the 1930s, Hoover's agency grew as part of the Roosevelt administration's war on crime. As the arrests and shootings of high-profile outlaws mounted, Americans responded with enthusiasm to the one government agency that seemed to be able to get things done. At the same time, Hoover's initial forays into public relations had yielded little in the way of publicity; then he encountered two journalists, Rex Collier and Courtney Ryley Cooper, who provided him with a useful template for public relations—an appealing set of themes that undermined critics' concerns about the FBI's legitimacy. For instance, whereas secret police agencies were subject to the whims of individuals and irresponsibly engaged in intrusive investigations, the FBI, according to the Collier-Cooper thesis, eliminated the possibility of corrupt individuals abusing the agency's power by relying on dispassionate science to solve crimes. In addition, the FBI was reluctant to get involved in local issues, and most important, Hoover was a trustworthy defender of civil liberties. In the 1930s, public relations helped Hoover keep his job and helped normalize the controversial notion of federal law enforcement.

Public relations pioneer Edward Bernays referred to persuasive communication based on an understanding of audience motivations as the "engineering of consent." Hoover's public relations team understood what motivated its audience of supportive journalists. Access to information from the FBI had professional benefits, allowing journalists to write and publish stories about the Bureau. At the same time, Hoover's iconic status and personal fame made friendship with the director a powerful motivator for his admirers, all of whom knew the personal and professional implications of a failure to cooperate. For the FBI, engineering consent among journalists meant metering their access based on their willingness to adhere to the Bureau's conditions (such as allowing their articles to be edited by agents in the Crime Records Division). In essence, the FBI, with its massive cache of valuable information, coerced the consent of reporters who were willing to play along.

The FBI was not alone in its efforts to cultivate beneficial relationships with reporters, editors, and publishers. The World War I Committee on Public Information undertook a coordinated effort to feed government information directly to journalists.[4] In 1922, Walter Lippmann outlined the role of publicity agents communicating with the news media to shape public opinion.[5] Bernays engaged the press in his early 1920s theatrical and corporate promotions.[6] By the late 1920s, large organizations such as AT&T were employing public relations tactics to build strategic relationships in communities around the country, including relationships with members of the press.[7]

No other contemporary organization, though, could match the cultural capital of Hoover's FBI, with its carefully constructed and highly popular stories of crime, heroism, and the triumph of good over evil. During Hoover's forty-eight-year tenure as director, thousands of FBI stories appeared in newspapers, magazines, and comic strips; on radio programs; in motion pictures; and ultimately, on television. Most of those stories were produced with the assistance, and often with the editorial input, of the Crime Records staff.[8] The Bureau had another powerful public relations tool: no other organization had a leader who could match the public profile of the iconic Hoover, a bureaucrat turned law enforcement giant whose name became synonymous with the FBI.

Whereas FDR intended his orders authorizing the Bureau to enter into the intelligence-gathering business to be limited mandates, Hoover saw an opportunity to consolidate power and counter his critics. The wiretaps, buggings, and surreptitious entries of the late 1930s and beyond allowed the director to cite the danger posed by the enemy within to normalize and legitimize his agency's work. With the rise of communism came a new "responsible" mission for the FBI, a mission that further marginalized concerns about the Bureau's power. To counter the potentially revolutionary communist movement forming within the United States, the logic went, the nation needed a secret force to uncover those communist cells. The Collier-Cooper thesis provided the nation with a trustworthy defender of civil liberties (Hoover) who would control any overzealous intelligence work.

Of course, the story of a scientific and careful FBI led by the trustworthy Hoover obscured the real nature of the Bureau's work from the 1940s to the 1970s. Meanwhile, the agency tasked with protecting the nation against subversion and crime expended enormous resources to investigate, monitor, and even actively undermine thousands upon thousands of people whose worldview did not mesh with Hoover's narrow and rigid conceptualization of Americanism. As has been demonstrated in this study and elsewhere, that group of "subversive" Americans included many members of the American press who were busily exercising their First Amendment rights. For Hoover, a focus on the press was an act of self-preservation. Friendly reporters provided the amplifier for the theme of a responsible, scientific FBI that need not be feared because the steady Hoover was at the helm. Unfriendly reporters who actively or even potentially undermined the Bureau's legitimacy through their criticism of the agency or its director were lumped together with communists and others who advocated the overthrow of the U.S. government. Criticism of the FBI was, in Hoover's mind, an un-American act and the first step toward a return to the anarchy that had sparked his rise to power.

Hoover's status as an American institution and his Bureau's reputation as America's indispensable law enforcement agency spanned decades, ending only with the director's death in 1972. Hoover and the work of his Bureau became legendary, a hagiography maintained by the FBI's tight control over the flow of information from its investigative files. The idea of a friendship with Hoover implied a certain exclusivity and glamour available to only a small group of insiders at the center of the government.

The relationships created and maintained through the FBI's public relations tactics (such as "personal" correspondence with Hoover) encouraged the individual targets of these messages to draw lines, identifying members and nonmembers of a community of meaning. Members of a community of meaning share a similar set of understandings about the organization and, ideally, are willing to act on those beliefs. The quest for excellence in the practice of public relations may be seen as an ongoing search for the perfect tactic and the perfect message to create those shared meanings. By fabricating the impression of close friendships with Hoover, the letter writers at the FBI strategically engaged a powerful community of meaning to promote and defend the Bureau.

According to the Collier-Cooper thesis, the FBI was a responsible, scientific agency led by the steady and trustworthy Hoover. Armed with that message, which characterized Bureau public relations throughout Hoover's tenure and beyond (in the form of *The F.B.I.* television series), the director built a formidable public relations infrastructure led by experienced officials who understood how to handle the news media. Key opinion leaders such as reporters, editors, publishers, and broadcasters were carefully "taught" the Collier-Cooper thesis through their access to FBI stories. Those who proved adept at amplifying the science, responsibility, and Hoover themes, particularly if they were strategically placed, became friends of the Bureau. Hoover's "friends" were courted and flattered, and in return, they became "objective" promoters and defenders of the FBI; some even became confidential informants.

One natural question that arises from a review of FBI public relations and its dealings with the news media is this: is democracy served when a government agency essentially manufactures consent by manipulating public opinion? The answer seems clear, particularly when that government agency is a massive law enforcement organization with extraordinary powers to monitor and investigate dissenters, including members of the press. Hoover's FBI, an often innovative law enforcement agency, used public relations to hide its more intrusive intelligence activities from the American public. Public relations constructed the facade that hid the framework of political intelligence gathering that eventually led to the active subversion of constitutionally protected dissent in America. Hoover used public relations as one tool to simultaneously normalize the idea of his agency and preserve his own position of power.

Journalists ostensibly serve as the public's agents, holding government officials accountable to standards of law and truth. But in their dealings with the FBI, journalists often failed to maintain a high standard of professionalism. Many journalists agreed to put their critical sensibilities on hold when it came to the FBI, perhaps acceding to Hoover's requirements for collaboration because of patriotism or ambition. As a result, the FBI's great misdirection scheme worked. The evocative science, responsibility, and Hoover themes promoted by the Bureau and amplified by compliant journalists succeeded in distracting Americans from real questions about the antidemocratic potential of centralized law enforcement and domestic intelligence power. When those questions did slip into the public sphere, Hoover's friends in newsrooms throughout America stood ready to silence that dissent, agreeing with the FBI that a "smear campaign" was under way to undermine democracy. In fact, those dissenters' concerns that the FBI was trampling on civil liberties and subverting democratic principles have proved true. Journalists, engaged as adjuncts through FBI public relations, provided the "objective" cover that Hoover needed to overcome his agency's ongoing crisis of legitimacy.

NOTES

Introduction

1. David T. Z. Mindich, *Just the Facts: How Objectivity Came to Define American Journalism* (New York: New York University Press, 1998), 5.

2. Michael Schudson, *Discovering the News: A Social History of American Newspapers* (New York: Basic Books, 1978).

3. Robert A. Hackett, "Decline of a Paradigm: Bias and Objectivity in Media Studies," *Critical Studies in Mass Communication* 1 (1984): 229–259.

4. Gaye Tuchman, "Objectivity as Strategic Ritual: An Examination of Newsmen's Notions of Objectivity," *American Journal of Sociology* 77, 4 (January 1972): 660–679.

5. Pamela J. Shoemaker and Stephen D. Reese, *Mediating the Message: Theories of Influence on Mass Media Content* (White Plains, N.Y.: Longman Publishers, 1996), 113.

6. Richard V. Ericson, Patricia M. Baranek, and Janet B. L. Chan, *Representing Order: Crime, Law, and Justice in the News* (Toronto: University of Toronto Press, 1991), 345.

7. Ibid., 349.

8. Todd Gitlin, *The Whole World Is Watching: Mass Media and the Making & Unmaking of the New Left* (Berkeley: University of California Press, 1980), 42.

9. Ibid., 269.

10. Leo Rosten, *The Washington Correspondents* (New York: Harcourt, Brace, 1937), 5.

11. Ibid., 111.

12. Ibid., 106.

13. Ibid., 252.

14. Leon Sigal, *Reporters and Officials: The Organization and Politics of Newsmaking* (Lexington, Mass.: D. C. Heath, 1973), 54–56.

15. Ibid., 55.

16. Bernard Roshco, *Newsmaking* (Chicago: University of Chicago Press, 1975), 75.

17. Warren Breed, "Social Control in the Newsroom: A Functional Analysis," *Social Forces* 33, 4 (May 1955): 328.

18. Ibid.

19. Gaye Tuchman, *Making News: A Study in the Construction of Reality* (New York: Free Press, 1978), 68.

20. Ibid., 68–69.

21. Sigal, *Reporters and Officials*, 181.

22. Ibid., 46.

23. Ibid.

24. Ibid., 182.

25. Ray Eldon Hiebert, *The Press in Washington* (New York: Dodd, Mead, 1966), 195.

26. Betty Houchin Winfield, *FDR and the News Media* (New York: Columbia University Press, 1994), 173.

27. Athan Theoharis and John Stuart Cox, *The Boss: J. Edgar Hoover and the Great American Inquisition* (Philadelphia: Temple University Press, 1988), 17.

28. Richard Gid Powers, *Secrecy and Power: The Life of J. Edgar Hoover* (New York: Free Press, 1987), 3.

Chapter 1. The FBI's Ongoing Crisis of Legitimacy

1. W. C. Sullivan to A. H. Belmont, "Molders of Public Opinion in the United States: Central Research Matter," March 18, 1959, FBI 100-401767. The original is maintained in the files of the FBI; I obtained a photocopy through the Freedom of Information Act.

2. Fred J. Cook, "The F.B.I.," *Nation*, October 18, 1958, 225.

3. Ibid., 222.

4. Don Whitehead, preface to *The FBI Story: A Report to the People* (New York: Random House, 1956), v.

5. Norman Thomas, "Agency of Justice," *Commentary*, April 1957, 384.

6. Whitehead, *FBI Story*, 286.

7. *The Mike Wallace Interview*, May 17, 1957, transcript from the Harry Ransom Center, University of Texas at Austin, http://www.hrc.utexas.edu/multimedia/video/2008/wallace/eaton_cyrus_t.html (accessed January 28, 2012).

8. William C. Sullivan, memorandum to Alan H. Belmont, December 18, 1958, FBI-unserialized (James A. Wechsler file), 2.

9. William C. Sullivan, memorandum to Alan H. Belmont, January 16, 1959, FBI 67-80006-1848.

10. P. G. Stillman, "The Concept of Legitimacy," *Polity* 7 (1974): 32–56; Edwin M. Epstein, "The Historical Enigma of Corporate Legitimacy," *California Law Review* 60 (1972): 1701–1717; R. A. Francesconi, "James Hunt, the Wilmington 10, and Institutional Legitimacy," *Quarterly Journal of Speech* 68 (1982): 47–59.

11. Gerald Turkel, "The 1980 Chrysler Loan Guarantee," *Research in Law, Deviance and Social Control* 4 (1982): 165–189.

12. Josh Boyd, "Actional Legitimation: No Crisis Necessary," *Journal of Public Relations Research* 12 (2000): 341–353.

13. Richard Gid Powers, *Broken: The Troubled Past and Uncertain Future of the FBI* (New York: Free Press, 2004), 48–61.

14. Ibid., 62.

15. Tim Wiener, *Enemies: A History of the FBI* (New York: Random House, 2012), 8.

16. Rodger Streitmatter, *Voices of Revolution* (New York: Columbia University Press, 2001), 115–125.

17. President Woodrow Wilson, Address to Congress, April 2, 1917, reprinted in Francis W. March, *History of the World War* (Philadelphia: United Publishers of the United States and Canada, 1918), 134.

18. Kenneth Ackerman, *Young J. Edgar: Hoover, the Red Scare, and the Assault on Civil Liberties* (Falls Church, Va.: Viral History Press, 2007), 39–130.

19. Ibid.

20. Athan G. Theoharis, Tony Poveda, Susan Rosenfeld, and Richard Gid Powers, eds., *The FBI: A Comprehensive Reference Guide* (New York: Oryx Press, 2000), 109–110.

21. "A Lawless Department of Justice," *New Republic*, March 29, 1922, 126.

22. Ibid., 127.

23. Cook, "The F.B.I.," 232.

24. Wiener, *Enemies*, 44.

25. Theoharis et al., *The FBI*, 128.

26. Frederick R. Barkley, "Critics Open Fire on Hoover's G-Men," *New York Times*, March 17, 1940.

27. Theoharis et al., *The FBI*, 10.

28. U.S. Senate Select Committee to Study Governmental Operations, *Intelligence Activities and the Rights of Americans, Book II* (Washington, D.C., 1976), 23.

29. Theoharis et al., *The FBI*, 11.

30. Alpheus Thomas Mason, *Harlan Fiske Stone: Pillar of the Law* (New York: Viking Press, 1956), 151.

31. Whitehead, *FBI Story*, 67.

32. Ackerman, *Young J. Edgar*, 8.

33. Ibid., 9.

34. *The Nation-Wide Spy System Centering in the Department of Justice* (New York: ACLU, 1924).

35. Wiener, *Enemies*, 60.

36. Ibid., 60–61.

37. Theoharis et al., *The FBI*, 333.

38. Eugene Lewis, *Public Entrepreneurship: Toward a Theory of Bureaucratic Political Power: The Organizational Lives of Hyman Rickover, J. Edgar Hoover, and Robert Moses* (Bloomington: Indiana University Press, 1980), 94.

39. Curt Gentry, *J. Edgar Hoover: The Man and the Secrets* (New York: W. W. Norton, 1991), 129–131.

40. Kenneth O'Reilly, "A New Deal for the FBI: The Roosevelt Administration, Crime Control, and National Security," *Journal of American History* 82 (December 1982): 642.

41. Milton S. Mayer, "Myth of the 'G-Men,'" *Forum* 94 (September 1935): 145.

42. O'Reilly, "New Deal for the FBI," 638–658.

43. Wiener, *Enemies*, 73, 74.

44. William Seagle, "The American National Police: The Dangers of Federal Crime Control," *Harper's Monthly Magazine*, November 1934, 751.

45. Ibid., 760.

46. Ibid.

47. Theoharis et al., *The FBI*, 176.

48. J. Edgar Hoover, testimony before the U.S. Senate Appropriations Subcommittee, April 11, 1936.

49. Theoharis et al., *The FBI*, 346.

50. Ibid.

51. Athan Theoharis and John Stuart Cox, *The Boss: J. Edgar Hoover and the Great American Inquisition* (Philadelphia: Temple University Press, 1988), 157.

52. Powers, *Broken*, 227.

53. Ibid., 138.

54. Sullivan, "Molders of Public Opinion," iii. This term for the press came into common usage around the turn of the century and had been used in a similar report Hoover requested in 1938. See no author, report attached to J. Edgar Hoover to Fulton Oursler, December 13, 1938, FBI 94-3-4-221-61. According to my research, the first published use of the term "molders of public opinion" was in *A Comprehensive Summary of the Press throughout the World on All Important Current Topics*, vol. 24 (New York: Public Opinion Company, 1898), 363.

55. D. Mickey Ladd, Inspection Report, May 30, 1945, FBI 67-205182-unserialized.

56. C. H. Carson, performance evaluation of William C. Sullivan, March 31, 1945, FBI 67-205182-unserialized.

57. Robert C. Hendon, memorandum to Clyde Tolson, May 25, 1944, FBI 67E-HQ-205182-unserialized.

58. William C. Sullivan, personal and confidential letter to J. Edgar Hoover, September 30, 1944, FBI 67-105182-109.

59. C. H. Carson, memorandum to D. Mickey Ladd, July 6, 1945, FBI 67-205182-119.

60. William C. Sullivan, personal letter to J. Edgar Hoover, April 19, 1948, FBI 67-205182-155.

61. J. Edgar Hoover, letter to William C. Sullivan, April 23, 1948, FBI 67-205182-156.

62. J. Edgar Hoover, handwritten note on J. E. Edwards, memorandum to Clyde Tolson, October 15, 1948, FBI 67-205182-157.

63. H. L. Edwards, memorandum to Mr. Glavin, January 19, 1949, FBI 67-205182-164.

64. William C. Sullivan, personal letter to J. Edgar Hoover, February 8, 1949, FBI 62-205182-167.

65. H. L. Edwards, memorandum to Mr. Glavin, December 8, 1949, FBI 67-205182-180.

66. William C. Sullivan, personal letter to Frederick C. Dumaine Jr., July 5, 1950, attached to William C. Sullivan, personal letter to J. Edgar Hoover, July 6, 1950, FBI 67-205182-191.

67. William C. Sullivan, personal letter to J. Edgar Hoover, August 11, 1951, FBI 67-205182-215.

68. M. A. Jones, memorandum to Louis B. Nichols, August 25, 1951, FBI 67-205182-216.

69. J. Edgar Hoover, handwritten note on H. L. Edwards, memorandum to Mr. Glavin, February 18, 1953, FBI 67-205182-239.

70. J. Edgar Hoover, handwritten note on H. L. Edwards, memorandum to Mr. Glavin, March 25, 1953, FBI 67-205182-252.

71. J. Edgar Hoover, letter to William C. Sullivan, August 10, 1953, FBI 67-205182-260.

72. J. Edgar Hoover, personal and confidential letter to William C. Sullivan, July 7, 1954, FBI 67-205182-281.

73. William C. Sullivan, personal letter to J. Edgar Hoover, October 25, 1957, FBI 67-205182-345.

74. William C. Sullivan, memorandum to Alan H. Belmont, December 16, 1958, FBI 67-205182-370.

75. Louis B. Nichols, memorandum to Clyde Tolson, October 23, 1957, FBI 67-205182-348.

76. J. H. Gale, memorandum to Clyde Tolson, December 10, 1963, FBI 67-205182-unserialized; John P. Mohr, memorandum to Clyde Tolson, March 24, 1964, FBI 67-205182-493.

77. William C. Sullivan, personal and confidential letter to J. Edgar Hoover, July 24, 1964, FBI 67-205182-501.

78. Theoharis et al., *The FBI*, 355.

79. J. Edgar Hoover, memorandum to Clyde Tolson, Mark Felt, et al., October 1, 1971, FBI 67-197055-578.

80. Thomas Bishop, memorandum to W. Mark Felt, October 5, 1971, FBI 67-205182-638.

81. H. N. Bassett, memorandum to Mr. Callahan, October 6, 1971, FBI 67-205182-643.

82. James A. Wechsler, "Hoover's Twilight," *New York Post,* October 6, 1971, 53.

83. Rowland Evans and Robert Novak, "Hoover's FBI Crisis," attached to U.S. Sen. Gordon Allott, letter to J. Edgar Hoover, November 9, 1971, FBI 67-205182-671.

84. Fulton Oursler, letter to J. Edgar Hoover, December 6, 1938, FBI 94-3-4-221-61.

85. J. Edgar Hoover, letter to Fulton Oursler, December 13, 1938, FBI 94-3-4-221-61.

86. Ibid.

87. Author unknown, Memorandum Re: The Assistance of the Press to Law Enforcement, December 13, 1938, attachment to FBI 94-3-4-221-61.

88. Ibid., 4.

89. Ibid., 5.

90. Author unknown, Memorandum Re: Press Interference and Successful Law Enforcement, December 13, 1938, p. 2, attachment to FBI 94-3-4-221-61.

91. J. Edgar Hoover, letter to Walter Winchell, April 17, 1936, FBI-unserialized.

92. "Editors Denounce 'Blanket Seizures,'" *New York Times,* April 19, 1936. All *Times* documents cited herein were accessed online at http://www.nytimes.com.

93. Michael Newton, *The Encyclopedia of Kidnappings* (New York: Facts on File, 2002), 187–188.

94. J. Edgar Hoover, letter to Walter Winchell, January 25, 1937, FBI 62-31615-56.

95. Sullivan, "Molders of Public Opinion," i. The report examined the following members of the press: Joseph Alsop, Max Ascoli, Alan Barth, [redacted], Winston Burdett, Al Capp, Horace Cayton, Marquis Childs, John Cogley, Henry Commager, Dorothy Day, Albert Deutsch, Fred Friendly, Marguerite Higgins, Philip Horton, Murray Kempton, Alexander Kendrick, Walter Kerr, Frederick Kuh, [redacted], Max Lerner, Walter Lippmann, John Martin, Herbert Matthews, Bill Mauldin, Carey McWilliams, Walter Millis, Edward R. Murrow, Drew Pearson, Richard Rovere, Dorothy Schiff, John Scott, Eric Sevareid, William Shirer, Edmund Stevens, I. F. Stone, Michael Straight, John Vandercook, James Warburg, and James Wechsler.

96. Ibid.

97. William C. Sullivan, memorandum to Alan H. Belmont, March 18, 1959, attached to "Molders of Public Opinion," FBI 100-401767.

98. Sullivan, "Molders of Public Opinion," i, ii.

99. Ibid.

100. Ibid., 14.

101. Ibid., 30, 74.

102. Matthew Cecil, "The Path to Madness: McCarthyism and *New York Post* editor James A. Wechsler's Battle for Press Freedom," *Journal of Communication Inquiry* 35, 3 (July 2011): 275–291.

103. Sullivan, "Molders of Public Opinion," i.

104. Using the Freedom of Information Act, I obtained and reviewed the FBI files of more than 400 American journalists and publications.

105. Matthew Cecil, "Friends of the Bureau: Personal Correspondence and the

Cultivation of Journalist-Adjuncts by J. Edgar Hoover's FBI," *Journalism and Mass Communication Quarterly* 88, 2 (Summer 2011): 267–284.

Chapter 2. A Bureau Built for Public Relations

1. Courtney Ryley Cooper, "Special Broadcast from the Federal Bureau of Investigation of the Department of Justice," radio script, July 17, 1935, FBI 62-21526-200.

2. Athan G. Theoharis, Tony Proveda, Susan Rosenfeld, and Richard Gid Powers, eds., *The FBI: A Comprehensive Reference Guide* (New York: Oryx Press, 2000), 11–12.

3. Jennifer Mnookin, "Fingerprints: Not a Gold Standard," *Issues in Science and Technology* 20, 1 (Fall 2003): 49; Simon A. Cole, "Witnessing Identification: Latent Fingerprinting Evidence and Expert Knowledge," *Social Studies of Science* 28 (October–December 1998): 695–696.

4. Theoharis et al., *The FBI*, 11–12.

5. Ibid., 208.

6. Gerald K. Haines and David A. Langbart, *Unlocking the Files of the FBI: A Guide to Its Records and Classification System* (Wilmington, Del.: Scholarly Resources, 1993), xii–xiii.

7. J. Edgar Hoover, memorandum to Mr. Dodge, May 6, 1929, FBI 62-21526-2.

8. Robert Stanton Lynd and Helen Lynd, *Middletown in Transition: A Study in Cultural Conflicts* (New York: Harcourt, Brace, 1937), 19–24.

9. J. Edgar Hoover, foreword to Don Whitehead, *The FBI Story: A Report to the People* (New York: Random House, 1956).

10. For a comprehensive and compelling review of the outlaw era, see Brian Burroughs, *Public Enemies: America's Greatest Crime Wave and the Birth of the FBI, 1933–1934* (New York: Penguin Books, 2004).

11. Richard Gid Powers, *G-Men: Hoover's FBI in American Popular Culture* (Carbondale: Southern Illinois University Press, 1983), 97.

12. Ibid., 41.

13. Curt Gentry, *J. Edgar Hoover: The Man and the Secrets* (New York: W. W. Norton, 1991), 174.

14. Drew Pearson, *Diaries, 1949–1959*, ed. Tyler Abell (New York: Holt, Rinehart & Winston, 1974), 284.

15. "Henry Suydam, 64, Press Aide, Dead," *New York Times*, December 12, 1955.

16. J. Edgar Hoover, memorandum to Clyde Tolson, November 2, 1934, FBI 62-21526-88X.

17. Pearson, *Diaries*, 284.

18. Carl Behrens, "Henry Suydam, 64, Dead; State Dept. Press Officer," *Washington Post and Times-Herald*, December 12, 1955, 16; Louis B. Nichols, handwritten note on above clipping, December 12, 1955, FBI 62-43811-29 (Henry Suydam file.)

19. There are myriad definitions of public relations. This study relies on a

composite definition I produced after reviewing popular public relations textbooks and scholarly articles. It is assumed in this book that public relations, as defined by Edward Bernays, the founder of the field, must include the gathering of insight into the audience, whether by formal or informal means. For an exploration of public relations definitions, see Dean Kruckeberg and Kenneth Starck, *Public Relations and Community: A Reconstructed Theory* (New York: Praeger, 1988), 16.

20. Edward Bernays, "The Engineering of Consent," *Annals of the American Academy of Political and Social Science* 250 (1947): 113.

21. Stuart Ewen, *PR! A Social History of Spin* (New York: Basic Books, 1996), 163.

22. For an assertion of Lee's "parenthood" of public relations, see Ray Eldon Hiebert, *Courtier to the Crowd: The Story of Ivy Lee and the Development of Public Relations* (Ames: Iowa State University Press, 1966).

23. Ewen, *PR!* 80.

24. For an examination of Lee's Declaration of Principles as a starting point for modern public relations, see Karen Miller Russell and Carl O. Bishop, "Understanding Ivy Lee's Declaration of Principles: U.S. Newspaper and Magazine Coverage of Publicity and Press Agentry, 1865–1904," *Public Relations Review* 35, 2 (June 2009): 91.

25. Edward Bernays, *Crystallizing Public Opinion* (New York: Liveright Publishing, 1923), 166–167.

26. Walter Lippmann, *Public Opinion* (New York: Harcourt, Brace, 1922), 3–32.

27. Margot Opdycke Lamme and Karen Miller Russell, "Removing the Spin: Toward a New Theory of Public Relations History," *Journalism and Communication Monographs* 11, 4 (Winter 2010): 354.

28. Ibid., 341–342.

29. Ibid., 355.

30. Roland Marchand, *Creating the Corporate Soul: The Rise of Public Relations and Corporate Imagery in American Big Business* (Berkeley: University of California Press, 1998), 194.

31. Henry Suydam, memorandum to J. Edgar Hoover, August 23, 1935, FBI 62-37036-6 (Neil "Rex" Collier file).

32. J. Edgar Hoover, memorandum (for the files), October 9, 1935, FBI 62-37036-10.

33. Henry Suydam, letter to George Janosik, October 10, 1935, FBI 62-37036-13.

34. Promotional materials for *War on Crime*, FBI 62-37036-32.

35. Louis B. Nichols, memorandum to Clyde Tolson, February 3, 1936, FBI 62-37036-20.

36. Neil "Rex" Collier, "Dillinger No. 46: A Woman's Tip," continuity for *War on Crime* comic strip, July 6, 1936, FBI 62-37036-59.

37. Richard Gid Powers, *Broken: The Troubled Past and Uncertain Future of the FBI* (New York: Free Press, 2004), 155.

38. Neil "Rex" Collier, "Equipment Lacking as Agents Battle Well Armed Gangs," *Washington Star*, April 29, 1934, FBI 80-64-A.

39. Neil "Rex" Collier, "Justice Agents Brush up on Sharpshooting with New Deadly Weapons for War on Gangs," *Washington Star*, June 19, 1934, FBI 80-64-unserialized.

40. J. Edgar Hoover, memorandum to Clyde Tolson, July 10, 1934, FBI 80-64-9 (Neil "Rex" Collier file); Clyde Tolson, memorandum to J. Edgar Hoover, July 9, 1934, FBI 80-64-74.

41. Neil "Rex" Collier, "Hoover, Their Chief, Says There Is No Mystery in Crime Detection, Merely Painstaking Work and Common Sense," *New York Times Magazine*, August 19, 1934, FBI 80-74-A.

42. Ibid.

43. Neil "Rex" Collier, "Was the G-Man Execution of Dillinger Wanton, or Justified," *Milwaukee Journal*, August 5, 1936, 1, 3.

44. "Aide of Buffalo Bill Sketches 'Circus Days' for Radio's Big Top," *New York Times*, October 22, 1933; Courtney Ryley Cooper, "The Elephant Forgets," in *O. Henry Memorial Award: Prize Stories of 1930*, ed. Blanche Colton Williams (Garden City, N.Y.: Doubleday, Doran, 1930), 111–128.

45. Powers, *G-Men*, 94–98.

46. Courtney Ryley Cooper, letter to J. Edgar Hoover, April 22, 1933, FBI 62-21526-9 (Courtney Ryley Cooper file).

47. Courtney Ryley Cooper, letter to J. Edgar Hoover, April 27, 1933, FBI 62-21526-9.

48. Courtney Ryley Cooper, telegram to J. Edgar Hoover, May 17, 1933, FBI 62-21526-11.

49. Courtney Ryley Cooper, "The Biggest Jail on Earth: As Told by J. Edgar Hoover, Director, United States Bureau of Investigation to Courtney Ryley Cooper," June 10, 1933, FBI 62-21526-22.

50. Courtney Ryley Cooper, "How Smart Is a Crook? As Told by J. Edgar Hoover, Director, United States Bureau of Investigation to Courtney Ryley Cooper," June 10, 1933, FBI 62-21526-22.

51. Courtney Ryley Cooper, letter to J. Edgar Hoover, August 3, 1933, FBI 62-21526-27.

52. J. Edgar Hoover, letter to Courtney Ryley Cooper, August 5, 1933, FBI 62-21526-27.

53. Courtney Ryley Cooper, "The Roots of Crime: An Interview with J. Edgar Hoover, Director, Division of Investigation, United States Department of Justice," October 30, 1934, FBI 62-21526-89, 2.

54. See, for example, Homer S. Cummings, letter to Courtney Ryley Cooper, December 21, 1936, in which Cummings thanks Cooper for a box of kumquats (accession 9973, box 88, Homer S. Cummings Papers, University of Virginia Library).

55. Courtney Ryley Cooper, "Cosmopolite of the Month: J. Edgar Hoover," *Cosmopolitan* 103, 5 (November 1937): 14.

56. Courtney Ryley Cooper, *Here's to Crime* (Boston: Little, Brown, 1937), 345–346.

57. Courtney Ryley Cooper to J. Edgar Hoover, August 3, 1936, 1, accession 9973, box 88, Homer S. Cummings Papers, University of Virginia Library.

58. Arthur C. Millspaugh, *Crime Control by the National Government* (Washington, D.C.: Brookings Institution, 1937; reprint, New York: Da Capo Press, 1972), 275–301.

59. Robert Van Gelder, "Book Review: *Ten Thousand Public Enemies*," *New York Times*, March 9, 1935, sec. I, p. 13.

60. Courtney Ryley Cooper, "Foreword," draft for J. Edgar Hoover, December 24, 1934, FBI 62-21526-113, 3.

61. W. H. Drane Lester, memorandum to Clyde Tolson, January 10, 1935, FBI 62-21526-119.

62. Clyde Tolson, memorandum to J. Edgar Hoover, January 11, 1935, FBI 62-21526-119.

63. Courtney Ryley Cooper, letter to Clyde Tolson, January 16, 1935, FBI 62-21526-124.

64. Edward Tamm, memorandum to J. Edgar Hoover, March 8, 1935, FBI 62-21526-150.

65. J. Edgar Hoover, memorandum to Assistant Attorney General William Stanley, March 9, 1935, FBI 62-21526-150.

66. T. D. Quinn, memorandum to Clyde Tolson, March 15, 1935, FBI 62-21526-151.

67. For example, James E. Grunig and Todd Hunt, *Managing Public Relations* (New York: Holt, Rinehart & Winston, 1984); David M. Dozier with Larissa Grunig and James E. Grunig, *Manager's Guide to Excellence in Public Relations and Communication Management* (Mahwah, N.J.: Lawrence Erlbaum Associates, 1995).

68. Dozier, Grunig, and Grunig, *Manager's Guide*, 7.

69. For a comprehensive review of the FBI's efforts to employ popular entertainment formulas as public relations tactics, see Powers, *G-Men*.

70. Burroughs, *Public Enemies*, 481.

71. Reinhard Bendix, *Max Weber: An Intellectual Portrait* (Berkeley: University of California Press, 1977), 423–425.

72. W. Mark Felt, *The FBI Pyramid: From the Inside* (New York: G. P. Putnam's Sons, 1979).

73. For an extensive review of the FBI's bureaucratic structure, see Theoharis et al., *The FBI*.

74. William C. Sullivan, *The Bureau: My Thirty Years in Hoover's FBI* (New York: W. W. Norton, 1979), 101.

75. Theoharis et al., *The FBI*.

76. Ibid., 335.

77. Ibid., 357.

78. Ibid.

79. J. Edgar Hoover, memorandum to Clyde Tolson et al., July 5, 1935, FBI 67-9529-195.

80. Memorandum for the Attorney General, March 12, 1940, FBI 94-34-690-8.

81. Theoharis et al., *The FBI*, 214.

82. For a discussion of practitioner roles, see Dozier, Grunig, and Grunig, *Manager's Guide*.

83. Glen M. Broom and George D. Smith, "Testing the Practitioner's Impact on Clients," *Public Relations Review* 5, 3 (Fall 1979): 47–59.

84. Sullivan, *The Bureau*, 83.

85. Cartha DeLoach quoted in Natalie Robins, *Alien Ink: The FBI's War on Freedom of Expression* (New York: Morrow, 1992), 109.

86. Sullivan, *The Bureau*, 15–16.

87. J. Edgar Hoover, letter to SAC, Boston, March 16, 1935, FBI 62-21526-160.

88. "C. R. Cooper, Author, Kills Himself Here," *New York Times*, September 29, 1940.

89. "Author Cooper Kills Self over FBI Spy Snub," *Washington Times-Herald*, October 12, 1940, FBI 94-3420-678.

90. J. Edgar Hoover, handwritten note on telephone message slip, September 30, 1940, FBI 94-3420-675.

91. J. Edgar Hoover, letter to Eleanor Patterson, September 30, 1940, FBI 94-3420-677X.

92. J. Edgar Hoover, memorandum to Edward A. Tamm, October 10, 1940, FBI 94-3420-675.

93. Louis B. Nichols, memorandum to Clyde Tolson, October 4, 1940, FBI 94-3420-676.

Chapter 3. Enforcing the Bureau's Image of Restraint

1. Ronald Kessler, *The Bureau: The Secret History of the FBI* (New York: Macmillan, 2003), 48.

2. *Topeka Daily Capital*, April 7, 1939, 1, 18.

3. Gerald B. Norris, personal and confidential letter to J. Edgar Hoover, April 7, 1939, FBI 7-2561-604X, 2–3.

4. Gerald B. Norris, Investigative Summary, April 8, 1939, FBI 7-2561-616.

5. Edward A. Tamm, memorandum to J. Edgar Hoover, April 7, 1939, FBI 7-2561-618X.

6. Ibid., 1–2.

7. J. Edgar Hoover, handwritten note on Tamm to Hoover, FBI 7-2561-618X.

8. Edward A. Tamm, memorandum to J. Edgar Hoover, April 8, 1939, FBI 7-2561-619, 1.

9. Transcript of Coroner's Inquest into the Death of Benjamin J. Dickson, St. Louis County, April 9, 1939, FBI 7-2561-820, 8.

10. Edward A. Tamm, memorandum to J. Edgar Hoover, April 8, 1939, FBI 7-2561-729, 2.

11. *Kansas City (Mo.) Journal*, April 7, 1939, 28; *Kansas City (Mo.) Star*, April 7, 1939, 1.

12. *Kansas City Journal*, April 11, 1939, 1.

13. *Topeka Daily Capital*, April 9, 1939, 1.

14. Victor P. Keay, Investigative Summary, April 22, 1939, FBI 29-100-651-31.

15. John W. Owens, "Monotonous Tale," *Baltimore Sun*, April 8, 1939, 6.

16. J. Edgar Hoover, letter to John W. Owens, April 14, 1939, FBI 7-2561-266X.

17. Jack Carley, editorial, *Memphis Commercial Appeal*, April 8, 1939, 4.

18. J. Edgar Hoover, letter to Jack Carley, April 19, 1939, FBI 7-2561-713X.

19. Frederick L. Collins, *The FBI in Peace and War* (New York: G. P. Putnam's Sons, 1943), 58.

20. Louis B. Cochran, *FBI Man: A Personal History* (New York: Duell, Sloan & Pearce, 1966), 187.

21. Coroner's inquest transcript, FBI 7-2561-820, 5.

22. "Orders Dismissal in Spanish War Case," *New York Times*, February 16, 1940.

23. John S. Bugas, memorandum to J. Edgar Hoover, "Details of the Arrest of Mary Paige," March 12, 1940, cited in Athan Theoharis, ed., *The Louis B. Nichols Official and Confidential File and the Clyde Tolson Personal File* (Bethesda, Md.: University Publications of America, 1990).

24. John S. Bugas, memorandum to J. Edgar Hoover, "Details of the Arrest of Dr. Eugene Shafarman," March 12, 1940, ibid.

25. John S. Bugas, memorandum to J. Edgar Hoover, "Details of the Arrest of Eugene S. Hartley," March 12, 1940, ibid.

26. J. Edgar Hoover, memorandum to Attorney General Robert H. Jackson, March 12, 1940, 5, ibid.

27. Athan G. Theoharis, Tony Poveda, Susan Rosenfeld, and Richard Gid Powers, eds., *The FBI: A Comprehensive Reference Guide* (New York: Oryx Press, 2000), 114.

28. "Norris Is 'Worried' at F.B.I. Activity," *New York Times*, February 27, 1940.

29. Tim Wiener, *Enemies: A History of the FBI* (New York: Random House, 2012), 77.

30. *Nardone v. United States*, 302 U.S. 379 (1937).

31. Theoharis et al., *The FBI*, 21.

32. Wiener, *Enemies*, 88.

33. Curt Gentry, *J. Edgar Hoover: The Man and the Secrets* (New York: W. W. Norton, 1991), 212–213. Hoover's November testimony before the House was also men-

tioned in "Justice Department Bans Wire Tapping; Jackson Acts on Hoover Recommendation," *New York Times*, March 18, 1940.

34. "Congress Should Investigate," *New Republic*, March 25, 1940, 393–394.

35. Julian Webb, "Spotlight on the G-Man," *New Masses*, March 26, 1940, 9; "Justice Department Bans Wire Tapping; Jackson Acts on Hoover Recommendation," *New York Times*, March 17, 1940.

36. "FBI Is No OGPU, Jackson Asserts," *New York Times*, March 31, 1940.

37. Franklin Delano Roosevelt, memorandum to Robert H. Jackson, May 21, 1940, box 94, folder 6, Robert H. Jackson Papers, Library of Congress.

38. Gentry, *J. Edgar Hoover*, 212–213.

39. Ibid., 216.

40. "Our Lawless G-Men," *Nation*, March 2, 1940, 296.

41. See, for example, Matthew Cecil, "'Press Every Angle': FBI Public Relations and the 'Smear Campaign' of 1958," *American Journalism* 19, 1 (Winter 2002): 39–58.

42. "OGPU Unthinkable Here, Says Hoover," *New York Times*, March 17, 1940.

43. Frederick R. Barkley, "Critics Open Fire on Hoover's G-Men," *New York Times*, March 17, 1940.

44. "American Ogpu," *New Republic*, February 19, 1940, 231.

45. "J. Edgar Hoover's Fishy Activities," *St. Louis Post-Dispatch*, March 1, 1940.

46. No author, "Memorandum re: Marquis William Childs," February 18, 1946, FBI 94-35425-1X (Marquis Childs file).

47. Edward A. Tamm, memorandum for the files, February 28, 1940, FBI 94-3-4-690-7.

48. Edward A. Tamm et al., "Statements Made with Regard to Various Charges Made against Representatives of the Federal Bureau of Investigation Arising from the Arrests of Eleven Persons at Detroit and One Individual at Milwaukee, on the Morning of February 6, 1940," March 12, 1940, FBI 94-3-4-60-8.

49. Senator George W. Norris to Attorney General Robert H. Jackson, February 22, 1940, FBI 94-4-4514-1X.

50. Stone quoted in Norris to Jackson, February 22, 1940.

51. Edward A. Tamm, memorandum to J. Edgar Hoover, March 1, 1940, 2, in Theoharis, *Louis B. Nichols Official and Confidential File*.

52. Ibid., 3.

53. Ibid., 4.

54. Ibid., 5.

55. Attorney General Robert H. Jackson to Sen. George W. Norris, March 1, 1940, FBI 94-9-24-unserialized.

56. Sen. George W. Norris to Attorney General Robert H. Jackson, March 10, 1940, in Theoharis, *Louis B. Nichols Official and Confidential File*.

57. Frederick R. Barkley, "Jackson Orders New FBI Inquiry," *New York Times*, March 15, 1940.

58. Earl Godwin, letter to J. Edgar Hoover, March 2, 1940, FBI 94-8-24-81.

59. R. C. Hendon, memorandum to Associate Director Clyde Tolson, March 2, 1940, FBI 94-8-24-88.

60. Walter Winchell, letter to J. Edgar Hoover, March 12, 1940, FBI 62-31615-161.

61. Ibid., enclosures.

62. Lewis's lunch with Nichols is detailed in Louis B. Nichols, memorandum to Clyde Tolson, March 7, 1940, FBI 94-4-2189-15.

63. Fulton Lewis Jr., letter to J. Edgar Hoover, March 16, 1940, FBI 94-4-2189-15.

64. Fulton Lewis Jr., letter to J. Edgar Hoover, March 20, 1940, FBI 94-4-2189-15X.

65. Transcript attached to J. Edgar Hoover, letter to all SACs, March 21, 1940, FBI 94-4-2189-16.

66. "Attack on the FBI," *Flint (Mich.) Journal*, February 24, 1940, FBI 94-8-79-6X.

67. "Defense of the FBI," *Flint (Mich.) Journal*, March 28, 1940, FBI 94-8-79-7.

68. Neil "Rex" Collier, "Attack by Innuendo," *Washington Star*, March 13, 1940, FBI 94-8-24-94.

69. J. Edgar Hoover, letter to Neil "Rex" Collier, March 13, 1940, FBI 94-8-24-100X.

70. Arthur Krock, "In the Nation: Some Unfair Penalties for Political Differences," *New York Times*, March 26, 1940, FBI 94-4-4101-2.

71. George E. Sokolsky, "Civil/Liberties," *New York Herald-Tribune*, March 25, 1940, in Theoharis, *Louis B. Nichols Official and Confidential File.*

72. William Randolph Hearst, "The Modern Revolutionists Are Seeking Not Freedom but Anarchy and Tyranny," *Washington Times-Herald*, May 1, 1940, FBI 80-63-106.

73. J. Edgar Hoover, letter to William Randolph Hearst, April 8, 1940, FBI 80-63-105.

74. Gentry, *J. Edgar Hoover*, 212–213.

75. J. Edgar Hoover, memorandum to Attorney General Robert H. Jackson, April 25, 1940, in Theoharis, *Louis B. Nichols Official and Confidential File.*

76. J. Edgar Hoover, memorandum to Attorney General Robert H. Jackson, April 30, 1940, ibid.

77. Henry A. Schweinhaut, "Report to the Attorney General Concerning Investigation of Arrests and Subsequent Procedure in Detroit Spanish Recruiting Cases," April 30, 1940, ibid.

78. "Jackson Backs FBI In Loyalist Case," *New York Times*, May 5, 1940.

79. Theoharis et al., *The FBI*, 115.

80. "D.A.R. Pledges Its Americanism," *New York Times*, April 18, 1940.

81. "FBI Attacks Laid to Reds by Hoover," *New York Times*, May 4, 1940.

82. "Attack on the FBI Laid to 'Left Wing,'" *New York Times*, April 26, 1940.

83. "Whoa, Now, Edgar, Let's Clarify!" editorial, *Des Moines Register*, April 20, 1940, FBI 94-8-137-56.

84. R. C. Hendon, memorandum to Clyde Tolson, April 20, 1940, FBI 94-8-137-56X.

85. Ibid.

86. J. Edgar Hoover, letter to Gardner Cowles, April 24, 1940, FBI 94-8-137-56X (note that related FBI documents often carry the same internal serial number).

87. E. R. Davis, letter to J. Edgar Hoover, March 14, 1940, FBI 94-8-137-52.

88. E. R. Davis, letter to J. Edgar Hoover, June 4, 1940, FBI 94-8-137-52; Hoover's handwritten note on ibid.

89. R. C. Hendon, memorandum to Clyde Tolson, April 22, 1940, FBI 94-8-137-57.

90. R. C. Hendon, memorandum to Clyde Tolson, August 1, 1940, FBI 94-8-24-unserialized.

91. George Seldes, *Witch Hunt* (1940), quoted in R. C. Hendon, memorandum to Clyde Tolson, December 11, 1940, FBI 97-424-10, 2.

92. George Seldes, "Hoover's FBI Repeats 1918 Wartime Terrorism; Attacks Opponents of Dictatorship and War," *In Fact*, June 2, 1941, 2.

93. Hoover's note on *Washington Times-Herald*, undated, 1942, FBI 94-4-4514-3X.

94. Milton A. Jones, memorandum to Louis B. Nichols, October 21, 1955, FBI 94-4-4514-5.

95. Milton A. Jones, memorandum to Louis B. Nichols, November 28, 1955, FBI 94-4-4514-6.

Chapter 4. Silencing a "Useful Citizen"

1. George Seldes, letter to J. Edgar Hoover, August 22, 1945, FBI 97-427-222, 1–2.

2. Ibid.

3. D. M. Ladd, memorandum to J. Edgar Hoover, August 28, 1945, FBI 94-427-221, 1–4.

4. J. Edgar Hoover, letter to SAC, New York, April 21, 1962, FBI 97-427-112.

5. Ladd to Hoover, August 28, 1945, 8.

6. J. Edgar Hoover, letter to George Seldes, September 10, 1945, FBI 94-427-219, 1.

7. Ibid., 2.

8. George Seldes, *Witness to a Century* (New York: Ballantine Books, 1987), 18.

9. George Seldes, *Freedom of the Press* (New York: Da Capo, 1935).

10. George Seldes, *Lords of the Press* (New York: Julian Messner, 1938), 10.

11. Ibid., 387–388.

12. William Dicke, "George Seldes Is Dead at 104: An Early, Fervent Press Critic," *New York Times*, July 3, 1995.

13. George Seldes, *You Can't Print That! The Truth behind the News, 1918–1928* (New York: Payson & Clark, 1929).

14. Seldes, *Lords of the Press*, 10.

15. George Seldes, *Witch Hunt: The Techniques and Profits of Redbaiting* (New York: Modern Age Books, 1940), ix.

16. A. J. Liebling, *The Wayward Pressman* (New York: Greenwood Press, 1972), 282.

17. "1941 Censorship Like 1917," *In Fact*, March 17, 1941, 1.

18. "Hoover's FBI Repeats 1918 Wartime Terrorism; Attacks Opponents of Dictatorship and War," *In Fact*, June 2, 1941, 2.

19. "The FBI Replaces Labor Spy Agencies," *In Fact*, May 12, 1941, 2.

20. Ben Bagdikian quoted in Rick Goldsmith, *Tell the Truth and Run: George Seldes and the American Press* (Harriman, N.Y.: New Day Films, 1996).

21. Seldes, *Witness to a Century*, 347.

22. Ibid., 377.

23. Stephen Early, memorandum to J. Edgar Hoover, November 25, 1940, FBI 97-427-1.

24. Blind memorandum, George Seldes, December 11, 1940, FBI 97-427-2.

25. Blind memorandum, *In Fact*, December 11, 1940, FBI 97-427-2.

26. SAC, New York, investigative report, January 23, 1941, FBI 97-427-5, 1.

27. D. D. Guttenplan, *American Radical: The Life and Times of I. F. Stone* (New York: Farrar, Straus & Giroux, 2009), 301.

28. Executive Sessions of the Senate Permanent Subcommittee on Investigations of the Committee on Government Operations, Eighty-Third Congress, First Session, 1953, vol. 2, 1208–1209.

29. Ibid.

30. Ibid., 1209–1210.

31. Harvey Klehr, John Earl Haynes, and Alexander Vassiliev, *Spies: The Rise and Fall of the KGB in America* (New Haven, Conn.: Yale University Press, 2009), 169.

32. SAC, New York, investigative report, January 23, 1941, 2.

33. A. H. Raskin, "Thug Hurls Acid on Labor Writer; Sight Imperiled," *New York Times*, April 6, 1956, 1.

34. Edward Ranzal, "Riesel on the Stand, Describes How Acid 'Deluge' Hit His Eyes," *New York Times*, December 4, 1956, 1; Lawrence Van Gelder, "Victor Riesel, 81, Columnist Blinded by Acid Attack, Dies," *New York Times*, January 5, 1995.

35. Pete Hamill, "The Lives They Lived: Victor Riesel and Walter Sheridan; In Defense of Honest Labor," *New York Times*, December 31, 1995.

36. Stanley Levey, "F.B.I. Solves Riesel Case; Reports Acid-Hurler Slain," *New York Times*, August 18, 1956, 1.

37. SAC, New York, investigative summary, January 23, 1941, FBI 97-427-5, 2.

38. Ibid.

39. J. Edgar Hoover, letter to Stephen Early, February 15, 1941, FBI 97-427-7.

40. J. Edgar Hoover, letter to Brigadier General Sherman Miles, February 21, 1941, FBI 97-427-9.

41. J. Edgar Hoover, memorandum to Attorney General Robert H. Jackson, March 27, 1941, FBI 97-427-10.

42. For example, J. Edgar Hoover, letter to Rep. Leland N. Ford, March 30, 1941, FBI 97-427-12.

43. George Seldes, "Hoover's FBI Repeats 1918 Wartime Terrorism; Attacks Opponents of Dictatorship and War," *In Fact*, June 2, 1941, 2.

44. J. Edgar Hoover, teletype to Earl J. Connelly, July 8, 1941, FBI 97-427-53.

45. SAC, New York, investigative report, June 7, 1941, FBI 62-1275-29, 2.

46. Ibid., 4.

47. Ibid., 5.

48. Ibid.

49. J. Edgar Hoover, telegraphic communication to Earl J. Connelly, July 8, 1941, FBI 62-1275-32.

50. George Seldes, letter to J. Edgar Hoover, July 21, 1941, FBI 94-427-57X.

51. R. C. Hendon, memorandum to Louis B. Nichols, July 23, 1941, FBI 94-427-57X.

52. J. Edgar Hoover, letter to George Seldes, August 30, 1941, FBI 94-427-57X, 1–2, 2, 3, 6, 8, 10, 11, 14–15.

53. Wendell Berge, memorandum to J. Edgar Hoover, August 13, 1941, FBI 97-427-60.

54. Percy E. Foxworth, letter to J. Edgar Hoover, September 12, 1941, FBI 97-427-79, 2.

55. Earl J. Connelly, letter to J. Edgar Hoover, September 26, 1941, FBI 97-427-67.

56. Louis B. Nichols, memorandum to Clyde Tolson, October 1, 1941, FBI 97-427-73.

57. List, September 23, 1941, FBI 97-427-71.

58. "Court Lifts Ban on 'Ulysses' Here," *New York Times*, December 7, 1933, 1.

59. Alden Whitman, "Morris Ernst, 'Ulysses' Case Lawyer, Dies," *New York Times*, May 23, 1976.

60. Morris Ernst, "Why I No Longer Fear the F.B.I.," *Reader's Digest*, December 1950, 27.

61. Morris Ernst, letter to Bruce Bliven, October 6, 1941, FBI 97-427-72.

62. SAC, New York, investigative report, October 22, 1941, FBI 65-1275-49.

63. SAC, New York, investigative report, February 17, 1942, FBI 65-1275-66.

64. [Redacted], New Haven, Conn., investigative report, February 25, 1942, FBI 65-1275-67.

65. Custodial Detention Index card, June 19, 1942, FBI 65-1275-77.

66. Athan G. Theoharis, Tony Poveda, Susan Rosenfeld, and Richard Gid Powers, eds., *The FBI: A Comprehensive Reference Guide* (New York: Oryx Press, 2000), 20–21.

67. Francis Biddle, memorandum to Hugh B. Cox, Assistant Attorney General, and J. Edgar Hoover, July 16, 1943, FBI 100-6270-195, 1.

68. Theoharis et al., *The FBI*, 21.

69. Security Index card, June 25, 1942, FBI 65-1275-101X.

70. R. C. Hendon, memorandum to Clyde Tolson, August 19, 1942, FBI 97-427-132.

71. [Redacted], memorandum to Mr. Mumford, November 5, 1942, FBI 97-427-14.

72. J. Edgar Hoover, letter to SAC, New York, April 21, 1942, FBI 65-1275-75.

73. SAC, Memphis, investigative report, September 25, 1942, FBI 65-1275-82.

74. J. Edgar Hoover, letter to SAC, New York, September 17, 1942, FBI 65-1275-81.

75. SAC, New York, letter to J. Edgar Hoover, October 7, 1942, FBI 65-1275-83, 1.

76. Ibid., 2.

77. J. Edgar Hoover, memorandum to SAC, New York, November 14, 1942, FBI 65-1275-91, 2.

78. SAC, New York, investigative report, January 1, 1943, FBI 65-1275-93, 2.

79. SAC, New York, investigative report, March 27, 1943, FBI 65-1275-100, 2.

80. Several Office of Censorship reports from 1943 are included in FBI 65-1275-114.

81. Eugene Lyons, "Mrs. Roosevelt's Youth Congress," *American Mercury* 49 (April 1940): 481–484.

82. Eugene Lyons, *The Red Decade: The Stalinist Penetration of America* (New York: Bobbs-Merrill, 1941).

83. SAC, New York, summary report, January 13, 1944, FBI 97-427-180.

84. George Seldes, "Editorial: To All Our Faithful Subscribers," *In Fact*, October 2, 1950, 1.

85. Ibid., 2.

Chapter 5. Investigating Critics on the Left

1. "'The Nation,' 'The New Republic,' the Communist Party," December 9, 1943, FBI 61-901-90 (*The Nation* file), 2.

2. Ibid.

3. Ibid., 3.

4. Ibid., 5.

5. Bruce Bliven, "What the FBI Is Doing," *New Republic*, April 30, 1941, 587.

6. John T. Flynn, "Who's Behind Hoover?" *New Republic*, March 11, 1940, 345.

7. Bliven, "What the FBI Is Doing," 587.

8. Athan Theoharis and John Stuart Cox, *The Boss: J. Edgar Hoover and the Great American Inquisition* (Philadelphia: Temple University Press, 1988), 151.

9. Ibid.

10. Ibid., 154.

11. J. Edgar Hoover, testimony, "Hearings on Emergency Supplemental Appropriations Bill for 1940," U.S. House of Representatives Committee on Appropriations, November 30, 1939, 304–305.

12. J. Edgar Hoover, testimony, "Hearings on Department of Justice Appropria-

tions Bill for 1941," U.S. House of Representatives Committee on Appropriations, January 8, 1940, 153.

13. Bliven, "What the FBI Is Doing," 588.

14. Ibid.

15. Ellen Schrecker, *Many Are the Crimes: McCarthyism in America* (Boston: Little, Brown, 1998), 110–111.

16. R. C. Hendon, memorandum to Clyde Tolson, January 9, 1941, FBI 100-8487-1 (Bliven file).

17. J. Edgar Hoover, "SAC Letter No. 50, Series 1950," July 31, 1950, FBI 66-04-1162 (SSC file).

18. [Redacted], memorandum to Clyde Tolson, March 26, 1954, FBI 62-21531-1093 (Special Correspondents List file).

19. Robert C. Hendon, memorandum to Clyde Tolson, April 22, 1940, FBI 94-8-137-57.

20. Ralph Ingersoll, "Volunteer Gestapo," *PM*, July 2, 1940, included in FBI 94-8-1003-10X (*PM* file).

21. Hugh M. Clegg, memorandum to J. Edgar Hoover, September 8, 1940, FBI 94-81003-29 (*PM* file).

22. D. D. Guttenplan, *American Radical: The Life and Times of I. F. Stone* (New York: Farrar, Straus & Giroux, 2009), 172n.

23. Victor Riesel, "Million-Dollar Daily Follows CP Line," *New Leader*, July 28, 1940, 4–5.

24. Edward A. Tamm, memorandum to J. Edgar Hoover, June 22, 1940, FBI 94-81003-11.

25. J. Edgar Hoover, handwritten note on Tamm to Hoover, June 22, 1940, FBI 94-81003-11.

26. Harold Ranstad, memorandum to Hugh M. Clegg, August 20, 1940, FBI 94-81003-13x.

27. Louis B. Nichols, memorandum to Clyde Tolson, June 3, 1940, FBI 94-81003-5.

28. Kenneth G. Crawford, "J. Edgar Hoover," *Nation*, February 27, 1937, 232–233.

29. Kenneth G. Crawford, "J. Edgar Hoover," *Nation*, March 6, 1937, 262.

30. SAC, New York, personal and confidential letter to J. Edgar Hoover, July 26, 1940, FBI 94-81003-14.

31. J. Edgar Hoover, handwritten note on Ike McAnally, telegram to J. Edgar Hoover, August 6, 1940, FBI 94-8-1003-16.

32. Louis B. Nichols, memorandum to Clyde Tolson, August 10, 1940, FBI 94-81003-23X.

33. Louis B. Nichols, memorandum to Clyde Tolson, August 15, 1940, FBI 94-81003-26.

34. R. C. Hendon, memorandum to Clyde Tolson, September 23, 1940, FBI 94-81003-32.

35. Ike McAnally, letter to J. Edgar Hoover, October 15, 1940, FBI 94-81003-45.

36. Louis B. Nichols, memorandum to Clyde Tolson, August 15, 1940, FBI 94-81003-25.

37. R. C. Hendon, memorandum to Clyde Tolson, November 5, 1940, FBI 94-81003-47.

38. J. Edgar Hoover, handwritten note on Edward A. Tamm, memorandum to J. Edgar Hoover, October 25, 1940, FBI 94-81003-50.

39. Louis B. Nichols, memorandum to Clyde Tolson, October 8, 1941, FBI 94-81003-76.

40. Kenneth G. Crawford, "Dept. of Justice Exposes the Great Dies Hoax . . . Finds Only 2 of 1121 He Called Communists Guilty," *PM*, August 31, 1942, 14.

41. Kenneth G. Crawford, "On the Great Dies Fiasco," *PM*, August 31, 1942, 4.

42. Attorney General Francis Biddle, memorandum to J. Edgar Hoover, August 31, 1942, FBI 94-71003-126.

43. J. Edgar Hoover, personal and confidential memorandum to Attorney General Francis Biddle, September 1, 1942, FBI 94-81003-126.

44. Edward A. Tamm, memorandum to J. Edgar Hoover, September 10, 1942, FBI 94-81003-unserialized.

45. Ralph Ingersoll, "Good for J. Edgar Hoover," *PM*, June 19, 1942, 3.

46. J. Edgar Hoover, letter to Ralph Ingersoll, June 20, 1942, FBI 94-8-1003-113X, 1–4.

47. J. Edgar Hoover, memorandum to Attorney General Francis Biddle, June 20, 1943, FBI 94-81003-113X1.

48. J. Edgar Hoover, SAC Letter No. 12, July 15, 1942, FBI 94-81003-120.

49. Ralph Ingersoll, letter to J. Edgar Hoover, July 2, 1942, FBI 94-81003-117.

50. Louis B. Nichols, memorandum to Clyde Tolson, July 16, 1942, FBI 94-81003-116.

51. "PM to Take 'Ads'; Ingersoll Quits," *New York Times*, November 5, 1946, 1, 30.

52. "Freda Kirchwey, 82, Dies; Long Editor of *The Nation*," *New York Times*, January 4, 1976.

53. Lewis Gannett, "Villard and His 'Nation,'" *Nation*, July 22, 1950, 80.

54. No author, memorandum to J. Edgar Hoover, July 29, 1941, FBI 100-37078-unserialized (I. F. Stone file).

55. J. Edgar Hoover, handwritten note on memorandum, July 29, 1941, FBI 100-37078-unserialized.

56. XXX, "Washington Gestapo," *Nation*, July 17, 1943, 65.

57. Ibid., 66.

58. XXX, "Washington Gestapo," *Nation*, July 24, 1943, 92.

59. Ibid.

60. Ibid., 95.

61. "Freda Kirchwey, 82, Dies."

62. "1,300 Here Honor Freda Kirchwey," *New York Times*, February 26, 1944.

63. Freda Kirchwey, "End the Inquisition," *Nation*, July 31, 1943, 117.

64. Ibid.

65. Roger N. Baldwin and Morris Ernst, letters to the editors, *Nation*, September 25, 1943, 362.

66. G. C. Callan, memorandum to D. M. Ladd, August 19, 1943, FBI 61-901-76.

67. Guttenplan, *American Radical*, 189–190n.

68. I. F. Stone, "XXX and the FBI," *Nation*, September 25, 1943, 342.

69. Ibid.

70. Ibid., 343.

71. J. Edgar Hoover, handwritten note, undated, FBI 100-37078-14. The note appears chronologically in *The Nation* file just after notification of the Stone article and is attached to the October 13, 1943, memorandum analyzing that article.

72. J. J. Starke, memorandum to J. Edgar Hoover, October 13, 1943, FBI 100-37078-14 (I. F. Stone file), 20.

73. Edward A. Tamm, memorandum to Clyde Tolson, September 20, 1943, FBI 61-901-84.

74. J. Edgar Hoover, letter to E. E. Conroy, September 20, 1943, FBI 61-901-84.

75. Peter B. Flint, "I. F. Stone, Iconoclast of Journalism, Is Dead at 81," *New York Times*, June 19, 1989.

76. Guttenplan, *American Radical*, 43.

77. Ibid., 43–70.

78. J. J. Starke, memorandum to J. Edgar Hoover, October 13, 1943, FBI 100-37078-14, 1.

79. D. M. Ladd, memorandum to J. Edgar Hoover, April 21, 1944, FBI 100-27078-9.

80. I. F. Stone, "Challenge to J. Edgar Hoover," *PM*, April 22, 1944, 2.

81. Alan H. Belmont, memorandum to D. M. Ladd, July 29, 1953, FBI 100-37078-130, 11–12.

82. Ibid.

83. Guttenplan, *American Radical*, 105.

84. "Summary of File References," December 22, 1950, FBI 100-27078-28.

85. Ibid., 48.

86. Ibid., 60.

87. Ibid., 63.

88. I. F. Stone, "Some Questions for J. Edgar Hoover," *PM*, October 6, 1946, 2.

89. "Summary of File References," December 22, 1950, FBI 100-27078-27, 340.

90. Ibid., 356.

91. SAC, New York, investigative summary, January 31, 1952, FBI 100-37078-85, 12–13.

92. SAC, Washington, memorandum to J. Edgar Hoover, August 17, 1954, FBI 100-37078-187.

93. Guttenplan, *American Radical*, 274.

94. SAC, New York, memorandum to J. Edgar Hoover, March 18, 1952, FBI 100-37078-92.

95. Ibid.

96. SAC, New York, investigative summary, October 29, 1951, FBI 100-37078-73, 5–8; surveillance logs, FBI 100-NY-90640, subsection A.

97. SAC, New York, memorandum to J. Edgar Hoover, October 29, 1951, FBI 100-37078-73.

98. J. Edgar Hoover, memorandum to SAC, New York, February 15, 1952, FBI 100-37078-85.

99. Guttenplan, *American Radical*, 285.

100. Ibid., 287.

101. I. F. Stone, advertisement, *New York Post*, December 7, 1952, reprinted in SAC, New York, investigative summary, January 23, 1953, FBI 100-37078-115, 2.

102. Harry S. Truman, "Veto of the Internal Security Bill," September 22, 1950, http://trumanlibrary.org/publicpapers/viewpapers.php?pid=883.

103. Guttenplan, *American Radical*, 290.

104. I. F. Stone, "Thank You, Daniel Webster," *I. F. Stone's Weekly*, February 7, 1953, 3.

105. J. Edgar Hoover, memorandum to SAC, New York, December 16, 1952, FBI 100-37078-113.

106. J. Edgar Hoover, memorandum to SAC, Washington, April 30, 1953, FBI 100-37078-118.

107. I. F. Stone, "Not a Secret Police?" *I. F. Stone's Weekly*, March 21, 1953, 3.

108. "Hoover Applauds Efforts," *New York Times*, August 24, 1953, 11.

109. I. F. Stone, "The J. Edgar Hoover–McCarthy Axis," *I. F. Stone's Weekly*, September 5, 1953, 1.

110. Ibid.

111. I. F. Stone, "The FBI, McCarthy and the Witch Hunt," *I. F. Stone's Weekly*, March 22, 1954, 1–2, 4.

112. Robert L. Benson, *The Venona Story* (Fort George G. Meade, Md.: Center for Cryptologic History, n.d.), distributed by the National Security Agency, http://www.nsa.gov/about/_files/cryptologic_heritage/publications/coldwar/venona_story.pdf.

113. Venona 1433, KGB, New York to Moscow, October 10, 1944, http://www.nsa.gov/public_info/_files/venona/1944/10oct_operational_report_sergej.pdf.

114. J. Edgar Hoover, letter to New York SAC, August 1, 1951, FBI 65-6065-1.

115. J. Edgar Hoover, handwritten note on SAC, Newark, memorandum to J. Edgar Hoover, April 22, 1954, FBI 100-37078-174.

116. J. Edgar Hoover, memorandum to Attorney General Herbert Brownell, May 11, 1954, FBI 100-37078-174.

117. I. F. Stone, "More Evidence of Liaison between the FBI and the Witch Hunt," *I. F. Stone's Weekly*, March 29, 1954, 4.

118. Guttenplan, *American Radical*, 322.

119. SAC, Washington, memorandum to J. Edgar Hoover, December 16, 1954, FBI 100-37078-194.

120. SAC, Washington, memorandum to J. Edgar Hoover, July 5, 1955, FBI 100-37078-198.

121. William C. Sullivan, memorandum to Alan H. Belmont, June 15, 1956, FBI 37078-240.

122. SAC, Washington, summary memorandum, March 29, 1963, FBI 100-37078-249.

Chapter 6. Dividing the Press

1. Transcript, "Telephone Conversation with Mr. Eckhouse, 5 p.m., Wednesday, May 6th," box 11, "DS-DS" folder, p. 1, James A. Wechsler Papers, State Historical Society of Wisconsin, Madison.

2. Ibid., 2.

3. Wolfgang Saxon, "James Wechsler, a Columnist and Ex-Editor of Post, Dies," *New York Times*, September 12, 1983, D13.

4. "Nancy F. Wechsler, One of First Women Admitted to Columbia Law School, Dies at 93," Columbia Law School news release, July 31, 2009, http://www.law.columbia.edu/media_inquiries/news_events/2009/july2009/wechsler.

5. Harold Ranstad, memorandum to Hugh Clegg, July 18, 1940, FBI 94-8-1003-13X (*PM* file).

6. Lawrence M. C. Smith, Justice Department, memorandum to J. Edgar Hoover, July 10, 1942, FBI 100-26441-7.

7. J. Edgar Hoover, letter to SAC, New York, July 16, 1942, FBI 100-26441-6.

8. Louis B. Nichols, memorandum to Clyde Tolson, June 14, 1948, FBI 100-26441-16, 2–3.

9. Ibid., 3.

10. J. Edgar Hoover, memorandum to SAC, New York, February 11, 1945, FBI 100-26441-13.

11. J. Edgar Hoover, memorandum to SAC, New York, March 8, 1945, FBI 100-26441-14.

12. John D. Norris, "Truman Creates Civil Rights Board," *New York Times*, December 6, 1946.

13. Ibid.

14. Alan H. Belmont, memorandum to Clyde Tolson, March 20, 1959, FBI 100-26441-unserialized.

15. Robert K. Carr, letter to Dorothy Schiff, May 19, 1959, accession 310, box 16, "Family" folder, Wechsler Papers.

16. J. Edgar Hoover, letter to SAC, Washington Field Office, April 13, 1948, FBI 121-4005-1.

17. James Wechsler, memorandum to Dorothy Schiff, September 23, 1952, accession 310, box 11, "JW Personal" folder, Wechsler Papers.

18. Herbert Shapiro, *White Violence and Black Response: From Reconstruction to Montgomery* (Amherst: University of Massachusetts Press, 1988), 370.

19. James A. Wechsler, "How to Rid the Government of Communists," *Harper's Magazine*, November 1947, 438–443.

20. Louis B. Nichols, memorandum to Clyde Tolson, April 27, 1948, FBI 121-4005-1X, 2.

21. Louis B. Nichols, memorandum to Clyde Tolson, February 7, 1948, FBI 100-26441-16.

22. Louis B. Nichols, memorandum to D. Milton Ladd, June 9, 1948, FBI 100-26641-16X.

23. Nichols to Tolson, June 14, 1948, 2–3.

24. James A. Wechsler, statement dictated to Louis B. Nichols, June 11, 1948, reprinted in M. A. Jones, memorandum to Louis B. Nichols, October 24, 1958, FBI 100-26441-49, 9.

25. Wechsler to Schiff, September 23, 1952.

26. "Memorandum: James Arthur Wechsler," January 23, 1952, FBI 100-26441-22X.

27. Transcript, *The Author Meets the Critics*, March 27, 1952, accession 310, box 5, "Lait and Mortimer" folder, Wechsler Papers.

28. Dorothy Schiff, memorandum for her files, April 1, 1952, accession 310, box 22, "DS-DS" folder, Wechsler Papers.

29. Alan H. Belmont to D. M. "Mickey" Ladd, April 13, 1953, FBI 62-31615-775, 2.

30. Ibid.

31. "Wechsler Implores ASNE to Speak out Eloquently," *Editor & Publisher*, May 9, 1953, 7.

32. Richard Rovere, *Senator Joe McCarthy* (New York: Harper & Row, 1959), 199.

33. Transcript, *Hearing before the Permanent Subcommittee on Investigations of the Committee on Government Operations United States Senate, Eighty-Third Congress, First Session*, April 24, 1953 (Washington, D.C.: Government Printing Office, 1953), 257.

34. Ibid., 258.

35. Ibid.

36. James Wechsler, "McCarthy up Close," *Progressive* 17, 6 (June 1953): 6.

37. Transcript, *Hearing*, April 24, 1953, 268.

38. Ibid., 260.

39. Alan H. Belmont to D. Milton "Mickey" Ladd, May 11, 1953, FBI 62-31615-29.

40. Alan H. Belmont to D. Milton "Mickey" Ladd, May 18, 1953, FBI 62-31615-33.

41. Alan H. Belmont to D. Milton "Mickey" Ladd, May 18, 1953, FBI 62-31615-30.

42. Transcript, *Hearing*, April 24, 1953, 260.

43. Transcript, *Hearing before the Permanent Subcommittee on Investigations of the Committee on Government Operations United States Senate, Eighty-Third Congress, First Session*, May 5, 1953 (Washington, D.C.: Government Printing Office, 1953), 267.

44. Ibid., 290.

45. Ibid., 309.

46. Ibid., 310.

47. Ibid., 299.

48. James A. Wechsler, FBI 100-26441.

49. "Wechsler Implores ASNE," 8.

50. George W. Healy to Sen. Joe McCarthy, August 18, 1953, box 13, "A.S.N.E." folder, Wechsler Papers.

51. Joseph Lee to J. Russell Wiggins (*Washington Post*), May 23, 1953, box 13, "A.S.N.E." folder, Wechsler Papers.

52. Reprinted in "Wechsler Implores ASNE," 7.

53. C. P. Kimball to the editor, *Editor & Publisher*, May 30, 1953, 45.

54. "Wechsler vs. McCarthy," *Editor & Publisher*, May 16, 1953, 38.

55. "'Free Press' Cry," *Editor & Publisher*, May 23, 1953, 34.

56. "Walters Refers Wechsler Protest to Special Group: Wiggins Sending Full Transcript of McCarthy Quiz to 10 Editors," *Editor & Publisher*, May 16, 1953, 9–10.

57. "Comment on the Wechsler Hearings by the Special Committee of the American Society of Newspaper Editors," August 13, 1953, 1, original in the New York Public Library.

58. Ibid., 4.

59. "Special ASNE Committee Says: Each Editor Is Sole Judge of McCarthy Quiz Threat; Wide Disagreement among Panel and Board Action Appears Unlikely," *Editor & Publisher*, August 15, 1953, 7–8. Members of the committee were Paul Block Jr. of the *Toledo Blade*, Herbert W. Brucker of the *Hartford (Conn.) Courant*, Raymond L. Crowley of the *St. Louis Post-Dispatch*, William H. Fitzpatrick of the *Wall Street Journal*, George W. Healy Jr. of the *New Orleans Times-Picayune*, L. D. Hotchkiss of the *Los Angeles Times*, Joseph W. Lee of the *Topeka (Kans.) State Journal*, James S. Pope of the *Louisville Courier-Journal and Times*, Eugene C. Pulliam of the *Indianapolis News*, and William Tugman of the *Eugene (Ore.) Register-Guard*.

60. "Additional Comment on the Wechsler Case," August 13, 1953, 4, original in the New York Public Library.

61. "Comments," *New York Post*, August 13, 1953, 4; "Special ASNE Committee Says: Each Editor Is Sole Judge," 7–8.

62. James A. Wechsler to Arthur Schlesinger Jr., June 1, 1953, box 13, "Rauh-Schlesinger" folder, Wechsler Papers.

63. Max Lerner, "When Is Press in Danger," *New York Post*, August 14, 1953, 20.

64. Robert Lasch, "I See by the Papers," *Progressive* 17, 11 (November 1953): 15.

65. Transcript, Elmer Davis commentary, "Radio Reports, Inc.," August 12, 1953, box 13, "Radio-TV Transcripts" folder, Wechsler Papers.

66. "ASNE Report," *Editor & Publisher*, August 15, 1953, 34.

67. McCarthy to seven members of the ASNE committee, August 14, 1953, quoted in James Aronson, *The Press and the Cold War* (New York: Bobbs-Merrill, 1970), 92.

68. Ibid., 8.

69. Remarks by James Kerney Jr., in *Problems in Journalism: Proceedings of the 1954 Convention of American Society of News Editors* (Washington, D.C.: ASNE, 1954), 98.

70. Ibid., 99.

71. Remarks by Sam Day, in *Problems in Journalism: Proceedings of the 1954 Convention*, 105–106.

72. Remarks by Irving Dillard, in *Problems in Journalism: Proceedings of the 1956 Convention of American Society of News Editors* (Washington, D.C.: ASNE, 1956), 63.

73. Remarks by Vermont C. Royster, in *Problems in Journalism: Proceedings of the 1956 Convention*, 69.

74. Remarks by James A. Wechsler, in *Problems in Journalism: Proceedings of the 1956 Convention*, 71.

75. V. P. Keay, memorandum to Alan H. Belmont, December 8, 1953, FBI 100-26441-36.

76. Milton A. Jones, memorandum to Louis B. Nichols, December 17, 1953, FBI 100-26441-unserialized.

77. Milton A. Jones, memorandum to Louis B. Nichols, February 1, 1954, FBI 100-26441-38.

78. Milton A. Jones, memorandum to Louis B. Nichols, October 24, 1958, FBI 100-26441-45.

79. Marilyn Nissenson, *The Lady Upstairs: Dorothy Schiff and the* New York Post (New York: St. Martin's Griffin, 2007), 217.

80. Milton A. Jones, memorandum to Louis B. Nichols, October 22, 1958, FBI 100-26441-43.

81. William C. Sullivan, memorandum to Alan H. Belmont, December 18, 1958, FBI 94-43457-8.

82. *NAM News*, February 20, 1959, reprinted in Nissenson, *The Lady Upstairs*, 218.

83. Walter Trohan, letter to James Wechsler, March 24, 1960, FBI 100-26441-unserialized.

84. Cartha D. DeLoach, memorandum to Clyde Tolson, November 3, 1959, FBI 94-8-173-317, 2.

85. Ibid., 10.

86. Ibid.

Chapter 7. Engaging Defenders in the Press

1. Hoover, handwritten note on George A. Nease, memorandum to Clyde Tolson, October 15, 1958, FBI 61-901-unserialized (*The Nation* file).

2. Milton A. Jones, memorandum to George A. Nease, May 26, 1958, FBI 61-901-unserialized (*The Nation* file).

3. Fred J. Cook, *Maverick: Fifty Years of Investigative Reporting* (New York: G. P. Putnam's Sons, 1984), 173.

4. "Boards and Bureaus: The Watchful Eye," *Time*, August 6, 1949, 12–16.

5. *Newsweek*, December 7, 1964, 21.

6. SAC, New York, memorandum to J. Edgar Hoover, February 18, 1959, FBI NY 100-87559.

7. Cited in Milton A. Jones, memorandum to Cartha DeLoach, November 9, 1962, FBI 62-100544-22.

8. "Eaton Sees Liberty Periled by Snooping," *New York Times*, May 5, 1958, 1, 20.

9. Alden Whitmen, "Cyrus Eaton, Industrialist, 95, Dies," *New York Times*, May 11, 1979, A1, A24.

10. J. Edgar Hoover, letter to Fulton Lewis Jr., May 8, 1958, FBI 94-4-2189-375.

11. Fulton Lewis Jr., "Washington Anti-Communist Circles Are Shocked," *Exclusive*, May 7, 1958, 1.

12. J. Edgar Hoover, letter to Fulton Lewis Jr., May 14, 1958, FBI 94-4-2189-unserialized.

13. Richard Gid Powers, *Secrecy and Power: The Life of J. Edgar Hoover* (New York: Free Press, 1987), 226.

14. Fred J. Cook, "The F.B.I.," *Nation*, October 18, 1958, 225.

15. Ibid.

16. Ibid., 250.

17. G. A. Nease, memorandum to Clyde Tolson, October 14, 1958, FBI 61-901-unserialized (*The Nation* file).

18. Milton A. Jones, memorandum to G. A. Nease, October 14, 1958, FBI 61-901-unserialized (*The Nation* file).

19. Ibid., 5.

20. G. A. Nease, memorandum to Clyde Tolson, October 15, 1958, FBI 61-901-unserialized (*The Nation* file).

21. G. A. Nease, memorandum to Clyde Tolson, October 22, 1958, FBI 61-901-unserialized (*The Nation* file.)

22. Ibid.

23. John Gibbons, "A Policeman Looks at the Communist Party," *World Marxist Review*, January 1959, 96–97.

24. J. Edgar Hoover, letter to Victor Lasky, March 11, 1959, FBI 100-370032-45.

25. G. A. Nease, memorandum to Clyde Tolson, October 23, 1958, FBI 61-901-unserialized.

26. Alan H. Belmont, memorandum to J. Edgar Hoover, October 15, 1958, FBI 61-901-unserialized (*The Nation* file).

27. J. Edgar Hoover, handwritten note on Belmont to Hoover, October 15, 1958.

28. Donald Whitehead, letter to J. Edgar Hoover, October 18, 1958, FBI 62-102051-unserialized (Whitehead file).

29. J. Edgar Hoover, letter to Donald Whitehead, October 24, 1958, FBI 61-901-unserialized.

30. Nease to Tolson, October 15, 1958.

31. Walter Trohan, telephone interview with the author, October 5, 2000.

32. Leo Rosten, *The Washington Correspondents* (New York: Harcourt, Brace, 1937), 111.

33. G. A. Nease, memorandum to Clyde Tolson, October 30, 1958, FBI 61-901-unserialized.

34. J. Edgar Hoover, handwritten note on G. A. Nease, memorandum to Clyde Tolson, October 17, 1958, FBI 61-901-unserialized.

35. G. A. Nease, memorandum to Clyde Tolson, October 16, 1958, FBI 61-901-unserialized.

36. Nease to Tolson, October 17, 1958, 2.

37. Nease to Tolson, October 15, 1958, 1–2.

38. G. A. Nease, memorandum to Clyde Tolson, October 20, 1958, FBI 61-901-unserialized.

39. SAC San Francisco, letter to J. Edgar Hoover, October 20, 1958, FBI 61-901-unserialized.

40. George N. Kramer, "Ten-Part Smear Bespatters FBI," *Tidings*, October 24, 1958, 1.

41. Advance copy, *Firing Line*, October 31, 1964, FBI 61-901 (*The Nation* file).

42. George Sokolsky, "These Days . . . The Attack on J. Edgar Hoover," *Washington Post and Times-Herald*, November 4, 1958, A15.

43. J. Edgar Hoover, letter to George Sokolsky, November 4, 1958, FBI 62-89885-175 (George Sokolsky file).

44. George Sokolsky, "These Days . . . J. Edgar Hoover," *Washington Post and Times-Herald*, November 20, 1958, A21.

45. J. Edgar Hoover, letter to George Sokolsky, November 20, 1958, FBI 62-89885-176.

46. [Name withheld], letter to J. Edgar Hoover, December 4, 1958, FBI 100-340810-26.

47. J. Edgar Hoover, letter to Fulton Lewis Jr., December 15, 1958, FBI 94-4-2189-393.

48. Don Whitehead to J. Edgar Hoover, October 18, 1958, FBI file 62-105051-unserialized.

49. *Congressional Record: Proceedings and Debates of the 86th Congress, 1st Session,*

105, part 16, January 7, 1959 to September 14, 1959 (Washington, D.C.: Government Printing Office, 1959), A1840, A1874, A2021, A2090, A2127, A2163, A 2261; *Efforts of the Communist Conspiracy to Discredit the Federal Bureau of Investigation and Its Director* (Washington, D.C.: Government Printing Office, 1959), GPO Catalog No. 861-1, S. Doc. 23, 15c, 1–27.

50. "The Great Conspiracy," *Nation*, June 13, 1959, 525–526.

51. Milton A. Jones, memorandum to Cartha DeLoach, June 11, 1959, FBI 61-901-194.

52. G. A. Nease, memorandum to Clyde Tolson, October 27, 1958, FBI 61-901-unserialized.

53. SAC Charlotte, N.C., letter to J. Edgar Hoover, November 21, 1958, FBI 94-8-713-23.

54. *Congressional Record: Proceedings and Debates of the 86th Congress*, January 15, 1959, 752–754.

55. Ibid.; *Congressional Record: Proceedings and Debates of the 86th Congress*, January 22, 1959, 1037–1038.

56. Quinn Tamm, memorandum to J. Edgar Hoover, October 15, 1958, FBI 61-901-unserialized.

57. Quinn Tamm, memorandum to Clyde Tolson, October 17, 1958, FBI 61-901-145.

58. SAC, New York, letter to J. Edgar Hoover, October 17, 1958, FBI 61-901-136.

59. William C. Sullivan, memorandum to Alan H. Belmont, December 24, 1958, FBI 61-901-176; H. B. Fletcher, memorandum to Quinn Tamm, December 30, 1958, FBI 61-901-unserialized.

60. G. A. Nease, memorandum to Clyde Tolson, October 17, 1958, FBI 61-901-131.

61. SAC, Washington, letter to J. Edgar Hoover, October 17, 1958, FBI 61-901-135.

62. Milton A. Jones, memorandum to G. A. Nease, November 6, 1958, FBI 61-901-167.

63. Nease to Tolson, October 16, 1958.

64. Nease to Tolson, October 17, 1958, FBI 61-901-unserialized, 3.

65. Fred J. Cook, "On Being an Enemy of the FBI," *Nation*, March 22, 1986, 428–429.

66. Nease to Tolson, October 27, 1958.

67. "'The Nation,' 'The New Republic,' the Communist Party," December 9, 1943, FBI 61-901-90.

68. R. R. Roach, memorandum to Alan H. Belmont, October 17, 1958, FBI 94-51742-1.

69. William C. Sullivan, memorandum to Alan H. Belmont, December 18, 1958, FBI 94-43357-8.

70. Roach to Belmont, October 17, 1958.

71. J. Edgar Hoover, handwritten note on Roach to Belmont, October 17, 1958.

72. Executive Conference, memorandum to Clyde Tolson, April 15, 1959, FBI 61-901-unserialized.

73. Milton A. Jones, memorandum to Cartha DeLoach, October 18, 1960, FBI 62-104779-31 (Fred J. Cook file).

74. Ibid., 3.

75. Cartha DeLoach, memorandum to John P. Mohr, February 7, 1964, FBI 62-104779-46.

76. Ibid.

77. Milton A. Jones, memorandum to Cartha DeLoach, February 28, 1964, FBI 62-104779-47.

78. Milton A. Jones, memorandum to Cartha DeLoach, March 18, 1964, FBI 62-104779-52.

79. Cartha DeLoach, memorandum to Clyde Tolson, April 22, 1964, FBI 62-104779-53.

80. Milton A. Jones, memorandum to Cartha DeLoach, April 24, 1964, FBI 62-104779-54.

81. Milton A. Jones, memorandum to Cartha DeLoach, June 11, 1964, FBI 62-104779-56.

82. Milton A. Jones, memorandum to Cartha DeLoach, June 24, 1964, FBI 62-104779-55, 4.

83. Milton A. Jones, memorandum to Cartha DeLoach, July 23, 1964, FBI 62-104779-58.

84. SAC Miami, memorandum to J. Edgar Hoover, August 31, 1964, FBI 62-104779-62.

85. Cartha DeLoach, memorandum to John P. Mohr, September 11, 1964, FBI 94-8-24.

86. Jerry O'Leary Jr., "Nobody Knows FBI Pictured in This Book," *Washington Sunday Star*, September 13, 1964 (included in Cook file as FBI 62-104779-65X).

87. Milton A. Jones, memorandum to Cartha DeLoach, September 23, 1964, FBI 64-104779-72.

88. Milton A. Jones, memorandum to Cartha DeLoach, September 29, 1964, FBI 62-104779-unserialized.

89. Milton A. Jones, memorandum to Cartha DeLoach, October 22, 1964, FBI 94-4-725-557.

90. SAC Miami [name withheld], telegram to J. Edgar Hoover, Cartha DeLoach, December 17, 1964, FBI 94-47606-24.

91. John McMullan, letter to J. Edgar Hoover, November 11, 1964, FBI 94-42674-14.

92. Milton A. Jones, memorandum to Cartha DeLoach, November 16, 1964, FBI 94-42674-15.

93. Milton A. Jones, memorandum to Cartha DeLoach, November 25, 1964, FBI 94-42674-18.

94. Ibid., 2.

95. J. Edgar Hoover, handwritten note on Milton A. Jones, memorandum to Cartha DeLoach, November 17, 1965, FBI 94-56619-5.

96. Milton A. Jones, memorandum to Cartha DeLoach, April 6, 1965, FBI 62-104779-106.

Chapter 8. Corresponding with Friends in the Press

1. John P. Foster, letter to the editor, *American Magazine*, January 1955, 11.

2. M. A. Jones to Louis B. Nichols, January 3, 1955, FBI 94-4-5977-unrecorded.

3. Sumner Blossom to Louis B. Nichols, January 11, 1955, FBI 94-4-5977-18.

4. J. Edgar Hoover to Sumner Blossom, January 18, 1955, FBI 94-4-5977-18.

5. Athan G. Theoharis, Tony Poveda, Susan Rosenfeld, and Richard Gid Powers, eds., *The FBI: A Comprehensive Reference Guide* (New York: Oryx Press, 2000), 229.

6. William C. Sullivan, *The Bureau: My Thirty Years in Hoover's FBI* (New York: W. W. Norton, 1979), 85.

7. [Redacted] to Louis B. Nichols, March 26, 1954, FBI 62-21531-1093.

8. William C. Sullivan to Alan H. Belmont, "Molders of Public Opinion in the United States," March 18, 1959, FBI 100-401767-7.

9. See, for example, Matthew Cecil, "'Monotonous Tale': Legitimacy, Public Relations, and the Shooting of a Public Enemy," *Journal of Communication Inquiry* 28 (April 2004): 157–170.

10. Theoharis et al., *The FBI*, 270.

11. See, for example, J. Edgar Hoover to Courtney Ryley Cooper, September 27, 1933, FBI 62-21526-unserialized. These and other early letters include a notation that "CT" (Clyde Tolson) was the author. Later, "LBN" (Louis B. Nichols) authored most of the letters to reporters, editors, and publishers.

12. J. Edgar Hoover to Courtney Ryley Cooper, September 11, 1934, FBI 62-21526-82.

13. J. Edgar Hoover to Courtney Ryley Cooper, October 11, 1934, FBI 62-21526-83.

14. J. Edgar Hoover to Courtney Ryley Cooper, April 16, 1935, FBI 6-21562-171.

15. J. Edgar Hoover to Courtney Ryley Cooper, October 15, 1935, FBI 62-21562-235.

16. Clyde Tolson to Gen Cooper, October 19, 1935, FBI 62-21526-236.

17. Courtney Ryley Cooper to J. Edgar Hoover, January 21, 1936, FBI 62-21526-254.

18. Courtney Ryley Cooper to J. Edgar Hoover, October 31, 1938, FBI 94-3-4-20-491.

19. J. Edgar Hoover to Courtney Ryley Cooper, November 9, 1938, FBI 94-3-4-20-491.

20. For an extensive discussion of Cooper's work for Hoover, see Richard Gid Powers, *G-Men: Hoover's FBI in American Popular Culture* (Carbondale: Southern Illinois University Press, 1983).

21. Louis B. Nichols, memorandum to Mr. Tolson, September 12, 1939, FBI 94-3-4-20-519.

22. "Fulton Oursler, Editor and Author of Books on Religious Themes," *Washington Star*, May 25, 1952, A-32; "Fulton Oursler, Author, Dies at 59," *New York Times*, May 25, 1952.

23. Fulton Oursler to J. Edgar Hoover, August 18, 1938, FBI 94-4-692-20.

24. J. Edgar Hoover to Fulton Oursler, August 19, 1938, FBI 94-4-692-17; J. Edgar Hoover to Grace Oursler, November 25, 1938, FBI 94-4-692-23X.

25. Fulton Oursler to J. Edgar Hoover, November 26, 1938, FBI 94-4-692-23X1.

26. Fulton Oursler, "Inked Out," original manuscript, FBI 94-4-692-30X, 11.

27. Fulton Oursler to J. Edgar Hoover, January 20, 1939, FBI 94-4-692-30.

28. J. Edgar Hoover to Fulton Oursler, January 31, 1939, FBI 94-4-692-30.

29. I have reviewed the FBI files of more than 200 individual reporters and approximately 100 publications, all obtained through the Freedom of Information Act.

30. Fulton Oursler to J. Edgar Hoover, February 20, 1939, FBI 94-4-692-32.

31. Fulton Oursler to J. Edgar Hoover, February 20, 1939, FBI 94-4-692-48.

32. Fulton Oursler to J. Edgar Hoover, May 19, 1939, FBI 94-4-692-51.

33. J. Edgar Hoover, telegram to Fulton Oursler, September 26, 1939, FBI 94-4-692-53.

34. J. Edgar Hoover to Fulton Oursler Jr., October 26, 1939, FBI 94-4-592-60.

35. Fulton Oursler, "Every Sheriff a Sherlock Holmes," original manuscript, FBI 94-4-692-74.

36. Fulton Oursler to J. Edgar Hoover, January 14, 1941, FBI 94-4-692-78.

37. L. B. Nichols, memorandum to Mr. Tolson, December 17, 1945, FBI 94-4-692-117.

38. Ibid.

39. For a full account of Hoover's relationship with Ernst, see Curt Gentry, *J. Edgar Hoover: The Man and the Secrets* (New York: W. W. Norton, 1991); Athan Theoharis and John Stuart Cox, *The Boss: J. Edgar Hoover and the Great American Inquisition* (Philadelphia: Temple University Press, 1988); and Harrison E. Salisbury, "The Strange Correspondence of Morris Ernst and John Edgar Hoover," *Nation*, December 1, 1984, 575–589.

40. Louis B. Nichols to Director, FBI, September 29, 1950, FBI 94-4-692-162.

41. J. Edgar Hoover to Fulton Oursler, May 2, 1952, FBI 94-4-692-211.

42. J. Edgar Hoover to Grace Oursler, May 27, 1952, FBI 94-4-692-212.

43. "Great Friend of FBI Passes Away," draft article for *The Investigator*, June 23, 1952, FBI 94-4-692-214.

44. "Death Ends Career of Jack Carley," *Memphis Commercial Appeal*, February 21, 1962, 1.

45. J. Edgar Hoover, handwritten note on Louis B. Nichols to Clyde Tolson, January 5, 1943, FBI 94-4-6119-4X.

46. D. S. Hostetter to J. Edgar Hoover, October 16, 1945, FBI 94-4-6119-not recorded.

47. J. Edgar Hoover, handwritten note on Louis B. Nichols to Clyde Tolson, June 22, 1950, FBI 94-4-6119-129.

48. J. Edgar Hoover to Jack Carley, July 7, 1950, FBI 94-4-6119-131.

49. D. S. Hostettler to J. Edgar Hoover, August 7, 1950, FBI 14-47554-unserialized.

50. Jack Carley to U.S. Sen. Kenneth McKellar (D-Tenn.), undated transcription from August 1951, FBI 94-4-6119-155.

51. M. A. Jones to Louis B. Nichols, October 28, 1954, FBI 94-4-6119-227, 2.

52. D. S. Hostettler to J. Edgar Hoover, November 15, 1954, FBI 94-4-6119-229X.

53. Louis B. Nichols, telephone conversation with Jack Carley, reported in Nichols to Clyde Tolson, February 14, 1956, FBI 94-4-6119-unserialized.

54. Louis B. Nichols to Clyde Tolson, February 16, 1956, FBI 94-4-6119-265X.

55. Louis B. Nichols to Clyde Tolson, February 21, 1956, FBI 94-4-6119-266.

56. Fred J. Cook, "The F.B.I.," *Nation*, October 18, 1958, 221–280.

57. Matthew Cecil, "'Press Every Angle': FBI Public Relations and the 'Smear Campaign' of 1958," *American Journalism* 19, 1 (Winter 2002): 39–58.

58. G. A. Nease, telephone conversation with Jack Carley, reported in G. A. Nease to Clyde Tolson, October 31, 1958, FBI 94-4-6119-315.

59. Jack Carley to J. Edgar Hoover, May 12, 1959, FBI 94-4-6119-329.

60. J. Edgar Hoover, handwritten note on Edward A. Tamm to Clyde Tolson, October 22, 1959, FBI 94-4-6119-342.

61. J. Edgar Hoover, statement on the death of Jack Carley, February 20, 1962, FBI 94-4-6119-405.

62. "Roy W. Howard, Publisher, Dead," *New York Times*, November 21, 1964, 1, 29.

63. J. Edgar Hoover, memorandum to Clyde Tolson, May 31, 1936, FBI 62-45525-X.

64. See, for example, Roy W. Howard, letter to J. Edgar Hoover, December 15, 1941, FBI 62-45525-3.

65. R. G. Fletcher, memorandum to H. M. Kimball, December 20, 1941, FBI 62-45525-7.

66. Roy W. Howard, letter to J. Edgar Hoover, January 6, 1942, FBI 62-45525-8.

67. Roy W. Howard, letter to J. Edgar Hoover, April 7, 1947, FBI 62-45525-17.

68. J. Edgar Hoover, letter to Roy W. Howard, April 19, 1947, FBI 62-45525-18.

69. Roy W. Howard, letter to J. Edgar Hoover, April 26, 1947, FBI 62-45525-19.

70. "Our First Line of Defense," *Washington News*, September 14, 1948, FBI 62-45525-20X.

71. J. Edgar Hoover, letter to Roy W. Howard, September 15, 1948, FBI 62-45525-21.

72. Roy W. Howard, letter to J. Edgar Hoover, August 5, 1949, FBI 62-45525-22.

73. Roy W. Howard, letter to J. Edgar Hoover, August 19, 1949, FBI 62-45525-23.

74. Attached to Howard to Hoover, August 19, 1949.

75. "The FBI's Big Job," *New York World Telegram and Sun*, February 27, 1950, FBI 62-45525-28.

76. "FBI and Commies," *New York World Telegram and Sun*, February 9, 1954, FBI 62-45525-37.

77. Louis B. Nichols, memorandum to Clyde Tolson, July 14, 1954, FBI 62-45525-38.

78. Roy W. Howard, letter to J. Edgar Hoover, October 27, 1959, FBI 62-45525-53.

79. Roy W. Howard, letter to J. Edgar Hoover, September 10, 1960, FBI 62-45525-59.

80. J. Edgar Hoover, letter to Walter Trohan, April 10, 1952, FBI 62-96885-unserialized (Trohan file).

81. Walter Trohan, letter to J. Edgar Hoover, November 19, 1957, FBI 62-96885-31.

82. Walter Trohan, letter to J. Edgar Hoover, April 3, 1952, FBI 62-96885-unserialized.

83. SAC Gerald B. Norris, teletype to J. Edgar Hoover, May 20, 1953, FBI 62-96885-unserialized.

84. J. Edgar Hoover, letter to John N. Speakes, February 3, 1954, FBI 62-96885-15.

85. J. Edgar Hoover, letter to Walter Trohan, March 25, 1955, FBI 62-96885-17; Legal Attaché, Rome, letter to J. Edgar Hoover, December 9, 1959, FBI 62-96885-63; J. Edgar Hoover, memorandum to Legal Attaché, Paris, May 23, 1961, FBI 62-96885-86; Legal Attaché, London, teletype to J. Edgar Hoover, May 1, 1962, FBI 62-96885-95; Legal Attaché, Paris, teletype to J. Edgar Hoover, April 30, 1963, FBI 62-96885-98; SAC, Washington, memorandum to J. Edgar Hoover, June 17, 1965, FBI 62-96885-109; J. Edgar Hoover, cablegram to Legal Attachés Paris, Rome, March 9, 1966, FBI 62-96885-111; J. Edgar Hoover, cablegram to Legal Attaché, Paris, May 6, 1968, FBI 62-96885-124; J. Edgar Hoover, cablegram to Legal Attaché, Rome, September 3, 1969, FBI 62-96885-130.

86. Walter Trohan, letter to J. Edgar Hoover, October 7, 1969, FBI 62-96885-134.

87. Office memorandum attached to J. Edgar Hoover to Walter Trohan, December 30, 1960, FBI 62-96885-unserialized.

88. Trohan obituary, *Baltimore Sun*, October 31, 2003, FBI 62-96885-unserialized.

89. Walter Trohan, "Chief of the G-Men Record of His Career," *Chicago Sunday Tribune*, June 21, 1936, 1.

90. Ibid.

91. Ibid.

92. Edward A. Tamm, memorandum to J. Edgar Hoover, July 15, 1936, FBI 62-96885-X.

93. J. Edgar Hoover, personal and confidential memorandum to Homer S. Cummings, July 9, 1936, FBI 62-96885-X.

94. Louis B. Nichols, memorandum to Clyde Tolson, March 30, 1955, FBI 62-96885-21X.

95. J. Edgar Hoover, letter to Walter Trohan, May 17, 1950, FBI 62-96885-X11.

96. Walter Trohan reviewed the book for an unidentified Washington, D.C., newsletter under the heading "Book Events." The review is included in Trohan's FBI file attached to J. Edgar Hoover, letter to Walter Trohan, November 28, 1950, FBI 62-96885-X12.

97. Walter Trohan, "Washington Scrapbook," *Chicago Tribune*, June 19, 1953, attached to Louis B. Nichols, memorandum to Clyde Tolson, September 22, 1953, FBI 62-96885-unserialized.

98. Clyde Tolson, handwritten note on ibid.

99. Louis B. Nichols, memorandum to Clyde Tolson, October 22, 1953, FBI 62-96885-11.

100. Walter Trohan, letter to Cyrus Eaton, May 12, 1958, FBI 62-96885-34.

101. Walter Trohan, letter to Cyrus Eaton, June 6, 1958, FBI 62-96885-46.

102. Walter Trohan, letter to Dorothy Schiff, October 14, 1959, FBI 62-96885-61.

103. J. F. Malone, memorandum to John Mohr, May 27, 1960, FBI 62-96885-76.

104. J. Edgar Hoover, handwritten comment on J. F. Malone, memorandum to John Mohr, June 1, 1960, FBI 62-96885-47.

105. Cartha D. DeLoach, memorandum to John Mohr, February 5, 1962, FBI 62-96885-94.

106. Anthony Lewis, "Panel Unanimous: Theory of Conspiracy by Left or Right Is Rejected," *New York Times*, September 28, 1964, 1, 14.

107. Walter Trohan, "Report from Washington," *Chicago Tribune*, September 30, 1964, 5.

108. Ben A. Franklin, "Hoover Assails Warren Findings," *New York Times*, November 18, 1964, 1, 28.

109. Max Frankel, "Quits on Report of Morals Case," *New York Times*, October 14, 1964, 1, 31.

110. Ben A. Franklin, "Hoover Assailed on Jenkins Case: Admirers' Criticism Centers on Bouquet from F.B.I.," *New York Times*, October 28, 1964, 1.

111. Milton A. Jones, memorandum to Cartha DeLoach, November 4, 1964, FBI 62-96885-107.

112. D. C. Morrell, memorandum to Cartha DeLoach, August 10, 1965, FBI 62-96885-110.

113. Walter Trohan, "Report from Washington," *Chicago Tribune* Press Service, December 21, 1966, enclosed in Trohan, letter to J. Edgar Hoover, December 21, 1966, FBI 62-96885-118.

114. Wolfgang Saxon, "William Loeb Is Dead at 75; Owned Conservative Newspapers," *New York Times*, September 14, 1981.

115. John P. MacKenzie, "High Court Told of Bugs, Wiretaps in Hoffa Plea," *Washington Post*, January 27, 1967, 6A.

116. Walter Trohan, letter to J. Edgar Hoover, December 31, 1966, FBI 62-96885-120.

117. Walter Trohan, letter to William Loeb, February 1, 1967, FBI 62-96885-120.

118. Walter Trohan, "Report from Washington," *Chicago Tribune*, December 31, 1969, FBI 62-96885-129.

119. Walter Trohan, "Washington Report: Friends' Campaign Bothers Hoover," *Chicago Tribune*, July 2, 1971, 10.

120. J. Edgar Hoover, letter to Walter Trohan, July 12, 1971, FBI 62-96885-138.

Chapter 9. Managing Friends in the Broadcast Media

1. [Redacted], letter to J. Edgar Hoover, January 30, 1956, FBI 94-4-2189-276.

2. J. Edgar Hoover, letter to Fulton Lewis Jr., February 8, 1956, FBI 94-4-2189-276.

3. George Seldes, "America's No. 1 Nazi Hires Two More Columnists," *In Fact*, February 28, 1944, 1.

4. "Fulton Lewis Jr. Is Dead at 63; Right-Wing Radio Commentator," *New York Times*, August 22, 1966.

5. Louis B. Nichols, memorandum to Clyde Tolson, July 1, 1938, FBI 94-4-2189-3.

6. J. Edgar Hoover, memorandum to Clyde Tolson, July 13, 1938, FBI 94-4-2189-5.

7. "George Sokolsky, Columnist, Dies," *New York Times*, December 14, 1962.

8. Alden Whitman, "Free-Swinging Critic," *New York Times*, June 25, 1969.

9. Ibid.

10. Louis B. Nichols, memorandum to Clyde Tolson, March 7, 1940, FBI 94-4-2189-15.

11. Ibid.

12. Fulton Lewis Jr., letter to J. Edgar Hoover, September 10, 1941, FBI 94-4-2189-25X.

13. J. Edgar Hoover, letter to Fulton Lewis Jr., September 16, 1941, FBI 94-4-2189-25X.

14. Fulton Lewis Jr., transcript provided to FBI, August 10, 1942, FBI 94-4-2189-34.

15. R. G. Danner, memorandum to J. Edgar Hoover, March 13, 1943, FBI 94-4-39.

16. D. M. "Mickey" Ladd, memorandum to Edward A. Tamm, December 1, 1943, FBI 94-4-2189-42.

17. D. M. "Mickey" Ladd, memorandum to Edward A. Tamm, December 2, 1943, FBI 94-4-2189-44.

18. "Fulton Lewis Jr. Fears Plot in Mystery Hotel Room Fire," *Los Angeles Times*, December 2, 1943, 1.

19. "Fulton Lewis Hot over Fire," *Los Angeles Daily News*, December 2, 1943, 1.

20. R. B. Hood, memorandum to J. Edgar Hoover, December 2, 1943, FBI 94-4-2189-47, 3.

21. Milton A. Jones, memorandum to Louis B. Nichols, May 19, 1945, FBI 94-4-2189-60.

22. R. C. Hendon, memorandum to Clyde Tolson, May 24, 1945, FBI 94-4-2189-77.

23. FBI transcript of Fulton Lewis Jr. on WOL radio, May 30, 1945, FBI 94-4-2189-unserialized.

24. Fulton Lewis Jr., promotional materials, September 28, 1945, FBI 94-4-2189-86.

25. J. Edgar Hoover, telegram to SAC, Honolulu, November 7, 1945, FBI 94-4-2189-88.

26. Telephone message, Fulton Lewis, Office of the Director, February 23, 1947, FBI 94-4-2189-95; Louis B. Nichols, memorandum to Clyde Tolson, February 24, 1947, FBI 94-4-2189-96.

27. Telephone message, Fulton Lewis, Office of the Director, December 30, 1948, FBI 94-4-2189-102; J. Edgar Hoover, letter to Fulton Lewis, December 30, 1948, FBI 94-4-2189-103.

28. Milton A. Jones, memorandum to Louis B. Nichols, January 20, 1950, FBI 94-4-2189-109.

29. Louis B. Nichols, memorandum to Louis B. Nichols, January 24,1952, FBI 94-4-2189-134.

30. Milton A. Jones, memorandum to Louis B. Nichols, November 12, 1952, FBI 94-4-2189-138.

31. Milton A. Jones, memorandum to Louis B. Nichols, October 8, 1953, FBI 94-4-2189-unserialized.

32. Fulton Lewis Jr., letter to J. Edgar Hoover, June 4, 1951, FBI 94-4-2189-130.

33. Louis B. Nichols, memorandum to Clyde Tolson, April 29, 1952, FBI 94-4-2189-unserialized.

34. FBI transcript of Fulton Lewis Jr. broadcast, May 2, 1957, FBI 94-4-2189-354.

35. Milton A. Jones, memorandum to Louis B. Nichols, September 16, 1957, FBI 94-4-2189-360.

36. "Friends of Fulton Lewis," *Human Events*, December 7, 1957.

37. Fulton Lewis, letter to J. Edgar Hoover, October 22, 1962, FBI 94-4-2189-484.

38. J. Edgar Hoover, letter to Fulton Lewis Jr., March 27, 1963, FBI 94-4-2189-495.

39. J. Edgar Hoover, telegram to Mrs. Fulton Lewis Jr., August 21, 1966, FBI 94-4-2189-546.

40. George Sokolsky, letter to J. Edgar Hoover, February 16, 1944, FBI 62-89885-11.

41. George Sokolsky, "These Days," February 8, 1946, original copy from King Features Syndicate, FBI 62-89885-14.

42. Louis B. Nichols, memorandum to Clyde Tolson, February 12, 1946, FBI 62-89885-15.

43. J. Edgar Hoover, letter to George Sokolsky, February 12, 1946, FBI 62-89885-15.

44. George Sokolsky, letter to J. Edgar Hoover, February 13, 1946, FBI 62-89885-16.

45. Louis B. Nichols, memorandum to Clyde Tolson, March 3, 1947, FBI 62-89885-25.

46. Ibid., 2.

47. J. Edgar Hoover, handwritten note on Nichols to Tolson, March 3, 1947, 2.

48. George Sokolsky, "These Days," *Washington Times-Herald*, October 7, 1948, FBI 62-89885-23.

49. Louis B. Nichols, memorandum to Clyde Tolson, October 7, 1948, FBI 62-89885-24.

50. J. Edgar Hoover, letter to George Sokolsky, October 7, 1948, FBI 62-89885-23.

51. Arthur J. Freund, "The Mass Media before the Bar," *Hollywood Quarterly* 4, 1 (Autumn 1949): 90–97.

52. Ibid., 95.

53. Ibid., 97.

54. J. Edgar Hoover, "Statement on Radio Crime Programs by John Edgar Hoover, Federal Bureau of Investigation, Released to the United Press on February 2, 1948," February 2, 1948, FBI 62-89885-27, 1.

55. Ibid., 2.

56. George Sokolsky, "These Days," *Washington Times-Herald*, February 1, 1949, 14.

57. J. Edgar Hoover, handwritten note on copy of George Sokolsky, "These Days," *Washington Times-Herald*, January 18, 1949, 14, FBI 62-89885-26.

58. Louis B. Nichols, memorandum to Clyde Tolson, January 19, 1949, FBI 62-89885-27, 1.

59. J. Edgar Hoover, letter to Arthur Freund, December 9, 1947, FBI 62-32517-71.

60. Nichols to Tolson, January 19, 1949, 2.

61. George Sokolsky, "The FBI," *New York Sun*, July 7, 1949, FBI 62-89885-29.

62. Ibid.

63. J. Edgar Hoover, handwritten note on copy of George Sokolsky, "These Days," *Washington Times-Herald*, July 7, 1949, 18, FBI 62-89885-30.

64. J. Edgar Hoover, letter to George E. Allen, Reconstruction Finance Corporation, November 13, 1946, FBI 62-25733-39.

65. Max Lowenthal, *The Federal Bureau of Investigation* (New York: William Sloane Associates, 1950), 447.

66. "Max Lowenthal, Lawyer, Dies; Book on F.B.I. Stirred a Storm," *New York Times*, May 19, 1971.

67. Summary memorandum, Max Lowenthal, April 27, 1945, FBI 62-25733-38.

68. George Sokolsky, "These Days," *Washington Times-Herald*, November 30, 1950, FBI 62-89885-32.

69. *Counterattack*, April 11, 1952, 1.

70. Louis B. Nichols, memorandum to Clyde Tolson, April 8, 1952, FBI 100-350512-463, 1.

71. Ibid.

72. John Crosby, "Black Mark for Television," *St. Louis Post-Dispatch*, November 30, 1951, FBI 62-9189-499.

73. Milton A. Jones, memorandum to Louis B. Nichols, April 11, 1952, FBI 94-39253-5, 1.

74. Ibid., 2.

75. Ibid.

76. Ibid.

77. J. Edgar Hoover, handwritten note on Jones to Nichols, April 11, 1952, 2.

78. Jones to Nichols, April 11, 1952, 2.

79. Louis B. Nichols, memorandum to Clyde Tolson, April 14, 1952, FBI 94-39253-6.

80. Ibid.

81. J. Edgar Hoover, letter to John Crosby, April 11, 1952, FBI 94-39253-24.

82. John Crosby, letter to J. Edgar Hoover, April 14, 1952, FBI 94-39253-25.

83. J. Edgar Hoover, telegram to [redacted], April 16, 1952, FBI 94-39253-21.

84. Louis B. Nichols, memorandum to Clyde Tolson, April 17, 1952, FBI 94-39253-7.

85. "Ogden Mills Reid of Herald Tribune, Dies of Pneumonia," *New York Times*, January 4, 1947, 1.

86. Louis B. Nichols, memorandum to Clyde Tolson, April 17, 1952, FBI 94-39253-7.

87. J. Edgar Hoover, handwritten note on Nichols to Tolson, April 17, 1952, 2.

88. Milton A. Jones, memorandum to Louis B. Nichols, April 11, 1952, FBI 94-39253-15.

89. Alan H. Belmont, memorandum to D. M. "Mickey" Ladd, April 16, 1952, FBI 94-39253-16.

90. Edward Scheidt, telegram to Louis B. Nichols, April 17, 1952, FBI 94-392543-14.

91. George Sokolsky, "These Days," *New York American*, April 22, 1952, 19.

92. Richard Gid Powers, *Not without Honor: The History of American Anticommunism* (New Haven, Conn.: Yale University Press, 1998), 246.

93. George Sokolsky, letter to Louis B. Nichols, April 23, 1952, FBI 62-89885-39.

94. J. Edgar Hoover, letter to George Sokolsky, May 13, 1952, FBI 62-89885-43.

95. George Sokolsky, letter to Louis B. Nichols, May 15, 1952, FBI 62-89885-45.

96. George Sokolsky, letter to Louis B. Nichols, May 26, 1952, FBI 62-89885-47.

97. See, for example, J. Edgar Hoover, letter to SAC, Los Angeles, June 9, 1952, FBI 62-89885-unserialized.

98. George Sokolsky, letter to [redacted], January 4, 1957, FBI 62-89885-139.

99. J. Edgar Hoover, letter to George Sokolsky, November 19, 1955, FBI 62-89885-121.

100. George Sokolsky, "These Days," *Washington Post and Times-Herald*, December 13, 1956, A25.

101. Milton A. Jones, memorandum to Cartha DeLoach, February 15, 1961, 66-1897-717.

102. George Sokolsky, "These Days," *New York Journal-American*, October 3, 1962, 32.

Chapter 10. Renewing the FBI Story in Bureau-Authorized Books

1. "The FBI: A Revolution in Law Enforcement," speech by Don Whitehead, 1, included as an enclosure with J. Edgar Hoover to Donald F. Whitehead, May 7, 1957, FBI 77-68669-39.

2. Ibid., 8.

3. J. Edgar Hoover, foreword to Don Whitehead, *The FBI Story: A Report to the People* (New York: Random House, 1956), viii.

4. Don Whitehead, preface to *The FBI*, v.

5. Norman Thomas, "Agency of Justice," *Commentary*, April 1957, 384.

6. Cabell Phillips, "Meet Mr. Hoover's Men," *New York Times*, December 16, 1956.

7. Ibid.

8. Irving Ferman, "The FBI and Civil Liberties," *New Republic*, December 10, 1956, 19.

9. Irving Ferman, letter to Louis B. Nichols, December 19, 1956, FBI 61-130-unserialized (ACLU file).

10. Irving Ferman, letter to J. Edgar Hoover, December 10, 1956, FBI 61-130-630.

11. Donald F. Whitehead to J. Edgar Hoover, undated [circa March 10, 1957], FBI 77-68662-50.

12. Stuart Ewen, *PR! A Social History of Spin* (New York: Basic Books, 1996), 80.

13. "Don Whitehead, Pulitzer Prize Winner for Dispatches on Korean War," *New York Times*, January 14, 1981.

14. Thomas, "Agency of Justice," 386.

15. Robert A. Hackett, "Decline of a Paradigm: Bias and Objectivity in Media Studies," *Critical Studies in Mass Communication* 1 (1984): 229–259.

16. Richard Hofstetter, "News Bias in the 1972 Campaign: A Cross-Media Comparison," *Journalism Monographs* 58 (1978): 5.

17. "Frederick Collins, Author and Editor: Writer of 'F.B.I. in Peace and War' Dies—Headed McClure Publications in 1911–20," *New York Times*, July 26, 1950.

18. J. Edgar Hoover, introduction to Frederick L. Collins, *The FBI in Peace and War* (New York: G. P. Putnam's Sons, 1943), xiv.

19. "John J. Floherty, Author, 87, Dies," *New York Times*, December 4, 1964.

20. John J. Floherty to L. B. Nichols, August 24, 1942, FBI 94-4-1018-6.

21. FBI NYC, telegram to J. Edgar Hoover, September 10, 1942, FBI 94-4-1018-5.

22. J. J. McGuire, memorandum to Mr. Nichols, September 10, 1942, FBI 94-4-1018-3.

23. L. B. Nichols, memorandum to Mr. Tolson, September 14, 1942, FBI 94-4-1014-4.

24. McGuire to Nichols, September 10, 1942.

25. Carroll Burleigh Colby to J. Edgar Hoover, November 23, 1953, FBI 94-46157-1; J. Hoover to Colby, November 30, 1953, ibid.

26. Colby family history, http://freepages.genealogy.rootsweb.ancestry.com /~colby/colbyfam/b153.html.

27. C. B. Colby to [redacted] FBI, April 3, 1942, FBI 65-47965-1.

28. Investigative summary, August 19, 1943, FBI 65-47965-6.

29. Hoover to Colby, November 30, 1953.

30. Carroll Burleigh Colby to Louis B. Nichols, December 11, 1953, FBI 94-46157-2.

31. SAC, New York, to J. Edgar Hoover, December 23, 1953, FBI 94-0-431.

32. M. A. Jones to Louis B. Nichols, January 4, 1954, FBI 94-46157-5.

33. M. A. Jones, memorandum to Mr. Nichols, January 19, 1954, FBI 94-34419-7.

34. Douglas Dales, "'Hero' of War Book Admits Exploits as Cloak-Dagger Spy Were Hoax," *New York Times*, November 15, 1953, 1, 45.

35. J. Edgar Hoover to James V. Forrestal, October 24, 1947, FBI 94-34419-10.

36. Blind memorandum attached to ibid.

37. Quentin Reynolds to J. Edgar Hoover, September 1, 1953, FBI 94-34419-18.

38. Louis B. Nichols, memorandum to Mr. Tolson, May 10, 1955, FBI 77-68662-51.

39. Ibid.

40. J. Edgar Hoover, telegrams to SACs, Richmond and Norfolk, Virginia; Honolulu, Hawaii; Detroit, Michigan; Louisville, Kentucky; Memphis and Knoxville, Tennessee; New York, New York; Washington, D.C., September 1, 1955, FBI 77-68662-3-11. An additional investigation was conducted at Baltimore, Maryland; see FBI 77-68662-17.

41. Summary memorandum, Donald Ford Whitehead, special inquiry, September 15, 1955, FBI 77-68662-24.

42. J. Edgar Hoover to John J. Floherty, October 13, 1942, FBI 94-4-1018-15.

43. Louis B. Nichols, addendum to J. J. McGuire, memorandum to Mr. Nichols, October 12, 1942, FBI 94-4-1018-15.

44. L. B. Nichols to John J. Floherty, November 25, 1942, FBI 94-4-1018-17.

45. "John J. Floherty, Author, 87, Dies."

46. M. A. Jones, memorandum to Mr. Nichols, February 12, 1954, FBI 94-46157-11.

47. C. B. Colby, *FBI: The G-Men's Weapons and Tactics for Combating Crime* (New York: Coward-McCann, 1954); captions enclosed with Jones to Nichols, February 12, 1954.

48. Carroll Burleigh Colby to Milton A. Jones, February 16, 1954, FBI 94-46157-12.

49. M. A. Jones, memorandum to Mr. Nichols, June 26, 1953, FBI 94-34412-17.

50. Ibid.

51. M. A. Jones, memorandum to Mr. Nichols, September 1, 1953, FBI 94-34419-20.

52. Louis B. Nichols, memorandum to Mr. Tolson, October 27, 1955, FBI 77-68662-25.

53. J. Edgar Hoover, memorandum to Mr. Tolson, Mr. Nichols, March 16, 1956, FBI 77-68662-26.

54. J. J. McGuire, memorandum to Mr. Nichols, December 14, 1942, FBI 94-4-1018-19.

55. J. Edgar Hoover to John J. Floherty, April 5, 1943, FBI 94-4-1018-27.

56. John J. Floherty to J. Edgar Hoover, March 19, 1943, FBI 94-4-1018-27.

57. Louis B. Nichols, handwritten comment on J. J. McGuire, memorandum to Mr. Nichols, March 30, 1943, FBI 94-4-1018-30.

58. M. A. Jones, memorandum to Mr. Nichols, April 22, 1954, FBI 94-46157-15.

59. L. B. Nichols, memorandum to Mr. Tolson, August 29, 1955, FBI 94-34419-21.

60. M. A. Jones, memorandum to Mr. Nichols, December 30, 1953, FBI 94-34417-25.

61. J. Edgar Hoover, memorandum to Mr. Tolson, Mr. Nichols, July 2, 1956, FBI 77-68662-unserialized.

62. Redmond P. Gibbons, book review, "The F.B.I. in Peace and War," *Journal of Criminal Law and Criminology* 34, 4 (November–December 1943): 282–283.

63. Fowler Hill, "An Alert Nemesis," *New York Times*, November 14, 1943.

64. J. Edgar Hoover, handwritten comment on M. A. Jones, memorandum to Mr. Nichols, December 29, 1951. FBI 94-4-1018-X24.

65. SAC Letter 54-49, September 14, 1954.

66. M. A. Jones, memorandum to Mr. Nichols, November 29, 1954, FBI 94-46157-46.

67. L. B. Nichols, memorandum to Mr. Tolson, August 5, 1955, FBI 94-334412-52.

68. SAC, Los Angeles, to C. D. DeLoach, June 22, 1965, FBI 94-60750-116.

69. M. A. Jones, memorandum to Mr. Nease (subject: Don Whitehead), December 5, 1958, FBI 77-68662-74.

70. Louis B. Nichols, memorandum to Clyde Tolson, September 25, 1944, FBI 94-1-31913-28X2 (*FBI in Peace and War* file).

71. Ibid.

72. Frederick L. Collins, letter to J. Edgar Hoover, September 28, 1944, FBI 94-1-31913-28X3.

73. Frederick L. Collins, memorandum to "J. E. H., re: revised radio script," September 28, 1944, FBI 94-1-31913-28X3.

74. Frederick L. Collins, letter to Clyde Tolson, September 28, 1944, FBI 94-1-31913-28X4.

75. J. Edgar Hoover, handwritten note on Louis B. Nichols, memorandum to Clyde Tolson, October 2, 1944, FBI 94-1-31913-28X7.

76. Louis B. Nichols, memorandum to Clyde Tolson, October 31, 1944, FBI 94-1-31913-29X.

77. Ibid., 2.

78. Frederick L. Collins, letter to Louis B. Nichols, January 12, 1945, FBI 94-1-31913-39.

79. Hilton H. Biow, letter to Louis B. Nichols, January 17, 1945, FBI 94-1-31913-40.

80. Louis B. Nichols, memorandum to Clyde Tolson, January 30, 1945, FBI 94-31913-41, 4.

81. Louis B. Nichols, memorandum to Clyde Tolson, February 2, 1945, FBI 94-31913-42, 1.

82. Louis B. Nichols, memorandum to Clyde Tolson, February 19, 1945, FBI 94-1-31913-44X.

83. Louis B. Nichols, memorandum to Clyde Tolson, April 25, 1947, FBI 94-1-31913-unserialized.

84. Louis B. Nichols, telegram to J. Edgar Hoover, April 26, 1947, FBI 94-1-31913-78.

85. J. Edgar Hoover, handwritten note on Winchell column, April 26, 1947, FBI 94-1-31913-77.

86. SAC, Los Angeles, telegram to J. Edgar Hoover, November 18, 1947, FBI 94-1-31913-83.

87. J. Edgar Hoover, telegram to SAC, Los Angeles, November 19, 1947, FBI 94-1-3193-83.

88. Letter transcribed in SAC, Los Angeles, telegram to J. Edgar Hoover, March 17, 1948, FBI 94-1-3193-unserialized.

89. [Redacted], memorandum to D. M. Ladd, November 7, 1949, FBI 94-1-3193-94X.

90. J. Edgar Hoover, handwritten note on Milton A. Jones, memorandum to Louis B. Nichols, December 15, 1949, FBI 94-1-3193-unserialized.

91. J. Edgar Hoover, handwritten note on Louis B. Nichols, memorandum to J. Edgar Hoover, January 31, 1949, FBI 94-1-3193-unserialized.

92. J. J. McGuire, memorandum to Mr. Nichols, March 30, 1943, FBI 94-4-1018-30.

93. John J. Floherty to J. Edgar Hoover, May 6, 1948, FBI 94-4-1018-80 (also filed as 1-2523-21).

94. Milton A. Jones, memorandum to Louis B. Nichols, May 17, 1951, FBI 94-4-1018-89.

95. J. Edgar Hoover, SAC Letter No. 2, series 1946, January 8, 1946, FBI 66-04-195 (Special Service Contacts file).

96. J. Edgar Hoover, SAC Letter No. 50, series 1950, July 31, 1950, FBI 66-04-1162.

97. J. Edgar Hoover, SAC Letter No. 54, series 1954, October 7, 1954, FBI 66-04-2118.

98. SAC, New York, memorandum to the Director, February 16, 1955, FBI 94-4-1018-153.

99. For example, Milton A. Jones, memorandum to Mr. Nichols, October 13, 1955, FBI 94-46157-58.

100. Milton A. Jones, memorandum to Mr. Nichols, August 3, 1956, FBI 94-46157-unserialized. The blind memorandum on Adler was attached.

101. Carroll Burleigh Colby to M. A. Jones, August 9, 1956, FBI 94-46157-66.

102. Carroll Burleigh Colby to M. A. Jones, November 16, 1956, FBI 94-46157-74.

103. M. A. Jones, memorandum to Mr. [Thomas] Bishop, January 7, 1969, FBI 94-46157-146.

104. M. A. Jones, memorandum to Mr. Bishop, February 1, 1970, FBI 94-46157-151.

105. Quentin Reynolds to Louis B. Nichols, July 29, 1955, FBI 94-34419-52.

106. Louis B. Nichols, memorandum to Mr. Tolson, August 5, 1955, FBI 94-34419-52.

107. Louis B. Nichols to Quentin Reynolds, May 17, 1956, FBI 94-34419-53.

108. J. Edgar Hoover, memorandum to Mr. Tolson, Mr. G. A. Nease, October 17, 1958, FBI 94-34419-unserialized.

109. L. B. Nichols to Don Whitehead, October 15, 1958, FBI 77-68662-69. For a complete review of the FBI's response to the 1958 critique, see Matthew Cecil, "'Press Every Angle': FBI Public Relations and the 'Smear Campaign' of 1958," *American Journalism* 19, 1 (Winter 2002): 39–58.

110. Don Whitehead to J. Edgar Hoover, October 18, 1958, FBI 62-105051-unserialized.

111. [Redacted], memorandum to Mr. Parsons, February 16, 1959, FBI 77-68662-80.

112. J. Edgar Hoover, memorandum to Mr. Tolson, Mr. Nease, February 4, 1960, FBI 77-68662-53.

113. For example, J. Edgar Hoover to Don Whitehead, May 18, 1960, FBI 77-68662-93.

114. SAC, Knoxville, memorandum to J. Edgar Hoover, June 15, 1961, FBI 77-68662-99X.

115. Don Whitehead to J. Edgar Hoover, August 16, 1962, FBI 94-55553-6.

116. C. D. DeLoach, memorandum to Mr. [John P.] Mohr, August 15, 1962, FBI 77-68662-104.

117. M. A. Jones, memorandum to Mr. DeLoach, November 19, 1964, FBI 77-68662-124.

118. C. D. DeLoach, memorandum to Mr. Mohr, December 1, 1964, FBI 77-68662-125.

119. M. A. Jones, memorandum to Mr. DeLoach, December 2, 1964, FBI 77-68622-126, 4.

120. For example, Don Whitehead, "Hoover Ridicules Retirement Talk, Defends FBI Role," *Washington Post*, December 5, 1964, A-4.

121. Don Whitehead, "Don Whitehead Reports on the FBI's Responsibility," *Knoxville News-Sentinel*, April 27, 1965, 4.

122. J. Edgar Hoover to Don Whitehead, May 4, 1965, FBI 77-68662-130.

123. A useful exploration of FBI narrative themes can be found in Richard Gid

Powers, *G-Men: Hoover's FBI in American Popular Culture* (Carbondale: Southern Illinois University Press, 1983).

Chapter 11. Building a Television Audience

1. Robert Windeler, "Hollywood Turns against Violence: Writers and Directors Sign Pleas for Less Film Gore," *New York Times*, June 17, 1968, 45.

2. Ibid.

3. *Times* article from "The F.B.I. TV Series" file, July 3, 1968, FBI 94-60750-809.

4. Jonathan Etter, *Quinn Martin, Producer: A Behind-the-Scenes History of QM Productions and Its Founder* (Jefferson, N.C.: McFarland, 2003), 62.

5. Richard Gid Powers, *G-Men: Hoover's FBI in American Popular Culture* (Carbondale: Southern Illinois Press, 1983), 243.

6. Louis B. Nichols, memorandum to Clyde Tolson, May 27, 1953, FBI 94-33693-unserialized.

7. Ibid.

8. Benjamin Kalmenson, letter to Cartha DeLoach, December 11, 1964, FBI 94-60750-1362.

9. Ibid.

10. "The FBI: Dipping into the Cookie Jar," *Time*, August 2, 1976, http://www.time .com/time/magazine/article/0,9171,914432,00.html.

11. Kalmenson to DeLoach, December 11, 1964.

12. Cartha D. DeLoach, memorandum to John P. Mohr, January 12, 1965, FBI 94-60750-unserialized.

13. Ibid., 2.

14. Ibid.

15. Ibid., 3.

16. Thomas W. Moore, letter to J. Edgar Hoover, January 12, 1965, FBI 94-60750-unserialized.

17. Quinn Martin, letter to J. Edgar Hoover, January 14, 1965, FBI 94-1-32254-315.

18. The FBI routinely tracked each episode's cost through the reports of its agent on the set. For example, see SAC, Los Angeles, letter to Cartha DeLoach, February 27, 1967, FBI 94-60750-585; Etter, *Quinn Martin*, 67.

19. Etter, *Quinn Martin*, 65–66.

20. Mr. Clayton, memorandum to Cartha DeLoach, July 28, 1966, FBI 94-60750-448.

21. Milton A. Jones, memorandum to Cartha DeLoach, May 18, 1965, FBI 94-60754-75.

22. Etter, *Quinn Martin*, 77. Examples of the vetting of actors for the first four episodes of the first season can be found in FBI 94-60750-14, 94-60750-28, 94-

60750-49, 94-60750-54, 94-60750-57, 94-60750-63, 94-60750-64, 94-60750-76, 94-60750-82, 94-60750-84, 94-60750-97, 94-60750-89, 94-60750-95, and 94-60750-119.

23. Etter, *Quinn Martin,* 77.

24. Milton A. Jones, memorandum to Thomas Bishop, August 26, 1968, FBI 94-60750-827.

25. Milton A. Jones, memorandum to Mr. Wick, January 7, 1966, FBI 94-60750-299, 2.

26. Hoover note on Washington Capital News Service teletype, January 7, 1971, FBI 94-60750-1129.

27. Milton A. Jones, memorandum to Cartha DeLoach, May 26, 1965, FBI 94-60750-93, 2.

28. Cartha DeLoach, memorandum to John P. Mohr, March 16, 1965, FBI 94-60750-13.

29. Milton A. Jones, memorandum to Mr. Wick, June 9, 1966, FBI 94-60750-427.

30. Cartha DeLoach, memorandum to Clyde Tolson, June 8, 1966, FBI 94-60750-422.

31. SAC, Los Angeles, letter to Cartha DeLoach, May 6, 1965, FBI 94-60750-61.

32. Milton A. Jones, memorandum to Cartha DeLoach, June 2, 1965, FBI 94-60750-107.

33. Milton A. Jones, memorandum to Cartha DeLoach, May 6, 1965, FBI 94-60750-50.

34. Milton A. Jones, memorandum to Cartha DeLoach, May 26, 1965, FBI 94-60750-98.

35. William Branigan, memorandum to William C. Sullivan, November 30, 1965, FBI 94-60750-268.

36. Milton A. Jones, memorandum to Cartha DeLoach, March 30, 1965, FBI 94-60750-43.

37. Cartha DeLoach, memorandum to John P. Mohr, April 30, 1965, FBI 94-60750-66, 2.

38. Milton A. Jones, memorandum to Cartha DeLoach, June 14, 1965, FBI 94-60750-124, 2.

39. Cartha DeLoach, memorandum to John P. Mohr, June 17, 1965, FBI 94-60750-113.

40. SAC, Los Angeles, letter to Cartha DeLoach, June 22, 1965, FBI 94-60750-116.

41. Milton A. Jones, memorandum to Cartha DeLoach, May 18, 1965, FBI 94-60750-91.

42. Milton A. Jones to Cartha DeLoach, August 12, 1965, FBI 94-60750-159X.

43. Ibid.

44. Clyde Tolson, memorandum to Cartha DeLoach, September 26, 1966, FBI 94-60750-unserialized.

45. Milton A. Jones, memorandum to Mr. Wick, February 16, 1966, FBI 94-60750-342.

46. Milton A. Jones, memorandum to Cartha DeLoach, December 17, 1965, FBI 94-60750-290, 2; Cartha DeLoach, memorandum to John P. Mohr, July 29, 1965, FBI 94-60750-147.

47. Milton A. Jones, memorandum to Mr. Wick, February 3, 1966, FBI 94-60750-331, 2.

48. J. Edgar Hoover, memorandum to Clyde Tolson, Cartha DeLoach, January 9, 1967, FBI 94-50750-517.

49. Cartha DeLoach, memorandum to Clyde Tolson, January 10, 1967, FBI 94-60750-513.

50. J. Edgar Hoover, memorandum to Clyde Tolson, Cartha DeLoach, Thomas Bishop, October 23, 1969, FBI 94-60750-966.

51. Thomas E. Bishop, memorandum to Cartha DeLoach, November 7, 1969, FBI 94-60750-974, 1–2.

52. Cartha DeLoach, memorandum to Clyde Tolson, November 10, 1969, FBI 94-60750-976.

53. Clyde Tolson, memorandum to Cartha DeLoach, Thomas E. Bishop, and [redacted], November 19, 1969, FBI 94-60750-973.

54. Ibid., 82.

55. Cartha DeLoach, memorandum to John Mohr, July 16, 1965, FBI 94-60750-130, 2 (revised).

56. Cartha DeLoach, memorandum to John P. Mohr, March 16, 1965, FBI 94-60750-13.

57. R. E. Wick, memorandum to Cartha DeLoach, June 9, 1966, FBI 94-60750-424.

58. Milton A. Jones, memorandum to Thomas Bishop, March 25, 1970, FBI 94-60750-1024.

59. Milton A. Jones, memorandum to Thomas Bishop, March 6, 1969, FBI 94-60750-904.

60. Milton A. Jones, memorandum to Thomas Bishop, March 29, 1971, FBI 94-60750-1147; Milton A. Jones, memorandum to Thomas Bishop, June 13, 1972, FBI 94-60750-1280.

61. Mr. Heim, memorandum to Mr. Marshall, May 4, 1973, FBI 94-60750-1374.

62. Mr. Malmfeldt, memorandum to Mr. Marshall, May 23, 1973, FBI 94-60750-1382.

63. Milton A. Jones, memorandum to Thomas Bishop, March 9, 1972, FBI 94-60750-1244, 2.

64. Milton A. Jones, memorandum to Thomas Bishop, December 13, 1968, FBI 94-60760-871.

65. Milton A. Jones, memorandum to Thomas Bishop, January 9, 1968, FBI 94-60750-746, 2.

66. Jack Gould, "Actors Cleared for F.B.I. Series," *New York Times*, June 1, 1965, 39A; Hoover's response, June 4, 1965, FBI 94-60750-97.

67. Cartha DeLoach, memorandum to John P. Mohr, June 1, 1965, FBI 94-60750-106.

68. "Davis Special for ABC," *New York Daily News*, June 3, 1965, 82.

69. "FBI Seizes Pair in Extortion Plot," *Washington Post*, January 26, 1966, A1.

70. R. E. Wick, memorandum to Cartha DeLoach, January 26, 1966, FBI 94-60750-unserialized.

71. Cartha DeLoach, memorandum to John P. Mohr, September 22, 1965, FBI 9-60750-219.

72. Milton A. Jones, memorandum to Mr. Wick, March 8, 1966, FBI 94-60750-355.

73. R. E. Wick, memorandum to Cartha DeLoach, June 10, 1966, FBI 94-60750-431.

74. R. E. Wick, memorandum to Cartha DeLoach, December 16, 1966, FBI 94-60750-512.

75. [Redacted], letter to J. Edgar Hoover, December 4, 1966, FBI 94-60750-521; Milton A. Jones, memorandum to R. E. Wick, December 13, 1966, FBI 94-60750-528; Milton A. Jones, memorandum to R. E. Wick, January 12, 1967, FBI 94-60750-558.

76. S. Samuel Di Falco, letter to J. Edgar Hoover, March 20, 1967, FBI 94-60750-611.

77. Milton A. Jones to R. E. Wick, February 24, 1967, FBI 94-60750-541; Milton A. Jones, memorandum to Thomas Bishop, March 13, 1968, FBI 94-60750-unserialized.

78. Milton A. Jones, memorandum to Thomas Bishop, July 26, 1968, FBI 94-60750-816.

79. Memoranda exploring the controversies raised by members of Congress can be found throughout the FBI TV Series file.

80. Milton A. Jones, memorandum to Thomas Bishop, November 20, 1970, FBI 94-60750-unserialized.

81. Milton A. Jones, memorandum to Thomas Bishop, November 23, 1970, FBI 94-60750-1116.

82. Milton A. Jones, memorandum to Thomas Bishop, November 24, 1970, FBI 94-60750-unserialized, 4.

83. Ibid., 5.

84. J. Edgar Hoover, letter to [redacted; likely Julius Duscha], March 27, 1967, FBI 105-246964. Hoover was responding to Julius Duscha, "Behind the Tube—This Is

'The FBI,'" *Potomac Magazine* (*Washington Post* supplement), March 19, 1967, 28–32.

85. J. Edgar Hoover, letter to [redacted], February 10, 1969, FBI 94-60750-891.

86. Thomas E. Bishop, letter to Jack Nelson, January 7, 1971, FBI 94-60750-unserialized, 4.

87. Milton A. Jones, memorandum to Cartha DeLoach, March 30, 1965, FBI 94-60750-35.

88. For example, J. Edgar Hoover, memorandum to SAC, Minneapolis, July 6, 1965, FBI 94-60750-128.

89. David Rintels, "How Much Truth Does 'The FBI' Tell about the FBI?" *New York Times*, March 5, 1972, D1.

90. Rintels himself was vetted in 1965. FBI Washington, urgent teletype to FBI Los Angeles, April 1, 1965, FBI 94-60750-28.

91. Rintels, "How Much Truth."

92. Milton A. Jones, memorandum to Thomas Bishop, March 8, 1972, FBI 94-60750-unserialized, 1–6.

93. J. Edgar Hoover, "How J. Edgar Hoover Felt about TV's 'The FBI,'" *TV Guide*, May 20–26, 1972, 28–30.

94. Terry Turner, "FBI Will Have Human Touch in New Series," *Chicago Daily News*, June 29, 1965, 39, FBI 94-60750-138, 2.

95. Jim Groth, "Burbank Bank Scene of 'FBI' Shooting," *Burbank Daily Review*, July 7, 1965, 7, FBI 94-60750-142.

96. ABC-TV news release, "'The F.B.I.' Is Global Success Story," March 25, 1970, FBI 94-60750-1026.

97. Etter, *Quinn Martin*, 63.

Conclusion

1. J. Edgar Hoover, testimony, U.S. Senate Appropriations Subcommittee, April 11, 1936.

2. Thomas E. Bishop, letter to Jack Nelson, January 7, 1971, FBI 94-60750-unserialized, 4.

3. Athan Theoharis and John Stuart Cox, *The Boss: J. Edgar Hoover and the Great American Inquisition* (Philadelphia: Temple University Press, 1988), 111.

4. Kevin Stoker and Brad L. Rawlins, "The 'Light' of Publicity in the Progressive Era: From Searchlight to Flashlight," *Journalism History* 30, 4 (Winter 2005): 183.

5. Walter Lippmann, *Public Opinion* (reprint, New York: Free Press, 1997), 218.

6. For an extensive exploration of Bernays's campaigns, see Larry Tye, *The Father of Spin: Edward L. Bernays and the Birth of Public Relations* (New York: Holt, Winston, 1998).

7. Arthur W. Page, "What Publicity and Advertising Can Do to Help Operation,"

speech presented at the AT&T General Operating Conference, May 1927, Arthur W. Page Center for Integrity in Public Communications.

8. For a concise review of the FBI in popular culture, see Athan G. Theoharis, Tony Poveda, Susan Rosenfeld, and Richard Gid Powers, eds., *The FBI: A Comprehensive Reference Guide* (New York: Oryx Press, 2000), 261–308.

SELECTED BIBLIOGRAPHY

FBI Files

ACLU, *American Mercury*, Cedric Belfrage, Bruce Bliven, Sumner Blossom, Jack Carley, Neil "Rex" Collier, Fred J. Cook, Courtney Ryley Cooper, *Counterattack*, Gardner Cowles, John Cowles, Kenneth Crawford, John Campbell Crosby, *Des Moines Register*, Benjamin Dickson, Stella Mae Dickson, Cyrus Eaton, FBI Book Reviews, FBI Do Not Contact List, *FBI in Peace and War* (Radio Show), FBI TV Series, Mark W. Felt, *Flint Journal*, William Randolph Hearst, *In Fact*, Ralph Ingersoll, Martin Luther King, Mervyn LeRoy, Fulton Lewis Jr., Max Lowenthal, Ike McAnally, Molders of Public Opinion, Clark R. Mollenhoff, *The Nation*, *The New Republic*, George Norris, Gerald B. Norris, John B. Oakes, Fulton Oursler, Andrew Pearson, *PM*, Victor Riesel, Dorothy Schiff, George Seldes, William V. Shannon, George Sokolsky, Special Service Contacts, I. F. Stone, Henry Suydam, Edward Allen Tamm, Walter Trohan, *Washington Star*, James A. Wechsler, Nancy S. Wechsler

Manuscript Collections

Homer S. Cummings Papers, University of Virginia Library
Robert H. Jackson Papers, Library of Congress
James A. Wechsler Papers, State Historical Society of Wisconsin

Books and Articles

Ackerman, Kenneth. *Young J. Edgar: Hoover, the Red Scare, and the Assault on Civil Liberties.* Falls Church, Va.: Viral History Press, 2007.

Bendix, Reinhard. *Max Weber: An Intellectual Portrait.* Berkeley: University of California Press, 1977.

Bernays, Edward. *Crystallizing Public Opinion.* New York: Liveright Publishing, 1923.

———. "The Engineering of Consent." *Annals of the American Academy of Political and Social Science* 250 (1947): 113–120.

Boyd, Josh. "Actional Legitimation: No Crisis Necessary." *Journal of Public Relations Research* 12 (2000): 341–353.

Breed, Warren. "Social Control in the Newsroom: A Functional Analysis." *Social Forces* 33, 4 (May 1955): 326–335.

Broom, Glen M., and George D. Smith. "Testing the Practitioner's Impact on Clients." *Public Relations Review* 5, 3 (Fall 1979): 47–59.

Burroughs, Brian. *Public Enemies: America's Greatest Crime Wave and the Birth of the FBI, 1933–1934.* New York: Penguin Books, 2004.

Cecil, Matthew. "Friends of the Bureau: Personal Correspondence and the Cultivation of Journalist-Adjuncts by J. Edgar Hoover's FBI." *Journalism and Mass Communication Quarterly* 88, 2 (Summer 2011): 267–284.

———. "'Monotonous Tale': Legitimacy, Public Relations, and the Shooting of a Public Enemy." *Journal of Communication Inquiry* 28 (April 2004): 157–170.

———. "The Path to Madness: McCarthyism and *New York Post* editor James A. Wechsler's Battle for Press Freedom." *Journal of Communication Inquiry* 35, 3 (July 2011): 275–291.

———. "'Press Every Angle': FBI Public Relations and the 'Smear Campaign' of 1958." *American Journalism* 19, 1 (Winter 2002): 39–58.

Cochran, Louis B. *FBI Man: A Personal History.* New York: Duell, Sloan & Pearce, 1966.

Colby, C. B. *FBI: The G-Men's Weapons and Tactics for Combating Crime.* New York: Coward-McCann, 1954.

Collins, Frederick L. *The FBI in Peace and War.* New York: G. P. Putnam's Sons, 1943.

Cook, Fred J. "The F.B.I." *Nation*, October 18, 1958.

———. *Maverick: Fifty Years of Investigative Reporting.* New York: G. P. Putnam's Sons, 1984.

Dozier, David M., with Larissa Grunig and James E. Grunig. *Manager's Guide to Excellence in Public Relations and Communication Management.* Mahwah, N.J.: Lawrence Erlbaum Associates, 1995.

Epstein, Edwin M. "The Historical Enigma of Corporate Legitimacy." *California Law Review* 60 (1972): 1701–1717.

Ericson, Richard V., Patricia M. Baranek, and Janet B. L. Chan. *Representing Order: Crime, Law, and Justice in the News.* Toronto: University of Toronto Press, 1991.

Ernst, Morris. "Why I No Longer Fear the F.B.I." *Reader's Digest* (December 1950): 27.

Etter, Jonathan. *Quinn Martin, Producer: A Behind-the-Scenes History of QM Productions and Its Founder.* Jefferson, N.C.: McFarland, 2003.

Ewen, Stuart. *PR! A Social History of Spin.* New York: Basic Books, 1996.

Felt, W. Mark. *The FBI Pyramid: From the Inside.* New York: G. P. Putnam's Sons, 1979.

Francesconi, R. A. "James Hunt, the Wilmington 10, and Institutional Legitimacy." *Quarterly Journal of Speech* 68 (1982): 47–59.

Gentry, Curt. *J. Edgar Hoover: The Man and the Secrets.* New York: W. W. Norton, 1991.

Gitlin, Todd. *The Whole World Is Watching: Mass Media and the Making & Unmaking of the New Left.* Berkeley: University of California Press, 1980.

Grunig, James E., and Todd Hunt. *Managing Public Relations.* New York: Holt, Rinehart & Winston, 1984.

Guttenplan, D. D. *American Radical: The Life and Times of I. F. Stone.* New York: Farrar, Straus & Giroux, 2009.

Hackett, Robert A. "Decline of a Paradigm: Bias and Objectivity in Media Studies." *Critical Studies in Mass Communication* 1 (1984): 229–259.

Haines, Gerald K., and David A. Langbart. *Unlocking the Files of the FBI: A Guide to Its Records and Classification System.* Wilmington, Del.: Scholarly Resources, 1993.

Hiebert, Ray Eldon. *Courtier to the Crowd: The Story of Ivy Lee and the Development of Public Relations.* Ames: Iowa State University Press, 1966.

———. *The Press in Washington.* New York: Dodd, Mead, 1966.

Hofstetter, Richard. "News Bias in the 1972 Campaign: A Cross-Media Comparison." *Journalism Monographs* 58 (1978).

Kessler, Ronald. *The Bureau: The Secret History of the FBI.* New York: Macmillan, 2003.

Klehr, Harvey, John Earl Haynes, and Alexander Vassiliev. *Spies: The Rise and Fall of the KGB in America.* New Haven, Conn.: Yale University Press, 2009.

Kruckeberg, Dean, and Kenneth Starck. *Public Relations and Community: A Reconstructed Theory.* New York: Praeger, 1988.

Lamme, Margot Opdycke, and Karen Miller Russell. "Removing the Spin: Toward a New Theory of Public Relations History." *Journalism and Communication Monographs* 11, 4 (Winter 2010).

Lewis, Eugene. *Public Entrepreneurship: Toward a Theory of Bureaucratic Political Power: The Organizational Lives of Hyman Rickover, J. Edgar Hoover, and Robert Moses.* Bloomington: Indiana University Press, 1980.

Liebling, A. J. *The Wayward Pressman.* New York: Greenwood Press, 1972.

Lippmann, Walter. *Public Opinion.* Reprint, New York: Free Press, 1997.

Lowenthal, Max. *The Federal Bureau of Investigation.* New York: William Sloane Associates, 1950.

Lynd, Robert Stanton, and Helen Lynd. *Middletown in Transition: A Study in Cultural Conflicts.* New York: Harcourt, Brace, 1937.

Lyons, Eugene. "Mrs. Roosevelt's Youth Congress." *American Mercury* 49 (April 1940): 481–484.

———. *The Red Decade: The Stalinist Penetration of America.* New York: Bobbs-Merrill, 1941.

Marchand, Roland. *Creating the Corporate Soul: The Rise of Public Relations and Corporate Imagery in American Big Business.* Berkeley: University of California Press, 1998.

Mason, Alpheus Thomas. *Harlan Fiske Stone: Pillar of the Law.* New York: Viking Press, 1956.

Mayer, Milton S. "Myth of the 'G-Men.'" *Forum* 94 (September 1935): 145.

Millspaugh, Arthur C. *Crime Control by the National Government.* Washington, D.C.: Brookings Institution, 1937. Reprint, New York: Da Capo Press, 1972.

Mindich, David T. Z. *Just the Facts: How Objectivity Came to Define American Journalism.* New York: New York University Press, 1998.

Nissenson, Marilyn. *The Lady Upstairs: Dorothy Schiff and the* New York Post. New York: St. Martin's Griffin, 2007.

O'Reilly, Kenneth. "A New Deal for the FBI: The Roosevelt Administration, Crime Control, and National Security." *Journal of American History* 82 (December 1982): 638–658.

Pearson, Drew. *Diaries, 1949–1959,* ed. Tyler Abell. New York: Holt, Rinehart & Winston, 1974.

Powers, Richard Gid. *Broken: The Troubled Past and Uncertain Future of the FBI.* New York: Free Press, 2004.

———. *G-Men: Hoover's FBI in American Popular Culture.* Carbondale: Southern Illinois University Press, 1983.

———. *Not without Honor: The History of American Anticommunism.* New Haven, Conn.: Yale University Press, 1998.

———. *Secrecy and Power: The Life of J. Edgar Hoover.* New York: Free Press, 1987.

Robins, Natalie. *Alien Ink: The FBI's War on Freedom of Expression.* New York: Morrow, 1992.

Roshco, Bernard. *Newsmaking.* Chicago: University of Chicago Press, 1975.

Rosten, Leo. *The Washington Correspondents.* New York: Harcourt, Brace, 1937.

Rovere, Richard. *Senator Joe McCarthy.* New York: Harper & Row, 1959.

Russell, Karen Miller, and Carl O. Bishop. "Understanding Ivy Lee's Declaration of Principles: U.S. Newspaper and Magazine Coverage of Publicity and Press Agentry, 1865–1904." *Public Relations Review* 35, 2 (June 2009): 91–101.

Salisbury, Harrison E. "The Strange Correspondence of Morris Ernst and John Edgar Hoover." *Nation,* December 1, 1984, 575–589.

Schrecker, Ellen. *Many Are the Crimes: McCarthyism in America.* Boston: Little, Brown, 1998.

Schudson, Michael. *Discovering the News: A Social History of American Newspapers.* New York: Basic Books, 1978.

Seagle, William. "The American National Police: The Dangers of Federal Crime Control." *Harper's Monthly Magazine,* November 1934, 751–761.

Seldes, George. *Freedom of the Press.* New York: Da Capo, 1935.

———. *Lords of the Press.* New York: Julian Messner, 1938.

———. *Witch Hunt: The Techniques and Profits of Redbaiting.* New York: Modern Age Books, 1940.

———. *Witness to a Century.* New York: Ballantine Books, 1987.

———. *You Can't Print That! The Truth behind the News, 1918–1928.* New York: Payson & Clark, 1929.

Shapiro, Herbert. *White Violence and Black Response: From Reconstruction to Montgomery.* Amherst: University of Massachusetts Press, 1988.

Shoemaker, Pamela J., and Stephen D. Reese. *Mediating the Message: Theories of Influence on Mass Media Content.* White Plains, N.Y.: Longman Publishers, 1996.

Sigal, Leon. *Reporters and Officials: The Organization and Politics of Newsmaking.* Lexington, Mass.: D. C. Heath, 1973.

Stillman, P. G. "The Concept of Legitimacy." *Polity* 7 (1974): 32–56.

Stoker, Kevin, and Brad L. Rawlins. "The 'Light' of Publicity in the Progressive Era: From Searchlight to Flashlight." *Journalism History* 30, 4 (Winter 2005): 177–188.

Streitmatter, Rodger. *Voices of Revolution.* New York: Columbia University Press, 2001.

Sullivan, William C. *The Bureau: My Thirty Years in Hoover's FBI.* New York: W. W. Norton, 1979.

Theoharis, Athan, and John Stuart Cox. *The Boss: J. Edgar Hoover and the Great American Inquisition.* Philadelphia: Temple University Press, 1988.

Theoharis, Athan G., Tony Poveda, Susan Rosenfeld, and Richard Gid Powers, eds. *The FBI: A Comprehensive Reference Guide.* New York: Oryx Press, 2000.

Thomas, Norman. "Agency of Justice." *Commentary*, April 1957, 384.

Tuchman, Gaye. *Making News: A Study in the Construction of Reality.* New York: Free Press, 1978.

———. "Objectivity as Strategic Ritual: An Examination of Newsmen's Notions of Objectivity." *American Journal of Sociology* 77, 4 (January 1972): 660–679.

Turkel, Gerald. "The 1980 Chrysler Loan Guarantee." *Research in Law, Deviance and Social Control* 4 (1982): 165–189.

Tye, Larry. *The Father of Spin: Edward L. Bernays and the Birth of Public Relations.* New York: Holt, Winston, 1998.

Wechsler, James A. "How to Rid the Government of Communists." *Harper's Magazine*, November 1947, 438–443.

Whitehead, Don. *The FBI Story: A Report to the People.* New York: Random House, 1956.

Wiener, Tim. *Enemies: A History of the FBI.* New York: Random House, 2012.

Winfield, Betty Houchin. *FDR and the News Media.* New York: Columbia University Press, 1994.

INDEX

345

The Federal Bureau of Investigation was an agency devoted to American ideals, professionalism, and scientific methods, directed by a sage and selfless leader—and anyone who said otherwise was a no-good subversive, bent on discrediting the American way of life. That was the official story, and how J. Edgar Hoover made it stick—running roughshod over those same American ideals—is the story this book tells in full for the first time.

From Hoover's first tentative media contacts in the 1930s to the Bureau's eponymous television series in the 1960s and 1970s, FBI officials labored mightily to control the Bureau's image—efforts that put them not-so-squarely at the forefront of the emerging field of public relations. In the face of any journalistic challenges to the FBI's legitimacy and operations, Hoover was able to create a benign, even heroic counter narrative, thanks in part to his friends in newsrooms. Matthew Cecil's own prodigious investigation through hundreds of thousands of pages from FBI files reveals the lengths to which Hoover and his lackeys went to use the press to hoodwink the American people. Even more sobering is how much help he got from so many in the press.

Conservative journalists like broadcaster Fulton Lewis, Jr. and columnist George Sokolsky positioned themselves as "objective" defenders of Hoover's FBI and were rewarded with access, friendship, and other favors. Some of Hoover's friends even became adjunct-FBI agents,